T

L

THE ARTS

OF

LEADING

*Perspectives from the Humanities
and the Liberal Arts*

EDITED BY EDWARD BROOKS AND

MICHAEL LAMB

GEORGETOWN UNIVERSITY PRESS / WASHINGTON, DC

The publisher is not responsible for third-party websites or their content. URL links were active at time of publication.

Library of Congress Cataloging-in-Publication Data

Names: Brooks, Edward W. R. L. (Edward William Randolph Llywelyn), 1979- editor. | Lamb, Michael, 1982- editor.
Title: The arts of leading: perspectives from the humanities and the liberal arts/ edited by Edward Brooks and Michael Lamb.
Description: Washington, DC: Georgetown University Press, 2024. | Includes bibliographical references and index.
Identifiers: LCCN 2024011622 (print) | LCCN 2024011623 (ebook) | ISBN 9781647124823 (hardcover) | ISBN 9781647124830 (paperback) | ISBN 9781647124847 (ebook)
Subjects: LCSH: Leadership. | Leadership in literature. | Leadership in art.
Classification: LCC HD57.7 .A7827 2024 (print) | LCC HD57.7 (ebook) | DDC 658.4/092—dc23/eng/20240807

LC record available at https://lccn.loc.gov/2024011622
LC ebook record available at https://lccn.loc.gov/2024011623

♾ This paper meets the requirements of ANSI/NISO Z39.48–1992 (Permanence of Paper).

25 24   9 8 7 6 5 4 3 2   First printing

Printed in the United States of America

Cover design by Brad Norr
Interior design by Westchester Publishing Services

CONTENTS

FOREWORD

Leading Stories and Stories of Leaders

Elleke Boehmer

Across human cultures, the life stories of exemplary leaders are motivational and inspiring. In the past, the lives of seers, saints, or sages may have provided compelling models. Today, biographies and memoirs of prizewinners, sports champions, media stars, and former presidents feature prominently in booklists and bookshops. These texts are quoted and promoted as part of political campaigns and in the build-up to sporting competitions. We often turn to these life stories, past and present, to find out about the energies, inspirations, and frustrations that drive exemplary leaders. What is their secret of leadership success? How did they cope with setbacks and hard times yet retain their focus on their goal or the good? In what ways, especially when it counted, did they rally their team, group, or nation?

The essays brought together here explore these and many other questions relating to leadership good and bad, but they do so by expanding the scope of what leadership is and who counts as a leader. Rather than looking only to business, politics, or sports, they plumb the depths of the arts and humanities, uncovering the life stories of a variety of leaders—both fictional and nonfictional—who challenge us to look at leadership anew. Rather than simply lifting up heroes and celebrities for easy imitation, they show the power of ordinary leaders whose acts of service and sacrifice changed society. And rather than focusing uniquely on leadership success, they highlight the complexity of extraordinary leaders whose flaws and foibles are often hidden by the gleam of collective nostalgia. In the process, they reveal the enduring and critical value of the arts and humanities in illuminating, interrogating, and shaping the complexity and diversity of the human condition.

It may be true, as the Anglo Irish poet W. B. Yeats once wrote, that an inspired and inspiring individual like a poet or a prophet or (sometimes) a politician is never "the bundle of accident and incoherence that sits down to breakfast" but more of an ideal to aspire toward and to learn from.[1] Nonetheless, in reading about the ordinary, day-to-day life of exemplary figures, most of us find we glean something of what it takes to be an outlier, in addition to the ten thousand hours of work and commitment that Malcolm Gladwell famously described.[2] In the past, when talking to audiences about my biography of Nelson Mandela (2008), I often observed how open people were to learning from an exemplary, though still flawed, life like his.[3] They were curious about the secrets of his charisma, sometimes called his "magic," but also intrigued about the darker sides of wielding power and influence that his experience illustrated—missteps, poor decisions, roads taken that, with hindsight, might better have been avoided.

The reliance on models and good examples counts for leaders themselves. Former UK prime minister Gordon Brown and former US president Barack Obama are among the leaders who cite Nelson Mandela's life story as inspirational, as they do Martin Luther King's. For them and many others, the title of Mandela's autobiography, *Long Walk to Freedom*, captures not only his vision and determination but also the sheer amount of time required to foster good leadership and the extent to which leadership depended on collaboration—a point many of the essays below make. Interestingly, the phrase "long walk to freedom" is itself taken from the autobiography of another influential postcolonial leader who, in his turn, inspired Mandela: Jawaharlal Nehru, the first prime minister of independent India.[4] And as *Long Walk to Freedom* makes clear, Mandela, too, across his long career drew on models and texts he took as salutary, including Shakespeare's *Julius Caesar*, Chinua Achebe's *Things Fall Apart*, and the perhaps unlikely yet stirring poem "Invictus" by the Scottish amputee imperialist W. E. Henley. When times were particularly dark, Mandela turned to "Invictus" for moral lessons in keeping faith in himself and his abilities. To quote from the poem, it taught him even "in the fell clutch of circumstance" how to keep his head "bloody, but unbowed."[5]

Always open-minded and intellectually curious, Mandela was interested in learning from transformational but also countervailing examples, like those we find in these pages. Across his years of incarceration as a political prisoner, even as he thought about models of resilience and overcoming, he also considered instances of malign and self-destructive leadership, as demonstrated by Achebe's autocratic hero Okonkwo, for instance, and by the tyrannical Creon in Sophocles's *Antigone*, the play discussed here by Edith Hall as "quantitatively the most influential ancient drama in performance of all time."[6] *The Arts of Leading* does not shy away from exploring such oppositional examples, including that of Richard III as captured in William Shakespeare's iconic play. They, too, teach valuable lessons about how a leader successfully relates to those they lead. Interestingly, in a 1970s Robben Island prison production of *Antigone*, Mandela chose to take the part of Creon—an exercise that allowed him as a one-time lawyer to reflect deeply on the damage inflicted by a tyrannical adherence to the law. He thought about what it was to appeal to the law above the law, as Antigone does in the play—and as Mandela himself had done when accused of sabotage in the 1960s.

Considering the complexities of all cultures, not least ours today, there is no single winning formula for effective leadership. As the editors Edward Brooks and Michael Lamb explain in their introduction to this book, leadership is as much of an art as it is a science. It deals in the complicated and unpredictable chemistry of human interaction. Indeed, even the science of leadership is founded on accumulated case histories. The prevalence of the object lesson or salutary story in leadership studies is an apt demonstration that perspectives from the arts and humanities fruitfully develop and deepen our understanding of leadership. How does a leader appeal to those they seek to lead? Why does a group turn to a certain leader, including leaders who play to our deepest anxieties and fears? Who are the often invisible leaders who actually make certain achievements possible with or without the person "out front" or "at the top"? These questions invite phenomenological responses, such as we find in the arts and humanities: answers to do with perceptions and understandings that are difficult, not to say impossible, exactly to quantify.

The key ingredients of leadership—vision, dynamism, determination, strength of character—exist in different proportions not only in different leaders, but in leaders at different points in history. Cultures change, as do the ways in which we interact with each other within our cultures and societies. The leaders who persuaded us a century ago, if alive today, might no longer impress us in the same way. In fact, as this wide-ranging book persuasively demonstrates, we may be at a tipping point in our understanding of leadership, with more diverse and inclusive kinds of leadership increasingly coming into prominence. Whereas the Victorian writer Thomas Carlyle saw "great men" like Frederick the Great as the drivers of history, many historians now lift up less visible leaders whose efforts were essential to the common project and emphasize how leading personalities interact with the social systems and structures of which they form a dynamic part. In the 2020s, heated debates about British World War II prime minister Winston Churchill, once almost universally admired, dramatize the extent to which our views of the lone patriarchal leader figure are changing. For some, Churchill remains a strong-voiced hero with a fine tactical sensibility who piloted Britain through its darkest hour. For others, Churchill's legacy is divisive. They point out that his achievements came at considerable cost to those deemed outsiders or strangers to Britain and its then empire—those he considered as not forming part of the white brotherhood of English-speaking nations.

The same historical reappraisal is currently taking place among other revered leaders from history. This volume's chapters on the US Civil War provide an apt example. Paul Escott critically examines the oft-celebrated leadership of Abraham Lincoln, noting his moral limitations while elevating the efforts of Black leaders whose persistent moral vision made the abolition of slavery possible. Meanwhile, Thavolia Glymph shines a spotlight on the women, refugees, and enslaved people whose courageous leadership during the war helped to effect their own emancipation, and David M. Lubin describes how one influential monument memorializes the leadership not only of a prominent white colonel but of the Black soldiers who comprised the Union's first Black regiment, thereby challenging the racism of the moment and inspiring others to pursue justice. These careful studies, made possible through the disciplinary lenses of the arts and humanities, highlight the dangers of memorializing heroic leaders without recognizing their flaws or the ways that other, perhaps more inclusive leaders made collective achievements possible.

These examples also further illuminate how humanistic approaches to leadership through the disciplines of history, philosophy, classics, modern literature, religious studies, music, theater, and the visual arts, as we find in *The Arts of Leading*, are effective in exploring such complex and nuanced debates about leaders' reputation and legacy over time. The idea that lessons can be learned from literature, history, and the arts runs as a common thread throughout the book. What is striking is that these disciplines not only illuminate new *content* about particular leaders but also provide valuable *methods*—ways of knowing, thinking, and seeing—that offer insights into how we conceptualize and practice leadership across a wide variety of contexts. These disciplines draw together knowledge and teaching from the past and open it up to informed critical inquiry and debate. Contributors lay emphasis on the "illuminating" tale and the object lesson, on "aspirational vision" and "pointed reflection" on historical parallels, literary texts, artistic practices, and cautionary tales—in effect, on the power of metaphor. As anthropologist-writer Barry Lopez put it, metaphor is "a tool of comparative inquiry" that appeals in a fundamental way to how our minds work—that is, through the "parallelism we finally call narrative."[7] So, too, for the physician and literary critic Rita Charon, narrative knowledge is a means of increasing understanding. By sharing stories from history, literature, philosophy, religion, and the arts, we are able to reevaluate our difficulties and recuperate our strengths.[8] Under oppressive conditions, as the 1970s South African Black Consciousness leader Steve Biko discerned, positive stories drawn from history allow us to "battle the doubt that these situations cast upon us."[9] The lessons Biko teaches in his core text *I Write What I Like* (1978) illustrate the power of the inspiring story to externalize negativity, transform our self-understanding, and build community.

If leadership is an art, as *The Arts of Leading* proposes across its length, then narrative is its indispensable medium, and reading its methodology. It is difficult to think of leadership without thinking in symbols and offering interpretations, even if only implicit ones. Moreover, there is no effective leader whose life does not, in some way, tell a persuasive story, even if that story may not yet be known. The studies of leadership we find in these pages generate in effect a narratology of exemplary stories—stories that work well as narratives but that also lay down important truths, truths that challenge the uncritical celebration of heroic leadership and uncover other leaders and forms that are too often neglected in traditional studies. The shape of these stories takes various forms—the onward-and-upward trajectory, the formative explosive moment, the step-by-step pattern of overcoming, the power and vision of a collective, and many others—but in all cases, they have the power to mold and remold our understanding of leadership for our time in ways that inspire, enliven, and surprise us, as the arts and humanities so often do.

NOTES

1. W. B. Yeats, "A General Introduction for My Work" (1937), *Essays and Introductions* (London: Macmillan, 1961).
2. Malcolm Gladwell, *Outliers* (London: Penguin, 2008).
3. Elleke Boehmer, *Nelson Mandela: A Very Short Introduction* (Oxford: Oxford University Press, 2008).
4. Jawaharlal Nehru, *The Discovery of India* (Oxford: Oxford University Press, 2002), 58–59.
5. Boehmer, *Nelson Mandela*, 84.
6. Hall, "Tragedies of Leadership," ch. 2 herein.
7. Barry Lopez, *Arctic Dreams* (1986; London: Vintage, 2014), 250.
8. Rita Charon, *Narrative Medicine* (New York: Oxford University Press, 2008), 5, 9.
9. Steve Biko, *I Write What I Like* (1978; London: Bowerdean Press, 1987), 29–30.

Humanizing Leadership

Reimagining Leadership as a Liberal Art

Edward Brooks and Michael Lamb

Our society is obsessed with leadership. Biographies of famous leaders top best-seller lists, while attempts to offer the latest leadership lessons line bookshelves, fill media articles, and populate popular podcasts. Colleges and universities offer programs and courses focused on leadership, corporations of all sizes organize leadership training programs to inspire and equip managers, and cadres of coaches and consultants earn a living advising people how to become better leaders. Across multiple sectors, leadership development has become a multibillion-dollar industry.[1]

Meanwhile, scholarly research on leadership has proliferated. Since the 1970s leadership theorists have advanced one model of leadership after another to respond to changes in culture and context, often drawing heavily on quantitative approaches in the social sciences to determine the nature of effective leadership and measure leader performance. Several academic journals have arisen to publish this cutting-edge research on leadership, including some that are climbing the rankings of applied psychology and management journals.[2]

Despite increased study and application, however, these important advances in the science of leadership have not prevented bad behavior or forestalled a lack of trust in our leaders. Public confidence remains low. In 2013, against a backdrop of high-profile leadership scandals, the Edelman Trust Barometer highlighted a global "crisis in leadership" as its central finding.[3] The last ten years have only underlined this assessment. In 2023 Richard Edelman diagnosed "a failure of leadership" as one of the major causes of a "deeply and dangerously polarized" world.[4] This crisis of leadership is even more concerning amid the set of urgent and interlocking ecological, economic, social, and political challenges that confront contemporary societies.

This book seeks to address these ongoing challenges and leadership failures by turning to the arts and humanities to reimagine leadership and leadership education. Introducing ideas, examples, and approaches from classics, history, literature, philosophy, religion, music, art, and theater, the volume gathers distinguished scholars to offer new perspectives on a topic that is perennially important but especially relevant in our uncertain age. By broadening our intellectual and ethical horizons beyond the science of leadership, the volume seeks to open diverse, fresh, and creative ways of thinking about leadership through disciplines especially equipped to grapple with cultural and ethical complexity. If some of the lessons of repeated leadership crises are that leadership needs to be humanized and that ethical purpose needs to be added to efficiency and effectiveness as the standards by which leaders are judged, then regrounding leadership and leadership education in the arts and humanities is a vital adjustment.

LEADERSHIP STUDIES AND THE LIBERAL ARTS

While leaders and leadership have been studied since the ancient world, only in the last century has leadership studies emerged as a discrete area of academic inquiry. The historian and political scientist James MacGregor Burns is widely recognized as one of the field's founders. Well known for his 1971 biography of Franklin D. Roosevelt, which won the Pulitzer Prize, Burns saw a gap in academic work on leadership. Rich historical reflection on classical, Confucian, and Christian traditions, Burns argued, had dissipated into "a superabundance of facts about leaders" and dozens of definitions of leadership without an overarching theory.[5] Burns turned his hand to such theoretical work in *Leadership* (1978), joining insights from history, philosophy, politics, and psychology to argue, fundamentally, that "we must see power— and leadership—as not things but as relationships."[6] Most influentially, he introduced the now famous distinction between "transactional" leadership, where a formal leader-follower relationship operates according to exchange and external agreement, and "transforming" (later "transformational") leadership, where leaders and followers are bound together by shared values in a relationship based instead on empowerment toward a common goal.[7]

In the forty years following Burns's influential book, manifold leadership theories and models have been advanced, all seeking to map some part of a puzzle that involves such aspects as personality, culture, communication, ethics, group dynamics, leader-follower relations, power structures, and embedded systems. While such study is inherently interdisciplinary, insights from the social sciences (often applied to organizational challenges in the business world) have predominated. This work has been immensely valuable, adding scientific rigor to theoretical models of leadership, uncovering skills that can be isolated and developed, and highlighting aspects of effective organizational management that can be replicated and scaled. This research has exposed the limits of hierarchical command-and-control models, illuminated the deeply contextual and relational nature of leadership, and helped us move beyond tired stereotypes of "good leaders" by making leadership a topic of serious scholarly study. Breaking open the black box of organizational leadership and analyzing its data have boosted confidence that leadership can be understood and that leaders can learn how to do more to improve performance and advance social purpose.

Yet, while the production of leadership literature and investment in leadership development has continued to increase, few executives are persuaded that their leadership development efforts are actually achieving results, much less fostering the trust needed to restore confidence in leaders in the face of repeated failures.[8] In response, scholars have placed a growing emphasis on "ethical leadership" and highlighted the human dimensions of character and identity as necessary foundations for leadership aimed at fostering trust.[9] As Mark Carney puts it, we need to think in terms not only of "what leaders do" but also "who leaders are," adding a strong focus on values and virtues alongside practical competence and managerial expertise.[10] This emphasis on the personal, interpersonal, and ethical aspects of leadership is reflected globally. According to a recent review of research in low- and middle-income countries, research on character-based approaches to leadership has increased more than tenfold since 2008.[11] And the human dimensions of leadership can be seen in a renewed focus on the inner journey of leaders by educators at prominent universities who have developed courses and programs that infuse leadership with key virtues of character, often by drawing insights from the arts and humanities into a discourse otherwise dominated by management studies.[12]

While this turn to the arts and humanities is no doubt a minority report, a nascent "dialogue of the disciplines" in leadership studies is under way.[13] A special edition of *Leadership Quarterly* featured perspectives on leadership from classics, theology, literature, theater, and philosophy.[14] Michael Harvey and Ronald Riggio's edited volume *Leadership Studies* also includes visual art and history, alongside contributions from sociology, psychology, and management studies.[15] Several collections have gathered historical, philosophical, and literary texts from various disciplines and traditions and highlighted the leadership lessons they contain.[16] Occasional articles in journals such as *Leadership Quarterly*, *Journal of Business Ethics*, and *Harvard Business Review* have brought fresh perspectives from the arts and humanities to bear on leadership, with occasional calls for a more thoroughgoing humanities-led renaissance in leadership education.[17]

This humanistic turn is to be celebrated, and this volume sits happily within this stream, paying concerted attention to the arts and humanities as important sources of insight that reveal diverse exemplars, alternative practices, and distinct ways of being and knowing.[18] But this volume also pushes against the tide of a somewhat one-sided, instrumentalizing approach that seeks to draw the arts and humanities into leadership and management studies without examining or interrogating core assumptions. In some expressions of this approach, a flow of insights from the arts and humanities is tapped and channeled to add philosophical, historical, literary, or artistic spice to a diet dominated by social science and management research. The danger is that the existing management structure of leadership studies goes largely unnoticed and often unchallenged, and the arts and humanities are pigeonholed into alien ways of knowing and standards of validity that do not recognize the complex ways that humanistic inquiry and modes of expression can inform, unsettle, and expand existing understandings of leading in various contexts. While an instrumentalizing approach helpfully brings the arts and humanities into leadership studies, this volume seeks to bring leadership into the arts and humanities to consider the idea and practice of leadership within the complexity, variety, and ambiguity of human life and to explore myriad ways that the arts and humanities can teach us how to lead well.

To this end, this volume intentionally includes scholars who are known primarily for their contributions to their respective disciplines rather than to leadership studies. By inviting distinguished scholars to engage this interdisciplinary inquiry, we hope to bring questions of leadership to the fore in the humanities while also expanding the diversity of perspectives, practices, and voices that can inform how we lead. In this way, we lift up humanities scholars and artists themselves as leaders who wield significant influence on culture and who—through their research, teaching, and practice—have the power to shape how we see the world and act within it. The academy is not separate from the "real world" but part of it, and its educational, cultural, and social power shapes daily how millions of people learn and live.

This humanistic focus, we should emphasize, need not diminish a properly scientific approach to leadership nor a concern with effective management, even if it must resist being co-opted by both. The value added by the arts and humanities is of a different kind. These disciplines prompt a broader set of questions and concerns, focusing our attention on ideas, beliefs, practices, and contexts that a scientific focus on efficacy and efficiency might otherwise overlook. In particular, the arts and humanities elevate questions of history, culture, language, and ethics to illuminate the interaction between leaders' motivations, values, goals, and relationships and the social, historical, political, and cultural contexts within which they live.[19] These ways of knowing offer new perspectives on leadership, presenting us less with theories, systems, and measures than with ideas, narratives, cautions, and questions that might fuel a constructive conversation with the social sciences. As recent work on dual processing in the human brain has shown, there is a place for both cool calculation *and* creative improvisation, analytical reasoning *and* artistic imagination. The emphasis should be on the right relationship between multiple modes of attention rather than the displacement of one mode by another.[20] We need the empirical insights of the science of leadership to serve and support the ethical purposes and practices of the arts of leading.

LEADERSHIP AS A LIBERAL ART

A central claim of this volume is that leadership itself is a liberal art.[21] In ancient Greece and Rome, "liberal arts" (*artes liberalis* in Latin) referred to those arts or skills that make human beings "free," with "liberal" drawing etymologically from the Latin word *liberalis*, meaning that which relates to, or is befitting of, a "free" person.[22] By fostering knowledge and critical inquiry, these "liberating arts" served to liberate human beings from subjugation, oppression, and domination and prepare them to be independent thinkers, active citizens, and virtuous friends.[23] In ancient Greece and Rome, an entire educational program was developed to serve this civic and social purpose, often in a democracy or republic where the good of the society depended on the virtue and skill of self-governing citizens. Given the common reliance on self-government and the importance of political representation, leading was—and is—a valuable art for helping people become and remain free.[24]

History supplies abundant examples of despotic and authoritarian leaders who threaten freedom and exercise tyranny over others, yet some approaches in political science have tended to downplay and displace attention to leadership by focusing helpfully but sometimes too narrowly on the institutions and structures of government.[25] Recognizing the role and authority of leaders, however, need not conflict with a proper focus on democratic governance. As feminist scholar Jo Freeman argues in a classic article, the absence of formalized leadership can itself foster a "tyranny of structurelessness," creating a vacuum that is inevitably filled by charismatic or privileged elites who exercise power and authority informally and often invisibly without accountability or responsibility.[26] In turn, this lack of formal accountability can lead to ineffectiveness, exclusion, discrimination, or domination. According to Freeman, making leadership roles explicit, open, and accessible to all; formally selecting leaders, distributing power, and assigning tasks; and specifying limits on a leader's power can encourage inclusion and accountability, along with more effective decision-making and collective action. We need leaders with the knowledge, power, skill, and authority to act on our behalf in various contexts, but we also need to ensure their authority is accompanied by vigorous and visible accountability to avoid tyranny and domination.[27]

While institutional checks and balances and clear rules and norms can help to foster a culture of accountability for leaders, external accountability is often not enough to preserve freedom or advance the common good. Crafty leaders can sometimes scuttle, subvert, or co-opt institutions, roles, or norms to increase their power and advance their self-interest. Alongside laws and institutions, we also need forms of internal accountability—moral virtue and ethical commitment—to encourage both leaders and followers to govern themselves in a way that preserves freedom, prevents domination, and promotes human flourishing.

Therefore, if leadership is to be a liberal art, it also requires the liberal arts.[28] Leaders need the knowledge, virtues, and skills fostered by a liberal arts education to lead in ways that empower free citizens and educate virtuous human beings. The liberal arts and humanities acquired their names because they comprise disciplines deemed essential to "cultivating humanity," educating the "whole person," and empowering human beings to flourish and become free.[29] The liberal arts and humanities open up new ways of acting, being, and knowing in the world, often in ways that challenge contemporary orthodoxies and yield fresh lenses on what it means to lead.

Indeed, one reason to engage the arts and humanities is that they offer different visions of what leadership might be, which is especially important in a world that is much more diverse than the "leaders" who typically represent it. Because of various and often intersecting forms of discrimination, injustice, and exclusion, those who are often perceived to be "leaders" in

Western societies have historically tended to be wealthy, white, and male, representing only limited and sometimes distorted experiences of what it means to lead. The proper scope of the arts and humanities is the *human*— in all its myriad forms and expressions, including those that might disrupt dominant cultural paradigms.[30] The arts and humanities invite us to consider different modes and expressions of humanity and thereby humanize conceptions of leadership, challenging us to explore how art, history, literature, music, philosophy, religion, and theater can inform, express, and expand how leadership is imagined, embodied, and practiced. At a time when many communities, organizations, and institutions are recognizing the value of diversity, equity, and inclusion in their leadership structures and practices, these ways of being and knowing can offer alternative perspectives while nurturing a form of critical and open inquiry that can prevent any one manifestation from being seen as universally normative for all others.

This commitment to diversity reflects one reason why this volume seeks to critically evaluate and decenter traditional representations of leadership and to elevate underrepresented voices and visions. Even when contributors engage traditional figures in their respective fields—from Plato and Cicero to Shakespeare and Lincoln—they do so not only to build on their insights but to highlight their limits and adapt their ideas to lift up leaders from marginalized communities, thereby opening up alternative ways of studying and imagining leadership. The diversity of authors in this collection contributes to this reimagining, embodying the value of diversity not only in the content of leadership studies but in the form those studies take. The volume includes scholars from various communities often underrepresented in their disciplines, and many of them explicitly take up questions of justice, equity, and inclusion, demonstrating the distinctive value of engaging questions of leadership in ways that both disclose and disrupt disciplinary norms.

This multiplicity of perspective is one advantage of an interdisciplinary edited volume over a monograph. A collection with multiple contributors from multiple disciplines brings multiple voices into conversation, enabling them to speak to a shared theme without necessarily requiring consensus or conformity.[31] This approach also allows authors to raise questions about the assumptions that supposedly characterize "common" conceptions of leadership and thereby challenge the reductionism that presumes leadership is manifest in a singular or homogeneous form. In both content and form, this volume expresses a fundamental commitment to inclusive forms of leadership that recognize a diversity of thought, perspective, and identity as valuable and necessary to the flourishing of human communities.

AN OVERVIEW

The volume is divided into six parts, with essays reflecting perspectives from classics, philosophy and religion, literature, history, the visual arts, and the performing arts. Given the limits of a single volume, this collection cannot adequately reflect the inexhaustible diversity of leaders and expressions of leadership across history, culture, or geography, or the limitless ways to approach these subjects within and across these fields. For the sake of thematic coherence and depth, we have limited the volume to two chapters from each humanistic area of inquiry and solicited contributions that engage a shared thinker, theme, or historical epoch. This focus ensures that the chapters are able to speak to and with each other, but it limits the range of topics covered within each field.

Another limitation is that most (but not all) of the chapters engage thinkers or themes of leadership from Western cultures and societies and thereby do not attend to the rich and valuable visions of leadership from non-Western societies. The volume does not seek to offer a comprehensive or final word on the arts of leading (as if such were possible), but only to make one limited contribution to the emerging conversation about how leadership might be reimagined to advance the flourishing of people and the planet in our time. Our hope is that this volume will encourage this conversation to grow within and beyond the disciplines, and within and beyond Western societies, and thereby join other efforts to expand comparative, cross-disciplinary, and cross-cultural examinations of leadership through the lens of the liberal arts and humanities.[32]

Classics

Some of the earliest humanistic accounts of leadership that appeared in Western intellectual traditions (at least in written form) emerged in ancient Greece and Rome, where leadership and character were constant preoccupations of philosophers, poets, dramatists, and orators. As the discipline focused on the careful study, contextualization, and interpretation of these ancient texts, classics illuminates perennial themes of leadership amid tragedy, tyranny, and precarity while providing a critical distance and imaginative lens that can enable us to see our contemporary age anew.[33]

In chapter 1, Joy Connolly examines insights from ancient Rome, focusing on how Cicero's "art of speaking" illuminates "an intriguing, aspirational vision of inclusive leadership for the twenty-first century." Rather than simply applying Cicero's ethical, rhetorical, and political thought directly to our contemporary context, Connolly seeks to "reinvent" his account of dialogue and decorum for an age defined by plurality and precarity. Emphasizing human sociality, the relational nature of leadership, and the capacity for communication to serve as "civic glue," Connolly advances an account of Ciceronian persuasion that requires leaders to be radically other-directed, self-aware, and self-controlled, recognizing the power of passionate speech while also restraining their behavior to avoid domination and attend humbly, patiently, and perceptively to a wide range of perspectives, especially of those on the margins. By engaging Cicero critically in conversation with Gloria Anzaldúa, Hannah Arendt, Judith Butler, and Jacques Rancière, among others, Connolly elevates a vision of inclusive leadership that is "conversant" in two senses: it reflects a deep familiarity with its audiences born of humble awareness, active listening, and empathetic imagination, and it is committed to authentic conversation through "turning together" to issues of common concern. Such conversant leadership, Connolly concludes, is necessary for sustaining radically plural forms of human community in our increasingly global age.

In chapter 2, Edith Hall finds relevant insights in ancient Greece—particularly in the works of Sophocles and Aristotle, who offer pointed reflections on tyrannical leadership. While Hall celebrates Aristotle's influence and insights, including his dual categorization of tyranny as both malevolent and benevolent, she argues that his theories rely on the work of Greek dramatists, especially Sophocles, the great tragedian of Greek civic life. Contextualizing Aristotle's engagement with the theater and offering a close reading of Sophocles's *Antigone*, Hall highlights how the despot of Sophocles's play, Creon, embodies the worst tendencies of Aristotle's malevolent tyrant. Creon exercises power unilaterally without restraint, challenges established laws and norms, issues false accusations and harsh punishments, refuses the advice and deliberation of the elders, and sows discord among citizens. Sophocles's vivid portrayal of Creon's tyranny—and Antigone's courageous resistance to it—has made the play "quantitatively the most influential ancient drama in performance of all time," informing not only how Shakespeare diagnosed tyranny in early modern England but also how contemporary activists have resisted apartheid, communism, and authoritarianism. At a time when emergent forms of tyranny create contemporary challenges across the globe, Hall concludes that a careful reading of Aristotle, Sophocles, and Shakespeare supplies leaders and citizens with "powerful tools with which to analyze and resist" tyranny.

Philosophy and Religion

Both Connolly and Hall highlight the power of philosophical thought to inform and illuminate various ways to lead. Philosophy has long served that function, fostering a "love of wisdom" that helps its practitioners cultivate the virtues needed to live and lead in ways that advance personal and societal flourishing. This function was especially prominent in ancient Greece and Rome, where philosophy was practiced not simply as an abstract academic discourse but as a disciplined "way of life" that supplied exercises and examples intended to educate human virtue and vision.[34]

In chapter 3, Noah Lopez turns to one of the classic texts of ancient philosophy, Plato's *Republic*, to highlight leadership lessons present in Plato's famous allegory of the cave. Unlike those who emphasize the leadership of the enlightened philosopher-king who returns to the cave to lead its prisoners out of darkness, however, Lopez identifies a second, neglected leader in the allegory: the guide who initially leads others out of the cave, the teacher who makes further acts of leadership possible. Lopez thus highlights pedagogy itself as an important "site of leadership," revealing the forms of authority, possibility, and power that often remain veiled in the contemporary educational process. For Lopez, such veiling not only prevents due consideration of patterns of leadership education that are mirrored in the forms of leadership we see in the world, but it also covers over the kind of leadership enacted in the classroom. Lopez points out the dynamics of compulsion and violence that are present in the pedagogy of the guide in the *Republic*, who drags a prisoner from the cave into the light outside. Contrasting this pedagogy of violent coercion with the idea of philosophy as the "love of wisdom," Lopez laments its too-frequent replication in contemporary philosophy classrooms. Situating the discussion of Plato in relation to forms of inequity and exclusion in higher education, Lopez highlights the need for a critical pedagogy that unmasks and resists structures of power, privilege, and exclusion and thereby enables the transformational learning needed to heal divisions and educate the inclusive leaders required to guide us out of our contemporary caves.

Alongside philosophy, some of the most historically influential sources for the interpretation and practice of leadership are found within the world's religions, where philosophy and ritual practice are often joined into robust moral traditions. A diversity of religious traditions and interpretations illuminate different understandings and visions of leadership as well as different models for critical engagement, consideration, and emulation—both across and within particular traditions. The essays that follow analyze perspectives from three of the world's major religious traditions: Judaism, Islam, and Christianity.

In chapter 4, Alan Mittleman examines Mosaic leadership, the multifaceted leadership of Moses as portrayed within the context of rabbinic thought. In this stream of the Jewish tradition, Moses is construed as "the first rabbi," an example to be emulated for his virtues, traits, and skills. Yet interpreters present the meaning of Moses's leadership in different ways. For example, Martin Buber portrays Moses as a worldly failure, subverting worldly patterns of accomplishment, while Niccolò Machiavelli presents Moses as a secular success, an "armed prophet" who is a model of violent action. While these presentations are not utterly devoid of legitimacy, Mittleman argues, they depict two extremes. The rabbis, by contrast, see Moses's leadership as lying between these extremes: an "effective leader whose success is based on his exemplary character traits, as well as his resilient faith in God and in his people." Mittleman's Rabbinic portrait reframes Moses's leadership within a sacred conception of reality where the leader's moral commitment grounds justice and service and enables reliance on reasoned persuasion rather than political coercion.

In chapter 5, Tahera Qutbuddin turns to Ali ibn Abi Talib, one of the most influential figures in early Islam, revered by Muslims across Islamic traditions. In a way that parallels Mittleman's account of Moses, Qutbuddin's presentation of Imam Ali's leadership undermines the common opposition between ethics and efficacy. According to Qutbuddin, Imam Ali exhibited political acumen, military strategy, and administrative skills that are crucial to the success of an individual's leadership yet are insufficient apart from a deeper moral foundation. Drawing on the prophet's sermons, letters, and sayings, Qutbuddin presents Ali's most important leadership qualification as the virtue of justice, which went "beyond simple equality to include a complex cluster of virtues." Ali's example of just leadership is presented under five main themes: consciousness of God; learning, reason, and wisdom; compassion and gentleness; integrity and freedom from corruption; and inclusion and pluralism. Since Ali is widely admired by Muslims from diverse traditions, Qutbuddin concludes, his wisdom "can be a lodestar for just leadership in Muslim-majority countries, many of which are fiercely divided today."

In chapter 6, Marla Frederick moves the focus from individual to community and from celebrated men to women whose leadership is often overlooked. In "Women's Work and the Question of Leadership," Frederick explores the leadership of First Baptist Missionary Church in Sumter, South Carolina. Founded in 1868, only three years after slavery was abolished, this Christian church was "a beacon of hope for Black people," built and rebuilt, so the standard story goes, under the leadership of a succession of powerful, charismatic, and celebrated men. Frederick uncovers a different story, found deep within the church's archives. The work of leadership she discovers through her research is the down-to-earth labor of three formerly enslaved women: Mary Mitchell, Minnie Blair, and Tilda Bush, who "organized the church," as the record reads. In recovering their untold story, Frederick highlights the importance of reimagining "what leadership looks like and what leadership means." When it comes to the history of Black churches in the United States, Frederick argues, "great leadership" is collaborative and communal. It is "not male-dominated but often constitutive of a vast and invisible female volunteer assemblage" whose "concerns tend to be rooted in the needs of the community." Frederick's account troubles an easy identification of the sacred dynamic of leadership with the personal charisma of anointed individuals. "One cannot look for leadership only in the polished photos adorning the halls of our institutions," she argues. "Leadership is about who gets the work done, advances the cause of the institution, and creates a vision for future generations."

Literature

If you ask for leadership literature in a bookstore, you will likely find yourself in the business section, faced with books detailing strategies and skills to improve leadership performance. While there is much to be learned from practical insights on how to become a more effective leader, the simpler the formula on offer, the less useful it is likely to be in the face of the complexity and uncertainty that characterize our times. Perhaps, for this reason, you might also find a number of recent works exploring leadership through literature, both ancient and modern.[35] Such works plumb beneath the surface of what it means to lead, probing inner lives and motives as well as powerful external forces in a way that recognizes human complexity.[36] As Joseph L. Badaracco puts it, "serious literature offers a view from the inside."[37] In this section, our contributors turn to Shakespeare, a guide to leadership whose works could well be taken as a literary curriculum for leadership studies. His plays, and the famous characters we meet within them, illumine both the role of leadership in shaping history and the psychology of leaders as they wrestle with primal desires and pangs of conscience and find themselves vulnerable to the powers they have sought to possess, often in ways that unsettle the traditional hierarchies of their age.[38]

In chapter 7, John Miles explores what Shakespeare has to say about leadership in two of his most famous characters, Hamlet and King Harry. Rather than rehearsing accounts of these characters commonly portrayed in the leadership literature, however, Miles parlays deft literary analysis to innovatively set their portrayal in Shakespeare's First Folio against their counterparts in earlier, sometimes "bad," versions of the plays. The comparisons are both intriguing and instructive. In contrast to the decisive yet unthoughtful "bad" Hamlet, the Hamlet of the First Folio appears more discerning and philosophical and, therefore, more reluctant to forfeit his ethical commitments to act in the violent and vengeful way expected of him as king. And while the Folio's King Harry is similar to earlier versions, the Folio's framing of *Henry V* is different. It includes substantial extratextual material—including a prologue, chorus, and epilogue that introduces the perspectives of a chorus and a prefatory address "To the Reader" that recruits the audience to ensure the book's success. The result is a clearer sense not only of Shakespeare's complex vision of leadership but of the lessons that we, as readers, may learn from it.

In chapter 8, Kristin M. S. Bezio highlights Shakespearean parallels to the political leadership of the United States since 2016. She also focuses on *Henry V* but sets the king against another famous Shakespearean leader, Richard III. Drawing out contrasts between Henry and Richard, Bezio explores Shakespeare's depiction of the dangers of populism, polarization, and demagoguery in relation to the election and continued support of Donald Trump. *Richard III*, Bezio argues, uncovers the nature of "toxic leadership," which is illustrated in a catalog of propagandist moves carried out by Richard and his cronies. Bezio suggests a host of comparisons between Richard and Trump, turning to Jean Lipman-Bluman's work *The Allure of Toxic Leaders* to provide a conceptual framework that can make sense of their popularity.[39] Bezio's aim, however, is not simply to find historical parallels but to prompt a rereading of *Richard III* as a cautionary tale for today. Taking readers back to the fraught sociopolitical context of late Elizabethan England, Bezio suggests that Shakespeare wrote *Richard III* in anticipation of the death of a glorious monarch as a warning of what could happen if the lessons of history were not taken to heart. The play can act as an antidote, Bezio argues, not simply to leaders like Trump, but to the toxic charismatic leadership they exemplify. It also reminds us that the people in a participatory political community, if active in resisting toxic leaders, can survive even the most dangerous divisions.

History

In the nineteenth century, Thomas Carlyle claimed that individual leaders make history, arguing infamously that "the History of the world is but the Biography of great men."[40] Carlyle's "great man" view of leadership as heroic, singular, and male has had a powerful and pernicious influence on the popular understanding of leaders and leadership. It has also shaped historical writing on leadership, delivering a narrow focus on famous battles and biographies.[41]

If Carlyle's view of history dominated many early studies of leadership, the rightful rejection of this view has characterized the recent study of history. Since the 1960s many historians have shifted their attention from the study of famous military and political leaders toward a more detailed exploration of social history, with a focus on structural change and the lived experience of "ordinary" people. On this view, leadership is less a function of heroic individuals than a dynamic of systems, structures, movements, and masses. This contrast highlights that the ways we view history and understand what leadership is, and even who the leaders are, are inseparably related. What's more, the leaders and leadership we see and celebrate in the past shape the leaders and leadership we see and celebrate in the present.

The essays in this section uncover the complex and dynamic ways that historical, social, and political contexts shape how we identify, analyze, and imagine leaders and leadership. To challenge Carlyle's approach, we turn to the US Civil War, often renowned for its great battles and great leaders. In particular, Civil War history tends to elevate Abraham Lincoln as the leader who preserved the Union and abolished slavery and to emphasize the military leaders who cunningly outwitted their enemies in battle. However, returning to the nineteenth century with a readiness to reexamine common assumptions illuminates Civil War–era realities that challenge ideas of leadership in ways that are relevant in our own time.

That Abraham Lincoln was a "great leader" is foundational in both the popular understanding of Civil War history and contemporary leadership writing, where he is often invoked as a model.[42] In chapter 9, Paul Escott reconsiders Lincoln's record in relation to the racism of his time. Escott's aim is neither to clear Lincoln nor condemn him, but to make plain his relationship to the prevalent white supremacy of his day and highlight the limitations of democratic leadership in a racist society with an almost exclusively white electorate. Through the 1850s, Lincoln positioned himself as a leading opponent of Southern slavery and a vocal critic of attempts to extend slavery in the North. Yet, while he opposed slavery as an injustice that contradicted liberty, Lincoln's position was configured in relation to the need to win support for the newly founded Republican Party within a context where white supremacy was assumed. Even as he moved into direct opposition to Southern slaveholding interests and toward war, Escott shows, Lincoln sought to distance himself from abolitionists and resisted their emphasis on social and political equality. Once elected president in 1861, Lincoln's failure to embrace racial equality continued, even as he worked toward emancipation to win the war. Seeking to preserve the unity of the nation, he took a conciliatory approach toward both rebellious Southern states and racist Northern Democrats, a vocal and sizable minority who attacked the Republicans as radical abolitionists. White supremacist beliefs were prevalent in the North, especially among the Democratic Party, and Lincoln was accused of upsetting the racial order and inciting insurrection in order to elevate enslaved people to citizens, a move that would break up the Union. In response, Lincoln and the Republican Party, infected by the racism around them, held back from asserting that "all men are created equal." Lincoln's position did turn in the final months of his life as he developed a more progressive moral vision, but as Escott powerfully shows, the limitations of Lincoln's democratic leadership in a virulently racist society meant that radical Black leaders were the ones who stepped up to advance the cause of racial equality, a vision embedded in the Declaration of Independence that is yet to be fulfilled.

In chapter 10, Thavolia Glymph maintains our focus on leadership in the Civil War era but turns our attention to "leadership from the ground." She celebrates the role of ordinary people—including enslaved people—who stepped up to lead in vital, if often unrecognized, ways. Numbering in the hundreds of thousands, people fleeing slavery affected both Confederate and Union plans, the former considering them enemies while the latter developed policies to accommodate or welcome them as allies. This grassroots approach to understanding history reveals a new roll call of Civil War leaders and surfaces battle sites where enslaved people enacted leadership and resistance—such as Magnolia Plantation and sites on the Combahee River—which are not customarily visited as part of executive leadership education tours. According to Glymph, the leadership roles of enslaved people and refugees have not yet been given the attention they warrant in historical accounts or leadership education, in part because of opposition to the work of some Civil War historians in the second half of the twentieth century. According to Glymph, academic opposition discouraged consideration of Black people as Civil War leaders, kept their names out of the history books, and rendered important battle grounds invisible. Glymph makes a strong case that the time has come for the cloak of invisibility to be removed. She even imagines a new series of leadership education tours, or "staff rides" such as those offered by the US Army War College, to sites where enslaved people exercised leadership, with the hope that "overlooked and ignored battlegrounds upon which Black people fought will be seen as hallowed ground not for magnolia and mint julep fantasies but for understanding leadership in the making of a new birth of freedom."

Visual Art

Leadership lessons from the nineteenth century continue in the chapters on art. Images and sculptures have long been an important aspect of leadership, constructing and extending a leader's presence and power. Today, famous leaders appear on currency, line the walls of palaces and public buildings, and stand on columns in city squares. Many of these leaders are dead, of course, but the works of art that have been commissioned and curated to honor them continue to present a normative vision of what good leadership is taken to be. For this reason, they have become controversial and recognized as potentially dangerous, particularly given that recent work on the physical and facial appearance of leaders has shown that a certain "look" can predict perceived success in business, politics, and the military, further reflecting and encoding biases based on race, gender, and ethnicity.[43] If surrounding ourselves with images of leaders shapes what we look for, it also shapes how leaders look in turn. As is clear from the portrayals of leadership in US history and politics in the next two chapters, art itself can play a leadership role.

David Lubin extends the Civil War lens on leadership by turning to art history. In chapter 11, Lubin focuses on Augustus Saint-Gaudens's famous sculpture of Colonel Robert Gould Shaw and the members of the Fifty-Fourth Massachusetts Voluntary Infantry, the North's first regiment of Black soldiers in the Civil War. Contrasting Boston's Shaw Memorial to heroic military sculptures from the past and situating it in light of Saint-Gaudens's earlier portrayal of Abraham Lincoln, Lubin highlights how the iconic and morally nuanced work of art—and the patrons and abolitionists who supported it—challenged racist attitudes and representations of the time. Rather than portraying Shaw gallantly alone on a horse, Saint-Gaudens crafts a bronze frieze that situates the white commander alongside the regiment's Black troops, whom the artist renders in exquisite detail not as an undifferentiated mass but as unique individuals, a sign of dignity and respect for their human personhood. Echoing Escott's and Glymph's elevation of Black Americans as agents of their own freedom and equality in chapters 9 and 10, Lubin argues that the Shaw Memorial not only recognizes the moral leadership of Colonel Shaw but presents the Black soldiers themselves as leaders who valiantly "lead their people out of bondage" and "the nation out of barbarism." According to Lubin, the memorial not only depicts a new model of leadership but also "played a leadership role" itself, shaping the cultural consciousness of a nation while inspiring the music of Charles Ives, the literature of Ralph Ellison, the poetry of Robert Lowell, and the leadership of Colin Powell, not to mention the 1989 film *Glory*, which depicted Shaw and members of the Fifty-Fourth Regiment as leaders who challenged racist stereotypes in their pursuit of justice. Ultimately, through a nuanced and contextualized account of the Shaw Memorial, Lubin illuminates the power of art to offer an "expanded view of leadership" that advances the cause of justice, emphasizes reciprocal relationships, and prioritizes the collective over the individual, themes that remain relevant in our century's ongoing debates around race, memory, and statues.

The importance of race in US history and politics continues to inform the context of leadership in chapter 12, where Gwendolyn DuBois Shaw elevates the role of portraiture in constructing leadership, identity, and power. Shaw focuses in particular on the role of art in the presidency of Barack Obama. Noting how the Obamas intentionally placed art in the White House to highlight its cultural power and represent a more diverse set of artists and images, Shaw traces how the Obamas selection of photography and portraiture communicated a refined aesthetic sensibility, encouraged a sense of belonging in a traditionally white space, and offered an inclusive vision of American life. After situating the Obamas' "visual leadership" within the history of art's presence in US politics, Shaw concludes by analyzing the portraits of President Obama and First Lady Michelle Obama by African American artists Kehinde Wiley and Amy Sherald. These paintings attracted national attention when they were unveiled, in part because they draw on rich and vivid images from the African American tradition to communicate the distinctive identity, power, and legacy of America's first Black First Family. In this way, Shaw, like Lubin, presents artists themselves as leaders, exercising a profound influence on politics and empowering others, including those of the next generation, to see themselves as "creators of culture."

Performing Arts

The benefits of experiential learning and a renewed focus on the performative aspects of leadership have spurred a growing movement that draws on theater, music, and dance in leadership education. It is not unusual to find executive leadership programs supplementing standard content and pedagogical methods with the creative introduction of improvisational drama, classical music, jazz, drumming, or dance. No doubt the performing arts offer powerful pedagogic resources that illustrate themes of collaboration and creative improvisation that are increasingly emphasized in writing on leadership. But do the arts simply convey the same content as a standard seminar in an alternate form, or does the form itself illumine facets of leadership that otherwise remain concealed? Might the dynamic and embodied nature of the performing arts introduce practices that reframe leadership, offering perspectives and insights that take us beyond more traditional intellectual and propositional modes of leadership inquiry? Case studies from classes at the University of Oxford and Stanford University explore these questions. In doing so, they not only illustrate the creative potential of performing arts in leadership education but also reveal the potential that exists in conceiving leadership itself as artistic performance.

In chapter 13, Pegram Harrison turns to Orlando Gibbons, one the great composers of a tumultuous period in early modern England. Born in Oxford in 1583, Gibbons became a leading figure in his field and also through it. Looking through the lens of leadership, the choral music he wrote was a projection of power that encoded faith, loyalty, and conformity. More than four hundred years after Gibbons music was first performed, Harrison, a humanities scholar and senior fellow in entrepreneurship at the University of Oxford's Saïd Business School, draws on Gibbons's eight-part setting of Psalm 47, "O clap your hands," to help students explore leadership through choral singing. By joining an expert rendition with participatory experience, musical performance provides both a pedagogy for leadership education and an induction into the mystery of music, which has the power to "articulate the ineffable" and take us where words struggle to go. Thus, rather than listing leadership lessons from musical performance, Harrison takes his readers on a journey into the musical realm. His first-person reflection affirms his conviction that one of music's contributions to leadership education is its prioritization of the personal and perspectival. The creativity and collaboration inherent in musical performance exposes the limits of mere imitation and debunks the hubristic application of command and control as a primary mode of leadership. Music calls for attention to patterns, an awareness of silence, and recognition of the contribution of others—all practices that create cohesion in an ensemble. The lessons are personal. They involve becoming aware of the limits of understanding and the need to trust the expertise of others; experiencing vulnerability and failure; and moving from a self-focus that obsesses with projecting competence and seizing control to a posture of humility that seeks to enable and empower others. These lessons are not cataloged since, as Harrison concludes, music is mysterious: we must "let the sound hang in the air." Therein lies an important lesson in a culture of command and control: leadership is like that too.

Chapter 14 takes us from music to theater as Melissa Jones Briggs explores how the adoption of mindsets and methods from stage performance can help leaders to "embrace the artistry" of their leadership roles. Like Harrison, Jones Briggs's work joins academic insight and creative pedagogy, drawing on performance art to "unlock creativity, confidence and compassion in everyday relationships." Theater, she contends, can "be a tool for social change," a dynamic that is illustrated in the chapter, which focuses on how techniques and theories from acting can support the practice of inclusive leadership. Inclusion is not simply an idea but a practice that incorporates "involvement, respect, and connection" and often requires leaders to stretch beyond the familiar and expected behaviors of their leadership roles. Pushing behavioral boundaries, however, is no easy task, particularly since leaders may fear or actually face forms of resistance or reprisal that cause them to "cover" or downplay stigmatized identities. Jones Briggs expands the idea of "covering" coined by sociologist Erving Goffman and developed by legal scholar Kenji Yoshino, arguing that it undermines inclusion and allows problematic cultural norms to remain unchallenged. The chapter draws on a case study of Briggs's popular class at Stanford, Acting with Power, to introduce performance strategies that can help to "uncover" buried selves and make it easier for others to "uncover" as well. The essay illustrates the power of theater to empower and embolden leaders to uncover their authentic identities and perform as artists within their roles.

In a concluding chapter, Corey D. B. Walker synthesizes common lessons and shared insights that emerge from the nuanced and textured accounts of leadership presented in each chapter. In particular, he highlights how the essays in this volume not only elevate a broad range of examples and forms of leadership but present new methods for understanding and ways of practicing leadership in different contexts. Modes of inquiry and imagination familiar to the humanities but less common in leadership studies illustrate what a "re/turn" to the humanities offers to the project of rethinking leadership for our complex moment of "planetary precarity." Yet rather than simply indulging a nostalgia about the humanities' past or present, Walker draws on the work of Charles H. Long to call for a critical interrogation of the humanities themselves and a reimagination of the very forms of human life that the humanities seek to articulate, express, and elevate. To advance this effort, Walker appeals to the *demos*—the people—which, he argues, offers a "theoretical freedom to rediscover a humanities without boundaries and a humanities open to multiple expressions of being human in the world." This "humanities for a new human" provides a foundation for reimagining both leadership and the humanities, democratizing both in order to renew our social and political life in a time of crisis.

Ultimately, the chapters in this volume elevate a vision of good leadership as relational, contextual, and inclusive, one that recognizes that good leadership can be exercised by a diverse range of leaders, including some who too often remain invisible or ignored. Good leadership cannot be constrained to positions of institutional power or authority, nor can it be reduced merely to skill, science, or technique. Rather, it must always attend to the complex and distinctively human elements of life. This is why the study and practice of leadership needs the arts and humanities to disclose new ways to understand human beings and doings. Yet, as Walker emphasizes, to resist calcification and premature closing, the arts and humanities, like the visions of leadership they yield, must also remain critical, open-ended, and dynamic, always unfolding, evolving, and expanding in response to new forms and imaginations of the human. In this way, among many others, studying the liberal arts and humanities remains essential to understanding and practicing the liberating and humanizing arts of leading.

NOTES

1. "Leadership Development Program Market," Future Market Insights, May 2022, https://www.futuremarketinsights.com/reports/leadership-development-program -market; Barbara Kellerman, "Introduction: Learning Leading—Lame Undertaking," *Professionalizing Leadership* (New York: Oxford University Press, 2018), 3, citing Gillian Pillans, "Leadership Development—Is It Fit for Purpose?," Corporate Research Forum, May 2015, 8.

2. See John Antonakis et al., "*The Leadership Quarterly*: State of the Journal," *Leadership Quarterly* 30, no. 1 (2019): 1–2.

3. The survey found that "less than one fifth of the general public believes business leaders or governmental officials will tell the truth when confronted with a difficult issue." Richard Edelman, *2013 Edelman Trust Barometer: Executive Summary*, 1, https://www .scribd.com/doc/121501475/Executive-Summary-2013-Edelman-Trust-Barome- ter. For other diagnoses of this leadership crisis, see, e.g., Pew Research Center, "Why Americans Don't Fully Trust Many Who Hold Positions of Power," September 19, 2019, https://www.pewresearch.org/politics/2019/09/19/why-americans-dont-fully-trust -many-who-hold-positions-of-power-and-responsibility/; Lee Rainie, Scott Keeter, and Andrew Perrin, "Trust and Distrust in America," Pew Research Center, July 22, 2019, https://www.pewresearch.org/politics/2019/07/22/trust-and-distrust-in-america/; Vipula Gandhi, "As COVID Continues, Employees Are Feeling Less Prepared," Gallup, July 2, 2020, https://www.gallup.com/workplace/313358/covid-continues-employees -feeling-less-prepared.aspx; Chris Pearse, "5 Reasons Why Leadership Is in Crisis,"

Forbes, November 7, 2018, https://www.forbes.com/sites/chrispearse/2018/11/07/5-reasons-why-leadership-is-in-crisis/.

4. Richard Edelman, *2023 Edelman Trust Barometer*, https://www.edelman.com/trust/2023/trust-barometer.

5. James MacGregor Burns, *Leadership* (1978: repr., New York: Harper, 2010), 2–3.

6. Burns, *Leadership*, 11.

7. Burns, 19–20.

8. Claudio Feser, Nicolai Nielsen, and Michael Rennie, "What's Missing in Leadership Development?" *McKinsey Quarterly*, August 1, 2017, https://www.mckinsey.com/featured-insights/leadership/whats-missing-in-leadership-development; Kellerman, *Professionalizing Leadership*.

9. See, for example, Nicola M. Pless and Thomas Maak, eds., *Responsible Leadership*, 2nd ed. (Abingdon: Routledge, 2021); Bill George, *Authentic Leadership: Rediscovering the Secrets to Creating Lasting Value* (San Francisco: Jossey-Bass, 2003); Robert K. Greenleaf, *Servant Leadership: A Journey into the Nature of Legitimate Power and Greatness* (New York: Paulist Press, 1977); Dirk van Dierendonck, "Servant Leadership: A Review and Synthesis," *Journal of Management* 37, no. 4 (2010): 1228–61; S. Alexander Haslam, Stephen D. Reicher, and Michael J. Platow, *The New Psychology of Leadership: Identity, Influence and Power* (New York: Psychology Press, 2011); Herminia Ibarra, Sarah Wittman, Gianpiero Petriglieri, and David V. Day, "Leadership and Identity: An Examination of Three Theories and New Research Directions," in *The Oxford Handbook of Leadership and Organizations*, ed. David V. Day (Oxford: Oxford University Press, 2014), 285–301; Adam Grant, *Give and Take: Why Helping Others Drives Our Success* (New York: Viking, 2013); Kim Cameron, "Responsible Leadership as Virtuous Leadership," *Journal of Business Ethics* 98 (2011): 25–35; Michael E. Brown, Linda K. Treviño, and David A. Harrison, "Ethical Leadership: A Social Learning Perspective for Construct Development and Testing," *Organizational Behavior and Human Decision Processes* 97 (2005): 117–34; Michael E. Brown and Linda K. Treviño, "Ethical Leadership: A Review and Future Directions," *Leadership Quarterly* 17 (2006): 595–616; Joanne B. Ciulla, ed., *Ethics, the Heart of Leadership*, 3rd ed. (Santa Barbara: Praeger, 2014).

10. Mark Carney, *Value(s): Building a Better World for All* (New York: HarperCollins, 2021).

11. Luna Wang and Edward Brooks, *Character and Global Leadership: A Survey of Character-Based Leadership Education and Research in Low- and Middle-Income Countries*, The Oxford Character Project, University of Oxford, 2023, 12.

12. For examples of scholars who teach courses at universities such as Harvard University and Columbia University, see, respectively, David Gergen, *Hearts Touched with Fire: How Great Leaders Are Made* (New York: Simon and Schuster, 2022); and Hitendra Wadhwa, *Inner Mastery, Outer Impact: How Your Five Core Energies Hold the Key to Success* (New York: Hachette, 2022). For examples of character-based leadership programs at universities, see the Oxford Character Project at the University of Oxford (https://oxfordcharacter.org/) and the Program for Leadership and Character at Wake Forest University (https://leadershipandcharacter.wfu.edu/). On the prevalence of management studies within leadership studies, see Joanne B. Ciulla, "Leadership Ethics: Expanding the Territory," in Ciulla, *Ethics, the Heart of Leadership*, 4.

13. Michael Harvey and Ronald E. Riggio, eds., *Leadership Studies: The Dialogue of the Disciplines* (Cheltenham: Edward Elgar, 2011).

14. Joanne B. Ciulla, ed., "Leadership: View from the Humanities," special issue, *Leadership Quarterly* 19, no. 4 (2008): 393–500.

15. Harvey and Riggio, *Leadership Studies*.

16. John K. Clemens and Douglas F. Mayer, *The Classic Touch: Lessons in Leadership from Homer to Hemingway* (Chicago: Contemporary, 1999); Joseph L. Badaracco Jr., *Questions of Character: Illuminating the Heart of Leadership through Literature* (Boston: Harvard Business School Press, 2006); Barbara Kellerman, ed., *Leadership: Essential Selections on Power, Authority, and Influence* (New York: McGraw Hill, 2010).

17. David K. Hurst, "Is Management Due for a Renaissance?" *Harvard Business Review*, May 30, 2014, https://hbr.org/2014/05/is-management-due-for-a-renaissance; Johan Roos, "The Renaissance We Need in Business Education," *Harvard Business Review*, July 2, 2014, https://hbr.org/2014/07/the-renaissance-we-need-in-business-education.

18. See also Joanne B. Ciulla, "Leadership Studies and 'the Fusion of Horizons,'" *Leadership Quarterly* 19 (2008): 393–95.

19. On the importance of attending to context in studying leaders and leadership, see Sandra J. Peart, "Overhauling How We Teach Leadership," *Washington Post*, February 12, 2013, https://www.washingtonpost.com/national/on-leadership/overhauling-how-we-teach-leadership/2013/02/12/aa85c70a-7527-11e2-aa12-e6cf1d31106b_story.html.

20. Iain McGilchrist, *The Master and His Emissary: The Divided Brain and the Making of the Western World* (New Haven, CT: Yale University Press, 2009); Iain McGilchrist, *The Matter with Things: Our Brains, Our Delusions, and the Unmaking of the World* (London: Perspectiva, 2021); Daniel Kahneman, *Thinking Fast and Slow* (New York: Farrar, Straus, and Giroux, 2011).

21. In recent decades, a number of scholars such as Peter Drucker have made a similar argument that management is a liberal art. See Peter F. Drucker, "Management as Social Function and Liberal Art," in *The New Realities: In Government and Politics, in Economics and Business, in Society and World View* (New York: Harper & Row, 1989): See also C. A. Nelson, "The Liberal Arts in Management," *Harvard Business Review* 36 (1958): 91–99; and James Maroosis, *Liberal Arts of Management: A Toolkit for Today's Leaders* (New York: Routledge, 2016).

22. For the Latin meaning of *liberalis*, see Charlton T. Lewis, *An Elementary Latin Dictionary* (New York: Oxford University Press, 2000), 469. For an influential history of the "liberal arts" in ancient Greece and Rome (and beyond), including their relation to freedom, status, and citizenship in both Latin and Greek, see Bruce A. Kimball, *Orators and Philosophers: A History of the Idea of Liberal Education*, expanded ed. (New York: College Entrance Examination Board, 1995), esp. 13–42, at 13–16.

23. See Jeffrey Bilbro, Jessica Hooten Wilson, and David Henreckson, eds., *The Liberating Arts: Why We Need Liberal Arts Education* (Walden, NY: Plough, 2023); Kimball, *Orators and Philosophers*, 13–16; Martha C. Nussbaum, *Cultivating Humanity: A Classical Defense of Reform in Liberal Education* (Cambridge, MA: Harvard University Press, 1997), 1–50, esp. 8–9, 19, 28–30; Joanne B. Ciulla, "The Jepson School: Liberal Arts as Leadership Studies," in Harvey and Riggio, *Leadership Studies*, 20–23; Michael S. Roth, *Beyond the University: Why Liberal Education Matters* (New Haven, CT: Yale University Press, 2014), 3–4; Fareed Zakaria, *In Defense of a Liberal Education* (New York: W. W. Norton, 2015), 40–71.

24. Further, Ronald E. Riggio draws on research that suggests that human beings, as "social animals," are "hard-wired" for leadership. See Ronald E. Riggio, "Introduction: The Dialogue of the Disciplines," in Harvey and Riggio, *Leadership Studies*, 3.

25. Gillian Peele, "Leadership and Politics: A Case for a Closer Relationship?" *Leadership* 1, no. 2 (2005): 187–204.

26. Reprinted as Jo Freeman, "The Tyranny of Structurelessness," *Women's Studies Quarterly* 41, no. 3/4 (2013): 231–46. See also Alanna Irving, "No Boss Does Not Mean No Leadership," *Medium*, July 5, 2015, https://medium.com/enspiral-tales/no-boss-does-not-mean-no-leadership-c4c97c660252.

27. For an insightful account of the relationship between leadership, authority, and accountability in a broad-based, democratic citizens' organization, see Jeffrey Stout, *Blessed Are the Organized: Grassroots Democracy in America* (Princeton, NJ: Princeton University Press, 2010).

28. On the "symbiotic" relationship between the core traits and practices of good leadership and the learning outcomes of liberal education, see Robert E. Colvin, "Leadership Studies and Liberal Education," *Journal of Leadership Education* 2, no. 2 (2003): 28–36. See also Kathy L. Guthrie and Kathleen Callahan, "Liberal Arts: Leadership Education in the 21st Century," *New Directions for Higher Education* 174 (2016): 21–33. For a powerful defense of the liberal arts in the context of leadership, see Drew Gilpin Faust, "To Be 'a Speaker of Words and a Doer of Deeds': Literature and Leadership," speech given at the United States Military Academy, West Point, NY, March 24, 2016, https://www.harvard.edu/president/speeches-faust/2016/to-be-a-speaker-of-words-and-a-doer-of-deeds-literature-and-leadership/.

29. Nussbaum, *Cultivating Humanity*; Roth, *Beyond the University*; Ciulla, "The Jepson School," 20–23.

30. For a critique of how the humanities have typically been practiced in the Western world and a call to expand their scope to other expressions of being human, see Charles H. Long, "The Humanities and 'Other' Humans," in *Morphologies of Faith: Essays in Religion and Culture in Honor of Nathan A. Scott, Jr.*, ed. Mary Gerhardt and Anthony C. Yu (Atlanta: Scholars Press, 1990), 203–14. We are grateful to Corey D. B. Walker for pointing us to this important essay.

31. Clare Bucknell makes a similar point about poetry anthologies: "Anthologies, with their diverse voices but convergent ideas, envision a public sphere in which solidarity doesn't require uniformity." See Clare Bucknell, "What Do We Want from Poetry in Times of Crisis?" *New Yorker*, December 22, 2020, https://www.newyorker.com/books/page-turner/what-do-we-want-from-poetry-in-times-of-crisis.

32. For an example of one effort to extend the study of leadership across disciplines and beyond the West, although through the lens of management, see Gregory P. Prastacos, Fuming Wang, and Klas Eric Soderquist, eds., *Leadership through the Classics: Learning Management and Leadership from Ancient East and West Philosophy* (New York: Springer, 2012).

33. For one account of what classics can teach about leadership, see Michael A. Genovese and Lawrence A. Tritle, "Leadership and the Classics," in Harvey and Riggio, *Leadership Studies*, 39–53.

34. Pierre Hadot, *Philosophy as a Way of Life: Spiritual Exercises from Socrates to Foucault*, ed. Arnold I. Davidson, trans. Michael Chase (Malden, MA: Blackwell, 1995).

35. Examples include Badaracco, *Questions of Character*; Jocelyn Davis, *The Greats on Leadership: Classic Wisdom for Modern Managers* (London: Nicholas Brealey, 2016); Jonathan Gosling and Peter Villiers, *Fictional Leaders: Heroes, Villains and Absent Friends* (London: Palgrave Macmillan, 2012); S. Manikutty and Sampat P. Singh, *The Essence of Leadership: Explorations from Literature* (New Delhi: Bloomsbury, 2015); Elizabeth D.

Samet, *Leadership: Essential Writings by Our Greatest Thinkers* (New York: W. W. Norton, 2015); John R. Shoup and Troy W. Hinrichs, *Literature and Leadership: The Role of the Narrative in Organizational Sensemaking* (Abingdon: Routledge, 2020).

36. Gosling and Villiers, *Fictional Leaders*, 1.

37. Badaracco, *Questions of Character*, 3.

38. Barbara Clarke Mossberg, "Literature and Leadership," in *Political and Civic Leadership: A Reference Handbook*, ed. Richard A. Couto (Thousand Oaks, CA: Sage, 2010), 1055.

39. Jean Lipman-Blumen, *The Allure of Toxic Leaders: Why We Follow Destructive Bosses and Corrupt Politicians—and How We Can Survive Them* (New York: Oxford University Press, 2005).

40. Thomas Carlyle, *On Heroes, Hero-Worship, and the Heroic in History*, in *"Sartus Restartus" and "On Heroes, Hero-Worship, and the Heroic in History"* (New York: E. P. Dutton, 1926), 266.

41. Carlyle's account was not unchallenged, even in the nineteenth century. Leo Tolstoy, for one, famously saw things in reverse. "Kings are the slaves of history," he wrote in *War and Peace*. According to Tolstoy, the idea that leaders make history is an illusion, an inference from their position in front of a movement that gives the impression that they draw great events in their wake. In fact, like a bow wave of a great ship, he argued, they are pushed along from behind. See Leo Tolstoy, *War and Peace*, trans. A. Briggs (London: Penguin, 2005), 670, 1340.

42. The notion that Lincoln is a model of good leadership is commonplace. A review of recent contributions to the *Harvard Business Review* highlights the point: Diane Coutu, "Leadership Lessons from Abraham Lincoln," *Harvard Business Review* 87, no. 4 (2009): 43–47; Nancy Koehn, "Reading List: Lincoln's Leadership Lessons," *Harvard Business Review*, February 19, 2010, https://hbr.org/2010/02/lincolns-leadership-lessons .html; Gautam Mukunda, "The Indispensable, Unlikely Leadership of Abraham Lincoln," *Harvard Business Review*, November 29, 2012, https://hbr.org/podcast/2012/ 11/the-indispensable-unlikely-lea; Doris Kearns Goodwin, "Lincoln and the Art of Transformative Leadership," *Harvard Business Review* 96, no. 5 (2018): 126–34; Nancy Koehn, "Real Leaders Are Forged in Crisis," *Harvard Business Review* online, April 3, 2020, https://hbr.org/2020/04/real-leaders-are-forged-in-crisis.

43. Panu Poutvaara, "Facial Appearance and Leadership: An Overview and Challenges for New Research," *Leadership Quarterly* 25, no. 4 (2014): 801–4.

PART I

Classics

CHAPTER 1

Conversant Leadership

Ciceronian Ideas for
Our Precarious Age

Joy Connolly

I want to persuade you that the writings of the first-century BCE Roman thinker and statesman Cicero can help us pursue a new mode of leadership in an age of precarity. Socially debilitating under any circumstances, precarity's effects are being aggravated around the world by increasing inequality and by leaders hostile to the poor and marginalized. The *ars dicendi* or "art of speaking" that Cicero practiced and examined in depth throughout his life offers an intriguing, aspirational vision of inclusive leadership for the twenty-first century.

Let me make it clear at the outset that I am not suggesting that the United States is some sort of latter-day Rome.[1] And I have no intention of calling on us to bring Ciceronian oratorical precepts back to life, even if such a thing were possible. Cicero himself, if we take his political activity and his values as a whole, is no exemplary model. Though he defended a limited role for non-elite citizens in republican politics, his political and personal values were unashamedly elitist.[2] His letters are as self-serving as they are learned and entertaining. In the course of trying to resolve conflicts between the leading men of Rome, he never lost sight of his own advantage, which he liked to equate with the good of Rome: it is telling that Julius Caesar's assassins chose not to include Cicero in their plans for the Ides of March. The risks he took by publicly attacking Caesar's right-hand man, Mark Antony, after Caesar's death, which led to his murder by Antony's henchmen, do not remedy his faults as a leader in his earlier career.

27

My approach to reading Cicero is rather an effort to open up his texts for dialogic deliberation and reinvention.[3] In doing this, I follow the humanist scholars of late medieval and early modern Europe. They lived in rapidly evolving socioeconomic conditions that made finding a secular discourse of politics an urgent necessity. Some of them took up the challenge, understanding that new models of leadership would have to mobilize the haves in search of power and glory as well as the have-nots seeking access to rule. Aware of and in some cases personally endangered by the conflicting interests of wealthy nobles and the Catholic church, these humanists discovered in Greek and Latin texts useful ideas about leaders and peoples—ideas strengthened and made safe for publication by the reverence conferred on ancient authors by the passage of time. From the Latin translation of Aristotle that allowed Marsilius of Padua to argue against papal rule in the early fourteenth century to the letters of Cicero and Pliny, which provided merchants and other non-nobles with models for a language of civil address, Greek and Roman thought helped humanists articulate new ideas about collective life and the role of leaders in it.[4]

None of these early moderns envisioned their own political communities as perfect analogs of Rome, even if they habitually used the language of inheritance and succession. Contemporary artist Vija Celmins offers a comparison that illuminates their method and mine. Starting in the late 1960s, Celmins began to produce marvelously detailed representations of ocean waves, desert sands, cloudscapes, and starscapes. At first glance, especially from across a room, her work can be difficult to distinguish from photographs. In fact, she works from photographs, and thanks to this, many critics have succumbed to the temptation to describe her work as copy-making. On the contrary, as she told one interviewer, to see her as a copyist misses the mark entirely: "it is precisely that I *reinvent* [the photograph] in other terms."[5] Celmins suggests that we see her hyper-realistic drawings not as replicas but as prompts for reflecting on memory, the passage of time, and the extraordinarily fertile way in which a single image generates countless meanings. Following up on Celmins's references to memory in her works' titles, curator and critic Stephanie Straine calls her works "ghostly memory traces" that can "endure many layers of superimposition."[6] Attempts to line up the "original" photograph with the completed drawing lead nowhere.

We cannot, and I presume we would not want to, "copy" a Roman text by claiming it for direct application to contemporary life. Greek and Roman writings, carrying a long history of loss and rediscovery, are both durably recognizable in their sameness over time and limitlessly multifold in their signifying capability, like the deserts and waves in Celmins's work. By now, as Marsilius and other humanists saw several centuries ago, the value of these texts rests in the ways they invite or possibly even compel what Celmins calls "reinvention." Cicero's work has been peculiarly apt for this activity. His writings on rhetoric and ethics were among the first and most frequently printed texts in the founding age of mass communication in Europe. While this popularity does not constitute proof of the value of his thought for us, it is worth noting that in that historically unprecedented age of change and socioeconomic mobility, from the fifteenth to the eighteenth centuries, Cicero consistently found a curious audience of what we would now call "change-oriented" readers.

In my decision to try to reinvent Cicero in the opening decades of the twenty-first century, I seek honestly to acknowledge and think through the traces Roman concepts and language have left on modernity. By analogy with Celmins's photographic "originals" and her drawings, the oscillation between a text originating in the past and current thinking that is prompted and shaped by that text heightens our awareness of our context, our history, our perspective, and our reliance on the past source. Does this mean, as one early reader of this essay suggested, that I am presenting "an invention of the kind of Cicero we might have wished existed, rather than really reflecting accurately the one who did"? Yes. The new interpretive text—the essay that you are reading now, including citations and quotations of a thinker whose values diverge sharply from ours—is at its core a *conversation*, an active engagement with another. This is a key term to which I shall return.

I begin from the German American thinker Hannah Arendt's assertion that the fundamental condition of human action and speech is plurality.[7] We humans are not and cannot be a singularity of one; we only imagine our-selves as one at enormous and often fatal cost. No period of human history has seen the tragic fruits of striving for oneness more clearly than the twen-tieth century—as Arendt, herself a refugee from Nazi Germany and wit-ness to the Eichmann trial, saw very clearly. Leadership today, if it is to be human and maximize human goods, must be pluralistic in conception and in practice.

What could all this possibly have to do with Marcus Tullius Cicero? Cicero gained the consulship, the highest office in the electoral politics of republican Rome, in the middle of the first century BCE, one of Rome's most tumultuous periods. By this time, the Roman empire stretched from Spain to Syria and from southern France to the northern African coast—a geo-graphical span almost as wide as the continental United States today. We find no evidence of concern for plurality in Roman historical sources: the com-peting ambitions of noble families, not popular interests, were the drivers of empire. During the three-quarters of a century leading up to Cicero's consulship in 63 BCE, the rich senatorial order's internal struggles had pushed the empire to its military and economic limits and, more than once, to civil war.

Though he spent his life navigating conventional Roman politics and values and many of his works suggest that Roman ways of doing things are superior, Cicero was not a member of a noble Roman family but from a well-off Italian family whose lands were about seventy-five miles away from the city. As the first in his line to win high political office, he was known as a "new man," a *novus homo*. Possibly prompted by his experience as a relative outsider, possibly because he made his career as a public speaker by talent and training, certainly because he thought for many years about the exercise and the civic significance of communication, his writings portray human lived experience as a dynamic assemblage of plural perspectives, convictions, obligations, desires, and hopes.

De Officiis, or *On Moral Duties*, the last book Cicero wrote before Mark Antony ordered his assassination, conceives its project—how to fulfill one's moral duties and thus live well—around a description of the human individual in relation to other people (*Off.* 1.12, 53). The implication is that only when the individual sees and understands those relations will he be in the position to exercise as best he can his judgment regarding what he owes to each.[8] This task is far from simple. Inhabiting separate bodies, we experience the world from that individuated perspective, so we find it difficult to understand or care about the perspectives of others: "Concern for other people's affairs is far from easy," Cicero remarks (*Off.* 1.30–31). Even when we establish strong relations with those closest to us, starting with our families and friends, our experiences in those groups invest us in them, making it difficult in turn to care about other groups. Divisive differences based in language, manners, class, political allegiance, or ethnicity emerge and do their damage. In Cicero's insistence that his readers see themselves embedded in ever expanding assemblages, from family and friends to national community and species, we see how deeply his thinking about individual moral duties is entangled with his conception of human beings as political by nature. *De Officiis* is a letter about the moral duties we owe to one another as essentially and naturally connected entities. It is not an exaggeration to say that Cicero sees individual human beings as fully human only when they are living in relationship to others—that is to say (given his view of the collective need for laws, for example), in political communities.

What links humans together despite all our differences, as individuals and across groups, is the capacity of speech. In every one of his ethical and rhetorical works, Cicero expresses his conviction in the power of speech to connect humans to one another. He does this not only through various arguments and acts of explication but through his choice of genre. *De Officiis* takes the form of a letter addressed to Cicero's only son, one act in an implied exchange. Many other works, notably *De Oratore*, or *On the Orator*, are dialogues among figures from recent Roman history or between Cicero himself and his friends. Each of his works was itself an item of exchange, dedicated to a friend or a friend's memory. Conversation, not the abstracted monotone of a treatise, is Cicero's preferred vehicle of thought.

From his earliest work, even before he chose dialogue as a genre, communication emerges in Cicero's thinking as civic glue, the stuff that made the fractious republic cohere. His technical treatise *On Invention*, written when Cicero was around twenty, draws on earlier Hellenistic Greek rhetorical works in its claim that civilization began when a man skilled in persuasion summoned people together out of the wilderness (1.5). Cicero anticipates his later thinking (and his practice throughout his political career) by framing speech as an activity that one man initiates, with everyone else listening and following. But as his own rhetorical works regularly and uneasily acknowledge, public speech has effects that are not perfectly predictable or controllable. Yet despite the risk the volatility of speech creates, Cicero understood and represented the Roman republic as a state of speech.[9]

We have already seen how individual moral duties merge into political ones in Cicero's thought. Thanks to his belief that the art of speaking is the sine qua non of republican politics, the circle of his thinking about virtue also embraces rhetoric. Cicero's accounts of the good speaker and his capacities constitute a handbook of civic virtue, accompanying ethical and political works like *De Officiis* and *De Republica*, or *On the Republic*.

In *De Officiis*, the most important virtues of the citizen-man are wisdom, justice, courage, and propriety. Most important of all is the last: propriety, literally, *decorum*, the Latin term Cicero uses to translate the Stoic Panaetius's Greek *to prepon*, "that which is fitting." The concept is broad, embracing how we understand ourselves, the families into which we are born, and our tendencies (to be solitary or gregarious, for instance) as well as clothing, posture, and tone of voice. It is profoundly bound up with Cicero's ideas about the civic art of speaking—which will shortly lead us to the speaker's good qualities as a leader.

First, though, it is important to acknowledge how deeply suspect a term "propriety" is and has always been for anyone attentive to inequality and difference in social and political life. Like most rules of social practice, propriety is not static, and those with wealth, authority, or ambition treat it as akin to their property. They may obey its rules when it suits them to do so, but they may also bend them, as the young Julius Caesar did when he wore a toga that trailed on the ground in extravagant, effeminate drapes. "Beware the loosely belted boy," the dictator Sulla was reported to have said to members of his own faction, presumably warning them that Caesar's disdain for Roman conventions of dress was a sign of his contempt of political tradition as well (Suetonius, *Julius* 45.3). Like civility, its close neighbor, propriety has a long tradition of being described as necessary for free civic discourse and then defined as a style of being and speaking that turns out to exemplify elite habits and excludes non-elites. Despite propriety's claim to be "just" another set of rules, it forms (in addition to the barriers of economic and political inequity) one more barrier to non-elite claims to authority and respect. Those who do not possess the "right" or "suitable" posture, clothes, and style of speech that signal "authentic" legitimacy and thus allow the exercise of full civic agency find themselves shut out.[10]

This way of conceiving propriety—as a guide for rules of social practice—is not what I have in mind here. Two elements in Cicero's arguments make it worth reconsidering and reinventing in a new contemporary model of leadership. First is Cicero's belief that virtue is incomplete without action. In the contest between living the life of Plato, a philosopher who advised kings but avoided active engagement in his home city of Athens, and living a life that mixes philosophical reflection with action in the civic sphere, Cicero decisively chooses and advocates for the latter (*Rep.* 1.2–5). So it is not sufficient for the good speaker simply to *know* what is fitting; insight must lead to action. Having learned what offends and what pleases his listeners, the speaker behaves accordingly.

In its most extreme conception, this process demands an almost self-consuming other-directedness and, at the least, consistent habits of giving deep attention to others through careful and intuitive listening and modifying one's own behavior to attune it to local conditions and expectations. In sum, for Cicero, a person who effectively persuades others must combine critical self-reflection with the capacity and desire to conform with social rules and moral norms through a flexible, knowledgeable command of local vocabulary and cultural values.[11] This is the embodiment of his advice in the beginning of *De Officiis*, that the individual see and conceive himself as constantly navigating an array of others: friends, family, fellow citizens, citizens of other nations, all members of the human species. He is himself and yet he is as others see him; to persuade them, he must manage their experience of him, making himself pleasing even as he figures out a way to be himself.

In addition to all of this, the good speaker must risk vulnerability in the face of uncertainty.[12] Cicero has much to say in his treatise *On the Orator* about the stage fright that afflicts good speakers, whose excellence derives in part from their keen awareness of their listeners' emotions and lines of thought—and their volatility (1.121–26). The orator will not persuade those who find him deeply offensive, and part of the common human sense of what is fitting, he implies, is the expectation of a certain level of self-awareness and self-moderation.

It is because he is distinctively self-aware and aware of others, and capable of embodying that awareness in modulated behaviors and tones, that the good speaker is distinctively fit to lead. Aware of himself as "a man just like other men" (1.127), he governs himself under the watchful, unpredictable gaze of the community, whose approval he needs to mount his persuasive powers and exert his authority. (We will come back to the problem of authority.)

The second reason to stop and reconsider Ciceronian propriety is Cicero's impatience with what we might call now plain or "low-key" speech, which he found bloodless and boring. He viewed the expression of emotion as key to effective communication because it strengthens the audience's sense of themselves as a collective in two senses—together with one another and together with the speaker. Further, Cicero notes, listeners tend to respond more readily to well-phrased passion than to carefully crafted rational arguments (*De Orat.* 1.134, 2.281, 2.485). Adopting an excessively plain and unemotional style takes too much for granted; it risks alienating the very people the orator needs to persuade. With these values in mind, Cicero dedicated one of his last treatises, *Orator*, a history of Roman speechmaking, to his close friend Marcus Junius Brutus, the man who would become Julius Caesar's assassin, with the implicit goal of convincing Brutus that Cicero's own habit of ornamental, emotional speech represented a better, more inclusive style than Brutus's flat, unadorned approach.

Examples of the power of emotional speech to invite listeners' sympathy and to engage their thoughts are many. In his 2007 memoir, Joseph Biden described a speech he gave at the Democratic convention in Jersey City in 1983, in which he praised the enduring influence of the Kennedy brothers' values: "I remember the feeling in the room when I delivered that line; its effect on the crowd washed back at me as a physical sensation. I could see people in the audience crying." Biden had discovered, one reader notes, that by channeling a powerful memory, he was giving listeners the chance to interpret his words in their own ways: "After all, each person has a little something different buried in a broken heart."[13]

To seek inclusivity and communal identity through expressions of human emotion is easy to praise, of course, when the emotions in question are benign. Sympathy, pity, and grief are difficult to weaponize. But as Cicero knew well, and as the inhabitant of the White House from 2016 to 2020 still reminds us, emotional speech also has the power to arouse violence.

This is one reason Cicero repeatedly apologizes for writing in such detail about style. On the one hand, he wants to describe for us a *vir bonus dicendi peritus*, a "good man skilled at speaking," a phrase that implies a quality of innate virtuousness: *boni* or "good men" is Latin shorthand for "the nobly born," the leaders of Rome, members of the rich senatorial order who dominated Roman politics. On the other hand, his good speaker commands techniques that undermine order in the self and in the republic. Cicero's anxiety about cultivating a moderately ornamented style extends beyond his purely social worry that his obedient readers might end up speaking like Greeks, the enslaved, the poor, or the effeminate—all groups whose social disempowerment forced them (at least in the elite male Roman imagination) to employ trickery and high exaggeration. It stems from his worry about the good speaker's power to unleash the most disordered and unpredictable impulses of his audience. With his praise of the effective speaker's ability to entertain his audience and to arouse emotion, Cicero is admitting that elections and the law—the underpinnings of the republic and its active virtue— are built to yield to pleasure, passion, and irrationality. The solution in the text, no surprise to those familiar with Cicero's self-regard, is Cicero himself, a living exemplar of *decorum*, the ideal middle way between ornamental and flat speaking (*Brut.* 21, 328).

Does this middle way offer us any remedy today? One of our main problems today is the intensified conditions of economic instability we have come to call precarity. While precarity has always been with us, it is a condition affecting more and more people in the industrial world. Thanks to social media and other factors, its impact is more visible now than in past decades. Precarity has a racial and a gendered dimension: whites and men are still more likely to be haves, women and people of color have-nots. Economic precarity is linked to political precarity. Those living in a precarious state are not just living outside of politics. They are "living out a particular form of political destitution" whose outlines reveal how the well-off and privileged police the boundaries of conventional politics.[14]

Elites are policing those boundaries right now with various calls, direct and indirect, for purity. Some of this is the old friend-enemy strategy— "you're with us or you're against us"—that we saw in the Bush administration and that we hear in Donald Trump's and his supporters' expressions of misogyny and racism. For many fans of Trump, the infantilism of Trump's anger serves as proof of the purity of his love for the republic. Cicero helps us understand this phenomenon. "You set the judge on fire with your speech," the orator Crassus tells Antonius in *De Oratore*, and Antonius explains that he is capable of convincing his audiences because he arouses himself to experience authentic passion and impassions his listeners in the process of his performance.

The American political left has its own problems with purity. But rather than get caught up in a debate over how pure our language should be, over safe spaces, comfort zones, and trigger warnings, let us tackle the problem another way. If our problem is precarity, the beginning of a fitting political response is to craft a new democratic politics of cohabitation: people in positions of comfort and power together with people experiencing conditions of precarity. To be clear, when it comes to political action, Cicero does not care about precarity or a politics of cohabitation. His practical aim was to consolidate senatorial power. But his treatment of passionate decorum (to use a pithy oxymoron that nonetheless accurately captures his thinking about effective speech) points to a tactical path forward.

Black Lives Matter and related political movements rightly insist that if a new politics is to be invented that gives a true part to those who have no part, as Jacques Rancière memorably puts it, we need to create space for all voices, views, and beliefs in the political conversation. This "aesthetics of politics" (remembering that propriety is an aesthetic term) consists "in the framing of a we" in the "collective demonstration whose emergence is the element that disrupts the [current] distribution of social parts. . . . [This] does not give voice to the anonymous. Instead, it reframes the world of common experience as the world of shared impersonal experience."[15]

The challenge is to create a conversational style of talk and action that allows for the marginalized to work with those already comfortable in the world of politics in conditions of non-domination, that is, without being appropriated or dominated by them. Cicero's good orator, reinvented for today, is a leader whose propriety manifests itself in a heterogeneous style of speech and manner that reflects the variety of their experiences in real life and in their imagination. "It is necessary for the orator to have seen and heard many things, to have gone over many subjects in reflection and reading," Cicero writes. "He must not take possession of these things as his own property, but rather take sips of them as things belonging to others. . . . He must explore the very veins of every type, age, and class, and of those before whom he speaks or is going to speak; he must taste of their minds and senses" (*De Orat.* 1.218, 223).

The truth Cicero recognizes and that I want to recuperate here is that the republic is not just any plurality. It is an *unchosen* assembly. We do not select our fellow citizens. And a republic is not a kin-group, so we do not necessarily resemble one another. Living in a state of relative unfamiliarity with our fellow citizens, we cannot reliably know what each of us believes or why, what we will think or do next. Plural political action means exposing ourselves to people and impressions we do not have a say over, even if and as we seek to influence others. Judith Butler notes that "we have not yet fully brokered" such conditions.[16] And indeed we must not. A genuinely plural politics—one that includes those in conditions of precarity—cannot emerge from agreements with preselected partners who already know how to play the game. We must learn to speak accordingly.[17]

Here is where a reinvented notion of propriety makes a useful intervention. For the speaker to be capable of assuming the shifts in plural perspective that make responsible and effective politics possible, Cicero believes that he must first be in control of himself. That is, he must not tread on the sensibilities of his listeners. He must make his priority the eradication of others' fear since, as Cicero knows from years of civil war, fear kills freedom and security. While to speak persuasively is to forcefully articulate one's views and try to impose them on others—and there is undoubtedly a coercive element in any attempt to convince another person to do or think something to which they may not be spontaneously inclined—to speak with self-control means restraining violent, over-reaching behaviors that increase public mistrust and fear.

As a term, "propriety" conjures up a world of urbane exclusivity. For now, if we can, let us set those associations aside and focus on the fact that anyone who wants to chart a mutually justifiable course for our unavoidably common life must take part in the quest for reasonable terms of social cooperation, setting the highest premium on effective communication and mutual respect. Here I am inspired by Iris Marion Young, who observes that the "perception of anything like a common good can only be an outcome of public interaction that expresses rather than submerges particularities."[18] Gloria Anzaldúa explores the "continual creative motion that keeps breaking down the unitary aspect of each new paradigm"—the "emancipatory exercise of the capacity to shift perspectives."[19] Cicero's emphasis on the importance of moderating behaviors that arouse fear among his fellow citizens is linked to his encouragement of something we can translate as a "plural self" or "multiple-voiced consciousness"—both terms used by feminist thinkers. These are arguments against complacency and certainty. This is the pursuit of a "we" in the speaking self, a "we" that seeks not to dominate but is specially attuned to the precariat, those whose voices are not (yet) heard and whose absence defines even as it deforms politics. Cicero's emphasis on the good speaker's sense of anxiety before the crowd can be translated into a deeper self-knowledge: the awareness that each of us is always missing something.

But what of the citizen living in precarity who is enraged and wants to protest violence? Or take a harder case: what if that citizen's protest is racist or misogynist? In the context of a short essay, I can only venture two answers. First, we can use the Roman political tradition and its comfort with antagonism—indeed, its general approach to politics as antagonism between the haves and have-nots—as a way to model a less comfortable but more honest and diverse field of discourse.[20] This is the path pursued by Étienne Balibar, who builds an argument for a politics of "antiviolence," which we might call "radical decorum," by pointing out that nonviolence naively ignores violence and counterviolence replicates it: only a strategy that acknowledges violence but chooses the difficult path of coalition-building holds the promise of true liberation.[21]

Second, the flexibility of mind and habits of responsive engagement that Cicero calls for in his good speaker also demand deep habits of conversation: listening to others and imagining the contexts in which others develop their views. Especially during times when his political career took him away from Rome—because he was governing a province, in exile, or escaping threats to his life—Cicero made a habit of intensive letter-writing. In many of these letters, he expresses the desire to hear from his friends—not only because he hopes for news, but because he relishes hearing their thoughts and exchanging ideas. Hearing from friends and engaging in conversation with them are essential for his understanding of the changing political conditions around him and his own role and responsibilities. Hannah Arendt also has in mind the scene of conversation when she argues that one crucial response to the human condition of plurality is imagination, which eases disagreements and enables the exchange of ideas that makes possible political action in the world. Noting that the process of making political judgments "finds itself always and primarily, even if I am quite alone, in an anticipated communication with others with whom I know I must finally come to some agreement," she describes an "enlarged way of thinking . . . [that] needs the presence of others 'in whose place' it must think, whose perspective it must take into consideration, and without whom it never has the opportunity to operate at all."[22] To imagine how best to convince one's fellows, as a plural and inclusive leader must do, involves imagining oneself in "communication," or conversation, with them. Because deep listening to others may moderate one's viewpoint, conversation limits the leader's sense of certainty and authority: it makes psychologically concrete the reality of leadership in a plurality.

In practice, this is far from easy, as I can say from my own experience as a leader in an academic context. As dean, provost, and acting college president, I spent considerable time listening and talking with faculty and students whose deep disagreements with me were fueled by their justified anger about financial constraints and about deeply rooted institutional habits of deference—for example, pay scales that tended to benefit older white faculty who were disproportionately male. As the leader of an institution hobbled by decades of underfunding, I was simultaneously fighting for increased support and absorbing blows because I was, and was seen to be, the person implementing precarity, deciding where the hardest blows would fall.

Administrators' calendars fill up quickly. In my first weeks in my first administrative position, I realized that if I were to hear multiple voices, including those of critics, I would have to make aggressive efforts to clear my calendar and to get out as much as possible instead of inviting people to come to my office, the site of institutional authority. A senior faculty member with a history of progressive activism early on advised me to seek out graduate students, who are at the most risk of being silenced by the traditional funding and advising systems. As I moved from a private to a public university where graduate students took part in most aspects of administration and governance, I saw firsthand the advantages of making inclusion a daily practice on the personal and institutional level. Because inclusive meetings usually move more slowly and involve more fact-checking and argument, they require patience, but there is no question in my mind that decisions made with graduate students at the table were made more justly and with closer attention to the least powerful people in the school.

One consequence of greater openness, inclusivity, and more argumentative public exchanges surprised me: the worry and fear expressed by members of all groups—faculty, students, staff, members of the Board—when the atmosphere grew emotional. Even in the comparatively safe space of a faculty meeting or all-school gathering, I learned, we are not used to disagreement when it pushes the borders of decorum. In these moments, verbally reminding everyone (including myself) of the advantages of honest if difficult conversation and the historical inequity wreaked by self-silencing helped ease the awkwardness.

Vija Celmins chooses to work with photographs because they evade the straightforward logic of reproduction. Their relation to what they represent—the fact that a photograph of waves seemingly captures a particular moment and a timeless, eternal essence at the same time—prompts reflection on the meaningful traces that things that are far distant in time and place nonetheless leave for and on us. Historically, the arts of rhetoric have helped make a lot of wealthy men leaders, and they have ordered the world for their own profit and pleasure. Cicero is no exception: he used his own talents to advance himself, not to share power with others. But as he knew well, rhetoric is an impure art, and his insights into how to work effectively within the system—managing rivals, holding violence at bay—turn out to prompt strategies about how to change unjust systems in ways more inclusive than he would ever have imagined. I have tried here to reclaim some of rhetoric's most useful impurities so that our vision of leadership may draw on the most provocative and inspiring seeds in his thinking.

Cicero's good speakers are conversant people. That is, they are knowledgeable about the affairs with which they concern themselves: this is the basic definition of "conversant." They concern themselves above all with their listeners; they train themselves to be intimately familiar with them, to understand their worries and hopes, along with the external conditions that constrain them. To take the term a little further, they are devoted to conversation, to talk, to "turning together," in the Latin etymology of the term, to matters of shared concern. To be a conversant leader, in my reinvention of Cicero's rhetorical, political, and ethical thought, is to speak passionately and plausibly to one's audience. But to do that one must first listen, and become familiar, all the while remembering one's obligations to the full array of groups in which one is embedded: not just the family or the racially identical group or even the nation, but the human species.

NOTES

1. I have explored one stretch of the Rome-US comparison territory in Joy Connolly, "The Romans Tried to Save the Republic from Men Like Trump. They Failed." *Village Voice*, January 17, 2017, but I typically avoid comparisons of the type made by Cullen Murphy, *Are We Rome?* (New York: Houghton Mifflin Harcourt, 2007).

2. See Robert Morstein-Marx, *Mass Oratory and Political Power in the Late Roman Republic* (Cambridge: Cambridge University Press, 2004), 216–28, for a rich review of Cicero's "mouthing" of popular slogans in his speeches in the Forum, by contrast to his characterization of the people as "dregs" in his private correspondence with fellow elites (121–22).

3. I discuss this in detail in Joy Connolly, *The Life of Roman Republicanism* (Princeton, NJ: Princeton University Press, 2014), 1–21. A comparable approach to Cicero may be found in Gary Remer, *Ethics and the Orator* (Chicago: University of Chicago Press, 2017).

4. See Cary Nederman, *The Bonds of Humanity: Cicero's Legacies in European Social and Political Thought, 1100–1550* (University Park: Pennsylvania State University Press, 2020).

5. Calvin Tomkins, "Surface Matters," *New Yorker*, September 2, 2019.

6. Stephanie Straine, "Dust and Doubt: The Deserts and Galaxies of Vija Celmins," *Tate Papers*, no. 14 (Autumn 2010), https://www.tate.org.uk/research/tate-papers/14/dust-and-doubt-the-deserts-and-galaxies-of-vija-celmins.

7. Hannah Arendt, *The Human Condition*, 2nd ed. (Chicago: University of Chicago Press, 1998), 175.

8. I use masculine pronouns when describing Cicero's thought to frankly acknowledge, not endorse, his own usage.

9. Joy Connolly, *The State of Speech: Rhetoric and Political Thought in Ancient Rome* (Princeton, NJ: Princeton University Press, 2007), 3, 27.

10. Linda Zerilli, ed., *Against Civility: A Feminist Perspective* (Cambridge: Cambridge University Press, 2014) criticizes the seductive, distracting power of quietist nostalgia. Sharika Thiranagama, Tobias Kelly, and Carlos Forment collect essays on the "uneasy" history of civility and propriety in *Anthropological Theory* 18, no. 2–3 (2018): 153–74. Alex Zamalin, *Against Civility: The Hidden Racism in Our Obsession with Civility* (Boston: Beacon Press, 2019) advocates for political and social practices that fight injustice with the tactics of shock and disorder, including strikes and protests. Teresa Bejan turns to Roger Williams and other "uncivil" or indecorous leaders and thinkers in the American tradition in her effort to define civility more expansively in *Mere Civility: Disagreement and the Limits of Toleration* (Cambridge, MA: Harvard University Press, 2019). See Matthias Hanses, "Cicero Crosses the Color Line: 'Pro Archia Poeta' and W. E. B. Du Bois's 'The Souls of Black Folk,'" *International Journal of the Classical Tradition* 26, no. 1 (2019): 10–26, especially 15–20, for W. E. B. Du Bois's attempt to write himself and Black Americans into the Ciceronian tradition—well aware that Blacks of "excellent mind and manliness" risked exclusion even when they followed white rules (15).

11. Connolly, *The State of Speech*, 130–36.

12. I use some of this language in my review of Remer's *Ethics and the Orator* in *Philosophy and Rhetoric* 52, no. 9 (2019): 189–95.

13. Fintan O'Toole, "The Designated Mourner," *New York Review of Books*, January 16, 2020, citing Joe Biden, *Promises to Keep* (New York: Random House, 2007).

14. Judith Butler, *Notes toward a Performative Theory of Assembly* (Cambridge, MA: Harvard University Press, 2015), 77.

15. Jacques Rancière, *Dissensus: On Politics and Aesthetics*, ed. and trans. Steven Corcoran (New York: Continuum International, 2010), 142.

16. Butler, *Notes toward a Performative Theory*, 152.

17. I explore this line of thought, and use some of this language, in "Dialogue Across Divides," *Academe* 106, no. 2 (2020): 30–37.

18. Iris Marion Young, *Justice and the Politics of Difference* (Princeton, NJ: Princeton University Press, 1990), 119, as cited and discussed in Susan Bickford, *The Dissonance of Democracy* (Ithaca, NY: Cornell University Press, 1996), 104.

19. Gloria Anzaldúa, *Borderlands/La Frontera* (San Francisco: Spinsters/Aunt Lute Press, 1987), 78–80, as cited and discussed in Bickford, *Dissonance of Democracy*, 122–23.

20. See further discussions in Connolly, *The State of Speech*, 262–73; and Connolly, *Life of Roman Republicanism*, 23–64.

21. I am rather brutally simplifying Balibar's careful construction of guardrails around his concept of antiviolence in *Violence and Civility: The Limits of Political Philosophy* (New York: Columbia University Press, 2016).

22. Hannah Arendt, "The Crisis in Culture," in *Between Past and Future* (New York: Penguin, 2006), 217.

CHAPTER 2

Tragedies of Leadership

Sophocles, Aristotle, and Shakespeare on Tyranny

Edith Hall

Renaissance scholar Stephen Greenblatt published in 2018 a book on autocrats in Shakespeare, titled, simply, *Tyrant*.[1] He tells us that it is his response to a particular political moment—indeed, a particular election—and that he believes that Shakespeare's portraits of tyrants can help us to understand our contemporary global politics.[2] Greenblatt dissects the features of tyranny as portrayed by Shakespeare—narcissism, paranoia, exemption from needing to traffic in facts or supply evidence, and moral corruption, which begins to infect every relationship in the state. He reveals the psychological complexity of the men in Shakespeare who acquire absolute power, whether Richard III or Macbeth or ancient Roman statesmen. The first detailed portraits of tyranny emerged, however, in the classical Greek writing of Herodotus, Aristotle, and, above all, Sophocles. In his book, Greenblatt is not addressing the classical provenance of much of Shakespeare's thought, although he acknowledges the presence of Plutarch's *Parallel Lives* in *Julius Caesar* and *Coriolanus*.[3] Here I argue that Sophocles, partly through his presence in Aristotle's thought, made every bit as important a contribution as Shakespeare did to world thinking on tyranny.

Importantly, Sophocles was highly respected not only as an artist but also as a political leader. He had a positive relationship with Pericles, the most prominent politician of his time, and served in at least three political offices himself. From 443 to 442 BCE, Sophocles oversaw the state finances as a treasurer before being elected a general in the Samian War. Later, in

413 BCE, he was invited to serve as a magistrate. Sophocles's experience as a leader informed his plays, especially in how they imagine leaders' responses to tragic conflicts and political emergencies. It is no surprise, then, that both *Oedipus Tyrannus* and *Antigone* illuminate the ways that leaders often tend toward autocracy once they come to possess power.[4]

Greek literature, from its dawn, puts the assessment of leaders at its center. Ouranos is castrated in Hesiod because he oppresses both his wife and his children.[5] Agamemnon in the *Iliad* is a selfish, mean-spirited, and at times incompetent leader, envious of the men he is expected to inspire. Odysseus in the *Odyssey*, as his lieutenant Eurylochus points out after his reconnaissance trip to Circe's palace, is cavalier about putting the lives of his own men in danger.[6] Aeschylus's *Persians* reveals how the young king Xerxes makes almost every mistake that Aristotle was later to catalog as the errors associated with the monarchical and tyrannical forms of government in his comparative discussion of the four types of constitution in the fifth book of his *Politics*—monarchy, tyranny, oligarchy, and democracy. This is informed by the Persian constitutional debate in Herodotus 3.80–82 but is more detailed. Aristotle's discussion has had an incalculable influence on Western political thought and practice: the vocabulary of European political theory was born when his *Politics* was first translated into modern languages.[7]

Aristotle's model underpins the political thought of key Roman authors such as Tacitus and subsequently medieval and Renaissance political theorists, especially Machiavelli. A month after the execution of Charles I in January 1649, John Milton's *The Tenure of Kings and Magistrates*, which justifies regicide where the king has made himself answerable only to God, uses Aristotle's definition of a monarch in the *Politics*.[8] But, rather earlier, Shakespeare is thought to have read the English translation of the *Politics* by an individual who signs himself I.D. and that was published in London by Adam Islip in 1598. By that date, the *Politics* had already penetrated deep into English cultural life through paraphrases, summaries, and discussions. "You cannot step into a scholar's study but (ten to one) you shall likely find open either Bodin's *de Republica* or Le Roye's *Exposition on Aristotle's Politics* or some other like French or Italian political discourses," wrote English intellectual Gabriel Harvey in about 1580.[9]

If Shakespeare derived some of his thinking on tyranny from Aristotle, then Sophocles's tyrants are implicitly present in the Renaissance theater, since there was a synergy between Sophocles's tyrants Oedipus and Creon and Aristotle's political and moral philosophy. Since the misfortune that Creon brings on Thebes in *Antigone* is entirely his responsibility (in contrast with unlucky Oedipus as presented in either *Oedipus Tyrannus* or *Oedipus at Colonus*), he was a perfect figure for Aristotle to use when thinking about how people's characters are to be judged by their words and deeds.[10] We know Aristotle thought hard about Sophocles's Creon because he specifically discusses his behavior in his *Poetics*.[11]

Indeed, repeated references to both *Oedipus* and *Antigone* in his *Poetics* prove that Aristotle knew them inside and out and assumed that his students and readers did too. A few scholars have ignored the apolitical tenor of the *Poetics* (in which Aristotle insists that poetry is a discrete craft which needs to be discussed in its own terms) to say that Aristotle thinks tragedy can be used to train its audiences to resist the undermining of democracy.[12] But how about the other way around? Little attention has been paid to what Aristotle learned about politics and ethics from his seminal encounters with the dramatists. I want to supplement a view often voiced by social scientists such as Roger Boesche, professor of politics at Occidental College in Los Angeles, who sparked Barack Obama's interest in politics. Boesche speaks for most of his discipline when he writes, "It is not exaggerating to say that Aristotle laid the groundwork for all subsequent theories of tyranny."[13] This is misleading. Aristotle continued the work, but he did not dig the foundations. Aristotle's discussion emerged from a tradition that went back to the fifth-century pre-Socratics such as Protagoras and Zeno and is already given sophisticated dialogue form in Herodotus. But it was given its most thrilling embodiment in Sophocles's Theban despots.

Aristotle's understanding of theater may have been informed by his analyses of science and ethics, but the influence was two-way. He likely frequented dramatic performances in a culture where theater was at the center. References to dramatic performances and texts in Aristotle's works are ubiquitous.[14] "In the *Poetics*," I have suggested elsewhere, "he shows such intense knowledge of contemporary tragedies as well as the 5th-century canonical repertoire that we know he must have watched plays constantly, as well as collecting papyrus texts of them to study."[15]

Aristotle's moral and political philosophy reflects his deep familiarity with theater:

His theory of the virtues occupying a middle position on a spectrum between excess and deficiency . . . often reads like an account of stock types in theater: the Spartan woman and the bombastic tyrant of tragedy, pimps and usurers who embody shameful profiteering, buffoons and [the] boor (*agroikoi*), the flatterer (*kolax*) and the grouch (*dyskolos*). . . . He shares specific vocabulary with the comic poets, like the sticky man or *glischros*, who is mean with money. . . . But the deep level at which tragedy seems to have informed his thinking about ethics and action is far more important. The relationship between intellectual activity, thinking things through, choice, and action which he observes in the *Poetics* actually underpin much of what he says in the *Ethics* about practical wisdom. . . . In his *Politics*, too, the analogy of the theatrical chorus occurs at important places when he is talking about relationships between citizens, and argues that *chorēgoi* should be public officials, as important as priests, ambassadors and heralds. The *Rhetoric* also reveals a powerful connection in his mind between civic speech in reality and in the fictional scenarios portrayed in drama.[16]

Aristotle recommends in his *Rhetoric* that speakers quote *Antigone* when appealing to "universal law."[17] There is corroborating testimony to the familiarity of Sophocles's *Antigone* in the fourth-century Athens, where Aristotle spent most of his adult life. No other surviving Greek tragedy features so prominently in Athenian public oratory: by a few decades after the play's composition, Athenian statesmen could rely on their audience understanding detailed comparisons of their real, contemporary situation with the situation in archaic mythical Thebes staged in *Antigone*.[18]

Aristotle's discussion of constitutions in his *Politics* rests both on intensive research (at the Lyceum, he and his students collected data on the history of dozens of Greek city-states) and an unusual range of lived experience in every kind of constitution. He was born and brought up in Stagira, then a free and autonomous city-state, which he later saw crushed by Macedon. He spent many years in democratic Athens. His whole life was spent in the shadow of the rising autocratic kingdom of Macedonia; his father was employed as a doctor by the royal family, and Aristotle was employed by Philip II for seven years in his forties until the king's assassination. But in 345–44 BCE, he also spent at least a year in Lesbos, which was almost certainly ruled by an oligarchy, after a couple of years with Hermias, his friend, the tyrant from Anatolia.

Assos was constitutionally a "tyranny." But the term did not always bear pejorative associations. A tyrant ruled not because he had inherited the throne but because he had come into sole power with the support of the masses, often in reaction to an unpopular monarch or oligarchy. A tyrant became sole ruler as a result of the will of the majority, as in a democracy, although by a coup rather than an election. Because tyrannies initially needed popular support, until the tyrant became repressive (which usually

happened), Aristotle notes that tyrannies share certain features with democ-
racies, including a greater freedom of conduct allowed to women, children,
and enslaved people.[19]

Aristotle's discussion identifies two categories of tyranny.[20] The traditional tyranny, as practiced by Periander of Corinth, relies on the tyrant
exterminating spirited members of the community, distrusting everyone,
prohibiting institutions likely to foster a sense of collective identity and
trust such as dining associations and educational organizations, scrutinizing
everything everyone says and does, and sowing dissent between friends, citizens, and social classes. These behaviors are the opposite of the nurturing
of the *homonoia*, like-mindedness or single purpose, praised by fifth-century
thinkers including Protagoras, Gorgias, Democritus, Euripides and Anti-
phon.[21] But another passage does not receive as much attention: "It is characteristic of a tyrant to dislike everyone who has dignity or independence;
he wants to be alone in his glory, but anyone who claims a like dignity or
asserts his independence encroaches upon his prerogative, and is hated by
him as an enemy to his power."[22]

The second kind of tyrant succeeds in holding on to supreme power,
however, by disguising himself as benevolent and avoiding any suggestion
of the characteristics Aristotle has identified in the traditional tyrant. The
"benevolent" tyrant tries to look as though he cares about public revenues.
He publishes his accounts transparently and pretends to be a steward of the
public interest. His demeanor is crucial: "He should appear, not harsh, but
dignified, and when men meet him they should look upon him with reverence, and not with fear." He must inspire respect, appear to be a great soldier,
and ensure that neither "he nor any of his associates should ever be guilty of
the least offense against modesty toward the young of either sex who are his
subjects." And "he should appear to be particularly earnest in the service of
the Gods; for if men think that a ruler is religious and has a reverence for the
gods, they are less afraid of suffering injustice at his hands, and they are less
disposed to conspire against him."[23]

The "benevolent" tyrant must honor people of merit, so they do not start
to think they might be more honored in a free constitution. Any punishments must be the business *not* of him but of the officers and courts of law. If
anyone needs to have their power reduced, then the process should be gradual rather than summary. Above all, the tyrant must abstain from outrage,
especially that wanton conduct toward the young. He needs to be careful in
his treatment of men who love honor, and if he does have to control them,
"he should be thought only to employ fatherly correction, and not to tram-
ple upon others; his acquaintance with youth should be supposed to arise

from affection, and not from the insolence of power."[24] The paradox with this kind of deliberately benign-looking, youth-friendly tyranny, of course, is that in a sense it stops being fully tyrannical and comes to resemble Aristotle's best kind of monarch.

The canonical tragedies about tyranny in the classical repertoire are set in Bronze Age Thebes. As I have noted elsewhere,

> The sumptuous edifice in the ancient citadel of Thebes, excavated in the early twentieth century, therefore housed an ancient nobility that, to Athenian democrats, had stood for everything they most disliked: an unshakeably aristocratic constitution, connivance with the invading Persians, and support of Spartan military activities in central Greece. The citadel was situated conspicuously in the hot, flat plains of Boeotia, remote from the sea, and just near enough to the Athenians—about eighteen hours' walk—to be a real psychological presence even across the Cithaeron mountain range. No wonder the ancient poets, including above all the playwrights of the maritime, culturally open, and noisy Athenian democracy, used the mysterious space contained within the walls of Thebes as the setting for such dark and politically profound tragedies as Sophocles's *Oedipus Tyrannus* and *Antigone*. The community there is portrayed as too introverted and suspicious of outside influence to be open to revitalization, change, and renewal, its ruling aristocracy prone to the secrets, incestuous relationships (whether literal or metaphorical), dogmatism, grudges, and internal power struggles that develop in any closed and unaccountable ruling class. There is always something wrong with the way the social order works in Thebes.[25]

If we read Sophocles's *Antigone* retrospectively in the light of Aristotle's tyrant, we see how Creon's Thebes adumbrates the unhappy state that Aristotle envisages suffering under his definitive traditional tyrant. The play begins with a scene showing how even the closest loving relationship between people who should be *philoi*, full sisters, is sabotaged by the behavior of the ruling tyrant. Antigone, forbidden by Creon from performing the ritual work of cleansing and singing, laments over the corpse of her brother Polynices and angrily argues with Ismene, her more compliant sister. Taking care of the body was the duty of Greek women, and Antigone's determination to carry out her role faithfully turned her into a spirited dissenter of the kind that the tyrant must handle with care. When Creon failed to perform his stipulated leadership duty as a man, which was to organize the funeral of kin, Antigone's honor bound her to intervene.

There is a corrosive vagueness in the constitutional power Creon wields. Antigone calls him a general, *strategos*. He seems to be called a tyrant, *turannos*, by Ismene, but she also says in a strange phrase that she and Antigone should not "in spite of the law go against the *vote* or power of tyrants" (*Antigone*, 59–60). Yet she implies that he *is* somehow identifiable with the will of the citizens, *politai* (78–79). The chorus, who have been handpicked by Creon as loyal to the royal family, call him a *basileus* (constitutional hereditary monarch) but also a "novice" who has only just started ruling and whose father never came near to holding royal power (155–56). The word "novice," *neochmos*, is startling, since elsewhere it applies not to people but to things—and usually with drastic or negative connotations.

The term used for the group that the chorus constitutes is also unusual. It is neither a "council" nor an "assembly" but a "talking-shop made up of handpicked old men." Creon's inaugural speech is peculiar. He says that he has selected these senior Thebans and separated them from the rest (164), thus using Caesar's policy of *divisa et impera*—dividing to rule, or sowing seeds of dissension between citizens. This is the opposite of nurturing *homonoia*. Antigone later addresses the chorus as the *koiranidai* of Thebes—an unusual word that must mean "members of the ruling houses" (perhaps the descendants of the Sown Men of Thebes?), implying an oligarchic constitution, meanwhile saying she is the only one left of the *royal* household (940–41). But now that her brothers are dead, Creon holds the whole power and throne according to what he calls "kinship closeness" to them (173–74). He does not say whether he sees himself as a *basileus* or a *turannos*.

When Creon tells the chorus that he has already delivered the proclamation about the burial policy, it is revealed as a fait accompli. Their response is unenthusiastic: that is his will, and he is entitled "to use any law" in regard to both the living and the dead (213–14). The ensuing dialogue becomes odder. Creon commands them to be "guardians" of what he has decreed (215). They take this literally, thinking he means they should physically keep watch over things, and ask him to refer this instruction to younger men. But he means it metaphorically: he responds that the guards are already stationed over the corpse. He has, clearly, been busy. What he actually means is that the elders should not "yield to those who disobey my commands" (219). Their response is ambiguous, setting the moral tone for the rest of the play (220): "There is no one so foolish as to crave death." They ostensibly mean that they do not think anyone will deliberately incur the death penalty by burying Polynices, but by putting the statement into a gnomic third person, they generalize the situation in Thebes so that it includes themselves. Creon makes no attempt to clear up the ambiguity in his response: "I assure you, that is the wage for disobedience."

Creon does almost everything which Aristotle says distinguishes the worst kind of tyrant: he delivers verdicts, determines the punishment (even by death) of actions he has unilaterally decided are crimes, and does not delegate such matters to any form of magistrate or court. He accuses the guard, on no evidence, of taking bribes; the guard cannot believe it when he escapes with his life. Thebans expect Creon to decree summary execution.

Creon decrees death to Ismene on no evidence whatsoever (488–90). He outrages domestic piety by interfering in the performance of duties between close kin: as Antigone says, "he has no right to keep me from my own" (48). His rule promotes secrecy, lies, and denunciations: Ismene begs Antigone to keep her deed secret (84–85). His rule promotes discord both internally to classes and between classes. The guards are so frightened of him that they fight among themselves when they see that the corpse has been buried rather than presenting a unified front: *homonoia*, even among members of the same class, is impossible under tyranny. In fact, everyone is terrified of speaking to him and voicing their views. Haemon says this explicitly: Creon's face is frightening, and the townspeople say things under cover of darkness that his father would dislike, such as praising Antigone's actions (690–95).

Moreover, Creon *omits* to do most of the things which Aristotle says distinguish the better kind of tyrant: the absence of any reference to him in the opening chorus implies he has done nothing to defend his city militarily. His reference to the gods at the beginning of his first speech is peremptory (162–63), just ten words. And when the chorus ponders whether there might be divine involvement in the strange things happening around Polynices's corpse, he shouts at them to be silent (278–81). Most illuminating of all is the sudden revelation, near the end, that his other son, Megareus, has recently died, in connection with yesterday's battle. The man we have been watching throwing his weight about so tyrannically in the public sphere has been personally bereaved from the beginning of the play. Demosthenes was criticized for appearing in public when his daughter had been dead only seven days.[26]

In Antigone, however, we have a Theban of considerable ability who is ambitious to gain honor for herself—the type of figure Aristotle says the tyrant needs to treat with care. She asks how she could have won a nobler glory than by giving burial to her own brother and says that everyone on stage would admit that they approved of her if fear did not silence them. But tyranny, she concludes, "has the power to do and say whatever it pleases" (504–7). Creon humiliates her as well as sentencing her to death for the very action that has brought her public admiration.

Finally, the emphasis on the theme of deliberation in the play will have attracted Aristotle's attention, since *euboulia*—giving and taking advice— is a hallmark of the great-souled man in the *Nicomachean Ethics*; Aristotle wrote a whole treatise, now lost, on the topic.[27] Furthermore, deliberative debate was a central feature of Athenian democracy:

> The Athenians heard detailed debates in the Assembly about the expediency of their policies before they voted to act on them. But the Athenian officials charged with deliberating the city's policies at length were the members of the "Council" (*Boulē*), since it was the place where deliberation took place. At the time of the drama competitions, these *bouleutai*, "councillors" or "deliberators," were symbolically privileged as thought leaders of the city since they sat together in seats of honor at the front of the theater. The importance of the *Boulē* in the Athenian democracy is underlined by the haste with which the oligarchs who took power in 411 BCE ousted the democratically elected *bouleutai* and took over their official seat, the *Bouleutērion*, as their own center of power. . . . The Council met almost every day (X. *Hell.* 2.3.11) and considered matters relating not only to the state's finances and the scrutiny of magistrates, but all its cults and festivals, its navy, its building program, and care for the sick, disabled, and orphaned. To serve as a councillor required accumulating information, assessing past actions and deliberating about future ones *virtually all day, every day, for a whole year*. The "quality of attention" required by service on the council seems breath-taking compared with what is required of politicians, let alone ordinary citizens, today.[28]

In *Antigone*, Creon's incompetent deliberation causes unnecessary chaos, several deaths in addition to those of Polynices and Eteocles, and desperate suffering. There is no consolation for the tragedy in the form of a beneficial new cult, as in some other plays. There is simply a mess. It has been caused not by Apollo's mysterious and unavoidable agenda, as in *Oedipus the Tyrant*, but by the wholly avoidable decisions made by a single fool who could have learned a thing or two by serving on the Athenians' democratic council.

Creon speaks frequently of "deliberations" (*bouleumata*, 179), but his practice is lacking. He states publicly that "anyone who while guiding the whole city fails to set his hand to the best counsels" (*bouleumaton*, 179) is the worst of men, yet there is a distinct absence of deliberation or consultation in the way he leads. He issues a decree prohibiting the burial of the dead, and when he learns that Antigone has defended the burial of her brother, he is outraged, suddenly deciding that "she and her sister shall not escape a dreadful death" (488–89). Later, when the chorus demands that he free Antigone, he relents, but by that stage, it is too late. In the final scene of the play, Creon himself even seems to recognize his own lack of judgment. It was his poor decisions (*bouleumaton*, 1265) and botched deliberations (*dusbouliais*, 1269), he concedes, that precipitated the death of Haemon.[29] As I observed in "The Necessity and Limits of Deliberation in Sophocles' Theban Plays":

> Creon's incompetence as a deliberator receives uniquely explicit comment, which may be one of the reasons why *Antigone* was so admired from a political perspective in antiquity and so intimately connected with the perception that Sophocles won high esteem as a statesman himself. . . . *Antigone* presents an incompetent deliberator offending the gods and thus creating avoidable tragedy.[30]

Creon makes much use of terms to do with deliberation, for example, the noun *bouleumata* ("deliberations," 179). Yet his decree proscribing burial of the enemy follows no deliberative or consultative process. In his first speech as newly self-appointed leader, he says the decree has been made for two reasons. The first is that a leader who does not take into account the best counsels (179) is the worst of men. He, however, ignores the chorus' sensible advice that the dust which has covered Polynices' cadaver has something to do with the gods (278–79).[31]

Creon takes another precipitate decision after hearing Antigone's defense and sentences both her and her sister to death (488–89), although he later changes his mind suddenly (771) and spares Ismene. As Haemon says, any benefits Creon might enjoy if he considered other people's opinions are canceled by his refusal to hear them (684–723). One of the most important lines in the play is Tiresias's statement that mistakes can often be rectified if a man who has erred realizes his error and corrects it (1026). This important concept is repeated when Tiresias responds to Creon's verbal assault on him that the most important of assets are good advice and deliberation (1050). The chorus soon afterward emphasizes that Creon should accept good advice and tells him to set Antigone free straightaway (1098). And, of course, he changes his mind too late. Creon himself acknowledges in the catastrophic final sequence that it was caused by his own poor deliberating

(1265, 1269). In *Antigone*, the tragedy is caused simply by an autocrat who is incompetent at decision-making.[32]

To return in conclusion to Shakespeare, it is now acknowledged, where it used to be emphatically and almost universally denied, that Shakespeare had access to Greek tragedies through the wide circulation of Renaissance Latin cribs.[33] Several Latin translations of Sophocles had circulated in the 1540s, and the complete seven plays had become available in Latin in 1550.[34] The edition circulated among European humanists. But *Antigone* has the unusual privilege of being translated, on its own, in 1581 by English scholar and poet Thomas Watson. Among the most widely accepted traces of Greek tragedy in Shakespeare are the glimpses of *Antigone*, especially in *King Lear*, the Shakespearean tragedy in which Greenblatt says the high cost of a strategy of resistance to tyranny is most starkly portrayed.[35] When Lear staggers onto the stage in despair and remorse, carrying the corpse of his child Cordelia, it is difficult not to imagine Shakespeare being impressed by Creon's closing entrance in *Antigone*, carrying the corpse of his son. Other details— Cordelia's hanging in prison, for example—are reminiscent of Sophocles's play. In the speech of the loyal Kent, the one courtier who tries to resist Lear's plans for carving up the kingdom and disinheriting and banishing Cordelia, sounds like the chorus, Tiresias, and Haemon all rolled into one: "And in thy best consideration check / This hideous rashness."[36] Like Sophocles's Thebes in *Antigone*, there is a conspicuous *lack* of state apparatus: as Greenblatt puts it, Lear's early British world "does not seem to have any institutions or offices—Parliament, Privy Council, commissioners, High Priests— to moderate or dilute royal power." Lear is said to be inconsistent—to have "inconstant starts."[37]

Greenblatt could indeed be summarizing *Antigone* when he writes, in general terms, of Shakespeare's portraits of tyranny in action:

> Shakespeare did not think that tyrants ever lasted for very long. However cunning they were in their rise, once in power they were surprisingly incompetent. Possessing no visions for the country they ruled, they were incapable of fashioning enduring support, and though they were cruel and violent, they could never crush all of the opposition. Their isolation, suspicion, and anger, often conjoined to an arrogant overconfidence, hastened their downfall.[38]

Just like Sophocles's Creon.

Antigone, whether in Sophocles's version, or adaptations of Jean Anouilh or Bertolt Brecht, is quantitatively the most influential ancient drama in performance of all time. It is also so in terms of political instrumentality: Antigone has protested on Robben Island against apartheid South Africa, in the dockyards of Gdańsk against authoritarian communism, in Argentina against the disappearance of young activists, and in the name of the independence movement in Manipur.[39] At a time when autocracy, the unaccountability of rulers (whether democratically elected or not), attacks on freedom of speech, promotion of social division, and an almost total absence of careful deliberation seem increasingly to characterize our global political culture, it is important to remember that the human race has survived such challenges in the past. Moreover, in the works of Aristotle and Shakespeare and, earlier than either of them, Sophocles, we have been given powerful tools with which to analyze and resist them.

NOTES

1. Stephen Greenblatt, *Tyrant: Shakespeare on Power* (London: Bodley Head, 2018).
2. Greenblatt, *Tyrant*, 191.
3. Greenblatt, 155.
4. See Edith Hall, *Greek Tragedy: Suffering under the Sun* (Oxford: Oxford University Press, 2010), 299–301; Edith Hall, "'Antigone' and the Internationalization of Theatre in Antiquity," in *"Antigone" on the Contemporary World Stage*, ed. Erin Mee and Helene P. Foley (Oxford: Oxford University Press, 2011), 50–51.
5. Hesiod, *Theogony*, lines 126–81.
6. Homer, *Odyssey*, 10.431–37; see Edith Hall, *The Return of Ulysses: A Cultural History of Homer's "Odyssey"* (London: I. B. Tauris, 2010), 103.
7. Edith Hall, *Aristotle's Way: How Ancient Wisdom Can Change Your Life* (London: Bodley Head, 2018), 171.
8. John Milton, *The Tenure of Kings and Magistrates: Proving, that it is lawfull, and hath been held so through all ages, for any, who have the power, to call to account a tyrant, or wicked king, and after due conviction, to depose, and put him to death* (London: Matthew Simmons, 1649), especially 10, 18.
9. See *Letter-Book of Gabriel Harvey, 1573–1580*, ed. Edward John Long Scott (London: Camden Society, 1884), 79; Robin Headlam Wells, *Shakespeare's Humanism* (Cambridge: Cambridge University Press, 2005), 132.
10. Aristotle, *Poetics*, 1450a–b.
11. Aristotle, 1454a.
12. E.g., Stephen G. Salkever, "Tragedy and the Education of the Demos," in *Greek Tragedy and Political Theory*, ed. J. Peter Euben (Berkeley: University of California Press, 1986), 274–303; Daniel DiLeo, "Tragedy against Tyranny," *Journal of Politics* 75 (2013): 254–65. On the missing *polis* in Aristotle's *Poetics*, see Edith Hall, "Is There a *Polis* in Aristotle's 'Poetics'?" in *Tragedy and the Tragic: Greek Theatre and Beyond*, ed. Michael S. Silk (Oxford: Oxford University Press, 1995), 294–309.
13. Roger Boesche, "Aristotle's Science of Tyranny," *History of Political Thought* 14 (1993): 1–25, at 22.

14. See Edith Hall, "Aristotle and the Idea of an Athenian University," *Parabasis* 15, no. 1 (2017): 93–103, esp. 98; Edith Hall, "'Master of Those Who Know': Aristotle as Role Model for the Twenty-First Century Academician," *European Review* 25 (2017): 3–19.

15. Hall, "Aristotle and the Idea of an Athenian University," 98.

16. See Victor Castellani, "Drama and Aristotle," in *Drama and Philosophy*, ed. James Redmond, Themes in Drama 12 (Cambridge: Cambridge University Press, 1990), 21–36. Aristotle, *Nicomachean Ethics*, 4.2.1122a24–25 and b22–26; *Politics*, 5.7.1309a17–20; 4.12; quoted from Hall, "Aristotle and the Idea of an Athenian University," 99.

17. Aristotle, 1.1375b.

18. Hall, "'Antigone' and the Internationalization of Theatre in Antiquity," 51–63.

19. See further Ivan Jordović, "Aristotle on Extreme Tyranny and Extreme Democracy," *Historia: Zeitschrift für Alte Geschichte* 60 (2011): 36–64.

20. Aristotle, *Politics*, 5.1313a18–1315a40.

21. See the references in Arnaldo Momigliano, "Camillus and Concord," *Classical Quarterly* 36 (1942): 111–20.

22. Aristotle, *Politics*, 5.1314a.

23. Aristotle, 5.1314b.

24. Aristotle, 5.1315a.

25. Quoted from Hall, "'Antigone' and the Internationalization of Theatre in Antiquity," 53–54, citing N. G. L. Hammond, "Plataea's Relations with Thebes, Sparta and Athens," *Journal of Hellenic Studies* 112 (1992): 144n1, and Froma Zeitlin, "Thebes: Theater of Self and Society in Athenian Drama," in Euben, *Greek Tragedy and Political Theory*, 101–41.

26. See Aeschines, *Orations*, 3.77; Hall, *Greek Tragedy*, 130.

27. See Hall, *Aristotle's Way*, ch. 3.

28. Quoted from Edith Hall, "The Necessity and Limits of Deliberation in Sophocles's Theban Plays," in *A Companion to Sophocles*, ed. Kirk Ormand (Oxford: Wiley Blackwell, 2015), 303–4. See Thucydides, *History of the Peloponnesian War*, 8.69–70.1; Aristotle, *Constitution of the Athenians*, 32.3; Julia Shear, "Cultural Space, Change and the Politics of Commemoration in Athens," in *Debating the Athenian Cultural Revolution: Art, Literature, Philosophy, and Politics, 430–380 B.C.*, ed. Robin Osborne (New York: Cambridge University Press, 2007), 102–3.

29. Hall, "The Necessity and Limits," 312–13.

30. Hall, 313.

31. See further Hall, 312.

32. Hall, 313.

33. See Inga-Stina Ewbank, "Striking Too Short at Greeks? The Transmission of *Agamemnon* to the English Renaissance Stage," in *"Agamemnon" in Performance*, ed. Fiona Macintosh, Pantelis Michelakis, Edith Hall, and Oliver Taplin (Oxford: Oxford University Press, 2005), 37–52.

34. See Louise Schleiner, "Latinized Greek Drama in Shakespeare's Writing of 'Hamlet,'" *Shakespeare Quarterly* 41, no. 1 (Spring 1990): 29–48.

35. Greenblatt, *Tyrant*, 140–47.

36. Shakespeare, *King Lear*, Act I, Scene 2, 148–49.

37. Shakespeare, Act I, Scene 1, line 296; Greenblatt, *Tyrant*, 116–17.

38. Greenblatt, *Tyrant*, 142.

39. See Mee and Foley, eds., *"Antigone" on the Contemporary World Stage*.

PART II

Philosophy and Religion

CHAPTER 3

Leadership Lessons from Plato's *Republic*

Noah Lopez

My first time in North Carolina, home to Wake Forest University, was as a participant in a week-long retreat, part of a two-year-long Buddhist dharma study and practice program for folks dedicated to promoting environmental well-being alongside justice, equity, and compassion in their communities. Our group of twenty-eight was diverse across age, ability, race, gender, geographic origin, cultural background, religious commitment, and more. Our conversations were often challenging. We talked about the relationship between personal identities and suffering, about the continuing damage of colonial language and thinking, about how to live well amid difference and plurality. During one of our conversations, a participant who had done work with South Africa's Truth and Reconciliation Commission invoked the commission's slogan: "Revealing is healing."

I mention this slogan now, at the beginning, because I think it is well applied in the leadership context of higher education, and higher education is the context with which I am most concerned here. As a philosopher whose work consists in promoting equity and critical inclusivity in university classrooms and culture, I want to offer Plato's *Republic* as a resource for leadership lessons. This will require some *revealing*—specifically in engagement with the allegory of the cave, a well-worn passage from Book VII of the *Republic*. I will suggest that the way this passage is often read and used in academic philosophical contexts tends to conceal pedagogy (how one teaches or facilitates learning) as a site of leadership. This concealing can inhibit *healing* in places where pedagogical practices and structures have brought about exclusion and harm. In order for healing to happen, we must reveal pedagogy as a site of leadership.

But what is to be healed? I have used the words "exclusion" and "harm"; we should get clearer on what these might refer to in the case of academic philosophy specifically and higher education more broadly. Indication of exclusion in academic philosophy is found in the preliminary results of the American Philosophical Association's 2018 Diversity and Inclusion Survey. The survey, intended to surface patterns and issues related to diversity and inclusion in the discipline, was sent out to 9,610 philosophy graduate students and graduates across the world. Ten and a half percent of contacted individuals responded, an overall participation rate akin to that of previous years.[1] The results show that, among current doctoral students and recent graduates in the field, there is notable underrepresentation of people of color, veterans, women, folks of nonbinary gender, and those of lower and lower-middle socioeconomic status.[2] Moreover, exclusion of scholarship representing these identities and others is a well-known problem in academic philosophy. As philosophers Luvell Anderson and Verena Erlenbusch note, there is wide agreement that philosophy has a "diversity problem," and syllabus diversification is a key way to address this problem.[3] In particular, syllabus reform can be a site of clarifying what academic philosophy's diversity problem actually consists in and addressing it accordingly: "How one chooses to approach syllabus diversification depends on just how one understands philosophy's diversity problem. Whether one takes it to be the result of an unfortunate presentation of content in philosophy courses or the consequence of a deeper conceptual problem that makes the content of philosophical debates unattractive or irrelevant for minorities will determine which approach one pursues."[4] Acknowledging that many academic philosophy syllabi exclude identities and voices also underrepresented in philosophy departments, Anderson and Erlenbusch highlight how exclusion at the level of the philosophy syllabus may signify various forms of exclusion throughout the discipline.[5]

Exclusion is thus manifest both in terms of who is doing the work of academic philosophy in departments and, intimately related, who is being studied within the canon and scholarship of academic philosophy. One can argue that this exclusion itself constitutes harm, but even beyond exclusion as harm, we find other overt manifestations of harm in academic philosophy. The list of cases involving an established male professor sexually harassing or intimidating a younger female graduate student, for example, is long. Charges of sexual harassment or assault have been brought by numerous female students against the likes of Thomas Pogge at both Yale and Columbia University, Colin McGinn at the University of Miami, and John Searle at the University of California–Berkeley. These are just a few of the higher-profile cases that received media attention on account of the status of the philosophy professor indicted in the charges.[6] The harmful effects of such experiences of sexual harassment or assault include increased symptoms of anxiety and depression, career and professional disruption, and diminished earning potential. These effects have been clearly articulated and are well documented.[7] And yet the story of this harmful dynamic between professor and student is so familiar that it has become a ready-made plotline, as demonstrated in Woody Allen's glamorization of the phenomenon in his 2015 film *Irrational Man*. Widely received as having a plot insensitive to the real harm that can result from gendered and sexualized power dynamics between professor and student, the Rotten Tomatoes critics' consensus reads: "*Irrational Man* may prove rewarding for the most ardent Joaquin Phoenix fans or Woody Allen apologists, but all others most likely need not apply."[8]

"But all others most likely need not apply" is an inadequate strategy for higher education, especially when we live in a society in which more education tends to correlate with higher earnings, increased rates of employment, and greater health and well-being.[9] Just because we philosophers deal primarily in ideas and arguments does not mean we get off the hook here. Moreover, these issues of exclusion and harassment are not just specific to philosophy; they cut across higher education. The manifestations range from poor mental health among college students to qualified scholars leaving academia due to the workplace climate.[10] Still, I want to suggest that the striking ideas, the provocative metaphors, and the deep questions studied and taught in philosophy have much to offer. We have some *revealing* work to do.

Of course, there are good reasons to be wary of beginning this revealing work by looking to Plato's *Republic* for leadership lessons. For one, the *Republic* is old—it dates to around 380 BCE—and is authored by a proverbial dead white man.[11] In these respects it is distant from the unique challenges and opportunities of pluralistic, diverse leadership today. Second, the work has been denounced for advocating totalitarian ideals. In the *Republic* Plato suggests the ideal leader of society should be a philosopher-king. In a well-visited critique, the philosopher Karl Popper takes Plato to task for this suggestion—support of autonomy, choice, and inclusivity are glaringly absent among this king's reigning values. Other of Plato's sociopolitical suggestions also cause alarm: that certain artists be exiled from the ideal city, for instance (*Rep.* 398a–b and 607a–b), or that the state take possession of all children under ten years old and raise them by its own laws and customs rather than those of their parents (540d–541b). For all of these reasons, one might feel quite wary of looking to Plato's *Republic* for insights on leadership!

But there are reasons to be wary of looking for leadership lessons in the usual places, too, confined as these can be to the worlds of business and politics. Where leadership today seeks to transcend mere concern for efficiency and a bottom line, there is need for resources to imagine, create, and sustain richer conceptions of leadership—leadership that seeks to ignite and mobilize diverse minds, hearts, and bodies; leadership that holds ongoing learning and wisdom as relevant and desirable aims. I chose the title "Leadership Lessons from Plato's *Republic*" with the belief that leadership lessons can and should take many forms. I will not end us at a place of bulleted takeaways or tips for leading, but I hope that shining light on pedagogy as a site of leadership will leave us with some fodder for considering leadership more critically and expansively.

PHILOSOPHY AND LEADERSHIP: THE ALLEGORY OF THE CAVE

I want to preface examination of the allegory of the cave by suggesting that this passage presents an image and story of transformational leadership. I use that term—"transformational leadership"—not in the technical sense cultivated by James MacGregor Burns, Bernard Bass, or other leadership theorists. I mean, on a very basic level, the kind of leading presented here aims at positive change in the personal and collective being of those who are led. This change is facilitated through a unique practice of education. As Plato describes it: "[Education] isn't the craft of putting sight into the soul. Education takes for granted that sight is there but that it isn't turned the right way or looking where it ought to look, and it tries to redirect it appropriately" (*Rep.* 518d). This is transformational leadership as pedagogy and pedagogy as transformational leadership; it asks the learner to aspire and move toward not just any future but one that is worthwhile, beautiful, and good.

The allegory of the cave is a passage at the start of Book VII of Plato's *Republic*, a wide-ranging work about justice and the ideal society. It is written in dramatic form, meaning that it is written as a conversation between characters, with the character Socrates occupying nearly all of the time at the mic. Socrates is the character who relays the allegory. He describes this scene: Prisoners in a cave are chained so that all they hear is echoes and all they see is a constant stream of shadows projected on the wall in front of them. The shadows and echoes come from a parade of puppeteers walking a path behind them. The puppeteers and their puppets are illuminated by the light of a fire beyond the path. The path itself leads treacherously up, out, into the blinding light of the sun. "They are like us," Socrates says (515a). And then this: a prisoner is unshackled. A guide drags this prisoner up the steep, rough path into the bright sunlight outside. It is hard to see at first; it takes time for the prisoner's vision to adjust and take in the objects of the outside world. Once the prisoner's eyes have adapted to the world's vibrance and beauty—seeing things as they really are, not just in flickering shadows—the prisoner is compelled to return to the darkness of the cave to share their newly wise vision and capacity for happiness with the still-shackled prisoners.

From experience teaching this passage, I have found that various permutations of dissatisfaction, alienation, and curiosity allow students—ranging from eighth graders to undergraduates—both intellectual and emotional access to the allegory's narrative of escape and transformation. I know that when I first read this passage for an English literature assignment as a thirteen-year-old, I certainly found the simile both thrilling and terrifying. It was not *so* hard to believe that we are all like prisoners in a cave. Early teenage life in suburban southern Arizona was permeated by flickering images (just switch on the TV or radio) and a general stagnation of thoughtful inquiry (we were thirteen). But there is a way out in the allegory; Socrates tells us it is called philosophy (521c). This mysterious practice or process or curriculum—we're not sure what it is exactly—can apparently lift one from a life of shadows and shackles to one of clear understanding, happiness, and, notably, the ability to lead others to the same.

LEARNING TO PHILOSOPHIZE: A SITE OF TRANSFORMATIONAL LEADERSHIP

There are actually two points at which leading is highlighted in the allegory. The first is when the guide leads the unchained prisoner up the steep path out of the cave. The prisoner would not become a philosopher if not for this initial leading; we might think of this moment of leading as the prisoner's Philosophy 101 course and beyond—their philosophical training. Leading is highlighted at a second point when the enlightened prisoner returns to the cave now in the new role of philosopher-king. Articles written about the allegory from a perspective interested in leadership tend to focus on the latter. They emphasize the enlightened prisoner's knowledge achievement and subsequent political action more than their process of knowledge acquisition. In other words, more attention is paid to the state of having learned, and the actions following from that, than to the learning process itself. Academic philosophers, too, have tended to write about the knowledge achievement and political action described in the passage, attempting to interpret what the various stages of the prisoner's ascent and descent represent. The guide often falls out of the conversation.[12]

But if philosophy is that by which a person ascends from the cave and comes to see the world in all of its vivid reality, then whomever this guide is, they are facilitating philosophical learning; in doing so, they are leading transformationally. Of course, the philosopher-king is *also* leading transformationally when they return to the cave. Socrates says, as if speaking directly to the philosopher-king: "the city will be governed, not like the majority of cities nowadays, by people who fight over shadows and struggle against one another in order to rule—as if that were a great good—but by people who are awake rather than dreaming" (520c). "We've made you kings in our city and leaders of the swarm . . . both for yourselves and for the rest of the city" (520b). In Socrates's words, the philosopher-king leads from the enlightened position of one who has already "become philosopher" (520a). So when thinkers interested in leadership pay attention only to the philosopher-king's leading within the allegory, we miss a crucial part of the picture. Leadership is not only exercised by those who have clearly "become philosopher"; it is exercised by those who, like the guide, whether or not we deem them "enlightened," facilitate a difficult process of learning to philosophize—a pedagogical process.

Attending to the guide's leading in the allegory, as opposed to the philosopher-king's, is a way of highlighting the significance of pedagogy as a site of leadership that both shapes and complements activities traditionally recognized as "leading": organizing community, managing political situations, formulating organizational strategies, and so on. When we neglect pedagogy as a site of leadership, not only do we unnecessarily narrow our understanding of leadership, but we lose the opportunity to become critical about the educational structures and processes that actually deeply influence what the more traditionally recognized forms of leading look like.

THE VIOLENCE OF PHILOSOPHICAL PEDAGOGY: CRITICAL CONSIDERATIONS FOR EDUCATORS

The allegory of the cave is a feel-good story. In truth, it is a liberation story, the liberator being philosophy. Here, Plato tells us in his characteristically creative fashion, is the suffering we are caught in, and here is philosophy, the activity that can free us. And yet there's an unpalatable aspect of this liberation story that drops out of the picture just as often as the guide's leadership, and that is the guide's violence. Consider this close reading of the guide's leading in the allegory:

1. When the prisoner is first loosed from their shackles: "When one of [the prisoners] was freed and suddenly *compelled* to stand up, turn his head, walk, and look up toward the light, he'd be *pained* and dazzled and unable to see the things whose shadows he'd seen before." (515c, emphasis added)
2. When the prisoner beholds the puppeteers for the first time: "if we pointed to each of the things passing by, asked him what each of them is, and *compelled* him to answer, don't you think he'd be at a loss and that he'd believe that the things he saw earlier were truer than the ones he was now being shown?" (515d, emphasis added)
3. When the prisoner first looks at the light of the fire: "And if someone *compelled* him to look at the light itself, wouldn't his eyes *hurt*, and wouldn't he turn around and flee toward the things he's able to see, believing that they're really clearer than the ones he's being shown?" (515d–e, emphasis added)
4. When the prisoner is compelled up the path leading outside: "And if someone *dragged* him away from there *by force*, up the rough, steep path, and didn't let him go until he had *dragged* him into the sunlight, wouldn't he be *pained* and irritated at being treated that way?" (515e, emphasis added)

The guide's philosophical pedagogy is characterized most prominently by compulsion and pain. Nowhere in the allegory is it explicitly argued that compulsion and pain are necessary for learning to philosophize, but the structure of the allegory sways it that way: the prisoners are enfeebled and the path is rough and steep—there is no getting around it. Perhaps this is fine for a philosophical fable, but the reality is that for many decades the allegory of the cave has been core to the canon studied by beginning students in North American and European philosophy departments. That being the case, we should consider the possible implications of this allegory's violent features for how we understand philosophical pedagogy and, I want to suggest, pedagogy more broadly.

Here are some observations. Nowhere in the allegory is there mention of the guide's relationship with the ascending prisoner (the learner); they never talk to each other about their progress or experience, and neither is there any mention of whether they like each other, hate each other, are obligated to each other, or relate to each other in any other way. Nowhere is there acknowledgment of the one-sidedness of how compulsion is applied; that is to say, there is no explicit acknowledgment that the guide is exercising a particular kind of authority and power in the prisoner's education. Accordingly, there is no acknowledgment of other possible ways that the prisoner might ascend the path—by their own will or delight, perhaps, or alongside the guide in a more collaborative fashion. What is made clear in the allegory is that the work is hard and oftentimes painful, and the prisoner must be compelled nonetheless.

The philosopher-king's totalitarian leadership has often been critiqued, but are their tyrannical tendencies really so surprising when their teachers operate in the same way?[13] This is why it is important to shine light on pedagogy as a crucial site of leadership: teachers and educators, just as the allegory's guide, can both shape and replicate broader sociopolitical dynamics of violence and exclusion. This thesis is, in a nutshell, the premise for the influential critical pedagogical work undertaken by philosophers and theorists like Paulo Freire, Henry Giroux, bell hooks, and Sara Ahmed. As Giroux says, "Critical pedagogy is central in drawing attention to questions regarding who has control over the conditions for the production of knowledge, values, and classroom practices. . . . [It acknowledges] the different ways in which authority, experience, and power are produced under specific conditions of learning."[14] The lesson is right here in Plato too—a 2,400-year-old lesson we are still learning.

CONCLUSION

The leadership lesson I have wanted to surface begins from a conviction that Plato's depiction of philosophy in the *Republic* has something to offer our thinking about leadership and from a deep concern about the fact that the allegory's prisoner—this philosophical learner—experiences compulsion and pain as the primary aspects of their transformational, supposedly liberatory education. The Greek *philosophia* means "love of wisdom," after all, but one might think that the compulsion and pain the ascending prisoner experiences signals not love but abuse.

Recognizing pedagogy as a site of leadership can create space for us to critically reflect here. If philosophical pedagogy, and indeed pedagogy in higher education more broadly, is a site of leading, then we can ask: How is leadership best exercised here? Where assumptions about authority, compulsion, and difficulty can remain veiled in the realm of teaching and learning, these are clear areas of consideration and debate in the realm of leadership studies and practice. And it is so important that these assumptions are revealed in the realm of teaching and learning because, whether it is persistent exclusion of certain voices in syllabi or repeated cases of sexual harassment in departments, healing is desperately needed.

For five years I had the pleasure of working at the Derek Bok Center for Teaching and Learning at Harvard University. At this center, I worked alongside undergraduates, graduate student teaching fellows, staff, administrators, and faculty from across the arts and sciences in an effort to make teaching and learning at Harvard more equitable and inclusive. This role involved facilitating conversations and creating programming in order to engage questions such as, How can we become more aware of and responsive to power dynamics in learning environments? What could a learning space be like in which diversity and difficulty are normalized? What might it look and feel like to occupy a position of teaching authority (leadership) while also prioritizing power sharing with students?

One of my favorite parts of this job was getting to mentor and work with a group of undergraduate fellows who develop and deliver workshops on student identities, power dynamics, and privilege in the classroom for departments across Harvard College. I once had a conversation in which one of these fellows (a senior philosophy major) told me—in near tears of happiness—about how this was the first semester in her whole four years at Harvard in which she felt excited about her classes because she could actually see herself in her teachers, in the content of her courses, and in the social issues being talked about in class. This was the first semester, she explained, in which she didn't feel as if she had to fight to be considered in class; her worldview did not feel excluded as "not properly philosophical." I wish I could say it was philosophy classes that had offered her this more expansive and inclusive experience, but it was actually classes at the Divinity School, in African American studies, and through the School of Public Policy. I really wish I could say she had been able to reflect on Afro-Latinx identity and consider the ethical muddle that is the US criminal justice system in a philosophical educational context that had felt more welcoming and empowering.

In her enthusiasm this undergraduate fellow pseudo-joked, "Is this what white people feel like in class?" We laughed, but the question is devastating; it points to exclusion that runs deep in the very structures of schooling. Some students feel more validated and more at home in certain disciplines and settings in higher education because of inherited pedagogical practices that tend to privilege their identities and perspectives. We need not look to philosopher-kings and the politics of the state to begin addressing these systems of exclusion and the harm they have generated. Learning spaces are sociopolitical spaces. So, acknowledging pedagogy as a site of leadership, how will we facilitate positive personal and collective change and refuse to replicate violence and exclusion? *Healing* is needed.

NOTES

1. M. A. Hunter, Patrice Cobb, Pablo Contreras Kallens, Z. A. Johnson King, Seth Robertson, A. C. Spivey, and Carolyn Dicey Jennings, "The Diversity and Inclusivity Survey for Philosophy PhD Students and Graduates: Preliminary Report," October 16, 2018, 6. Of the responses, 77.5 percent came from graduate students or graduates from US-based philosophy programs, so demographic information from the United States is used as the point of comparison for the respondents in the study.
2. Hunter et al., "Diversity and Inclusivity Survey," 7.
3. Luvell Anderson and Verena Erlenbusch, "Modeling Inclusive Pedagogy: Five Approaches," *Journal of Social Philosophy* 48, no. 1 (Spring 2017): 6–19.
4. Anderson and Erlenbusch, "Modeling Inclusive Pedagogy," 6.
5. Anderson and Erlenbusch, 8. The authors point out that exclusivity at the level of the philosophy syllabus can be both pragmatically and philosophically problematic at the level of the discipline as a whole: pragmatically problematic because "syllabi consisting of overwhelmingly white men . . . deter members of underrepresented groups," and philosophically problematic because "overwhelmingly white and male syllabi . . . represent the socially situated perspectives of some people as universal."
6. On the history of charges brought against Thomas Pogge, see Katie J. M. Baker, "The Famous Ethics Professor and the Women Who Accused Him," *BuzzFeed News*, May 20, 2016, https://www.buzzfeednews.com/article/katiejmbaker/yale-ethics-professor. On Colin McGinn, see Jennifer Schuessler, "A Star Philosopher Falls, and a Debate over Sexism Is Set Off," *New York Times*, August 2, 2013, https://www.nytimes.com/2013/08/03/arts/colin-mcginn-philosopher-to-leave-his-post.html. On John Searle, see Sarah Brown, "Harassment Allegations against a Star Scholar Put a Familiar Spotlight Back on Berkeley," *Chronicle of Higher Education*, March 24, 2017, https://www.chronicle.com/article/Harassment-Allegations-Against/239598. It should be noted that although gender and sexual identities and expressions are certainly a part of the power dynamics at play in such cases of sexual harassment, they are not so in a way that determines the harassment always occurs between a heterosexual male professor and a female student, as evidenced in the case of sexual harassment charges brought against NYU professor Avita Ronell, who identifies as queer, by a male graduate student who identifies as gay; see Katherine Mangan, "New Disclosures about an NYU Professor Reignite a War over Gender and Harassment," *Chronicle of Higher Education*, August 16, 2018, https://www.chronicle.com/article/New-Disclosures-About-an-NYU/244278.
7. As pertains to the case of academic philosophy in particular, see Janice Dowell and David Sobel, "Sexual Harassment in Philosophy," *PEA Soup: Philosophy, Ethics, Academia*, August 29, 2019, https://peasoup.princeton.edu/2019/08/first-of-a-two-part-series-on-sexual-harassment-in-philosophy/.
8. *Irrational Man* (2015), Rotten Tomatoes, accessed January 2019, https://www.rottentomatoes.com/m/irrational_man.

9. "Earnings and Unemployment Rates by Educational Attainment, 2021," US Bureau of Labor Statistics, last modified September 8, 2022, accessed January 2023, https://www.bls.gov/emp/chart-unemployment-earnings-education.htm; Véronique Irwin et al., "Report on the Condition of Education 2022," US Department of Education (Washington, DC: National Center for Education Statistics, 2022), https://nces.ed.gov/pubs2022/2022144.pdf; Anna Zajacova and Elizabeth M. Lawrence, "The Relationship between Education and Health: Reducing Disparities through a Contextual Approach," *Annual Review of Public Health* 39 (2018): 273–89.

10. Pierpaolo Limone and Giusi Antonia Toto, "Factors That Predispose Undergraduates to Mental Issues: A Cumulative Literature Review for Future Research Perspectives," *Frontiers in Public Health* 10 (2022): 1–12; Heather McLaughlin, Christopher Uggen, and Amy Blackstone, "The Economic and Career Effects of Sexual Harassment on Working Women," *Gender & Society*, 31, no. 3 (2017): 333–58, https://doi.org/10.1177/0891243217704631.

11. All direct quotes are taken from Plato, *Republic*, trans. G. M. A. Grube, rev. C. D. C. Reeve, in *Plato: Complete Works*, ed. John M. Cooper (Indianapolis: Hackett, 1997), henceforth abbreviated as *Rep.* with citations in the text.

12. Even scholars who explicitly acknowledge the guide as a leader give little attention to the nature or details of the guide's leading as compared to that of the enlightened prisoner. See Dominic Scott and R. Edward Freeman, "The Teacher," in *Models of Leadership in Plato and Beyond* (Oxford: Oxford University Press, 2021), ch. 5.

13. While Scott and Freeman do not explicitly acknowledge the violent aspects or possible non-cognitive dimensions of this educational process, they align with me in observing that the process is clearly intended to shape the student (the ascending prisoner) in the image of the teacher (the guide): "For Plato, the teacher aspires to raise the student to the same cognitive level as themselves. This is clear in the allegory, where the role of the educator appears twice: initially, when the person turns around from the wall of the cave, there is someone who forces him to look at the fire and then drags him out of the cave; but then the released prisoner himself is seen as an educator when we imagine him attempting to do for the prisoners what his educator did for him. The student has become the teacher" (Scott and Freeman, "The Teacher," 83).

14. Henry Giroux, *On Critical Pedagogy* (London: Bloomsbury, 2011), 5–6.

CHAPTER 4

Mosaic Leadership

Alan Mittleman

In this chapter, I want to explore some characteristics of Moses's leadership as conceived by the rabbinic tradition. It is true that Jewish thought found Moses utterly unique; Jews believed that Moses achieved a higher level of intimacy with the Ultimate than any other human being. As a fourteenth-century liturgical hymn puts it, "No one has since arisen among Israel like Moses. He alone was a prophet who gazed upon the visage of God." Portraying Moses as a prophet, as did Maimonides on whose thought the hymn is based, associates his work with an established category of biblical leadership, but it also puts him out of reach. For rabbinic Judaism, prophecy has ceased (b. Sotah 48b).[1] The prophet qua prophet cannot be emulated.

Categorizing Moses as a prophet is not the only tack that the Jewish tradition took. Far more common is to see Moses as a rabbi. Indeed, in traditional circles Moses is frequently referred to as Moshe Rabbenu, "Moses our rabbi." While forfeiting none of his uniqueness, the rabbinic construal of Moses makes him a far more accessible, intelligible, and emulable character. Moses became the first rabbi, the master of all subsequent rabbis, and so a fount of virtues, traits, and skills his innumerable rabbinic disciples sought to acquire. Moses as a leader in the rabbinic mode was self-sacrificing, justice-seeking, empathetic, compassionate, practical, and bold, yet humble. His success was due to his realism, his passion for justice, and his love of God, Torah, and the people of Israel.

Before we consider Mosaic leadership within the context of rabbinic thought, it is worth looking briefly at two portrayals of Moses as a leader that wholly depart from the traditional Jewish framework. The characteristics of the rabbinic approach will become more salient through the comparison.

One portrayal, that of Martin Buber, sees Moses as the paradigm of biblical leadership and sees biblical leadership essentially as a failure, at least as
evaluated from the point of view of ordinary history. Moses is a paragon of
failed leadership. The other portrayal, that of Machiavelli, sees Moses as an
"armed prophet," a successful founder of a new political order comparable
to Cyrus and Romulus. Judged in ordinary historical terms, Moses exem-
plifies successful leadership, the kind of leadership Machiavelli promotes in
The Prince. Between these extremes of worldly failure and secular success,
the rabbis see Moses as a supremely effective leader whose success is based
on his exemplary character as well as his resilient faith in God and in his
people.

Buber's central claim is that biblical leaders should not be compared to
the kind of leaders we find in secular history. Biblical leadership is against
nature and history; it knows nothing of heroism, cunning, luck, or strategy.
The true biblical leader, such as Abraham, Moses, or the prophets, is one
who is led.[2]

> [The Bible] knows nothing of [the] intrinsic value of success. On
> the contrary, when it announces a successful deed, it is duty-bound
> to announce in complete detail the failure involved in the success.
> When we consider the history of Moses we see how much failure is
> mingled in the one great successful action, so much so that when we
> set the individual events which make up his history side by side, we
> see that his life consists of one failure after another.[3]

Although it is true that Moses brought the people out of Egypt—his
one great successful action—he is subsequently always defeated by the
people. Moses's story is less that of the exodus than of wandering in the
wilderness.

Why does Buber emphasize failure? For him, the goal of history—the
kingdom of God—is discontinuous with ordinary history or, at least, with
the surface appearance of ordinary history. The kingdom comes not as
a result of continuous historical political work but in defiance of the frag-
mentary, misguided efforts of historical political leaders. Redemption is a
subterranean process, marked by outward failure but equally by intermit-
tent dialogue with God and fellow human beings. There is a hidden history
of redemption being written in the failed—but not false—work of Moses,
the prophets, Jesus, and the hasidic rebbes. Thus, for Buber, whatever we
might find to emulate in biblical leaders, including Moses, cannot be their
historical accomplishments but a dialogue with God that is masked from

view. Buber effectively negates the possibility of taking biblical leaders as paradigms of character and conduct. What remains to them is their inner disposition toward being led by God, toward dialogue with the divine You.

One hundred and eighty degrees from Buber is Machiavelli's characterization of Moses as an "armed prophet" who succeeds dramatically due to "his own ability and not by fortune," and especially by his own force of arms. Although Machiavelli demurs that Moses should properly not be compared with other military-prophetic founders due to his unusual closeness with God, he ignores his own advice and portrays Moses in a pervasively realistic way. Moses faced the same problem as other founders: he wanted to start an unprecedented new order. His opponents would therefore include all those who did well under the old order while his defenders would be only the few willing to take a chance on something untried. The prophet of the new order therefore needs to rely mostly on himself and on the force that he can accrue to bring others to his side: "Hence it is that all armed prophets have conquered, and unarmed ones have been destroyed. . . . If Moses, Cyrus, Theseus, and Romulus had been unarmed they could not have enforced their constitutions for long."[4] Machiavelli evidently has in mind the slaughter, which Moses sanctioned, of the three thousand Israelites who worshipped the golden calf, as well as the destruction of Korah and his company of 250 rebels. Moses becomes a model of Machiavellian *virtù*—poles apart from a Buberian failure or a rabbinic sage.

Buber was not wrong to point to Moses's trust in dialogue, nor was Machiavelli wrong to see Moses as given to decisive, even violent action. The way these traits are portrayed in rabbinic literature, however, is quite at variance with Buber or Machiavelli. We turn now to the rabbinic treatment, in classical biblical interpretation (midrash) and medieval biblical commentary (*parshanut*), of several episodes in Moses's career.

Let us first consider Moses's dramatic break with his Egyptian upbringing and radical identification with the suffering Israelites—his extrajudicial killing of the Egyptian taskmaster who was beating the Hebrew slave: "Some time after that, when Moses had grown up, he went out to his kinsfolk and witnessed their labors. He saw an Egyptian beating a Hebrew, one of his kinsmen. He turned this way and that and, seeing no one about, he struck down the Egyptian and hid him in the sand" (Exodus 2:11–12). Moses considered the slave "one of his kinsmen"—why he did so is not clear from the text. How did he come to identify with the Hebrew as a brother rather than with the Egyptian, since his whole upbringing and socialization was among the Egyptian elite? The written Torah does not tell us, opening the door to subsequent rabbinic speculation. The great medieval exegete R. Solomon ben Isaac (known as Rashi, d. 1105) provides an answer based, as is often the case with rabbinic exegesis, on a grammatical peculiarity. The text at Exodus 2:11, "witnessed their labors" or "looked on their burdens," uses the Hebrew letter ‎ב‎ ("in") as a prefix to the word "burdens." Translated literally, the text says, "he saw *in* their labors." That is, he saw *himself in* their labors; he empathized with them and grieved for them.[5] For Rashi and the ancient midrash from which he draws, Moses was disposed to identify with the victim; he empathized with the subject of injustice. He was animated by a passion for rescue. These stirrings of moral outrage brought Moses to recognize the Israelites as his kinsmen. We might say that Moses had moral imagination. He could overcome cultural distance and see in the face of the vulnerable other, a person like himself.

Other midrashim push Moses's identification with the Israelites further back and introduce new valued traits of character. When Moses went out to look upon their burdens, "R. Eleazar son of R. Yose the Galilean said: He saw heavy burdens put upon small people, and light ones upon big people; men's burdens upon women, and women's burdens upon men; the burden that an old man could carry on a youth, and that of a youth on an old man. So he would . . . step away from his retinue and rearrange the burdens, making believe that his intention was to be of help to Pharaoh."[6] Moses acted stealthily, convincing his Egyptian retinue that he was furthering Pharaoh's interest rather than that of his distressed brethren. In the view of this midrash, Moses tried to work "within the system" to alleviate the Israelites' distress. His action was far less radical than extrajudicial killing. Perhaps the inadequacy of merely rearranging burdens more equitably convinced him that more dramatic steps were necessary.

Another midrash has him intercede directly with Pharaoh, subtly manipulating him in order to help the Israelites. After seeing the Israelites bearing their burdens, he goes to Pharaoh and reasons with him: "When a man has a slave and the slave does not rest at least one day during the week, the slave will die. These are your slaves. If you do not let them rest one day during the week, they will surely die." Pharaoh replied, "Go and do with them as you say." Thus, Moses not only mitigated the slaves' most extreme misery; he also ordained the Sabbath for them before the giving of the Ten Commandments. This interpretation portrays Moses in the manner of a Talmudic sage who uses reasoned argument with a skeptical or hostile interlocutor, persuading Pharaoh that he is acting in his own interest while furthering the interest of others. It emphasizes Moses's belief in rational argument as well as in the necessity of a rhetoric that appeals to self-interest. On more than a few occasions, Moses will appeal to God's self-interest to dissuade Him from destroying His people and beginning again. This is not what Buber meant by dialogue, but it is a typical feature of the rabbinic portrayal of Moses.

Although both the biblical text and the rabbinic interpretation thus far show Moses as a highly self-confident man, both Bible and midrash dwell on Moses's doubts and hesitations about his own fitness as well. Moses becomes known in Judaism for his humility. When God charges Moses with his mission of liberation at the burning bush, Moses responds, "Who am I that I should go to Pharaoh and free the Israelites from Egypt?" (Exodus 3:11). Despite repeated assurances that God will be with him and will perform miracles on his behalf, Moses still voices his reluctance, admitting that he is "slow of speech and slow of tongue" and asking God, whose anger he thereby provokes, to appoint someone else. God relents and appoints Aaron, Moses's brother, to stand by him and compensate for Moses's perceived inadequacies (Exodus 4:10–15). In the hands of Rashi's grandson, R. Samuel ben Meir (known as Rashbam, d. 1174), Moses's reluctance was motivated not simply by his humble belief in his own relative unimportance but rather by his belief in the unavailability of good arguments on behalf of freeing the Israelites. Rashbam has Moses say: "Even if I were worthy of entering Pharaoh's presence . . . as far as freeing the Israelites goes, what could I say to Pharaoh that he would accept? Is Pharaoh foolish enough to listen to me and send a huge people, who are his slaves, away free from his land?"[7] Once again, the sages' transformation of Moses into a rabbi puts a premium on rational persuasion, on good arguments as the currency effective leaders use to transact political or moral business. Even when dealing with a tyrant, one needs good reasons and effective arguments to prevail. It is as if the rabbis turned the sphere of high-stakes political encounter into the give-and-take of the talmudic academy.

One of the crises of Moses's career comes in Numbers 16 when he is forced to confront an organized rebellion led by disgruntled Levites. In the biblical source text, Korah, Dathan, Abiram, and 250 leading Israelites accuse Moses and Aaron of going too far: "For all the community are holy, all of them, and the Lord is in their midst. Why then do you raise yourselves above the Lord's congregation?" (Numbers 16:3). The challenge seems anarchistic or perhaps democratic—if Israel as such is a "kingdom of priests and a holy nation," what business does it have with leaders who claim exceptional status for themselves? But as Jewish tradition understands the challenge, Korah and his Levite brethren are neither anarchists nor democrats; they are aristocrats. They are objecting to a priesthood set apart from and ranked higher than their own Levitical status. Korah does not want to level down but to level up. He cynically agitates the people, however, to undermine Moses.

In the midrashic elaboration of the story, Korah himself acts like a rabbi by putting difficult legal questions to Moses and trying to trip him up. His goal is to show that Moses has invented the law on his own, that he has no special relationship with God. This is a superficially principled but deeply cynical challenge to the basis of Moses's authority. Since the section immediately preceding the Korah story deals with the commandment to put fringes, one of which should be blue, on one's garment, the midrash has Korah challenge Moses on just this point. Korah asks Moses what the law should be if one's garment is already entirely blue. Would it not be otiose to add a blue fringe to it? Moses flatly asserts that the blue fringe is still obligatory. Korah then asks him what the law is with respect to a house full of Torah scrolls. Would it still require a little container (mezuzah) on the door with two sections of Torah (Deuteronomy 5:4–9; 11:13–21) in it? Korah deploys the biblical version of a reductio ad absurdum argument. He tries to humiliate Moses and show the capriciousness of his alleged revealed law.[8]

Yet Moses was not without argumentative resources of his own. Moses challenges Korah: "Hear me sons of Levi. Is it not enough for you that the God of Israel has set you apart from the community of Israel by giving you access to Him, to perform the duties of the Lord's Tabernacle, and to minister to the community and serve them? Thus, He advanced you and all your fellow Levites with you; yet you seek the priesthood too!" (Numbers 16:8–10). Moses sees through Korah's pretensions and finds nothing more than a naked power play. His argument with Korah is tu quoque: you accuse me of precisely what you are trying to do yourself. The midrash comments that Moses was not trying to humiliate Korah, as Korah did toward him, but rather trying to win him over. Moses wanted him to realize his hypocrisy, which the tu quoque argument would unmask. Thus, Moses continued to trust in the power of reason to conciliate an opponent and forestall disaster. But Korah does not answer Moses. The midrash ascribes an internal dialogue to him: "If I answer Moses, I know that, being resourceful, he will certainly overwhelm me with his arguments, so that I might find myself reconciled with him against my will. It is better for me not to respond." Korah chooses will over reason, stubbornness over repentance. When Moses saw that Korah was incorrigible and could not be dissuaded, he parted from him. The miraculous doom of Korah and his company proceeded apace.

Unlike Machiavelli, Moses saw violence as a last resort. It is not always wrong, but it is a sign of something that has gone horribly wrong. It follows the breakdown of leadership, real or imagined. It is not a tool of legitimate leadership. We see this in the most spectacular episode of Mosaic violence— Moses's response to the worship of the golden calf. While Moses in the end commands a violent purge of the people, resulting in the deaths of thousands, he also puts his own life at risk to save the Israelite nation before the violence commenced. The episode (given in Exodus 32) begins with the people despairing that Moses would ever return to them from Mount Sinai. They accost Aaron and demand that he make a god to lead them. Aaron does not resist; he enjoins the people to give him their golden jewelry, which he melts down and forms into the image of a calf. The people in utter faithlessness proclaim, "This is your god, O Israel, who brought you out of the land of Egypt" (Exodus 32:4). As God becomes aware of this massive betrayal, he tells Moses, "Hurry down, for *your* people, whom *you* brought out of Egypt, have acted basely." God disclaims responsibility for Israel and shifts the blame for their waywardness to Moses. He is done with Israel, disgusted by their infidelity. He does not want Moses to persuade Him to relent, announcing that Moses should "let Me be." He plans to obliterate the faithless nation and make Moses a great nation in Israel's place.

At this point, Moses steps into the breach and, at risk of his own life, engages God in dialogue: "Let not Your anger, O Lord, blaze forth against *Your* people, whom *You* delivered from the land of Egypt." Moses carefully reverses the referent of the pronoun. While God ascribed leadership of and therefore responsibility for the people to Moses, Moses returns it entirely to God. In the Bible, Moses goes on to argue with God. He appeals, in a way, to God's self-interest; he persuades God to realize that the remaining Egyptians will mock Him, saying "it was with an evil intent that He delivered them only to kill them off in the mountains." Moses reminds God that His reputation is at stake. God relents, and Moses descends to the camp where a slaughter of the malefactors soon ensues. Moses has saved the nation as such, but there is still a terrible price to be paid for their apostasy. And Moses is the instrument of terror—a problem that we consider later.

In the midrashic treatments of the story, Moses goes much further in his dialogue with God. After God, commanding Moses to leave his presence, says "let Me be" (Exodus 32:10), R. Abbahu comments that "if Scripture had not been explicit, this would be impossible to say. For the verse implies that, like a man who grabs his fellow by his coat, Moses grabbed hold of the Holy One and brazenly said to Him: Master of the Universe, I will not let You be until You pardon and forgive Israel."[9] Here the full force of Moses's heroism, daring, and willingness to sacrifice his own well-being for the common good appears. Moses aims not only to persuade, but to force God to relent.

Nonetheless, Moses still needs more than insistence and determination to appease God's anger and make Him change His plan. He needs an argument. The midrash is not content with the argument from self-interest in Scripture. Moses's rabbinic tactic is more subtle: he brings God to understand His own complicity in Israel's betrayal. By emphasizing that God brought them up from Egypt, Moses reminds God that He brought them down to Egypt in the first place and allowed them to remain there. "Master of the universe, You ignored the entire world and deliberately enslaved Your children in Egypt where the inhabitants worship calves; and so Your children learned from the Egyptians and now have made a calf for themselves." As if the point were not crystal clear, the midrash adds a parable. A sage opened a perfume shop for his son in the street of prostitutes. The street plied its trade, as did the perfume business. And so did the son. He followed his natural inclination. His father caught him one day with a prostitute and began to shout: "I'll kill you." But the sage's friend was there and spoke with him. "You yourself ruined your son and now you are yelling at him! You ignored all other occupations and taught him to be a perfumer. You ignored all other streets and deliberately opened a shop for him on the street of prostitutes!"[10] What did you expect to happen? Thus, Moses, through reasoned dialogue, appeased God's anger and saved the people Israel at great risk to himself. He doubly denied any motive of self-interest. Neither his own personal survival nor being the father of a new, great nation moved him. He was wholly devoted to the *torat ha-klal*, the common good of the people whom he sustained as "a nursing father" (Numbers 11:12).

This image of Moses, which is inspiring and benign, rests uneasily with the Moses praised by Machiavelli. Yet there is no denying the biblical basis of Machiavelli's laudation: Moses and his Levite followers initiated a slaughter of the Israelites ("about three thousand men") who worshipped the golden calf. Michael Walzer describes Moses's move as "the first revolutionary purge."[11] Walzer writes:

> The rabbis tended to talk of the "purgings" of the wilderness period as if they were a kind of law enforcement, but even they saw in the killing of the idol worshippers at the foot of Mount Sinai a political act of a special kind. For them, its extraordinary character was revealed by an omission in the text. "And [Moses] said unto them: thus saith the Lord God of Israel, put every man his sword by his side . . ." But God's command is not given; God nowhere orders the killing of the idol worshippers. Did Moses invent the command? Was he . . . a Machiavellian prince and liberator? This is the Moses that Machiavelli describes in his *Discourses*: "He who reads the Bible with discernment will see that, in order that Moses might set about

making laws and institutions, he had to kill a very great number of men . . ." And isn't it easier to do what in any case must be done if the prince can claim divine authority?[12]

A rabbinic text actually portrays Moses as *inventing* a divine command to motivate the Levites to slaughter their idol-worshipping fellow Israelites.[13] But mainstream commentators fight shy of such a cynical depiction of Moses. For Rashi, the commandment Moses was carrying out had already been enunciated at Exodus 22:19: "Whoever sacrifices to a god other than the Lord alone shall be proscribed." Rashi and his sources exemplify the tendency that Walzer criticizes; Rashi renders the punishment of the Israelites judicial rather than extrajudicial and so, in Walzer's view, not political. Rashi normalizes the "purge," domesticating it to the halakhic system of criminal law. In the latter, a proper death sentence requires that the would-be criminal be forewarned of the capital consequences of his intended action and that he be seen by fit witnesses. Noting that the Israelites died in three different ways (by the sword, by plague, and by being forced to drink water mixed with the dust of the golden calf), Rashi states that those who were killed by the swords of the Levites were the ones who were warned that they were about to commit a crime and did so anyway before valid witnesses. Violators who were not warned but were seen by witnesses were killed by a divine plague (Exodus 32:35). Violators who were neither warned nor seen by witnesses were tested, like the woman suspected of adultery (Numbers 5:19–23), by the gold-laced water and, if guilty, did not survive the ordeal. In Rashi's view, Moses was no Machiavellian prince but a rabbinic judge duly carrying out the procedures of justice however tragic the circumstances.

Nachmanides disagrees with Rashi. He acknowledges the emergency nature of Moses's action. There were so many violators to bring to court that it was not possible to follow normal criminal procedure; advance warning was not necessary. The Levites knew who the idolaters were. For Nachmanides, however, Moses did not suspend Jewish law as much as act upon another principle of it: the emergency decree (*hora'at sha'ah*).[14] In his view, Moses's decision-making remains within the sphere of law. Moses remains a rabbi, not a founder or a prince.

Moses's leadership, as portrayed by the rabbis, recalls Max Weber's comments about the political vocation: it is a constant boring through thick boards. Moses, while often angry at his ungrateful, wayward, foolish people, never despairs of them. He always works for their collective good, even if that involves stern judgment and punishment. He suppresses his own interests in favor of theirs. He is driven by a moral passion for rescue. He cannot abide injustice, even if it leads him into violence that raises formidable problems of justice on its own. Most striking in the rabbinic portrayal is his reliance on reasoned argument, on an orientation toward moral persuasion rather than political coercion. This latter feature, so typical of rabbinic discourse, makes Moses familiar to us as a kind of constitutional leader. Neither an armed prophet nor a worldly failure whose excellence lies in being led, the rabbinic Moses balances power with an ever-renewed obligation to justify the legitimacy of that power. He enacts this time after time in a dialogue that pursues mutually intelligible, morally transparent reasons.

NOTES

1. But note that this standard view has been challenged by Frederick Greenspahn, "Why Prophecy Ceased," *Journal of Biblical Literature* 108, no. 1 (Spring 1989): 37–49; and Benjamin Sommer, "Did Prophecy Cease? Evaluating a Reevaluation," *Journal of Biblical Literature* 115, no. 1 (Spring 1996): 31–47.
2. Martin Buber, "Biblical Leadership," in *Israel and the World: Essays in a Time of Crisis* (New York: Schocken, 1978), 132.
3. Buber, 125.
4. Machiavelli, *The Prince*, ch. 6. For a study of Machiavelli's comprehensive treatment of Moses in his various works, see John H. Geerken, "Machiavelli's Moses and Renaissance Politics," *Journal of the History of Ideas* 60, no. 4 (1999): 579–95.
5. Using the translation/interpretation of Michael Carasik in Carasik, ed. and trans., *The Commentators' Bible: Exodus* (Philadelphia: Jewish Publication Society, 2005), 12.
6. Hayim Nahman Bialik and Yehoshua Hana Ravnitzky, *The Book of Legends (Sefer Ha-Aggadah)*, trans. William Braude (New York: Schocken, 1992), 61 (based on *Exodus Rabbah* 1:27–28).
7. Carasik, *The Commentators' Bible*, 18 (s.v. Exodus 3:11).
8. Bialik and Ravnitzky, *The Book of Legends*, 91 (based on *Numbers Rabbah* 18:3).
9. Bialik and Ravnitzky, 84 (based on b. Berachot 32a).
10. Bialik and Ravnitzky, 85 (based on *Exodus Rabbah* 43:7).
11. Michael Walzer, *Exodus and Revolution* (New York: Basic, 1985), 59.
12. Walzer, 59–60.
13. From *Tanna d'bei Eliyahu*, cited in Walzer, 60.
14. See Nachmanides on Exodus 32:27. For suspending the normal protections of Jewish law in times of duress, see Alan Yuter, "Hora'at Sha'ah: The Emergency Principle in Jewish Law and a Contemporary Application," *Jewish Political Studies Review* 13, no. 3–4 (Fall 2001).

CHAPTER 5

Just Leadership in Early Islam
The Teachings and Practice of Imam Ali

Tahera Qutbuddin

According to Ali ibn Abi Talib (d. 661 CE)—the first imam after the Prophet Muhammad according to the Shia, the fourth caliph according to the Sunnis, and one of the most revered leaders in Islam—true leadership is contingent on a leader's justice. Although political acumen, military strategy, and administrative skills are also crucial to the success of an individual's leadership, the most important qualification by far is the virtue of justice. Luminaries across human history have deemed justice a cornerstone of leadership, but there are many brands of justice. What is Imam Ali's understanding of just leadership? As argued in broad strokes in this chapter, a just leader for Ali is one who possesses a composite of several qualities. A just leader is not simply one who is fair and equitable to all his subjects. That is only the beginning. A just leader also possesses wisdom, shows compassion to the weak, shuns corruption, and promotes pluralism. Most importantly, a just leader is at all times conscious of their accountability to God.[1]

ALI IBN ABI TALIB: EXEMPLAR OF JUST LEADERSHIP

Ali was the cousin, ward, and son-in-law of the Prophet Muhammad and the first male to accept Islam.[2] The Shia believe him to be the prophet's direct successor in both his spiritual and temporal roles, while Sunnis regard him as the fourth and last "Rightly Guided Caliph." Both Shia and Sunni Muslims revere him for his deep loyalty to Muhammad, his valorous role in establishing Islam in its nascent stage, and his profound piety, learning, and

78

justice. They study and cite his sermons, epistles, and aphorisms.[3] They laud his wisdom and eloquence.[4] They recount numerous sayings of the prophet praising him. Famously, they report Muhammad to have said, "I am the city of knowledge and Ali is its gateway," and "You, Ali, are my brother in this world and the next."[5] Particularly relevant to the topic at hand, they report that Muhammad said, addressing his companions, "The most just among you is Ali."[6]

Muhammad died in 632 CE, and Ali took a back seat in government for the next twenty-five years during the caliphates of Abu Bakr, Umar, and Uthman. In 656 he received the pledge of allegiance from the Muslim community and ruled as caliph until 661, when he was assassinated. Ali's words, and the anecdotes I quote in this chapter, are from these difficult times. In these four years, Ali was forced to fight three pitched battles against Muslim rebels, many of them prominent figures in the community who disagreed with his strict ideas of justice and equality. He fought the Battle of the Camel in Iraq against three powerful individuals from Medina; the Battle of Siffin against the Damascus governor, Mu'awiyah; and the Battle of Nahrawan against a renegade group from his own army called Kharijites. In the wake of a sham arbitration following the Battle of Siffin, most of his army pulled back, and he spent his last few months persuading them to resume the fight. Meanwhile, Mu'awiyah was going from strength to strength. He already had Syria; he now took over Egypt and sent raiding parties into Arabia and even Iraq, quite close to Ali's capital, Kufa (a suburb of Najaf in the south of present-day Iraq). Throughout, Ali faced the hard consequences of his ideals. Ultimately, he gave his life for them, killed—while praying in the Kufa mosque at dawn on the nineteenth of Ramadan—by a rebel Kharijite's poisoned sword.

One of the best characterizations of Ali is given soon after his death. It is remarkable because it is given by one of Ali's close companions, a man named Dirar al-Nahshali, in the presence of Ali's arch-enemy Mu'awiyah. Dirar went to Damascus to make some request of Mu'awiyah, who was now caliph. Mu'awiyah, presumably curious about his deceased foe, asked Dirar to describe Ali. Dirar pleaded to be excused from answering. Mu'awiyah insisted and Dirar yielded. This is what Dirar said:

> Ali was farsighted and strong. When pronouncing judgment, he was discerning. When commanding, he was just. Knowledge gushed from his person. Wisdom spoke upon his tongue. He shied away from the ornaments of this world, taking solace in the lonely night. He wept copiously in prayer, thought deeply, and turned his hands

one over the other, admonishing himself before admonishing others. He favored simple food and plain clothes. He lived among us as one of us, responding when asked, and answering when questioned. But despite our intimacy, we would approach him with reverent awe, hesitating to call him out for a casual conversation. He respected the pious and was kind to the poor. The powerful did not dare presume upon a favorable ruling and the weak never despaired of his justice.[7]

Flattery of leaders is not uncommon, but here we see something different. Here is a man Mu'awiyah knows to be Ali's stanch supporter praising Ali to Mu'awiyah's face, in what could easily be viewed as a strong rebuke of Mu'awiyah himself. This is a situation in which Mu'awiyah could arbitrarily command Dirar's execution—as he had of some of Ali's other supporters. Yet when Dirar is pressed to describe Ali, he cannot hold back his reverence and love.

In the 1,400 years since, Ali's legacy has lived on. In Ali's own words, "Those who hoard wealth are dead even as they live, whereas the learned remain for as long as the world remains—their persons may be lost, but their teachings live on in the hearts of men."[8]

ALI'S CONCEPT OF JUST LEADERSHIP

Ali's concept of just leadership is rooted in the Qur'an and the teachings of the Prophet Muhammad, which sought to end the negative tribalism and unjust practices of the so-called Age of Ignorance.[9] Justice, especially for the downtrodden, is a refrain in Ali's sermons and the hallmark of his rule. Ali preached justice, and as ruler, he practiced the justice he preached. In addition, he instructed his governors, commanders, and tax collectors to be scrupulously fair—but this is something scholars have already spoken of at length.[10] What I would like to add to that ongoing conversation is that Ali's ideas on justice go beyond simple equality to include a complex cluster of virtues. Drawing on the texts and contexts of his best-known sermons, letters, and sayings, I identify five principal rubrics of his multifaceted vision of justice:

- consciousness of God
- learning, reason, and wisdom

- compassion and gentleness
- integrity and freedom from corruption
- inclusion and pluralism

The large collection of Ali's teachings describes numerous further characteristics of good leadership, which range from the major and general to the
smaller and more specific. These characteristics include (without following
any particular sequence) the following:

- consultation
- keeping company with good people
- appointing only worthy representatives
- avoidance of nepotism
- being wary of the rich and powerful
- understanding the needs and roles of different categories of people
- tolerance and open-mindedness
- ensuring the prosperity of the populace rather than focusing on
  revenue-collection
- close supervision of appointees to safeguard against corruption
- special attention to the disadvantaged such as the orphan and the
  destitute
- efficient governance and hard work
- making yourself available to the people and listening to their
  complaints
- looking always to make peace, not war
- honoring people of knowledge and virtue
- being watchful against punishing unjustly
- humility, maturity, and deliberation.[11]

Two further caveats: First, the five main rubrics are in reality intertwined,
and sermons cited under one could equally apply to one or more of the others; I separate them only for clarity. Second, just governance has many legal
aspects, including criminal, personal, and property law, conflict resolution,
and, in the context of early Islam, the law of religious ritual. Although I touch
on some of these aspects, these are complex issues, and much more can be
said about each.

In a larger study, all these qualities and issues, and more, should be
addressed. In this chapter, I highlight five characteristics that showcase Ali's
essential framework for just leadership.

CONSCIOUSNESS OF GOD

Justice for Ali is a mandate from God, in step with the Qur'an verse, "God commands you to be just and good."[12] Thus, Ali's worldview anchors a leader's justice in accountability to God, indeed, in consciousness of God. In Ali's thought more broadly, as I have discussed in detail elsewhere, virtue is inextricably linked with piety (Arabic: *taqwā*). Just as godfearing piety is required of all who would be virtuous, virtue is required of all who would be pious; virtue and piety are two sides of the same coin.[13] For a leader in the community, this combination is all the more urgent. If a leader transgresses, if he oppresses, he will answer to the Divine Judge. Regarding his own governing practice, Ali says: "I would prefer to lie on a bed of three-pronged Sa'dan thorns, to be dragged along the ground in iron fetters, than to meet God and His Messenger on the Day of Resurrection having oppressed any of His servants, or having usurped any part of any person's property."[14]

Referencing justice (Arabic: *'adl*) in the above declaration by its opposite, namely, the vice of oppression or tyranny (Arabic: *ẓulm*), Ali sets up his ideas of justice in terms of virtue rather than expediency, of principles rather than laws empty of morality. Here again, he can be seen responding to the Qur'an in its warning, "As for the person who oppresses, we shall punish him."[15] Echoing this virtue-based approach to characterizing justice, medieval Arabic lexicons and works of philosophy explicitly define the term "justice" in contrast to "oppression." "Oppression" they define as "putting a thing in a place not its own."[16] "Justice" they define as "the opposite of oppression," thus, "putting a thing in its rightful place."

Connecting justice with consciousness of God, we see Ali declaring that if not for the dictates of piety, he would be more cunning than Mu'awiyah.[17] He also lays out this issue in some detail:

> We have entered an age when the public equates betrayal with intelligence, and the ignorant deem those who practice it the most resourceful. What is wrong with them? May God punish them! The man with a discerning heart knows well how to practice cunning, but God's commands and prohibitions prevent him from doing so. He deliberately refrains though he sees the possibility clearly in front of his eyes and has the full capability to implement it. It is the man who has no religion, no scruples to hold him back, who exploits the opportunity.[18]

We know from the sources that Mu'awiyah—together with his associate Amr ibn al-As—was proverbial for cunning. He riled up the people of Syria against Ali with a ruse when he raised a bloody shirt on the pulpit declaring that it belonged to "the murdered caliph Uthman" and placed the blame for the murder—falsely—on Ali. When the tide was turning against Mu'awiyah at Siffin, he raised Qur'an pages on spears as a ploy to halt the battle, supposedly turning to the Qur'an as arbiter when he had rejected any arbitration earlier. Whenever he felt the need, he disbursed illegal moneys from the state treasury to buy allegiances. Ali, on the other hand, refused to hand out treasury money, use dishonest tactics in war, or lie ever or at all, in absolute black-and-white terms. For Ali, the end did not justify the means. Pragmatism was not a driver you should heed; piety was. In Ali's terms, what was important at the end of the day was not whether you won the battle. What was important was how you conducted yourself during the battle, how you conducted yourself during your life. The be-all and end-all was responsibility to God.

LEARNING, REASON, AND WISDOM

Ali further underpins his concept of justice with three aspects of human discernment: learning, reason, and wisdom. Among his many sayings promoting these virtues, one lauds learning: "Knowledge is a noble legacy."[19] Another extols reason: "The best wealth is intelligence and the greatest poverty is foolishness."[20] A third that I particularly like for its openness to new ideas and its Arabian imagery exalts wisdom: "A word of wisdom is the believer's own lost camel—he should seize it where he finds it."[21] For those who would lead, Ali presents a combination of all three virtues as an essential prerequisite.

Among Ali's core requirements of a leader is deep learning. In one sermon, he proclaims, "Whoever puts himself forward as a leader among his people should begin by teaching himself before attempting to teach others."[22] In another lengthy sermon, he criticizes the man who, without acquiring sufficient knowledge, sets himself up as judge. After censuring this man's cobbling together of random pieces of information, he says of his ensuing rulings, "The blood of those executed screams from his oppressive rulings and inheritances cry out from his injustice."[23] Furthermore, Ali vaunts knowledge as a natural path to leadership. In one famous sermon, after setting up a multipoint comparison between knowledge and wealth, he says,

"Knowledge rules, while wealth is ruled over." Then, pointing to his own breast, he continues, "Truly, abundant knowledge is housed here!"[24]

So what kind of learning does Ali advocate for a leader? Given that Ali's teachings are mostly oral materials rather than written books, we should expect that they do not enclose a normative inventory. But we can sift through them to produce a rudimentary list of recommendations. Overall, as shown at the outset of this section, Ali's idea of learning is open and broad, and he encourages his audience to acquire wisdom from all sources. In particular, he advocates studying the Qur'an, the words of the Prophet Muhammad, the rules of the Islamic sharia, and his own teachings. He also instructs his governors to gain the full context about people among whom they judge and the full history of places they govern.[25]

Hand-in-hand with learning, Ali advocates reason as the route to leadership. "A man's reason," he says, "determines his rank."[26] For Ali, the one implies the other. Learning may be essential for a leader, but rote learning, devoid of critical thinking, is not real learning. Ali emphasizes rationality in all aspects of human existence. In one instance, he says, "Knowledge is of two kinds: innate and acquired; there is no benefit to be had from the acquired in the absence of the innate."[27] In another place he says, "Absorb any hadith you hear with mindful attention, not by rote learning. There are many narrators of knowledge, few its true custodians."[28] Yet elsewhere he says, "A learned man is sometimes killed by ignorance, and his learning fails to come to his aid."[29]

In addition to learning and reason, Ali speaks of wisdom—which he presents on some occasions as an aggregate of the two—as an essential part of justice. Indeed, he presents all three collectively as a fundamental element of faith. In one famous sermon, he first lists justice as one of four pillars of faith (the others are forbearance, conviction, and struggle against evil). Then he further parses justice into four supporting columns, of which three are the virtues of discernment that we are concerned with here: knowledge (learning), comprehension (reason), and wisdom; the fourth is restraint. Essentially, Ali makes faith contingent on justice, and justice contingent on comprehension, knowledge, and wisdom. Further along in the sermon, he explains why they are indispensable to justice, saying, "Whoever possesses comprehension understands particulars from the generalities of knowledge. Whoever knows the path of wondrous wisdoms is guided to the repositories of self-control and does not stray."[30] In these lines, Ali presents a hierarchy in which comprehension validates knowledge and wisdom validates comprehension. Wisdom—about which the Qur'an says, "Whoever is given wisdom is given immense good"[31]—emerges in Ali's sermon as the full flowering of rationality and learning and the most important support for justice.

In this connection, too, the medieval Arabic lexical tradition bears examining, for it affirms the culture's linking of wisdom, justice, and leadership. The lexicons note that the words denoting "wisdom," "judgment," and "rule"—*ḥikmah*, *ḥukm*, and *ḥukūmah*—are cognates derived from the same root, ḤKM. In fact, they show that the single, multivalent term, *ḥukm*, brings together all three concepts: although used most frequently to connote "judgment," *ḥukm* also means "rule" and "wisdom."[32]

But how does one become wise? Among the avenues that Ali recommends—for all people and especially for those who would lead—is learning from history, from the world around you, and, most importantly, from the example of God's prophets. Ali praises Muhammad as a true guide, and alongside Muhammad's hadith and the Qur'an, he holds up Moses, David, Solomon, and Jesus as exemplars of wisdom.[33] Ali himself was fully invested in teaching his followers, and his erudition was legendary even among his enemies. In speeches at Siffin, for example, even as they drew swords against Ali, Mu'awiyah's supporters were forced to admit that Ali was just, brave, pious, and wise.[34]

COMPASSION AND GENTLENESS

Two connected virtues that Ali presents as drivers of justice are compassion and gentleness. He frequently urges his followers to be compassionate and gentle, in sayings like, "Gentle character is a sign of nobility," and, in an iteration of the Golden Rule, "How you wish to be treated should be the measure of how you treat others."[35] In particular, if we study Ali's instructions to his governors, we find that he frequently pairs injunctions to justice with directives to kindness. For example, in his appointment letter for his ward Muhammad ibn Abi Bakr as governor of Egypt, he enjoins him to be both kind and fair to the people, saying, "Lower your wing over them, offer them your softer side, show them your face, and give equal attention to all in glance and look."[36]

Ali is uniformly described by the sources as a champion for the weak. While he encourages his governors to be kind and just to all, he urges them to be extra vigilant in protecting the rights of the poor. His famous and lengthy letter appointing his close associate Malik al-Ashtar as governor of Egypt includes a lengthy section on protecting the destitute, providing for their needs, and ensuring they get justice. Within this section, he writes:

Beware God's wrath and do not forsake the people of the lowest strata who have no other recourse—the poor, the needy. . . . Protect their rights for the sake of God, for He has entrusted them to you. . . . Appoint a special, trusted agent, a man who is godfearing and humble, to care for their needs. Have him bring you their concerns and respond to them in a manner that will earn you God's pardon on the day you meet Him. Of all your subjects, these are most in need of your justice.[37]

Ali did not just preach justice for the disadvantaged; he also practiced it. As Dirar said of him, "The powerful did not dare presume upon a favorable ruling and the weak never despaired of his justice."[38]

In yet another aspect of Ali's compassionate governance, we find he is especially forgiving of sins of fleshly temptation. In one famous saying, he declares, "If I saw a believer engaging in an immoral act, I would conceal him with this cloak that I am wearing."[39] On the other hand, he is severely unforgiving of transgressions committed by people in power, both his own officials and leaders of his opposition. In other words, while he is exceptionally benevolent in the face of sins of weakness, he is harshly intolerant of sins of strength.[40] He holds people in power to stringently high standards, presumably because the transgressions they commit in their capacity as leaders bring grief and pain to the community as a whole. He refuses to compromise with the powerful even though he knows the consequences will be dire, and we see this time and again. We see it in his flat-out refusal to renew Mu'awiyah's appointment as governor of Syria, which led to his rebellion and the Battle of Siffin. We see it in his refusal to grant the Medinese nobles Talhah and Zubayr higher stipends than the rest of the community, which led to their raising an army against him at the Battle of the Camel. We see it in his rebuke of his cousin and governor Ibn Abbas, who had used treasury funds for personal needs,[41] which led to a falling out among Ali's own supporters. But yet again, when Ali has defeated his enemies and brought them to account, we see time and again that he simply pardons them. He pardons the remaining insurgents after the Battle of the Camel. He pardons the Kharijites who withdraw from the Battle of Nahrawan. In his last moments, after having been struck a death-blow, he even pardons his own murderer, the Kharijite Ibn Muljim.

INTEGRITY AND FREEDOM FROM CORRUPTION

The examples just cited of Talhah and Zubayr, and of Ibn Abbas, are about *amānah* (honesty, integrity), and this leads us to another pillar of Ali's conception of justice: zero tolerance of corruption. It is reported that Ali would enter the treasury after the Friday prayer and declare, "O gold, O silver, tempt someone other than me!"[42] Then he would distribute stipends and have the space swept to ensure that not a single coin remained. According to another report, Ali addressed the world saying, "I have divorced you thrice-over and there can be no reversal!"[43] A mob had killed Ali's caliphal predecessor, Uthman, on charges of corruption and nepotism. Ali's own views against corruption are even more stern due to this chronology. His emphasis on integrity is seen further in his repeated exhortations to governors to be scrupulous regarding state property, in accordance with the Qur'anic injunction, "God commands you to hand over the trusts with which you have been entrusted to their rightful owners."[44]

In yet another report, Ali's own brother Aqil, who had a large family and many dependents, came asking for funds from the treasury. Not only did Ali refuse, but he brought a live firebrand close to Aqil's body, and when Aqil screamed from pain and fear, Ali said to him, "Do you scream from a firebrand, while expecting me to give myself over to the flames of hell?"[45] These and many more anecdotes accompany the vast trove of Ali's sermons strongly rejecting corruption and preaching a life of piety and virtue in this world in preparation for the eternal hereafter.[46]

INCLUSION AND PLURALISM

A large proportion of the people in Ali's realm were Christians and Jews. In Egypt the majority were Coptic Christians. Among Muslims a large proportion were not Ali's particular Shia followers. Yet he made no distinction between these groups in terms of rights in the state, and his directions for just and kind government applied equally to all. All were accorded safety of life, honor, and property under Ali's rule. On this issue, as with the others discussed in this chapter, Ali draws on Qur'anic teachings and the sayings of the Prophet Muhammad, who, in a famous hadith, declares, "All humans are children of God, and God loves best those who most benefit his children."[47]

In step with the prophet's hadith and speaking to his own pluralist ideas, Ali is reported to have proclaimed: "If seated to rule, I would pass judgment among the people of the Torah from the Torah, among the people of the Gospel from the Gospel, and among the people of the Qur'an from the Qur'an. These judgments would shine forth in the presence of God Almighty, and they would exclaim to him: Lord, Ali has judged among your creatures with your judgment."[48] The lines are usually cited as a testament to Ali's extraordinarily wide range of knowledge, but they also illustrate his broadminded governance.

It is important to remember that Ali preached his message of pluralism and inclusive justice from a position of power while he ruled one of the largest empires in the world. He could have taken a much different route, but he preached pluralism because he believed it to be the right thing to do. His story shows that, although he was not expecting to wave a magic wand and resolve all differences, he believed that we can and should learn to respect each other's beliefs. Indeed, Ali had his own strong faith; in one text he says, "I have never doubted the truth ever since it was shown to me."[49] Elsewhere, he declares, "Removing the veil of the body at death will not increase my conviction."[50] But from this conviction sprang inclusiveness, openness, and tolerance. In a letter to his tax collectors, for example, Ali instructed them to extend their justice and compassion to all people in the realm, Muslims as well as people of other faiths, writing: "Do not come between a man and his needs. . . . Do not whip anyone for silver. Do not seize the property of a single individual, whether Muslim, Christian, or Jew."[51] In his earlier cited letter to Ashtar, Ali wrote: "Clothe your heart with compassion, love, and kindness toward your subject. Do not be like a ravening lion who devours their flesh, for people are of two kinds: they are either your brothers in faith or your peers in creation."[52]

CONCLUSION

Ali's uncompromising position on just leadership is particularly interesting from someone who was simultaneously a religious leader, an ascetic, a caliph, and a military commander, someone who had charge of a far-flung empire and faced relentless rebellion and intrigue—thus, someone who was fully cognizant of the exigencies of realpolitik. Notwithstanding considerations of pragmatism, however, for Ali, leadership is evident only through the leader's justice, in the holistic sense that I have discussed.

As a savant revered by Muslims of all denominations, Ali's teachings can be a lodestar for just leadership in Muslim-majority countries, many of which are fiercely divided today. If these leaders were to take Ali's teachings to heart, they would be conscious of their accountability to God and their responsibility to their people and govern all in their realm with fairness. My hope is that scholars of political thought and modern Middle Eastern history, alongside leaders in education and politics, will build on this research to take that next step to bridge the gap on the ground.

As universal teachings of ethics, Ali's words transcend his time, place, and religious affiliation, and they embody the best values we all possess as humans. For leaders everywhere, Ali's teachings are a lofty vision for a just, rational, compassionate, principled, and pluralistic vision of governance that upholds the rights and looks after the needs of all in their domain. For, as Ali put it, "they are either your brothers in faith or your peers in creation."

NOTES

All translations in the article are my own. To balance accessibility with clarity, diacritical marks are omitted for names of people and places in the text of the narrative, but they are used for Arabic terms therein and for authors and titles in the notes.

1. Sermons, sayings, epistles, and some verses attributed to Ali have had enormous currency through the ages and are copiously represented in works of early Islamic history and literature. From these, they have been collected in tens of collections running into thousands of pages. Three major extant medieval compilations are al-Sharīf al-Raḍī, *Nahj al-balāghah*, ed. and trans. Tahera Qutbuddin as *Nahj al-balāghah: The Wisdom and Eloquence of ʿAlī* (Leiden: Brill, 2024); al-Qāḍī l-Quḍāʿī, *Dustūr maʿālim al-ḥikam wa-maʾthūr makārim al-shiyam*, Jāḥiẓ, *Miʾat kalimah*, both ed. and trans. Tahera Qutbuddin in a single volume as *A Treasury of Virtues: Sayings, Sermons, and Teachings of ʿAlī, with the One Hundred Proverbs of al-Jāḥiẓ* (New York: New York University Press, 2013). Citations in this chapter are mostly from these sources.

2. There are numerous primary and secondary works on Ali's career and character in a large number of Islamic languages such as Arabic, Persian, Urdu, and Turkish. For a concise biography of Ali and further references, see Robert Gleave, "ʿAlī ibn Abī Ṭālib," in *Encyclopaedia of Islam*, 3rd ed., ed. Kate Fleet, Gudrun Krämer, Denis Matringe, John Nawas and Devin J. Stewart (Brill online, 2008); and Tahera Qutbuddin, "ʿAli ibn Abi Talib," in *Dictionary of Literary Biography*, vol. 311, *Arabic Literary Culture, 500–925*, ed. Michael Cooperson and Shawkat M. Toorawa (Farmington Hills: Thomson Gale, 2005), 68–76. Historical analyses of Ali's career and standing include Wilferd Madelung, *The Succession to Muḥammad: A Study of the Early Caliphate* (Cambridge: Cambridge University Press, 1997), 141–310.

3. For an overview of Ali's oeuvre, see Tahera Qutbuddin, "Introduction," in Raḍī, *Nahj al-balāghah*. It should be noted that, as collected oral materials, one cannot be certain in absolute terms of their attribution to Ali. However, many of the texts cited here have an early and wide provenance, and they also conform to the historical and literary context of Ali's time. For an overview of the early Islamic oration genre, including a detailed discussion of the orality and authenticity of these materials, see Tahera Qutbuddin, *Arabic Oration: Art and Function* (Leiden: Brill, 2019).

4. On the aesthetics of Ali's oration, see Tahera Qutbuddin, "Sermons of Ali: At the Confluence of the Core Islamic Teachings of the Qurʾan and the Oral, Nature-Based Cultural Ethos of Seventh Century Arabia," *Anuario de Estudios Medievales* 42, no. 1

(2012): 201–28; and Tahera Qutbuddin, "A Sermon on Piety by Imam ʿAlī ibn Abī Ṭālib: How the Rhythm of the Classical Arabic Oration Tacitly Persuaded," in *Religion and Aesthetic Experience: Drama—Sermons—Literature*, ed. Sabine Dorpmüller, Jan Scholz, Max Stille, and Ines Weinrich (Heidelberg: Heidelberg University Press, 2018), 109–24.

5. Cited widely, including al-Qāḍī l-Nuʿmān (Shia), *Sharḥ al-akhbār fī faḍāʾil al-aʾimmah al-aṭhār* (Qum: Muʾassasat al-Nashr al-Islāmī, 1991), 1:89, 97; Tirmidhī (Sunni), *Sunan al-Tirmidhī*, ed. A. M. Shākir (Cairo: Muṣṭafā l-Bābī l-Ḥalabī), §3720, §3725, §3730, §3731; Ibn Saʿd (Sunni), *al-Ṭabaqāt al-kubrā*, ed. M. ʿA. ʿAṭā (Beirut: Dār al-Kutub al-ʿIlmiyyah, 1997), 3:16–18; Ibn Mājah (Sunni), *Sunan Ibn Mājah*, ed. M. N. al-Albānī (Riyadh: Maktabat al-Maʿārif, 1997), §121: (أنا مدينة العلم وعليّ بابها), (أنت يا عليّ أخي في الدنيا والآخرة).

6. Or: "the best judge." References include Nuʿmān, *Sharḥ al-akhbār*, 1:91; Ibn Mājah, *Sunan*, §154: (أقضاكم عليّ).

7. Citations include Qālī, *Kitāb al-Amālī* (Cairo: Dār al-Kutub al-Miṣriyyah, 1926), 2:147; Nuʿmān, *Sharḥ al-akhbār*, 2:391–92.

8. Quḍāʿī, *A Treasury of Virtues*, §4.3; Raḍī, *Nahj al-balāghah*, §3.133: (مات خزّان الأموال وهم أحياء) (والعلماء باقون ما بقي الدهر أعيانهم مفقودة وآثارهم في القلوب موجودة).

9. Several studies discuss the concept and practice of justice in Islam, and they draw on materials from the Qurʾan and Hadith. See, e.g., Mohammad Hashim Kamali, *Freedom, Equality, and Justice in Islam* (Cambridge: Islamic Texts Society, 2002); Majid Khadduri, *The Islamic Conception of Justice* (Baltimore: Johns Hopkins University Press, 2002); Muntasir Mir, "Twelve Verses from the Qurʾān," in *Justice and Rights: Christian and Muslim Perspectives*, ed. Michael Ipgrave (Washington: Georgetown University Press, 2009), 27–31; and Khalid Abou El Fadl, "Qurʾanic Ethics and Islamic Law," *Journal of Islamic Ethics* 1 (2017): 7–28.

10. For Sufi-oriented presentations of Ali's justice, see Reza Shah-Kazemi, *Justice and Remembrance: Introducing the Spirituality of Imam ʿAlī* (London: I. B. Tauris, 2006); M. Ali Lakhani, with Seyyed Hossein Nasr, Reza Shah-Kazemi, and Leonard Lewisohn, *The Sacred Foundations of Justice in Islam: The Teachings of ʿAli ibn Abi Talib* (Vancouver: World Wisdom and Sacred Web, 2006). For a comparison with Western systems of justice, see Ali Paya, "Imam ʿAli's Theory of Justice Revisited," *Journal of Shiʿa Islamic Studies* 6, no. 1 (2013): 5–30. Studies on Ali's justice in Middle Eastern and South Asian languages abound.

11. For Ali's injunctions to governors about these qualities, see Raḍī, *Nahj al-balāghah*, passim, esp. §2.53, known as "Ashtar's testament."

12. Qurʾan, Naḥl 16:90: (إِنَّ ٱللَّهَ يَأْمُرُ بِٱلْعَدْلِ وَٱلْإِحْسَانِ). Other Qurʾan verses enjoining justice include Nisāʾ 4:58, Naḥl 16:76.

13. Tahera Qutbuddin, "Piety and Virtue in Early Islam: Two Sermons by Imam Ali," in *Self-Transcendence and Virtue: Perspectives from Philosophy, Psychology, and Theology*, ed. Jennifer A. Frey and Candace Vogler (London: Routledge, 2019), 125–53.

14. Raḍī, *Nahj al-balāghah*, §1.221: (والله لئن أبيت على حسك السعدان مسهّدًا وأجرّ في الأغلال مصفّدًا أحبّ إليّ من أن ألقى الله ورسوله ظالمًا لبعض العباد أو غاصبًا لشيء من الحطام).

15. Qurʾan, Kahf 18:87: (أَمَّا مَن ظَلَمَ فَسَوْفَ نُعَذِّبُهُ).

16. (وضع الشيء في غير موضعه). See, e.g., Edward William Lane, *An Arabic-English Lexicon* (London: Williams and Norgate, 1863–1893), s.v. "ẒLM"; Ibn Manẓūr, *Lisān al-ʿArab*, ed. ʿA. ʿA. al-Kabīr et al. (Cairo: Dār al-Maʿārif, 1985), s.v. "ẒLM"; al-Muʾayyad fī l-Dīn

al-Shīrāzī, *al-Majālis al-Muʾayyadiyyah*, vols. 1–4, ed. Ḥ. Ḥamīd al-Dīn (Oxford and Mumbai: World of Islam Studies, 1975–2011), vol. 2, *majlis* §4.

17. Raḍī, *Nahj al-balāghah*, §1.198: "By God, Muʿawiyah is not more astute, but he deceives and sins. If not for my dislike of deceit, I would be the most cunning of people" (واللہ ما معاوية بأدهى مِنّي ولكنّه يغدر ويفجر ولولا كراهية الغدر لكنت من أدهى الناس); Ibn Shuʿbah al-Ḥarrānī, *Tuḥaf al-ʿuqūl ʿan āl al-rasūl* (Beirut: Dār al-Murtaḍā, 2007), 80: "If not for the dictates of piety, I would be the most cunning of the Arabs (لو لا التقى لكنت أدهى العرب).

18. Raḍī, *Nahj al-balāghah*, §1.41: (ولقد أصبحنا في زمان قد اتّخذ أكثر أهله الغدر كيسًا ونسبهم أهل الجهل فيه إلى حسن الحيلة ما لهم قاتلهم اللہ قد يرى الحُوّل القلب وجه الحيلة ودونها مانع من أمر اللہ ونهيه فيدعها رأي عين بعد القدرة عليها وينتهز فرصتها من لا حريجة له في الدين).

19. Raḍī, §3.2; Quḍāʿī, *A Treasury of Virtues*, §1.80: (العلم وراثة كريمة).

20. Raḍī, *Nahj al-balāghah*, §3.33; Quḍāʿī, *A Treasury of Virtues*, §1.168: (أغنى الغنى العقل وأكبر الفقر الحمق).

21. Raḍī, *Nahj al-balāghah*, §3.71; Quḍāʿī, *A Treasury of Virtues*, §1.128; Jāḥiẓ, *One Hundred Proverbs*, §61: (الحكمة ضالّة المؤمن حيث وجدها ألتقطها).

22. Raḍī, *Nahj al-balāghah*, §3.65: (من نصب نفسه للناس إمامًا فليبدأ بتعليم نفسه قبل تعليم غيره).

23. Quḍāʿī, *A Treasury of Virtues*, §6.2: (تبكي منه الدماء وتصرخ منه المواريث); Raḍī, *Nahj al-balāghah*, §1.17: (تصرخ من جور قضائه الدماء وتعجّ منه المواريث).

24. Quḍāʿī, *A Treasury of Virtues*, §4.3; Raḍī, *Nahj al-balāghah*, §3.133: (العلم حاكم والمال محكوم عليه), (إنّ ههنا لعلمًا جمًّا). The sermon begins: "Knowledge is better than wealth: Knowledge protects you, whereas you have to protect wealth. Wealth decreases with spending, whereas knowledge increases with it."

25. See Raḍī, *Nahj al-balāghah*, §2.53.

26. Quḍāʿī, *A Treasury of Virtues*, §1.124: (مرتبة الرجل بحسن عقله).

27. Raḍī, *Nahj al-balāghah*, §3.323: (العلم علمان مطبوع ومسموع ولا ينفع المسموع إذا لم يكن المطبوع).

28. Raḍī, §3.88 (اعقلوا الخبر إذا سمعتموه عقل رعاية لا عقل رواية فإنّ رواة العلم كثير ورعاته قليل).

29. Raḍī, §3.98 (رُبّ عالم قتله جهله وعلمه معه لا ينفعه).

30. Raḍī, §3.26; Quḍāʿī, *A Treasury of Virtues*, §5.14. For the text, translation, and analysis of this sermon, see Qutbuddin, "Piety and Virtue," 128–35.

31. Qurʾan, Baqarah 2:269 (وَمَن يُؤْتَ الْحِكْمَةَ فَقَدْ أُوتِيَ خَيْرًا كَثِيرًا).

32. See, e.g., Lane, *Lexicon*; and Ibn Manẓūr, *Lisān*, s.v. "ḤKM."

33. Quḍāʿī, *A Treasury of Virtues*, §2.10.3. The Qurʾan also praises these and other prophets for their wisdom, e.g., David (Qurʾan, Ṣād 38:20), Moses (Qaṣaṣ 28:14), John the Baptist (Maryam 19:12).

34. Such as the oration by Muʿawiyah's general Dhu l-Kalaʿ al-Himyari, cited in Naṣr ibn Muzāḥim al-Minqarī, *Waqʿat Ṣiffīn*, ed. ʿA. M. Hārūn (Cairo: Maktabat al-Khānjī, 1981), 240–41. See further references in Qutbuddin, *Arabic Oration*, 511 (oration §46.1), and discussion of the issue in Qutbuddin, *Arabic Oration*, 305–7.

35. Quḍāʿī, *A Treasury of Virtues*, §1.115: (من الكرم لين الشيم), and §4.1.9: (اجعل نفسك ميزانًا فيما بينك وبين غيرك). This counsel is similar to the Biblical dictum "Do unto others as you would have them do unto you" (Matthew 7:12); and the Confucian rule "Do not impose on others what you do not wish for yourself."

36. Raḍī, *Nahj al-balāghah*, §2.27.1: (فأخفض لهم جناحك وألن لهم جانبك وأبسط لهم وجهك وآس بينهم في اللّحظة والنظرة).

37. Raḍī, §2.53.14: (ثَمّ اللہ اللہ في الطبقة السفلى من الذين لا حيلة لهم والمساكين والمحتاجين . . . وأحفظ للہ ما أستحفظك من حقه فيهم . . . ففرّغ لأولئك ثقتك من أهل الخشية والتواضع فليرفع إليك أمورهم ثمّ أعمل فيهم بالإعذار إلى اللہ تعالى يوم تلقاه فإنّ هؤلاء من بين الرعيّة أحوج إلى الإنصاف من غيرهم). See also

oration §37: "The weak are mighty in my eyes, as I strive to restore their rights. The mighty are weak in my eyes, as I strive to wrest those rights from them" (الذليل عندي عزيز حتّى آخذ الحقّ له والقويّ عندي ضعيف حتّى آخذ الحقّ منه).

38. Citations include Qālī, *Kitāb al-Amālī* (Cairo: Dār al-Kutub al-Miṣriyyah, 1926), 2:147; Nuʿmān, *Sharḥ al-akhbār*, 2:391–92.

39. Ismāʿīl ibn Mūsā ibn Jaʿfar al-Ṣādiq, *al-Jaʿfariyyāt* (also titled *al-Ashʿathiyyāt*), ed. M. Ṣ. al-Muẓaffar (Karbala: al-ʿAtabah al-Ḥusayniyyah Qism al-Shuʾūn al-Thaqāfiyyah, 2013), 2: 258, §1606: (لو وجدت مؤمنًا على فاحشة لسترته بثوبي).

40. I thank my sister Dr. Bazat-Saifiyah Qutbuddin for this insight.

41. Yaʿqūbī, *Tārīkh al-Yaʿqūbī* (Beirut: Dār Ṣādir, 1960), 2: 205. Note that the issue is complicated by Ibn Abbas's thinking he was entitled to a share from the Qurʾanic *khums* (fifth) share, allocated from the public treasury to the Prophet Muhammad and his family. After Ali's rebuke, Ibn Abbas returned the money he had taken.

42. Ibn Abī l-Ḥadīd, *Sharḥ Nahj al-balāghah*, ed. A. Ibrāhīm (Cairo: Dār Iḥyāʾ al-Kutub al-ʿArabiyyah, 1965), 1.22: (يا صفراء ويا بيضاء غرّي غيري).

43. Raḍī, *Nahj al-balāghah*, §3.69: (طلّقتك ثلاثًا).

44. Qurʾan, Nisāʾ 4:58: (إِنَّ ٱللَّهَ يَأْمُرُكُمْ أَن تُؤَدُّوا۟ ٱلْأَمَٰنَٰتِ إِلَىٰٓ أَهْلِهَا). Further instructions by Ali to his governors enjoining *amānah* include Raḍī, *Nahj al-balāghah*, §2.5, 2.26, 2.40, 2.41, 2.53.

45. Raḍī, *Nahj al-balāghah*, §1.221. Sadly, Aqil went over to Muʿawiyah to ask for money; however, he regretted his act almost immediately and returned to Ali without accepting Muʿawiyah's largesse (Nuʿmān, *Sharḥ al-akhbār*, 2: 100–102).

46. For an analysis of Ali's overarching theme of the hereafter, see Tahera Qutbuddin, "ʿAli's Contemplations on this World and the Hereafter in the Context of His Life and Times," in *Essays in Islamic Philology, History, and Philosophy*, ed. A. Korangy, Wheeler M. Thackston, Roy P. Mottahedeh, and William Granara (Berlin: De Gruyter, 2016), 333–53; see also Ali's instructions to his governor Uthman ibn Hunayf rebuking him for pandering to the rich (Raḍī, *Nahj al-balāghah*, §2.45); and his rebuke to his judge Shurayh for purchasing a large house (Raḍī, *Nahj al-balāghah*, §2.3; Quḍāʿī, *A Treasury of Virtues*, §7.7).

47. Al-Qāḍī l-Quḍāʿī, *Light in the Heavens: Sayings of the Prophet Muḥammad* (*Kitāb al-Shihāb*), ed. and trans. Tahera Qutbuddin (New York: New York University Press, 2016), §9.54: (الخلق عيال الله وأحبّ الخلق إلى الله أنفعهم لعياله).

48. Ibn Abī l-Ḥadīd, *Sharḥ Nahj al-balāghah*, 20:283: لو كسرت لي الوسادة لحكمت بين أهل التوراة بتوراتهم وبين أهل الإنجيل بإنجيلهم وبين أهل الفرقان بفرقانهم حتّى تزهر تلك القضايا إلى الله عزّ وجلّ وتقول يا ربّ إنّ عليًّا قضى بين خلقك بقضائك). Cited after Madāʾinī, in Ibn Abī l-Ḥadīd, *Sharḥ Nahj al-balāghah*, 2:136, with a variant ending. The word used in the quote to denote the Qurʾan is Furqān (lit., Demarcator), one of its several names.

49. Raḍī, *Nahj al-balāghah*, §3.168: (ما شككت في الحقّ مذ أريته).

50. Jāḥiẓ, *One Hundred Proverbs*, §1: (لو كشف الغطاء ما زددت يقينًا).

51. Raḍī, *Nahj al-balāghah*, §2.51: ولا تحشموا أحدًا عن حاجته ولا تحبسوه عن طلبته . . . ولا تضربنّ (أحدًا سوطًا لمكان درهم ولا تمسّنّ مال أحد من الناس مصلّ ولا معاهد).

52. Raḍī, §2.53.3: وأشعر قلبك الرحمة للرعيّة والمحبّة لهم واللّطف بهم ولا تكوننّ عليهم سبعًا ضاريًا تغتنم (أكلهم فإنّهم صنفان إمّا أخ لك في الدين وإمّا نظير لك في الخلق). With slightly different phrasing in Nuʿmān, *Daʿāʾim al-Islām*, 1: 354. UN Secretary-General Kofi Anan quoted these lines in his address at Tehran University in 1997 (Press Release SG/SM/6419 OBV/34 at www.un.org/press/en/1997/19971209.SGSM6419.html).

CHAPTER 6

Women's Work and the Question of Leadership

Marla Frederick

Growing up in Sumter, South Carolina, I knew for decades that there were great pastors who had led my home church—*men* of God who guided the congregation through the aftermath of slavery and the horrors of Jim and Jane Crow. I had heard of the great shepherds of the flock, those who had marched with King and helped undergird the Progressive Baptist Convention, the denomination that split from the National Baptist Convention, the largest Black denomination in the country at the time. Its leader, Rev. Joseph Jackson, rejected Martin Luther King Jr.'s vision of civil disobedience and refused participation in the civil rights movement.[1] From thus sprung the Progressives. I knew some of this history.

Founded in 1868, just three years after slavery, First Baptist Missionary Church was a beacon of hope for Black people in this ninth largest city in South Carolina. Organized 105 miles west of Charleston, First Baptist Missionary was likely established with some angst. The founders certainly knew the dangers of launching out on their own. Perhaps they knew the story of Emanuel African Methodist Episcopal Church in Charleston and of Denmark Vesey's planned slave revolt there in 1822.

Denmark Vesey, a freedman whose family remained enslaved, and five of his co-conspirators were executed after a secret trial because of reports that they planned an insurrection. Weeks afterward, another thirty people were executed. Angry white mobs burned down Emanuel AME, the church where Vesey allegedly organized. Fearing further organization in houses of worship, the white-run city of Charleston outlawed all Black churches. Emanuel

AME would not rebuild its sanctuary until after emancipation. It is likely that enslaved people across South Carolina knew of the story, given that the point of terror campaigns was to strike fear in the hearts of other potential rebels.

Despite this history, First Baptist Missionary Church (the "Missionary" later added to distinguish it from the all-white First Baptist Church in town) opened anyway. As a young person, I never knew many details about the church's history, but in the vestibule of the church we could see portraits of its great leaders. The iconography spoke for itself. Portraits of the church's pastors lined the wall, as they do in many other churches. And, as histories go, monumental moments in an institution's history are marked by who occupies the position of leadership at the time. Under this pastor, the church was built; under that pastor, the sanctuary was rebuilt. The great work of this church, like that of countless churches across the country, has often been identified with powerful and charismatic male leaders.

It was not until I was asked to participate in the church's 149th anniversary in 2017 that I learned a new narrative. It is in the kind of information that comes from the archives and ethnographic research—the stories of the day-to-day, the who, what, when, where, and why—that we understand the truest constellation of great leadership. After all, the foundations of great leadership are often not hierarchical but collaborative. They are most certainly not male-dominated but often constitutive of a vast and invisible female volunteer assemblage, and their concerns tend to be rooted in the needs of the community. At least that is the overarching history of Black churches in the United States. Great leadership, I learned, is transformative because of these women's ideals.

As I began to prepare to participate in the anniversary celebration, I asked for more details on the church. The church secretary sent me the data that they had compiled through a bit of archival research in preparation for the 150th anniversary the following year. As it turns out, First Baptist Missionary Church, now at the corner of Washington and Dingle, was not founded by men but by a group of formerly enslaved *women*. Mary Mitchell, Minnie Blair, and Tilda Bush "organized the church," as the record reads, at the corner of Bee and South Main Streets in Sumter. Initially called Shiloh Baptist Church, the church was later relocated and renamed First Baptist Missionary Church. Interestingly, the record also reads that "those founders were led by the church's first pastor, Rev. Ben Lawson." Now, *how* one writes history is important. From the phrasing, it is difficult to tell whether the pastor was there from the beginning or whether the three women called Pastor Lawson to head the church *after* they organized. Nevertheless, we know that three women were the seeds of this extraordinary church.

In the telling of this story as in the narration of similar stories, we learn something not only about leadership but also about how history records leadership. Consequently, this written history often informs our understanding of what leadership looks like and what leadership means. In the absence of these women's photographs from the walls of the sanctuary *and* in the absence of their story from the printed histories, their contributions are erased to time. In his monumental work, *Silencing the Past: Power and the Production of History*, anthropologist Michel-Rolph Trouillot argues that "history is the fruit of power, but power itself is never so transparent that its analysis becomes superfluous. The ultimate mark of power may be its invisibility; the ultimate challenge, the exposition of its roots."[2] To expose these women's stories is to unmask the power inherent in the initial telling of the church's history itself.

Although First Baptist was established in 1868 in what historians call a "hush harbor," it was not until 1877 that members built their own edifice. As they grew, they and other Baptists across the state knew that they wanted more for themselves and their community. Outlawed from attending the University of South Carolina or any of the other white colleges in the state, they began to organize, like other freed Black people in other states, to build their own school. By 1909 Morris College, located in Sumter, was established "for the Christian and Intellectual Training of Negro youth."[3] It was the first and only Black Baptist college in South Carolina organized by the descendants of the formerly enslaved. Its founding was striking in its ambition. It was not established by white missionaries from the Northern Baptist Association, who had established other Black schools across the South as an extension of their abolitionist efforts.[4] Morris College was established by African Americans themselves.

The story of its earliest days is instructive. Once the edifice of the First Baptist Missionary Church was built in 1877, the State Baptist Education and Sunday School Convention (which became the Baptist Education and Mission Convention, or BEMC) was organized at First Baptist around the same time. This body was the impetus for the founding and ongoing support of Morris College. Yet it was the Women's Baptist Educational and Missionary Convention of South Carolina (WBEMC), organized in 1888, that was truly instrumental in the support of the college. According to one history of Black Baptist women's work in South Carolina, "The WBEMC's most significant and ongoing endeavor was its support for Morris College."[5] Over the years, and particularly in its earliest days, they worked hard to sustain the college, not on the resources of millionaires, but on the sacrifices of saints—sharecropping men and women, washerwomen, and teachers—some of whom knew they might never attend college yet who dreamed of an education for their children.

The men of the convention knew, based on other state conventions like those in Kentucky, North Carolina, and Alabama, that the best way to raise money and support for their initiatives, like education, was to help organize the women.[6] At their 1886 meeting, they issued a report requesting, first, "that each minister, on his return home, organize the female members of his church into a society, to be known as 'The Women's Missionary Society.'" But the catch was revealed in the second urging, "that the moneys collected in said societies be turned over, quarterly, to the Secretary of the Baptist State Convention."[7]

Male leaders of the time knew that women were central to the success of any campaign seeking to build an institution. And, although the pastors and presidents of churches and colleges are often celebrated, it is critical to underscore the sacrificial work of women in building these institutions. Too often they are written out of history. As W. E. B. Du Bois opined, "despite the noisier and more spectacular advance of my brothers, I instinctively feel and know that it is the five million women of my race who really count."[8] Near the turn of the twentieth century, Du Bois estimated that women raised three-fourths of the money used to acquire church property. This story is shored up in the notes of the WBEMC.

Although the Women's Baptist Educational and Missionary Convention of South Carolina was established in 1888 with the support of the BEMC, by the early 1900s the WBEMC was a fully functioning and independent organization. In 1906 "the South Carolina WBEMC . . . received a recommendation from the BEMC that it become an auxiliary to the men's organization in order for it 'to be in harmony with the National Baptist Convention and all other State Baptist Conventions.'" The BEMC also recommended that the WBEMC turn over all of its money in order to help the BEMC carry on its work. The WBEMC's Committee on Recommendations responded with the following statement: "Feeling that while it may be right for our convention to unite with our brethren's convention of this State, that at the present time, it would not be the expedient thing to do, we ask therefore that the recommendation from the various sources asking for said cooperation or union be tabled indefinitely."[9] One might translate their reservation as extreme caution about what might come of their resources given their laser focus on establishing a college for Black youth, a bridge to the future for generations to come. With these reservations, they declined the opportunity to come under the BEMC. And, to this day, they continue to decline.

Women like those in the WBEMC have helped to establish and ensure the longevity of Black colleges across the nation—schools from which

women and men such as contemporary political leaders US Vice President
Kamala Harris, Senator Raphael Warnock of Georgia, and Stacey Abrams of
Georgia, have all graduated.[10] But we would not know the history of Morris
College, nor the history of the founding of First Baptist Church out of which
it comes, were it not for archivists, historians, and oral historians.

The stories of these Baptist women and women like them tell us at least
two important things about leadership. First, they tell us that portraits hanging on walls can be deceptive. One cannot look for leadership only in the
polished photos adorning the halls of our institutions. Leadership is about
who gets the work done, advances the cause of the institution, and creates
a vision for future generations. Documenting the efforts of African American women who have done this work has been the work of religious studies scholars like Evelyn Brooks Higginbotham, Judith Weisenfeld, Barbara
Savage, Cheryl Townsend Gilkes, and Anthea Butler.[11] They go behind
the pulpit to tell the stories of the everyday women leaders of the church
who organize, fundraise, and push forward the vision of community. In my
research in Halifax County, North Carolina, I have found that women organized beyond the purview of documented history and often in the shadows
of public church leadership.[12] It is what anthropologist Judith Casselberry
refers to as the "labor of faith," the often discounted but critical work done
by women to make an institution function.[13] I called my study *Between Sundays* in part because so much of the work of faith was done outside of Sunday
morning services—organizing youth, leading Bible studies, planning visits
to the sick and shut-in, taking care of the elderly—the work of building sup-
portive community.

If historians have given us an appreciation for bottom-up narratives of
histories, or histories from the perspectives of those on the margins of society, anthropologists have given us ethnographies that tell of the agency of
seemingly powerless subjects. In the humanities and social sciences over the
last four decades (not uncoincidentally as more women and people of color
have entered into fields once dominated by white men), less-known subjects
have come to the center of our inquiries. And these new stories, as some
women's historians note, do not have an additive quality but rather a multi-
plicative quality in that they change the entire texture and tone of the narrative.[14] Ann Braude argues, for example, that attending to women's history in
the study of religion might just change three grand narratives that have come
to inform religious history—declension, feminization, and secularization.[15]
To study women's history might cause us to rethink our assumptions of religious decline, revisit the idea that women were not always already present
in the practice of religion, or reconsider the idea that secularism replaced

deep commitments to the divine. Women's stories thus are not merely additions to a predetermined story line. From these new histories we can not only ask better questions about who did what to attain a certain goal, but we can better understand how the goal itself was altered and who indeed led the initiative.

While I study Christian communities, much of the same can be said in thinking about how African American women have operated in other religious institutions, such as Muslim spaces. The research of scholars such as Carolyn Rouse, Jamillah Karim, and Debra Majeed all ask us to rethink the types of leadership roles that Islamic women occupy both within and beyond the space of the mosque.[16] What is particularly striking, for example, is their role in helping to interpret the Qur'an and the Hadith for younger Muslim women in the United States. They help them find women's power in the lines of the text, at times questioning the prevailing assumptions of male leaders.

Second, if the humanities compel us to ask what it means to be human, what it means to appreciate human difference, and how humans come to understand ourselves and our place in the world, then studying the lives of Black religious women in one of the poorest counties in eastern North Carolina teaches us a lesson on what sacrificial leadership looks like. It is the type of leadership that serves others without the expectation of reward in return, often because those whom you serve are not necessarily equipped with resources with which to reward you. It is not the neoliberal version of leadership often celebrated today, one given over to market-driven self-help individualism that looks for ways to advance its own financial interests. It is not the type of leadership needed to maintain a global competitive edge or to amass millions of television followers if you are a televangelist, like the ones I study in my later work. Rather, it is a leadership that is based upon interdependency, one that accounts for the real limitations in access to resources for everyday folks.

When I conducted ethnographic field research in Halifax County, I talked with the women who helped to launch the health clinic in Tillery, North Carolina—women who coordinated visits with medical doctors, who weekly prepared food for community elders, and who visited them in their homes or took them to their doctors' appointments. They were committed to establishing a space where those who were often older and less resourced could still find community, despite the fact that many of their children had migrated years earlier to cities east, west, north, or south for better opportunities.

One day while conducting research, I had the privilege of riding with "Ms. Sylvia," one of the coordinators. She arranges transportation for seniors both for the meetings and other events throughout the week, including doctor's appointments, trips to the grocery store, and so on. Ms. Sylvia picks up and drops off "Cousin Ellie," a term of endearment used by everyone in the center, every week before and after the meeting, or secures a ride for her. One week, I had an opportunity to escort Cousin Ellie to the doctor; I went with Ms. Sylvia the week before to ensure I knew exactly what to do. We dropped Cousin Ellie off at the end of the seniors' meeting, turning down the dirt road leading to the seniors' complex and eventually walking her inside the one-bedroom first-floor apartment. As I describe in *Between Sundays*:

> The walk from the car to the apartment was enough for me to gain an appreciation for the unrecognized work Ms. Sylvia performs. I walked on one side of Cousin Ellie, Ms. Sylvia on the other. For every step we took, she would take five or six tiny steps. We talked and waited while Cousin Ellie, never saying a word, caught up with our progression. When we finally reached the inside of her apartment, Ms. Sylvia instructed me to get a cold glass of water for Cousin Ellie so that she could have it beside her bed and would not have to make her way to the kitchen. I went to the refrigerator and found inside the lone jug of water alongside a pitcher of tea. A Styrofoam container with leftover food sat on the second shelf, with a few condiments in the refrigerator door. It was obvious that Cousin Ellie no longer cooks and has few, if any, visitors. We dressed her for the day, taking off her meeting clothes and putting on a cool house dress for her to lounge. Ms. Sylvia gave her some instructions about who would be coming over later to bring her dinner and what she needed to do in the meantime. We soon left, Ms. Sylvia taking her key and locking the door behind us.[17]

While others might point to the city councillors who meet regularly and for years had denied access to city water to this small community of African Americans on the outskirts of their town as the leaders of the community, I saw Ms. Sylvia as one of the unsung leaders of the small community. It was her who had actually made a difference in the lives of those unable to return the favor.

For me, documenting her story was about ensuring that this vision of service and care, this vision of leadership in community building, was not erased to the annals of time. Studying the lives of Black women of faith ultimately taught me that sometimes our categories as scholars do not always fit neatly. Terms like "activist" or "feminist" work for progressive, liberal spaces, but they do not always map onto the lives of the women with whom we conduct our research. As I collected stories from Baptist women in eastern North Carolina and participated in their civic events, one of my lingering questions centered on the role of faith in how they understand themselves as social actors. What was most interesting was that none of them saw themselves as activists. When they were on the picket line protesting the infiltration of industrialized hog farms in their community, when they protested in Washington, DC, against the loss of Black land, and when they went to local city council meetings to encourage council members to extend the city lines to annex a small part of the county where residents did not have running water, they simply saw themselves as doing "God's work." "Activists" were another group of people. This is striking in an age where critiques of Black church activism abound as scholars decry a perceived decline in Black church engagement. Women who engaged socially did not necessarily represent themselves as agents of the church but rather as agents of God. They were not tied to certain ministries of the church as they went about their day in service and organizing, although they were all largely active members of their respective congregations. To find "activism," it seems, we might have to look with a different lens at those who act and at the means by which they act.

The women from my home church in South Carolina who built the church and undergirded the college, and the women from Halifax County who advocate for the poor and care for the seniors—these women walk in the shoes of great leaders. They walk in paths worn by Fannie Lou Hamer, Coretta Scott King, and Septima Clark, among countless other women, who have helped to build institutions, enliven movements, and affect change in their communities, often in the shadows of history. To think about leadership through the purview of these women's lives is to revisit several questions: How do we understand true leadership? How does recognizing unsung leaders change our view of leadership? What ethical vision must leaders have for their communities? What type of sacrificial service are they willing to execute to make that vision a reality? And how do the narrators of the great stories shape our understanding of leadership? These are the pertinent questions and the indispensable lessons that the stories of Black religious women illuminate.

NOTES

1. C. Eric Lincoln and Lawrence H. Mamiya, *The Black Church in the African-American Experience* (Durham, NC: Duke University Press, 1990). See also Wallace Best, "'The Right Achieved and the Wrong Way Conquered': J. H. Jackson, Martin Luther King Jr.,

and the Conflict over Civil Rights," *Religion and American Culture: A Journal of Interpretation* 16, no. 2 (2006): 195–226.

2. Michel-Rolph Trouillot, *Silencing the Past: Power and the Production of History* (Boston: Beacon Press, 1995), xxiii.

3. "The Morris Experience," Morris College, accessed March 2023, https://www.morris .edu/our-college/history.

4. In South Carolina, Benedict Institute, the first Black Baptist college, had already been founded in 1870 by Bethesda A. Benedict from Rhode Island. She named the school after her late husband, Stephen Benedict. The school was largely supported by Northern Baptists who were a part of the American Baptist Home Mission Society. See also Ralph E. Luker, *The Social Gospel in Black and White: American Racial Reform, 1885–1912* (Chapel Hill: University of North Carolina Press, 1991).

5. W. Marvin Dulaney, ed., with Damon Fordham and Muima A. Shinault-Small, *Born to Serve: A History of the Woman's Baptist Educational and Missionary Convention of South Carolina* (Charleston, SC: Historical Commission by the Woman's Baptist Educational and Missionary Convention and the Avery Research Center for African American History and Culture at the College of Charleston, 2006), 20.

6. Dulaney, Fordham, and Shinault-Small, *Born to Serve*, 15.

7. Dulaney, Fordham, and Shinault-Small, 16.

8. W. E. B. Du Bois, "The Damnation of Women," in *Darkwater: Voices from within the Veil* (1920; reprint, New York: Washington Square Press, 2004), 179, as cited in Barbara Dianne Savage, *Your Spirits Walk Beside Us: The Politics of Black Religion* (Cambridge, MA: Harvard University Press, 2008), 26–27.

9. Dulaney, Fordham, and Shinault-Small, *Born to Serve*, 17.

10. Three of the most high-profile African American political leaders of this generation are graduates of HBCUs—Vice President Kamala Harris from Howard University, Raphael Warnock from Morehouse College, and Stacey Abrams from Spelman College. Although her bids for governor were unsuccessful, Abrams was the first African American woman to win the gubernatorial nomination of a major party, and her organization, Fair Fight, registered thousands of Georgia residents, who helped turn the state blue in the election of Warnock and President Joe Biden.

11. Evelyn Brooks Higginbotham, *Righteous Discontent: The Women's Movement in the Black Baptist Church, 1880–1920* (Cambridge, MA: Harvard University Press, 1993); R. Marie Griffith and Barbara Dianne Savage, *Women and Religion in the African Diaspora: Knowledge, Power, and Performance* (Baltimore: Johns Hopkins University Press, 2006); Judith Weisenfeld, *African American Women and Christian Activism: New York's Black YWCA, 1905–1945* (Cambridge, MA: Harvard University Press, 1997); Judith Weisenfeld and Richard Newman, *This Far by Faith: Readings in African-American Women's Religious Biography* (New York: Routledge, 1996); Anthea D. Butler, *Women in the Church of God in Christ: Making a Sanctified World* (Chapel Hill: University of North Carolina Press, 2007); Savage, *Your Spirits Walk Beside Us*; Cheryl Townsend Gilkes, "*If It Wasn't for the Women...*": Black Women's Experience and Womanist Culture in Church and Community* (Maryknoll, NY: Orbis, 2001).

12. Marla Faye Frederick, *Between Sundays: Black Women and Everyday Struggles of Faith* (Berkeley: University of California Press, 2003).

13. Judith Casselberry, *The Labor of Faith: Gender and Power in Black Apostolic Pentecostalism* (Durham, NC: Duke University Press, 2017).

14. Anne Braude, "Women's History Is American Religious History," in *Retelling US Religious History*, ed. Thomas A. Tweed (Berkeley: University of California Press, 1997), 1–11; Catherine Brekus, "Introduction: Searching for Women in Narratives of American Religious History," in *The Religious History of American Women: Reimagining the Past* (Chapel Hill: University of North Carolina Press, 2007), 1–50; and Evelyn Brooks Higginbotham, "African-American Women's History and the Metalanguage of Race," *Signs* 17, no. 2 (1992): 251–74. See also Kimberle Williams Crenshaw, "Mapping the Margins: Intersectionality, Identity, and Violence against Women," *Stanford Law Review* 43, no. 6 (1991): 1241–99.

15. Braude, "Women's History."

16. Dawn-Marie Gibson and Jamillah Karim, *Women of the Nation: Between Black Protest and Sunni Islam* (New York: New York University Press, 2014); Carolyn Moxley Rouse, *Engaged Surrender: African American Women and Islam* (Berkeley: University of California Press, 2004); Debra Majeed, *Polygyny: What It Means When African American Muslim Women Share Their Husbands* (Gainesville: University Press of Florida, 2015).

17. Frederick, *Between Sundays*, 76.

PART III

Literature

CHAPTER 7

Shakespeare, His Books, and Leadership

John Miles

On the frontispiece of the 1615 edition of Thomas Kyd's *The Spanish Trag-edy*, the title reads: *The Spanish Tragedie: Or, Hieronimo is mad againe.*[1] The eponymous Hieronimo bears a torch and a sword and is portrayed discov-ering the murder of his son, Horatio, while Bel-imperia calls for his help. As a revenge hero, Kyd's popular lead character embodies a trope well trod-den by a range of playwrights and authors by the time this particular edi-tion was published: the leader as a heroic and decisive executor of revenge. Ambiguity is not a problem Hieronimo must face; his situation and ensu-ing course of action are clear: his son has been hanged, and he must bring those responsible to justice. By the end of the play, justice has become ret-ribution, and Hieronimo, Bel-imperia, Lorenzo, Balthazar, and the Duke lie dead after a mock play-within-a-play depicting murderous revenge turns real. Hieronimo's approach represents a kind of leadership that would be seductive if it were not so utterly disastrous. He takes the initiative, assem-bles an intricate plan, puts the various players in place (as unwitting co-conspirators in the play-within-the-play bloodbath), and executes the final act decisively.

Kyd's revenge hero was likely an inspiration for Shakespeare's own ver-sion of the revenge hero, Hamlet, and Hieronimo's decisiveness certainly resonates with the willingness to act demonstrated by Shakespeare's most celebrated exponent of successful leadership, King Harry in *Henry V*. But Shakespeare's leaders are more sophisticated beings who find themselves in much more complicated situations. The nature of this sophistication, and the perspectives on leadership encapsulated in their actions and experiences, becomes clearer when we compare them with their forebears like Hieron-imo. It is yet clearer, I will argue here, when we compare them with their counterparts not only in other plays and sources but also in the earlier versions of their own plays.

"BAD" SHAKESPEARE

The early books of Shakespeare published during and just after his lifetime emerged from a world full of intrigue, populated with shady characters but also visionaries and entrepreneurs. As witnesses to Shakespeare's works, the books themselves tell a story: from edition to edition they often vary in astonishing ways from what is now putatively "canonical" or "authentic" Shakespeare.[2] Isolating and understanding the differences in their accounts is useful for all kinds of purposes, from identifying the intricacies of staging and printing practices to exploring Shakespeare's creative process over the course of his career.

Alongside the earlier, smaller, single-play quarto editions in the pantheon of Shakespeare's books, and most famous of all of them, is the Shakespeare First Folio. F1, as it is known to Shakespeare scholars, usually makes the headlines when it is either stolen, rediscovered, or being auctioned for millions.[3] It was published in 1623, seven years after Shakespeare's death, and collects thirty-six of his plays.[4] The First Folio's publishers, John Heminge and Henry Condell, characterize their book—somewhat ironically—as a collection of "True Originall Copies," versus previous "Surreptitious copies, maimed and deformed by the frauds and stealths of injurious imposters."[5]

There are many extraordinary variations between the Folio's versions of Shakespeare and those contained in the earlier quarto-sized books of individual Shakespeare plays. Some of the quartos are regarded in a similar light to the Folio as generally trustworthy textual witnesses, and some are as problematically structured as they are questionable in their origins. Several of these more dubious early books of Shakespeare's plays were labeled by early twentieth-century Shakespeare editors such as A. W. Pollard as "bad" quartos.[6] These hastily produced books of Shakespeare have been argued to be the work of unscrupulous intermediaries who had witnessed the plays on the early modern stage rushing out a pirated version to make a quick buck, or traveling troupes wishing to fashion a cut-down version of a play for touring performance, or others who managed to access and exploit Shakespeare's early drafts.[7]

"BAD" HAMLET

Perhaps the most conspicuous example of an early problematic text of Shakespeare, and one where we can begin to talk about leadership, is the 1603 edition of *Hamlet*, often derided as a "bad" quarto. In this case, the later and much longer 1623 Folio version, purportedly based on the author's manuscript, is usually taken to be the more reliable text. The First Folio version of Hamlet's most famous speech, for instance, will be familiar:

> To be, or not to be, that is the Question:
> Whether 'tis Nobler in the minde to suffer
> The Slings and Arrowes of outragious Fortune,
> Or to take Armes against a Sea of troubles,
> And by opposing end them: to dye, to sleepe
> No more; and by a sleepe, to say we end
> The Heart-ake, and the thousand Naturall shockes
> That Flesh is heyre too? 'Tis a consummation
> Deuoutly to be wish'd. To dye to sleepe,
> To sleepe, perchance to Dreame; I, there's the rub,
> For in that sleepe of death, what dreames may come.[8]

It is generally agreed that the earlier "bad" version of this play presents a text that was reconstructed by an unknown auditor or auditors. Tiffany Stern argues compellingly that audience note-taking played an important part in these reconstructive efforts.[9] The "bad" version of Hamlet's famous speech sounds when read aloud almost as though an auditor—perhaps an audience member or actor—is trying to recall the speech and a scribe is taking down the results verbatim. Together our imaginary duo has recorded Hamlet's ontological dilemma quite differently. "Bad" quarto Hamlet says: "To be, or not to be, *ay, there's the point.*" As if that line were not surprising enough to a modern reader, the auditor seems openly to be struggling to re-create the rest of the passage:

> To die, to sleep, is that all? Ay, all.
> No, to sleep, to dream, ay, marry, there it goes,

Before gaining some momentum at last:

> For in that dream of death, when we awake,
> And borne before an everlasting judge,

From whence no passenger ever returned,
The undiscovered country, at whose sight
The happy smile, and the accursèd damned.[10]

In the act of recalling Hamlet's speech, the intermediary responsible for this surreptitious copy of the play (most likely produced "by the eare" in some way or other) has thoroughly defaced the text they are trying to reconstitute. And in their anxiousness to capture faithfully and reproduce Shakespeare's original, they have destabilized its meaning, corrupting it with an inevitable interpretative bias. Here Hamlet's "undiscovered country" is imagined in the overtly Christian terms of the "happy" elect and the "accursed" reprobate, and the embattled Dane spares no time to consider the "slings and arrows of outrageous fortune," moving straight on to a less abstract philosophical main course, and dispensing with it in far fewer lines than his Folio counterpart.

The "bad" quarto's sweet prince is more robust than our more familiar Folio Hamlet: he cuts straight to the chase, sounding more like the conventional revenge hero that his father's ghost, his family, and his society expect him to be. As Lukas Erne argues, "The considerable difference in pace between Q1 and Q2/F *Hamlet* raises the intriguing possibility that the time-honored belief that procrastination and delay are central to the play has much to do with the text readers have studied but little to do with the play Elizabethan theater-goers would have witnessed."[11] Indeed, as a type of leader, this is a Hamlet more consistent with both the early modern revenge hero genre and the expectations of his early audience than his counterpart in the later edition of the play. He is "bad" Hamlet, in all senses of the word. And he calls to mind Kyd's earlier hero Hieronimo, holding his torch and sword, the man of action. Although "bad" Hamlet never quite reaches those heights, he is nevertheless more simplistically realized than his equivalent in the Folio edition of the play, whose text is nearly twice as long. "Bad" Hamlet is more quickly moved to perform what we might now call the "alpha" leadership role, acting fast, righting wrongs, with a less complicated moral code than his Folio counterpart and the eventual willingness to do what has to be done—that is, murder his own uncle and take his rightful place as king of Denmark. Which, as we know, does not end well.

"Bad" Hamlet marches swiftly through his most important speeches. Philosophy *itself* is the obstacle he must overcome in order to carry out his revenge: his procrastination is plainly *because* of his philosophy. His particular tragedy is borne of his personal failure to act, and the play's denouement, its resolution, is in his final struggle toward murderous revenge. This early version of Hamlet is closer to the conventional revenge hero archetypes that were so popular in Shakespeare's time, whose narrow perspectives on leadership are characterized by binary constructions like action versus inaction; happy versus accursed; success versus failure; sacrificial bravery versus quibbling, philosophizing cowardice.

The Hamlet of later texts is a more profound invention than this, of course, and this is made clearer when considered next to his predecessor. For Hamlet in the Folio, his indecision is indivisible from his philosophical consideration of "this sterile promontory" and of the "whips and scornes of time" to which he is so utterly subject.[12] Folio Hamlet's philosophy *enables* his consideration of the world and his fate within it, such that his eventual capitulation and weary yet rash action at the end of the play is anything but a straightforward journey of a reticent prince becoming a king and leader. His tragedy is that he convinces himself, or at least half convinces himself, that murdering his own uncle is a line of action that must be taken *because* of his moral philosophy, not in spite of it. As Wolfgang von Goethe concluded in the late eighteenth century, Hamlet is like an "oak-tree planted in a costly jar, which should have borne only pleasant flowers in its bosom: the roots spread, the jar is [shattered]."[13] For Folio Hamlet, "To be or not to be" is the question, not the point. But he exists in an environment with conditions toxic to the more considered, thoughtful, empathetic, objective, and progressive type of leadership we glimpse in his frustrations and philosophizing, and which he could fulfill if only he were allowed to do so. Something is truly rotten in the state of Denmark.

WE FEW: KING AND CHORUS IN *HENRY V*

King Harry in *Henry V* is perhaps the most often-cited example of inspirational, charismatic leadership in Shakespeare. Harry is now so famous for this that he has become a regular stopping-off point for executive leadership courses.[14] After all, here is a leader who unites a disparate people under a common goal—that is, conquering France in the face of abject provocation. To achieve this (and here is some management-speak for you), he builds consent and establishes a clear vision and mission. He identifies naysayers and critics and manages them effectively, even isolating traitors and making difficult decisions to ensure the key goal is always kept in sight. He gathers and motivates demoralized troops, wields power with wisdom beyond his tender years, and puts in place rational plans for what comes after France surrenders and the goal is achieved.

Harry is a character who has a highly developed sense of the relationship between a leader and those they lead. On the eve of the Battle of Agincourt, he assumes a disguise and walks among his troops, stopping to debate the topic of a leader's accountability with one of his soldiers, named Williams (potentially a reference to the author). Williams asks the disguised Harry to look upon his soldiers, saying: "if these men doe not dye well, it will be a black matter for the King, that led them to it; who to disobey, were against all pro-portion of subiection." For Williams, a leader holds ultimate responsibility, and the burden of ultimate judgment, for the fates of his followers, especially when they have no choice but to follow. For this "Soule," leadership operates through subjection and subjugation. Yet Harry argues that this logic is flawed, saying that obedience, when *earned* by those asking for it, makes every man accountable only for himself: from his perspective, "Euery Subiects Dutie is the Kings, but euery Subiects Soule is his owne."[15]

Harry's leadership is underpinned, of course, by powerful, inclusive, persuasive oratory, the most famous passage of which is spoken on the morning of the Battle of Agincourt:

> Crispine Crispian shall ne're goe by,
> From this day to the ending of the World,
> But we in it shall be remembred;
> We few, we happy few, we band of brothers:
> For he to day that sheds his blood with me,
> Shall be my brother: be he ne're so vile,
> This day shall gentle his Condition.
> And Gentlemen in England, now a bed,
> Shall thinke themselues accurst they were not here;
> And hold their Manhoods cheape, whiles any speakes,
> That fought with vs vpon Saint Crispines day.[16]

Like Folio Hamlet, Folio Harry has a counterpart in an early problematic edition. But in this case the spirit of the Folio version is much more recognizable in the earlier text. For the purposes of comparison, here is the same part of the speech in the 1600 First Quarto of *Henry V*:

> This story shall the good man tell his sonne,
> And from this day, vnto the generall doome:
> But we in it shall be remembred.
> We fewe, we happie fewe, we bond of brothers,
> For he to day that sheads his blood by mine,

Shalbe my brother: be he nere so base,
This day shall gentle his condition.
Then shall he strip his fleeues, and shew his skars,
And say, these wounds, I had on Crispines day:
And Gentlemen in England now a bed,
Shall thinke themselues accurst,
And hold their manhood cheape,
While any speak that fought with vs
Vpon Saint Crispines day.[17]

When compared with the variations of Hamlet's speeches in the early editions of *Hamlet*, the import of Harry's speeches is relatively consistent across early editions of *Henry V*. Regardless of the printed book in which the character appears, he is a decisive leader whose inspiration to his followers comes not just from his rhetoric but also from his investing of agency and responsibility in them.

What changes in *Henry V* from edition to edition, and what changes our perspective on King Harry's leadership, is the textual framework surrounding and delimiting the play. The 1600 quarto's title makes it clear that this early version of the play is a "Cronicle History of Henry the fift": its publishers place the play squarely into the English chronicle genre made famous by Raphael Holinshed and others, a genre not renowned for its dramatic complexity and one that at the time was in decline.[18] When we read the early quarto editions of *Henry V*, we are untroubled by extratextual interlocutors addressing us directly and commenting on the action. As it would be for a contemporary chronicle, reading or watching the play is a passive act, and the play's artifice is not commented upon explicitly or exposed by any character. By contrast, extratextual interlocuters and dramatic complexity are exactly what we get in the 1623 Folio version of *Henry V*. The Folio's *Henry V* possesses an entire extratextual apparatus consisting of prologue, chorus, and epilogue, all spoken by the same chorus figure. This chorus survives only because it was published in a new version of *Henry V* in Heminge's and Condell's 1623 collection. It is entirely absent from earlier printed editions of the play.

The chorus's perspectives on the play's action are not always reliable. Andrew Gurr notes that "in varying degrees the events of each act belie the claims made by the Chorus that introduces it."[19] Yet it completely changes *Henry V*. It is still reasonable to refer to Folio Harry as a gifted leader and to read brilliance into his efforts in the French campaign, but the chorus makes it clear that the success of the entire enterprise depends on us, too. We must "Peece out" the "imperfections" of the play.[20] Unless we "worke, worke our thoughts,"[21] playing our own parts in reconstructing the imaginary dramatic spectacle, the mighty Battle of Agincourt will be rendered down to a few players prancing farcically on the stage. As Stern notes, "Shakespeare utilises the spectators so that they become, unwittingly, part-actors in the plays that they are observing. They can supply the massed army that the *Henry V* prologue could not come up with."[22] The dramatic effect goes beyond this. As Catherine Belsey argues, "these pre-Enlightenment texts propel their audience towards the unpresentable, the possibility of histories made by the people."[23] We can read Henry's famous pronouns as being inclusive of us. "We in it shall be remembred," "We few, we happy few, we band of brothers," along with the characters, Shakespeare, his players, and his audiences, then, now, and in the future. To read *Henry V* in the Folio is to remember them, but also to remember ourselves.

As brothers (and sisters) in arms, we are invested with the same responsibility and agency by the chorus as Harry invests in his soldiers. And the reason this is so important is told by the "crooked Figure" of the chorus in its epilogue:

> Thus farre with rough, and all-vnable Pen,
> Our bending Author hath pursu"d the Story,
> In little roome confining mightie men,
> Mangling by starts the full course of their glory.
> Small time: but in that small, most greatly liued
> This Starre of England. Fortune made his Sword;
> By which, the Worlds best Garden he atchieued:
> And of it left his Sonne Imperiall Lord.
> Henry the Sixt, in Infant Bands crown"d King
> Of France and England, did this King succeed:
> Whose State so many had the managing,
> That they lost France, and made his England bleed:
> Which oft our Stage hath showne; and for their sake,
> In your faire minds let this acceptance take.[24]

Harry's achievements were squandered by the dissension of his descendants. This parting shot is a warning to those who idolize great leaders and look back nostalgically on past victories: hagiographical hang-ups will lead to collective failure. *Henry V* challenges us to recognize our individual parts in the continuance and sustainability of good leadership. For the chorus—ungendered, text incarnate, many voices as one, objectivity personified—leadership must happen everywhere.

THE READER AS PATRON

The chorus's empowerment of their patrons in *Henry V* is echoed, consciously or unconsciously, in the approach Heminge, Condell, and the rest of the First Folio's contributors and architects take to the patrons of the book as a whole. What by all accounts should come first in the 1623 Folio (after the title and frontispiece) is an address to the volume's patrons and funders, who have underwritten the hugely costly and resource-intensive three-year journey of the Folio into print. Up until this point it was an inviolable and ineluctable rule that a patron should be addressed first to indicate their status and importance. The most obviously comparable books preceding the Folio, those collecting the works of Samuel Daniel (1601–2) and Ben Jonson (1616), both address their patrons before anyone else. In the First Folio, however, Jonson's address "To the Reader" is the first prefatory text the reader encounters (even before the title and frontispiece in this case), and it sets the tone for the entire anthology. Using a large typeface, which helps it to dominate the page, the poem takes the sentiments expressed only five pages later in the address "To the Great Variety of Readers" (also quite possibly written by Jonson, although signed by Heminge and Condell) and compresses them into ten short lines:

To the Reader.

This Figure, that thou here seest put,
    It was for gentle Shakespeare cut;
Wherein the Grauer had a strife
    with Nature, to out-doo the life:
O, could he but haue drawne his wit
    As well in brasse, as he hath hit
His face; the Print would then surpasse
    All, that was euer writ in brasse.
But, since he cannot, Reader, looke
    Not on his Picture, but his Booke.
B. I.

Contrary to the convention of addressing one's patrons before anyone else, here it is the reader who is addressed first. Jonson, who brilliantly calls Shakespeare "Soule of the Age" *and* "for all time" in another prefatory poem attributed to him in the Folio, adopts an idiom which levels and empowers the Folio's subjects as ahistorical readers. In this way the Folio resonates from its very first page with King Harry's and *Henry V*'s modus operandi: like those who fought with him on St. Crispin's Day, the reader lives forever, captured in time but for all time, and is the ultimate "soule" responsible for the Folio's success and Shakespeare's remembrance. Even, that is, if their first act is so simple as to indulge Heminge's and Condell's plea to, "what euer you do, Buy" the book.[25]

LEAD YOURSELVES, AND OTHERS

Placing the early books of Shakespeare adjacent to each other makes it clearer than ever that the Elizabethan author's leaders are complex creations, even in the two short examples considered here. Contemplated in the light of his earlier "bad" cousin, a simplistic reading might conclude that Hamlet is even more obviously unsuitable for leadership than we first thought, busying himself procrastinating when his predecessor is quicker to move toward decisive action. But "bad" Hamlet's relative lack of sophistication speaks otherwise and brings into sharper relief Hamlet's paradox: he is expected by all around him to act and to exert himself as a leader fit to be the king of Denmark, but to do so he must abandon his moral philosophy and become the type of leader that perpetuated the tragedy's events in the first place. And although King Harry's rousing rhetoric and open-minded perspective are present in both the editions considered here, the drama he inhabits is profoundly different in the Folio. This later text still provides a rosy portrait of a classical "man of action," but the play has more than that to say about the dynamic between leaders and those they lead. The chorus makes it clear that the French campaign, the play on the stage, and the text on the page will not succeed unless we all literally play our part. With the chorus in place, voicing the perspective of the text, the drama itself is the source of democratizing, inspirational leadership: something that will live well beyond old stories of long-dead kings.

These Shakespearean examples speak to the idea that good leadership starts with ethical and moral consideration as the heart of one's approach rather than as something that must be circumvented in order to succeed. They also suggest that good leadership requires recognition of the value of your soldiers, or followers, or readers, or users as your siblings in arms, and that it demands you give them a stake in your collective success. Lest we conclude that Hamlet is a failure, shirking leadership, or that King Harry alone says everything that *Henry V* has to say about leadership, we should turn to Heminge and Condell's solicitation to us in their poem "To the Great Variety of Readers" of the 1623 Folio: "Reade him, therefore; and againe, and againe: And if then you doe not like him, surely you are in some manifest danger, not to vnderstand him." For Shakespeare's two compatriots, to whom we owe so much, the role of the reader as a leader is clear. Signing off and drawing the reader's attention to the other prefatory poetry in the volume, they say: "And so we leaue you to other of his Friends, whom if you need, can bee your guides: if you neede them not, you can leade your selues, and others. And such Readers we wish him."

NOTES

1. Thomas Kyd, *The Spanish Tragedie: Or, Hieronimo is mad againe* (London: W White, 1615), British Library copy, A1r.

2. For an introduction to the thoroughly discussed question of authenticity in the Shakespearean context, see Stephen Orgel, "The Authentic Shakespeare," *Representations* 21 (Winter 1988): 1–25.

3. In 1998 a copy of the First Folio was famously stolen from the University of Durham. Anthony West, who authenticated the copy on its return and stood as a witness during Raymond Scott's trial, recounts the episode in Anthony James West, "Proving the Identity of the Stolen Durham University First Folio," *The Library* 14, no. 4 (December 2014): 428–40. According to the police, when summoned to answer bail, Scott arrived to their astonishment in a stretch Humvee, with a cigar and bottle of champagne in one hand and a Pot Noodle in the other. Such is the strange world of Shakespeare Folios!

    The most recent recovery at the time of writing has been from the library at Mount Stuart on the Isle of Bute. The copy was authenticated by Emma Smith in 2016 ("Shakespeare Folio Confirmed as Genuine," *Mount Stuart Blog*, April 13, 2016, https://www.mountstuart.com/shakespeare-first-folio-confirmed-genuine/). The last round of auctions was timed to coincide with the four-hundredth anniversary of Shakespeare's death in 2016 (see "A Landmark Sale to Mark the 400th Anniversary of Shakespeare's Death," *Christie's*, March 17, 2016, https://www.christies.com/features/Shakespeare-first-four-folios-to-be-auctioned-at-Christies-on-the-400th-anniversary-7163-1.aspx).

4. For a concise and insightful introduction to the bibliographical background, publishing, and printing process of the Shakespeare First Folio, see Peter Blayney, *The First Folio of Shakespeare* (Washington: Folger Library, 1991). Emma Smith argues that, even if its texts are less problematic compared to some of the previous editions, reading the Folio can still at times constitute an "immersive experience of confusion" due to the many errors it contains (Emma Smith, "Reading the First Folio," in *The Cambridge Companion to Shakespeare's First Folio*, ed. Emma Smith [Cambridge: Cambridge University Press, 2016], 156).

5. William Shakespeare, *Mr. William Shakespeares Comedies, Histories, & Tragedies. Published according to the True Originall Copies* (London: printed by Isaac Jaggard and Edward Blount, 1623), British Library copy, C.39.k.15, A1r, A3r.

6. A. W. Pollard, *Shakespeare Folios and Quartos: A Study in the Bibliography of Shakespeare's Plays, 1594–1685* (London: Methuen, 1909), 64–80.

7. Reviled by early twentieth-century editors as unscrupulous, illegitimate, and inaccurate "pirated" texts, these volumes have since been reconsidered by modern scholarship and are now viewed as a useful source of stage directions and other performance-related paratexts that are not preserved in the other early texts of Shakespeare's plays. The intermediaries that compiled them have also been subject to critical reappraisal and have now been acknowledged as the first in a long line of editors of Shakespeare. See Lukas Erne, *Shakespeare as Literary Dramatist* (Cambridge: Cambridge University Press, 2003); and Sonia Massai, *Shakespeare and the Rise of the Editor* (Cambridge: Cambridge University Press, 2007).

8. William Shakespeare, *Mr. William Shakespeares Comedies, Histories, & Tragedies. Published according to the True Originall Copies* (London: printed by Isaac Jaggard and Edward Blount, 1623), Wadham College copy, 005r.

9. Tiffany Stern, "Sermons, Plays and Note-Takers: Hamlet Q1 as a 'Noted' Text," *Shakespeare Survey* 66 (2013): 1–23. For an alternate perspective arguing that Q1 constitutes an early draft, see Terri Bourus, "Enter Shakespeare's Young Hamlet, 1589," *Actes des congrès de la Société française Shakespeare* 34 (2016): 1–14.

10. William Shakespeare, *The tragicall historie of Hamlet Prince of Denmarke by William Shake-speare. As it hath beene diuerse times acted by his Highnesse seruants in the cittie of London: as also in the two vniuersities of Cambridge and Oxford, and else-where* (London: Printed for Nicholas Ling and John Trundell, 1603), British Library copy, D4v–E1r.

11. Erne, *Shakespeare as Literary Dramatist*, 239.

12. Shakespeare, *Mr. William Shakespeares Comedies, Histories, & Tragedies*, Wadham College copy, 005r.

13. Wolfgang von Goethe, *Wilhelm Meister's Apprenticeship and Travels, Vol. 1*, trans. Thomas Carlyle (New York: A. L. Burt, 1824), 223.

14. See, for instance, "Inspirational Leadership Training—*Henry V*," Olivier Mythodrama, accessed March 1, 2019, https://www.oliviermythodrama.com/programmes/inspirational-leadership. *Henry V* has, of course, been "celebrated—and then reviled—as an exercise in patriotism and jingoism." See Brian Vickers, "'Suppose You See': The Chorus in *Henry V* and *The Mirror for Magistrates*," in *Shakespearean Continuities*, ed. John Batchelor, Tom Cain, and Claire Lamont (London: Palgrave Macmillan, 1997), 1.

15. Shakespeare, *Mr. William Shakespeares Comedies, Histories, & Tragedies*, Wadham College copy, i2v.

16. Shakespeare, i4r.

17. William Shakespeare, *The Cronicle History of Henry the fift. With his battel fought at Agin Court in France. Togither with Auntient Pistoll. As it hath bene sundry times playd by the Right honourable the Lord Chamberlaine his seruants* (London: Thomas Millington and John Busby, 1600), George III copy, British Library, E2r.

18. Shakespeare, *The Cronicle History*, A2r; Daniel R. Woolfe, "Genre into Artefact: The Decline of the English Chronicle in the Sixteenth Century," *Sixteenth Century Journal* 19, vol. 3 (1988): 321–54.

19. Andrew Gurr, "Introduction," in *Henry V*, ed. Andrew Gurr (Cambridge: Cambridge University Press, 2005), 7. See also Anthony S. Brennan, "That within Which Passes Show: The Function of the Chorus in 'Henry V,'" *Philological Quarterly* 58 (1979): 40–52.

20. Shakespeare, *Mr. William Shakespeares Comedies, Histories, & Tragedies*, Wadham College copy, h1r.
21. Shakespeare, h5r.
22. Tiffany Stern, *Making Shakespeare: From Stage to Page* (London: Routledge, 2004), 28. See also Ewan Fernie, "Action! Henry V," in *Presentist Shakespeares*, ed. Hugh Grady and Terence Hawkes (London: Routledge, 2006), 106.
23. Catherine Belsey, "Making Histories," in *Shakespeare's History Plays: "Richard II" to "Henry V,"* ed. Graham Holderness (Basingstoke: Palgrave Macmillan, 1992), 118.
24. Shakespeare, h1r, k2r.
25. Shakespeare, *Mr. William Shakespeares Comedies, Histories, & Tragedies*, British Library copy, C.39.k.15, A3r.

CHAPTER 8

Crooked Politics

Shakespeare's Richard III and Leadership in the Twenty-First-Century United States

Kristin M. S. Bezio

Since November 2016, scholars, pundits, journalists, and others have repeatedly attempted to identify and explain the highly partisan state of modern American politics. In particular, the four years of Donald J. Trump's presidency from 2017 to 2021 have been compared to the regimes of various Latin American, Asian, and Middle Eastern despots and demagogues and even to the rise of Adolf Hitler. These are intellectually interesting comparisons (for differing reasons), but the problem of toxic masculine authoritarianism has roots in English politics of the medieval and early modern eras as well, perhaps best described and known from the plays of William Shakespeare. We should be wary of dismissing Trump's four years as an anomaly—regardless of personal politics—but should instead see his presidency as a part of a cycle of rulership created not by the singular ego of this leader or that, but as a product of the larger problem of polarization and civil conflict—circumstances that also appear in Shakespeare's extended historical tetralogies, from the events of *Richard II* to the close of *Richard III*, including the *Henry IV* and *Henry VI* plays.

It is a long-standing cliché that "those who do not learn from history are doomed to repeat it," but like so many clichés, this one rests on the fundamental truth that we can and should look to the past as a means of understanding and grappling with our present (and future). One of the primary ways we seek to disseminate such lessons is through the creation of cultural media artifacts centered on historical narratives, such as those written by

Shakespeare. Shakespeare's King Henry V, for instance, is often held up as a paragon of charismatic leadership, and his tyrant Richard III is lambasted as an exemplum of what *not* to do, whether in politics, business, or education. There may well be such lessons in the plays—for instance, murder (Richard III's modus operandi) is rarely a good solution to the problem of interfering middle managers. That being said, Shakespeare's warnings in the historical tetralogies about sixteenth-century England and the impending death of Elizabeth I can help the modern United States (and other parts of the world) come to terms with the twenty-first-century rise of populist neo-liberalism and alt-right conservatism, such as that under the presidency of Trump, which was a backlash against the perceived liberality of the Obama era and which led, in 2020 and 2021, to a contested election, a brief insurrection, and continued instability in American politics in the midst of a global pandemic.

During the 2010s, much of the Western world—specifically, the United States and Europe—saw a significant increase in populist movements that resulted in widespread "rejections of dominant (or perceived-as-dominant) social, political, economic, and religious paradigms."[1] In the midst of this populist surge came the "surprising and unusual" 2016 presidential campaign of Donald Trump.[2] Psychologist George R. Goethals explains that Trump's Electoral College victory was "the greatest popular vote versus electoral vote mismatch in US history," a disparity between popular opinion and election results that inaugurated subsequent months and years of protests, including the "Blue Wave" election movement in 2018 to replace Republicans in the House of Representatives and Senate with more progressive Democrats in an attempt to countermand Trump's presidency.[3] Given the significant disparity between the popular vote and the 2016 election results, we are left wondering, perhaps, *how* Trump was successfully elected to the White House.* Aside from the complexities of the American electoral system, a variety of psychological explanations—including racism, sexism, and feelings of disenfranchisement among the working classes—have been proffered.[4]

Goethals's description of Trump's "surprising and unusual" ascent to power could similarly apply to the dramatized elevation of Richard III to the throne of England in Shakespeare's pseudohistorical play.[5] As the youngest (third) son of the Duke of York, Richard would not have been expected to end up on the throne, and he is portrayed as profoundly disliked, even by his

---

*At the time of writing, Trump has declared his candidacy for the 2024 election while simultaneously being tried for a variety of criminal charges. Despite this, Trump is the favorite for the Republican nomination.

own mother, so his ascent is both "surprising and unusual." For our purposes, Richard's assumption of power provides an interesting parallel to the Trump presidency in large part because of the paradox of its predictability and unexpectedness, and also because it was not an isolated event but rather the product of an extended period of polarization and political oscillation.

In Shakespeare's first tetralogy, *Richard III* is the final play in the extended historical sequence that includes the Henriad. In the plays' chronology, it is the eighth play in the sequence and is framed—within the narrative of the Tudor Myth—as the inevitable culmination of the reigns of Richard II, Henry IV, Henry V, Henry VI, and Edward IV (and Edward V, although his "rule" was painfully short).[6] In our contemporary moment, Donald Trump's presidency came about, similarly, not as a lightning strike from nowhere, but as the consequence of years of polarization that one might argue date back to the 1970s and the disillusionment of the American populace with the government that lied to them about American involvement in Vietnam and the scandal surrounding Watergate. In both teleologies, the authoritarian leader, whether Richard or Trump, is produced by years of increasing polarization: in one, the deposition of Richard II and the later Wars of the Roses; in the other, fluctuating political radicalism and conservatism following Vietnam leading into the Reagan era, then the politicization of 9/11 followed by an economic recession under the first Black American president, Barack Obama.

What we can draw from these parallels, then, is both comfort and warning—the same message Shakespeare sought to convey to his own audience in his era: war, conflict, and polarization are, it seems, an inevitable part of history, but we have weathered them before and undoubtedly will again. For Shakespeare's audience, this was meant to provide comfort in the face of the impending (sooner or later) death of Elizabeth and the end of the Tudor dynasty. For a modern audience, the historical tetralogies show us that we are a part of the inevitable cycles of history that oscillate between division and unity, but they also remind us that we, as citizens, have agency in determining the extremity of those poles, and that we have the ability to choose leaders who will shepherd us away from civil conflict rather than toward it. Shakespeare's warning against tyranny can serve us in the twenty-first century as a caution against not only permitting but authorizing authoritarianism and toxicity through elections. Unlike the vast majority of Shakespeare's audience, we have the capacity not only to rebel against—and thereby censure—our leaders but to not elect them into office in the first place. Before we can turn to the plays themselves, however, we need to look at the sociopolitical context in which they were written and produced.

A HISTORY BEHIND SHAKESPEARE'S HISTORIES

The close of the sixteenth century in England was a time in which political participation formed a central component of the identity of English citizens, whether common or noble. Although we typically consider citizen participation in terms of modern democratic processes—such as voting—early modern England in Shakespeare's day also possessed a participatory form of government. Historically, England was (and had been) a limited participatory monarchy: in medieval and early modern England, the monarch drew power by means of a contract-style structure in which the monarch vowed (in the coronation oath) to protect and uphold the rights of the people, who, in turn, swore obedience.[7] We can see this in action as early as the 1014 *Anglo-Saxon Chronicle*, which placed restraints on then-king Æthelred via his counselors' statement that he should "be a gracious lord" who would "improve each of the things which they all hated" about his rule in exchange for future fealty.[8] This practice extended into the reign of Elizabeth I (up until the late eighteenth century, when the role of prime minister became entrenched) and is therefore useful in our consideration of Shakespeare's Richard III.[9]

In Shakespeare's England, citizen participation largely took the form of approval or revolt. During Elizabeth's tenure, the Northern Rising (1569) demonstrated the dissatisfaction of the northern earls with Elizabeth's ecclesiastical policies (and sought to replace her with Mary Queen of Scots), which, although suppressed, exacerbated tensions between the queen and her Catholic subjects.[10] By 1593 England had not seen a full-scale revolt in more than twenty years (though there were scattered plots against the queen). However, in the final decade of the sixteenth century, London was nevertheless characterized by political, social, and religious tensions. In 1570 Queen Elizabeth I had been declared excommunicate by Pope Pius V in the bull *Regnans in Excelsis*, compounded by the Jesuit mission launched in 1580 that sought to depose the queen and restore England to the Catholic fold. Although the English navy—with the assistance of a fortuitous storm— had defeated the Spanish armada in 1588, Spain nevertheless remained a source of international concern, while the French Wars of Religion across the English Channel further exacerbated tensions in the region between Catholics and Protestants.

Elizabeth herself provided an additional source of domestic anxiety by steadfastly refusing to name an heir. By 1590 the queen was long past the age when she could be expected to marry or bear children, and England found itself facing an impending monarchical crisis. Elizabeth's Privy Council faced a similar situation. As her councillors aged and died, Elizabeth refused to replace them, and power became increasingly consolidated in the hands of fewer and fewer men. Compounding the problems at court, England at the close of the sixteenth century also faced considerable domestic and international strain. The lords of Ireland staged repeated rebellions requiring English military intervention, and the Netherlands remained a site of contention between English Protestants and Spanish Catholics. In the New World and the Atlantic, England repeatedly clashed with Spain over territories and at sea.

Domestically, Parliament levied heavy wartime taxes; able-bodied young men were pressed into military service (taking them away from farms and businesses); inflation rose above income for merchants, nobles, gentry, and commons; and the court was a hotbed of competition for Elizabeth's favor and advancement in rank.[11] People of all classes were concerned about the rising cost of living and the perennial threat of plague, which surged hot and cold throughout London well into the seventeenth century.

The sociopolitical situation in which Shakespeare began writing his first four-history-play series—known as the "first tetralogy" and beginning with *Henry VI, Part I* around 1590—was fraught. It can come as no surprise, then, that the topic of the series was similarly contentious: the Wars of the Roses, which pitted the House of Lancaster against the House of York in the aftermath of the death of Henry V, the "mirror of all Christian kings" (*H5* 2.0.6).[12] The concluding play of Shakespeare's first tetralogy, *Richard III* was most likely composed and performed in 1593 at London's first professional outdoor playhouse, The Theatre, by the Lord Pembroke's Men. It was the last in a series of enormously popular history plays and would have been eagerly anticipated by audiences who were already intimately familiar with the story. The second half of the historical series—which depicted the first half of the chronology—appeared from 1595 to 1599, illustrating the histories of Richard II and his deposition by Henry IV, the rebellions under Henry IV, and the rise of Henry V, and ending with Henry V's glorious victories in France, but promising the downturn of English fortunes by reminding the audience that Henry V's reign ends with his death and the Wars of the Roses (the events of the first tetralogy). With Shakespeare anticipating the death of yet another glorious monarch, the tetralogy can be read as a cautionary tale of what might happen if the lessons of history were to go unlearned.

Shakespeare's focus on a villainous Richard and valorized Henry was both critical and propagandist. Richard III was the last non-Tudor monarch to hold the English throne before the accession of King Henry VII,

Elizabeth's grandfather. It is a long-standing view of many scholars that Shakespeare's tetralogy supports the historical legend of the Tudor Myth, an understanding of history that teleologically leads to the accession of the Tudor dynasty and the golden age of England under Elizabeth. As E. M. W. Tillyard explains, "the main business of the play is to complete the national tetralogy and display the working out of God's plan to restore England to prosperity."[13] In this paradigm, Richard serves in the role of the Scourge of God, a near-demonic figure whose purpose is to cleanse England of corruption through his own villainy in order to prepare the nation for the rise of the Tudors, while Henry V stands as the last-written (although chronologically central) model of the ideal king.

The chronology of the two tetralogies is noteworthy. Although the historical trajectory (from Richard II to Richard III) seems to point us toward hopelessness and carnage, it is important to remember that the compositional order moves us from war and carnage to victory under the "mirror of all Christian Kings," beginning with *Henry VI, Part 1* and ending with *Henry V* on the threshold of a new century. What this tells us is that although Shakespeare is issuing a warning, he does so with optimism rather than pessimism, especially because, even historically, the end of *Richard III* is not the triumph of a tyrant, but his downfall and the establishment of a new dynasty. Yet, as the end of *Henry V* reminds us, we cannot rest upon the laurels of an Elizabethan golden age:

> CHORUS Thus far, with rough and all-unable pen,
> Our bending author hath pursued the story,
> In little room confining mighty men,
> Mangling by starts the full course of their glory.
> Small time, but in that small most greatly lived
> This star of England. Fortune made his sword
> By which the world's best garden he achieved,
> And of it left his son imperial lord.
> Henry the Sixth, in infant bands crowned King
> Of France and England, did this king succeed,
> Whose state so many had the managing
> That they lost France and made his England bleed,
> Which oft our stage hath shown; and for their sake
> In your fair minds let this acceptance take. (*H5* Ep.1–14)

The closing chorus of *Henry V* reminds us of the impending civil war, the Wars of the Roses that "made his England bleed," a caution against feeling too triumphant in an age of prosperity and peace because all it would take to disrupt that idyllic state is the death of a monarch. And in 1599, Elizabeth was sixty-six years old, and her councillors—including Robert Dudley, Francis Walsingham, and William Cecil—had mostly died of age and infirmity. In the invocation of the first tetralogy—"which oft our stage hath shown"— Shakespeare reminds his audience that what follows glory is often strife, a trope tied in the medieval and early modern imagination to Fortune's Wheel, which dragged individuals and nations through periods of prosperity followed by dearth, peace followed by war, unity followed by conflict and polarization.

(UN)-KINGLY CHARISMA

As I have suggested before, Henry V "epitomizes both traditional and individual charisma: royal charisma as the fusion of *Heil* and martial heroism."[14] Yet in addition to aligning with the medieval notion of quasi-divinity and heroism, Henry also embodies our more modern understanding of leadership charisma, in that he rhetorically expresses an emotional dedication to his followers, shows drive and confidence in achieving his goals (first the crown and then France), eloquently urges his followers to victory, and responds to his followers' needs (particularly Williams and Flewellen).[15]

By contrast (although perhaps not as much contrast as we would like), Shakespeare's Richard provides a key example of a leader frequently characterized as a "toxic charismatic" (an attractive yet damaging leader). As Jean Lipman-Blumen explains in *The Allure of Toxic Leaders*, "Although it is hard to believe, we tend to *prefer* toxic leaders for a host of tantalizing reasons."[16] We are driven to follow these toxic charismatics because they understand how to play to our fears, convincing us that they alone can provide safety and belonging.[17] Toxic leaders, she observes, engage in a serious of "destructive behaviors," including deteriorating the conditions in which followers find themselves, abusing human rights, using deception and outright falsehood to coerce followers, feeding followers' fears, silencing criticism, undermining systemic checks and balances on power, engaging in totalitarian behaviors, creating division and encouraging out-group discrimination and violence, and "promoting incompetence, cronyism, and corruption."[18] Richard repeatedly engages in these toxic behaviors, and, in our twenty-first-century context, so did Trump. This comparison serves less as a condemnation of one particular politician (though it may do so) and more as a reminder of the persuasive power of unchecked toxic charisma—and of the importance of continuing to peer, as Shakespeare allows us to do, behind the political curtain to see whether our leaders are motivated by ego or (at least partially) by altruism.

So why would we choose or enable leaders like Shakespeare's Richard? The answers are complex, Lipman-Blumen argues, but essentially rest on ideas of safety, authority, and belonging.[19] Toxic leaders—like nontoxic leaders—provide a sense of security, assume a position of (ostensibly benevolent) authority, and appeal to our fear of ostracization and need to be a part of a community. Both Richard and Trump possess the ability to create a fictional context in which they occupy the role of savior, albeit in somewhat different ways. Lipman-Blumen calls such rhetorical context "illusions," which, she says, "are the umbilical cord linking leaders and followers."[20] These illusions provide a framework in which the leader is the sole source of safety, authority, and community, and anyone who seeks to reject them as such becomes an enemy to be summarily destroyed, either literally (in the case of Richard) or rhetorically (Trump).

As a character, Richard himself—who begins the play as plain Richard of Gloucester—had already appeared in *Henry VI, Part 3*, in which he openly declares his murderous intent:

> RICHARD Why, I can smile, and murder whiles I smile,
> . . .
> And wet my cheeks with artificial tears,
> And frame my face to all occasions.
> . . .
> I can add colours to the chameleon,
> . . .
> And set the murderous Machiavel to school.
> Can I do this, and cannot get a crown?
> Tut, were it farther off, I'll pluck it down. (*3H6* 3.2.182, 184–85,
>   191, 193–95)[21]

The audience for the original play would have been fully aware that the Richard they were paying to see in the final play was absolutely, unequivocally, a villain.[22]

Yet even though Henry V is the (nontoxic) charismatic "mirror of all Christian kings," his charisma is made transparent by Shakespeare, something that unsettles us as members of the audience and has bothered critics for centuries. For instance, Nina Taunton and Sara Munson Deats complain of his violence and self-aggrandizement, and Malcom Pittock charges Henry with "moral inauthenticity" for refusing to accept full "responsibility for his own actions" throughout the Henriad.[23] In "deliberately exposing the machinery of image creation—a necessary component of royal charisma—Shakespeare draws the audience's attention to the inherent fictiveness and instability of royal charisma," a move designed not to destabilize monarchy but to remind the audience that the illusion of grandeur that accompanies it is precisely that: a performative illusion.[24] Exposing this illusion is important in terms of understanding the relationship between leader and followers: when charisma is understood as a tool rather than an innate gift, the leader becomes more recognizably human and less likely to command absolute obedience. For Shakespeare, this lesson acts as a reminder to his audience that monarchs may be censured; for us, four centuries later, it tells us that not much has changed, but that it is important not to place our leaders on an authoritarian pedestal, even if we might not always be able to see behind the proverbial curtain.

As Prince Hal in *Henry IV, Part 1*, Henry tells the audience directly how he plans to assume the throne, not rhetorically or ambitiously unlike Richard:

> HENRY So when this loose behavior I throw off
> And pay the debt I never promised,
> By how much better than my word I am,
> By so much shall I falsify men's hopes;
> And, like bright metal on a sullen ground,
> My reformation, glittering o'er my fault,
> Shall show more goodly and attract more eyes
> Than that which hath no foil to set it off.
> I'll so offend to make offence a skill,
> Redeeming time when men think least I will. (*1H4* 1.2.198–207)[25]

Henry's princely persona is here revealed to be a deliberate construction, which he intends to "throw off" upon becoming king so that he will "show more goodly and attract more eyes." In essence, Henry understands the value of impression management, recognizing that cultivating a particular image will be conducive to his success—a Machiavellian move that enables him to be later perceived more positively, something Shakespeare reminds us of at the start of *Henry V*:

> CANTERBURY Consideration like an angel came
> And whipped th'offending Adam out of him,

Leaving his body as a paradise
T'envelop and contain celestial spirits.
Never was such a sudden scholar made. (*H5* 1.1.28–32)

Henry's reformation is here confirmed by the archbishop of Canterbury, not so that we understand anything about Henry per se, but so that we recognize the success of his campaign to convince others of his new persona. He remains "transformed" for the remainder of the play, unwavering in his new commitment to piety and responsibility.

Yet as many scholars have also noted, Richard (alongside Henry) is also one of Shakespeare's most charismatic as well as loquacious figures (he has more lines than any other character at 1,599).[26] While we have no accounts of Shakespeare's original audience's reaction, we know that Richard was played by the talented leading man of the company, Richard Burbage, and that the play was enormously popular, playing for at least three consecutive years following its introduction. Burbage would also, it is worth noting, have played the later Henry V, in his incarnations as both Prince Hal and King Henry. This metatheatrical similarity—being portrayed by the same actor—would also have likely produced sympathetic resonance between the two characters, both bringing Henry "down" and, in later productions, raising Richard "up."[27]

It is well worth reemphasizing that both Henry and Richard are charismatics—kings whose language and skill at inspiring their followers to action draws in the audience despite the fact that both engage in less than savory actions. Although Henry—in his earlier incarnation as Prince Hal—does not engage in outright murder (as does Richard), he does lie, cheat, steal, and debauch, all with a view to manipulating his image as reformed when he takes the throne. It is often the case that scholars and audience members want to suggest that Richard is the more violent of the two kings, but, in truth, Henry is *also* rather bloodthirsty, engaging in combat in *Henry IV, Part 1* in support of his father, executing three men for treason at the start of *Henry V*, going to war with France, executing his own former friend (Bardolph) for looting, threatening the town of Harfleur (including women and children), and convincing his men to engage in a battle (Agincourt) in which they are vastly outnumbered. Now Henry does not—as Richard does—stoop to outright murder, which makes Richard more culpable in the eyes of many, but he is nevertheless responsible for the loss of many lives in war.[28] So what do we *do* with these seeming contradictions of characters and plays? How do we translate Shakespeare's charismatic king plays—and the characters of Richard and Henry—into something meaningful for leadership in the twenty-first century?

An analysis of Shakespeare's kings within the context of the twenty-first-century United States enables us to consider both patterns of toxicity or charisma on the part of the central leading figure, but also the social structures and movements which arise to support and undermine that leader. Leadership scholar Bert Alan Spector tells us that "people seek a narrative structure that brings legitimacy to abstractions, offers coherence in response to apparent chaos, and asserts human agency in the face of seemingly unmanageable complexity."[29] Such a "narrative structure" may be found in both Shakespeare's tetralogies. Shakespeare sought to make use of story and history to convince his audience of their "role in the political *communitas*" as participating citizens whose purpose was not simply to obey, but to ratify and, when necessary, sanction their monarch.[30] Some four hundred years later, we, too, can use Shakespeare's analysis—both of his own history and his present—as a historical and literary tool to reflect on *our* present. We, too, can make use of "narrative structure" (story and history) to first recognize and then react to our present situation in such a way as to avoid civil breakdown and violence by instead choosing unity over division.

CROOKED POLITICS AND (TOXIC?) CHARISMA

In the twenty-first century, despite our smartphones and Twitter/X accounts, we are not all that different from our medieval and early modern forebears. We are as likely to fall victim to Lipman-Blumen's idea of toxic charisma as were medieval nobles or early modern playgoers, and we have the misfortune of not only applauding the performance of our Richard but having even elected him to high political office. Toxic leaders are attractive precisely because they promise those things that followers feel (or fear) are under threat: economic stability, security and safety, in-group cohesion, certainty, and control.[31] They invoke the need for increased income (or reduced taxes), job security, border and immigration control, and an us-versus-them mentality concerning national or party identity; they confirm what their followers "know" to be true; and they seek to empower those followers to "take back" what they have lost—for example, to "Make America Great Again."

To be clear, I am not suggesting that, like Richard, Donald Trump is a murderer, or even that he is as clever a manipulator as Richard or Henry. Rather, I want us to read certain patterns of (toxic?) charismatic behaviors against those showcased in Shakespeare's play and to use them to recognize Shakespeare's warning against polarization and civil conflict. Specifically, I want to call attention to the one fundamental difference between Richard and Henry: although both are charismatics who use similarly manipulative methods, Richard and Henry differ in how they apply their focus—Henry bends his will toward bringing together classes and ranks by eliding the differences between himself and his followers, while Richard emphasizes them as a way to drive a wedge between those he views as loyal to him and those who are not. And it is in this distinction that Shakespeare ultimately finds Henry to be the better king—because no matter the lies and deception, Henry ultimately seeks to unify his people and call them his "brothers" (H5 4.3.60). For instance, Henry allows any who do not wish to fight for him to go home unmolested:

> HENRY he which hath no stomach to this fight,
> Let him depart; his passport shall be made
> And crowns for convoy put into his purse. (H5 4.3.35–37)

On the other hand, Richard terms the Englishmen who will not fight in his name "vagabonds, rascals and runaways, / A scum of Bretons and base lackey peasants" (R3 5.3.315–16).[32] In the former, Shakespeare suggests that acceptance and mutual respect make a king, while disdain and division are what make the latter a tyrant.

Turning to the examples I have already quoted from Richard, taken from *Henry VI, Part 3*, in which Richard states outright his intention of deceiving the public and taking the throne, and Henry, in which he announces how he will trick his followers into seeing him as saintly by contrast to his former behavior in *Henry IV, Part 1*, we know that both men sought to use politics and wordplay to gain their respective thrones. We have a similar history from Trump, in fact, although he focuses on his future rhetorical methodology in interviews with Oprah in 1988, with *Playboy* in 1990, and with Larry King in 1999. Trump clearly states that if he were to run, he would do so on a working-class platform, and he would win:

> I think I'd win. I tell you what, I wouldn't go in to lose. I've never gone in to lose in my life. And if I did decide to do it, I think I would be inclined—I would say, I would have a hell of a chance of winning, because I think people—I don't know how your audience feels, but I think people are tired of seeing the United States ripped off. And I can't promise you everything, but I can tell you one thing, this country would make one hell of a lot of money from those people that for 25 years have taken advantage. It wouldn't be the way it's been, believe me.[33]

Here, Trump's assertion that the United States has been "ripped off" functions as an appeal to a populist audience who can be convinced to vote for him in order to safeguard their perceived identity and economic security—an example of leading through division rather than unity. As Goethals and I have suggested, in a populist context—like that facing Trump or Richard—"status anxiety and the need for positive self-esteem [act] as the underlying dynamic leading to the appeal of authoritarian leadership."[34] Richard, in evoking the Wars of the Roses, and Trump, by summoning the image of having been "ripped off," seek to create anxiety in their respective followings in order to provide the solution. By contrast, Henry's focus is on himself and how he will alter his *own* behavior to meet the expectations of his people, alleviating rather than exacerbating their fears. Henry, Trump, and Richard understand their appeal to their respective audiences, and all appear to be perfectly willing to leverage the needs and desires of those audiences in order to get what they want. Yet there is a clear disparity between Shakespeare's two kings—one that must cause us to ask why it is that Henry remains the hero while Richard becomes the villain, and which can help to reveal that the political poles of Lancastrian (Henry) and York (Richard) are perhaps not so far apart as they might seem.

What we find in the culmination of the two tetralogies—mostly contained within *Richard III*—is the legacy of polarization and civil war. The play itself begins with the famous "Now is the winter of our discontent / Made glorious summer by this son of York" (*R3* 1.1.1–2), the Ricardian parallel to the exhortation to "Make America Great Again." The situation of the play is the end—or so it seems—of a war and the return of troops to their homes and families, a situation not unlike that in the United States following the withdrawal of troops from Iraq or, indeed, Afghanistan. In Shakespeare's play, the country seems mostly stable but not perfect. The nobility is moderately discontent, and the monarch—Edward IV—struggles with an economy and society ravaged by the Wars of the Roses. Again, this situation is not dissimilar to the United States in the 2010s or to Shakespeare's England in the 1590s. The United States in the 2010s was in the long process of recovery from a significant economic recession. Like Henry V's rule, Barack Obama's early presidency provided political stability. However, the social underpinnings of both Edward's reign and Obama's later years are highly divided along partisan lines: Lancaster versus York and liberal versus conservative.

In *Richard III*, when Edward dies, England is plunged into a crisis, pulled between two factions: those supporting Elizabeth Woodville, Edward's wife and queen mother to the very young Edward V; and those supporting

Richard of Gloucester, the lord protector and brother of the deceased king. The tail end of the Obama presidency in 2014 similarly seems, therefore, to represent the end of an era. Since 2014, in particular, anti-immigrant (particularly anti-Muslim) sentiment has surged in the United States and Europe as "right-wing populist and extremist parties have been gaining ground."[35] In hindsight, it marks a significant divide between politics as largely centrist— as in the 1990s—and as highly polarized, just as England of the fifteenth century was split by the Wars of the Roses and Shakespeare's England by religious or courtly loyalties.

Taking the parallel further, we also see a dichotomization between a toxic charismatic male leader and an aspiring female leader following in a lineal tradition. In *Richard III*, Elizabeth remains the dowager queen— mother to Edward V and widow of Edward IV. In 2016 we saw the rise of Hillary Clinton, a politician in her own right but also the wife of a former president. Opposed to each is a radical male leader with a penchant for performance, demagoguery, and witch hunts—Richard himself and Donald Trump, both of whom otherize their opposition in order to increase their power. This behavior—the ostracizing of the perceived enemy by the toxic leader—provokes fear in followers that they (like Elizabeth or Clinton) will become the leader's next target.[36]

Yet Richard was not the only charismatic king to turn on his ostensible allies. Henry, too, turns against those who demonstrate disloyalty: Cambridge, Scroop, and Grey, who are accused of—and admit to—treason at the start of *Henry V*. Yet there is a distinct difference between the actions and accusations of the two kings. Henry brings the accused before him and asks how they would have him deal with a man "That railed against our person" (*H5* 2.2.41). Henry initially recommends mercy, saying that "It was excess of wine that set him on, / And on his more advice we pardon him" (*H5* 2.2.42–43). But the three traitors (not yet aware that Henry knows their guilt) urge Henry to "Let him be punished, sovereign, lest example / Breed, by his sufferance, more of such a kind" (*H5* 2.2.45–46). Henry takes their advice but leverages it against them so that when he reveals that he knows of their treachery, their own pleas for mercy are ignored. We justify Henry's actions because, through them, he exposes the hypocrisy of those around him; nevertheless, it is worth recognizing that although he speaks of mercy, Henry ultimately does not show it. His claims of merciful action are revealed, therefore, to be performative lies—yet the fault for his behavior is shifted away from himself and onto the three traitors because they had the opportunity (and failed) to embrace mercy and (hypothetically, anyway) earn it from Henry.

In *Richard III*, however, Richard levels (unsubstantiated) accusations of infidelity at Elizabeth, claiming that her sons—Edward V and the young Richard of York—are bastards. He follows this claim with another accusation, this time of witchcraft:

> Look how I am bewitched! Behold, mine arm
> Is like a blasted sapling withered up;
> And this is Edward's wife, that monstrous witch
> Consorted with that harlot, strumpet Shore,
> That by their witchcraft thus have marked me. (*R3* 3.4.67–71)

The audience will have seen Richard—and his withered arm, which he admits to having in the play's first scene—not only in this play but in two previous plays, and they therefore know that Richard's accusations are false, unlike Henry's, which are confirmed not only by others but by the traitors themselves. Nevertheless, Richard uses his claims as the means to secure the downfall of skeptics—Hastings objects and is sentenced to death—and to tarnish Elizabeth's reputation and declare her children illegitimate and unfit to rule.

The distinction lies not in whether or not the leader in question makes accusations, but in the presence of evidence (Henry has it, Richard does not) and the intention behind the accusation. In the case of Richard (and, one might argue, Trump), the motivation is not the security of the realm but the desire to eliminate a rival or silence the opposition. In Henry's case, Cambridge, Scroop, and Grey are guilty of treason, and their elimination serves not only to protect Henry but also to maintain national stability. It is certainly possible to see the evidence of Clinton's misuse of email servers as evidence—since they were, in fact, misused—and the repeated mention of those emails as valid concerns about national security. Yet the rhetoric of "Lock her up," suggestions that she had "low energy" or "lacked stamina," and the contradictory claims that she is both "sensitive" and has "no emotion" move beyond factual concerns and into the rhetorical realm of inflated accusation, not unlike Richard's charges of adultery and witchcraft.[37]

In *Richard III*, partly in retaliation and partly out of frustration, Elizabeth bands together with the other women of the court, including Richard's mother, the Duchess of Gloucester; his wife, Anne; and Margaret, the ostracized wife of the former King Henry VI, killed by Richard. These women come together in mutual fear and hatred of Richard, and they curse him for murdering their families (including Elizabeth's brother and sons, Richard's own brother, Anne's first husband, and Margaret's son and husband) and for corrupting the throne:

> QUEEN MARGARET I had an Edward, till a Richard killed him;
> I had a husband, till a Richard killed him.
> Thou hadst an Edward, till a Richard killed him.
> Thou hadst a Richard, till a Richard killed him.
> . . .
> QUEEN ELIZABETH O thou, well skilled in curses, stay awhile
> And teach me how to curse mine enemies. (R3 4.4.40–43, 116–17)

Along with Anne and the Duchess, Elizabeth and Margaret form a community of women in order to find support to counteract Richard's threat. They are among the only noble characters who are unwilling to acquiesce to Richard's usurpation of the throne—what we might today call a "hostile takeover," secured with the support of those at court (both commoners like Catesby and Tyrell and nobles like Buckingham) who hope to profit from his rise to power. In doing so, they demonstrate Lipman-Blumen's advice for countering toxic leaders by "finding the common core of humanity in [themselves] and others," reaching across their familial and political allegiances "to foster the leadership potential of others" besides Richard.[38]

By contrast, the fostering of leadership potential is something at which Henry—unlike Richard—excels in a positive (rather than obstructive) sense. While Richard promotes backstabbing and division within the ranks of his followers, Henry (rhetorically and performatively) levels the proverbial playing field, equating himself with his followers and elevating them in the process. In perhaps his most famous speech, he says,

> HENRY We would not die in that man's company
> That fears his fellowship to die with us.
> . . .
> This story shall the good man teach his son,
> And Crispin Crispian shall ne'er go by
> From this day to the ending of the world
> But we in it shall be remembered,
> We few, we happy few, we band of brothers.
> For he today that sheds his blood with me

Shall be my brother; be he ne'er so vile,
This day shall gentle his condition. (*HS* 4.3.38–39, 56–63)

In exhorting his men to battle—although in a stage production, this is mostly the gathered nobles and a handful of others—Henry guarantees passage and coin to any who are not willing to fight, allowing them the agency to make the choice without threat of vilification or condemnation for desertion. Instead, he promises the elision of class divisions if they stay: "he today that sheds his blood with me / Shall be my brother; be he ne'er so vile, / This day shall gentle his condition," is a promise of status elevation that brings them in line with the nobility, bringing unity across demographics.

The contrast between Henry and Richard specifically rests on the scission between division and unification; Henry's use of group cohesion is arrived at through the deployment of positive, unifying rhetoric, while Richard's is by virtue of establishing an us-versus-them framework that creates *internal* cohesion among his followers but does nothing to grow their ranks. This is not to suggest that manipulating out-group biases isn't effective; it absolutely is, and that is why leaders (toxic and nontoxic) employ it, particularly in times of war or strife. But at the same time, the danger of divisive language comes when there are not enough followers to compensate for the necessary enemies made by such rhetorical moves—as is the case with Richard. Ultimately, there are *more* people in the anti-Richard camp (which must fairly be recognized as anti-Richard and not pro-Richmond) than there are in the pro-Richard one.

Yet this divisiveness is also effective when it allows leaders to play off followers' fears, and both Richard and Trump are able to gain the support of followers who aid them in achieving high office. Throughout Trump's presidential campaigns, he sought to establish himself as distinct from traditional American politics, claiming—beginning in October 2016—that "it is time to drain the swamp in Washington, DC. This is why I'm proposing a package of ethics reforms to make our government honest once again."[39] As Peter Overby of NPR suggests, "The phrase 'drain the swamp' didn't originate with the Trump campaign. Advocates of tougher laws on political money and lobbying have used it for years," with reference to the way in which economics rather than ethics, seems to drive decision-making in American politics.[40] Trump promised to remove lobbyists from Washington and to reduce business's influence over legislative procedure, and many pundits suggest that this campaign "is a central topic to why President Trump won this election."[41] The rhetoric that surrounded this idea situated Trump as uniquely able to do this by virtue of not being a "Washington insider";

his separation from politics (prior to his presidential campaign) allowed him, suggests Thomas Gallagher, to claim an "image as a Washington outsider representing 'the forgotten man and woman' (Trump, 2016) and vowing to 'drain the swamp' in Washington on their behalf."[42] This assertion of commonality with the so-called average American (presumably white and working-class) and as a "Man of the People" comes in spite of Trump's actual position as one of the wealthiest men in the country with vested interests in Big Business. It may be worth noting that, from the 2016 to 2020 elections, lobbying actually increased, and Trump—who claimed a desire to remove business interests from Washington—refused to divest himself of his own business holdings and continued to profit from shuttling political events and vacations to his own hotels, resorts, and companies while in office.[43]

Shakespeare, too, understood an appeal to commonality as a successful leadership strategy—albeit one that worked differently in early modern England than it does in the twenty-first-century United States. For Shakespeare, being popular among the low-class commons was a double-edged sword. On the one hand, Shakespeare's common audience would have approved of such popular characters, like Henry IV's "Hal" incarnation in *Henry IV, Part 1*. On the other, however, Shakespeare was deeply critical of such popularity as evidence of effective leadership, which is why, at the close of *2 Henry IV, Part 2*, Henry casts off his Hal persona in order to become King Henry V. In *Henry V*, Henry's former tavern companions are torn about being forced to enlist in the army to serve under their erstwhile friend-turned-monarch:

> NYM The King hath run bad humours on the knight, that's the even
> of it.
> PISTOL Nym, though has spoke the right;
> His heart is fracted and corroborate.
> NYM The King is a good king, but it must be as it may.
> (*H5* 2.1.121–26)

"The knight" in the discussion is Falstaff, Henry's former closest companion whose heart has been broken by the king's rejection of him, at least according to the hostess's line, "The King has killed his heart" (*H5* 2.1.88). Yet the audience understands that Hal cannot be king, and that Henry the king cannot be a common man. As a "good king," he must leave behind the actions of a commoner: as Nym says, "it must be as it may." In this, Shakespeare's view of appropriate leadership differs from that of many Americans. For Shakespeare, a leader cannot act as a commoner; for many Americans, a leader should be someone they can "have a beer with," as satirist Mike Toole snarks in a 2019 piece speculating about the relative electability of possible Democratic candidates for the 2020 election.[44] The phrase, taken from George W. Bush's 2000 campaign, encapsulates the "Man of the People" claims echoed and magnified in Trump's 2016 campaign.

Yet despite targeting those outside of the political sphere, Trump's support base includes—as does Richard's, in *Richard III*—members of the conservative religious right, the new "alt-right," and so-called Big Business. Most of his top 2020 contributors were corporate entities, and his support base for the 2020 election was predominantly white men (62 percent) and women (47 percent), ideologically conservative (98 percent), and Christian (56 percent), particularly evangelical Protestants (77 percent), who attend services at least weekly (58 percent). Non-whites (particularly Black and Hispanic voters, at 6 percent and 28 percent supporting) and non-white Christians (3 percent of Black Protestants and 19 percent of Hispanic Catholics), by contrast, did not support Trump.[45] These numbers tell us that Trump's support base is predominantly white, Christian, and male, the same character demographics who provide support for Richard's rise to the throne. This is noteworthy because it suggests that supporters of both are interested in preserving an oppressive status quo; both Richard and Trump elevate an ideological stance that helps to maintain power (and wealth) for those already in power (such as the white Christian elite, in the twenty-first-century United States, and the lord mayor and bishops, in Shakespeare's version of fifteenth-century England).

Yet despite Shakespeare's hesitancy to align Henry with the tavern denizens in *Henry V*, he also clearly emphasizes the need for the people—common and noble—to respect and be drawn to their king. Henry is characterized as unifying his men rather than standing entirely apart from them, yet he is not *like* them:

CHORUS O now, who will behold
The royal captain of this ruined band
Walking from watch to watch, from tent to tent,
Let him cry 'Praise and glory on his head!'
For forth he goes and visits all his host,
Bids them good morrow with a modest smile,
And calls them brothers, friends and countrymen.
Upon his royal face there is no note
How dread an army hath enrounded him,
Nor doth he dedicate one jot of colour

Unto the wearing and all-watched night,
But freshly looks and overbears attaint
With cheerful semblance and sweet majesty. (*H5* 4.0.28–40)

The description given to the audience by the chorus emphasizes Henry's charismatic ability to appear confident in his vision, to relate to his followers' emotions, and to respond to their needs by not exacerbating their fears. He crosses boundaries of class and rank but does not lower himself, maintaining his "sweet majesty" even as he shares common conditions. When the chorus describes him, they speak of his "modest smile," focusing on positivity, inclusivity, and humility, something Richard is able to pretend temporarily but does not actually possess.

In the play, Richard is able to garner support and campaigns for the ratification of the lord mayor and his council by convincing them of his belief in Christian morals and his love for England. Just as Trump leveraged his lack of political experience as a positive through the "Drain the swamp" slogan, Richard—unlike Henry—claims humility as a means of self-aggrandizement:

RICHARD I would rather hide me from my greatness,
Being a bark to brook no mighty sea,
Than in my greatness covet to be hid
And in the vapour of my glory smothered. (*R3* 3.7.160–63)

This convoluted speech—which seems to indicate a lack of political ambition while repeating "great" and "glory"—concludes with Richard's insistence that he will accept the throne "against my conscience and my soul . . . / For God doth know, and you may partly see, / How far I am from the desire of this" (*R3* 3.7.225, 234–35). One imagines Richard winking at the audience, to whom he admits, both in the previous play and immediately at the start of this one, that he would "pluck down" the crown.

In contrast to the nobility, who are taken in by Richard's actions, many of the common people remain unconvinced by Richard. In *Richard III*, the third citizen says, "O, full of danger is the Duke of Gloucester" (*R3* 2.3.27), and the citizens discuss fears of impending doom, war, and hardship:

THIRD CITIZEN When clouds are seen, wise men put on their
   cloaks;
When great leaves fall, then winter is at hand;
When the sun sets, who doth not look for night?

Untimely storms make men expect a dearth.
All may be well; but if God sort it so,
'Tis more than we deserve, or I expect.
SECOND CITIZEN Truly, the hearts of men are full of fear.
You cannot reason almost with a man
That looks not heavily and full of dread. (*R3* 2.3.32–40)

In this scene, the people are deeply uncertain about Richard and the rumors he has spread about the bastardy of the young Edward V—not unlike the rumors Trump's campaign spread about Clinton or those Trump himself encouraged claiming that Obama was born in Kenya. Yet Trump—like Shakespeare's version of Richard—managed to convince just enough of the representatives of the people that he would be "good for the country" that they elected him to take power.

After Richard's confirmation by the lord mayor, in spite of the apprehension of the citizens, comes his "Inauguration Day." Buckingham proclaims him king, and the people—not those who raised Richard to the throne, but the *people*—refuse to confirm him:

RICHARD: How now, how now, what say the citizens?
BUCKINGHAM: Now by the Holy Mother of our Lord,
The citizens are mum, say not a word.
. . .
And when mine oratory drew toward end,
I bid them that did love their country's good
Cry, "God save Richard, England's royal King!"
RICHARD: And did they so?
BUCKINGHAM: No, so God help me, they spake not a word,
But like dumb statues or breathing stones
Stared on each other, and looked deadly pale. (*R3* 3.7.1–3, 20–26)

In response, Buckingham bribes some of the audience to cheer:

BUCKINGHAM: When he had done, some followers of mine own
At lower end of the hall hurled their caps,
And some ten voices cried, "God save King Richard!"
And thus I took the vantage of those few:
"Thanks gentle citizens and friends," quoth I;
"This general applause and cheerful shout
Argues your wisdom and your love to Richard." (*R3* 3.7.34–40)

This scene is one in which the crowds are scarce and mostly silent, in which the majority of citizens look upon Richard's reign "full of fear," "heavily and full of dread," wiser than the nobles who helped to place Richard on the throne. This scene is not far distant from the Trump inauguration, with attendance rates well below those of 2009 and 2013, with clear visible patches of empty pavement at the National Mall in front of the Capitol building.[46] The emphasis Shakespeare places on cronies initiating cheers is also germane to the Trump administration, given the presence of applauding staffers in various press conferences and the administration's removal of spectators whose appearance or responses do not reflect well on the former president.[47]

In *Henry V*, however, we see Henry not only moving among his men, seeking to comfort them, but also learning from them what he must do to be a respected leader. In one of the more hotly debated scenes of the play, Henry adopts a disguise so that he might learn what his people really think of him. Claiming the alias of Harry le Roy, Henry engages some of his common soldiers in conversation about their present circumstances and is somewhat surprised by the response:

> KING Methinks I could not die anywhere so contented as in the
>   King's company, his cause being just and his quarrel honourable.
> WILLIAMS That's more than we know.
> BATES Ay, or more than we should seek after, for we know enough
>   if we know we are the King's subjects. If his cause be wrong, our
>   obedience to the King wipes the crime of it out of us.
> WILLIAMS But if the cause be not good, the King himself hath a
>   heavy reckoning to make when all those legs and arms and heads
>   chopped off in a battle shall join together at the latter day and
>   cry all "We died at such a place." . . . Now if these men do not
>   die well it will be a black matter for the King, that led them to it,
>   who to disobey were against all proportion of subjection. (*H5*
>   4.1.126–46)

In short, Henry learns that he not only leads his men but bears eternal responsibility for their souls—something he was not fully prepared to have laid at his feet. The enormity of it leads Henry to a soliloquy that serves a dual purpose: first, he accepts (though unhappily) his responsibility, and second, he reveals that there is no division "save ceremony . . . general ceremony" (*H5* 4.1.236) between himself and a common man. In this admission, Shakespeare reveals to us the most essential part of the historical tetralogies: that kings are like common men, but also that a leader's humanity is at once their greatest strength and weakness. Henry's acceptance of his own fallibility allows him to act with the recognition that he can make mistakes and therefore must make deliberate decisions and cultivate the support and respect of all of his citizens, both high and low.

Richard, by contrast, seeks to maintain followers through otherizing the out-group rather than expanding the in-group. It is in this dichotomization that we find even more links to *Richard III* in Trump's push to further polarize the nation by riling up the bigotry of his most enthusiastic supporters, including accusing his "enemies" of collusion with foreign powers (Richard blames Henry VII for collusion with France and labels him a foreigner; Trump declared Obama a foreign national and a Muslim). Richard also encourages his followers to spy on and engage in violence against their neighbors for wearing the wrong color rose (red instead of white), while Trump and some of his supporters condemn the opposition for being liberal, Democratic, gay, disabled, Muslim, Jewish, or a person of color—for being politically blue instead of red. For instance, Trump's imitation of *New York Times* reporter Serge F. Kovaleski resulted in widespread backlash for his mockery of Kovaleski's physical disability, though it earned the applause of supporters at the rally where it was conducted.[48] Political scientists Brian F. Schaffner, Matthew MacWilliams, and Tatishe Nteta argue that racism and sexism both played a significant role in electing Trump in 2016, with a high correlation between those espousing support of Trump also demonstrating antipathetic attitudes toward minorities and women.[49] Furthermore, Griffin Sims Edwards and Stephen Rushin conducted a study using data from the Federal Bureau of Investigation that suggests "it was not just Trump's inflammatory rhetoric throughout the political campaign that caused hate crimes to increase. Rather, we argue that it was Trump's subsequent election as President of the United States that validated this rhetoric in the eyes of perpetrators and fueled the hate crime surge."[50] In this case, we see both Richard and Trump trying—and failing, to a degree—to silence opposition through the threat of ostracization and the attempt to construct an illusion of heroism and centrality.[51] Despite their lackluster success, these tactics are clear demonstrations of toxicity and serve in both cases as harbingers to the future of each administration.

The 2019 government shutdown and Trump's refusal to negotiate over his border wall also provide an eerie echo to Buckingham's conversation with Richard over the deaths of the princes:

RICHARD Why, Buckingham, I say I would be king.
BUCKINGHAM Why so you are, my thrice renowned liege.

RICHARD Ha! Am I king? 'Tis so—but Edward lives.
BUCKINGHAM True, noble prince.
RICHARD O bitter consequence
That Edward still should live 'true, noble prince'!
Cousin, thou wast not wont to be so dull.
Shall I be plain? I wish the bastards dead,
And I would have it suddenly performed.
What sayest thou now? speak suddenly. Be brief.
BUCKINGHAM Your grace may do your pleasure.
RICHARD Tut, tut, thou art all ice; thy kindness freezes.
Say, have I thy consent that they shall die? (R3 4.2.12–23)

Buckingham refuses to give Richard the answer he wants—like Congress to Trump—and Richard proceeds to hire a murderer to do the job for him, commissioning Tyrell to make the princes "disappear."

When Buckingham returns, he asks that Richard grant the promise made when Buckingham agreed to help him achieve the throne:

BUCKINGHAM What says your highness to my just request?
RICHARD I do remember me, Henry the Sixth
Did prophesy that Richmond should be king,
When Richmond was a little peevish boy.
A king, perhaps, perhaps—
BUCKINGHAM My lord.
RICHARD How chance the prophet could not at that time
Have told me, I being by, that I should kill him?
BUCKINGHAM My lord, your promise for the earldom—
RICHARD Richmond! When last I was at Exeter,
The mayor in courtesy showed me the castle
And called it Rougemont, at which name I started,
Because a bard of Ireland told me once
I should not live long after I saw Richmond.
BUCKINGHAM My Lord—
RICHARD Ay, what's o'clock?
BUCKINGHAM I am thus bold to put your grace in mind
Of what you promised me.
RICHARD Well, but what's o'clock?
BUCKINGHAM Upon the stroke of ten.
RICHARD Well, let it strike.
BUCKINGHAM Why let it strike?

RICHARD Because that, like a jack, thou keep'st the stroke
Betwixt thy begging and my meditation.
I am not in the giving vein today. (*R3* 4.2.93–114)

Richard's answers to Buckingham's demands that he fulfill his promise are non sequiturs, almost nonsensical at times, and unrelated to the question Buckingham repeatedly puts to him—a scene all too familiar from press conferences and other occasions throughout the Trump presidency. Buckingham recognizes, too late to save himself, that Richard has turned on Buckingham just as he turned against his brother, his nephews, and his wife. Buckingham, too, is charged with treason and led to the block, a bleak parallel to news accounts of people in deeply Republican districts in Florida, for example, whose lives have been damaged by Trump's refusal to negotiate and threats to employ disaster funding to build the border wall: "'I voted for him, and he's the one who's doing this,' one Florida woman said of Mr. Trump. 'I thought he was going to do good things. He's not hurting the people he needs to be hurting.'"[52] The list of Trump officials who were removed from their positions—including Steve Bannon, Sean Spicer, John Bolton, John Kelly, Jeff Sessions, Rex Tillerson, Reince Priebus, and Sally Yates, among others—is lengthy, with a turnover rate of approximately 80 percent.[53] Obviously, unlike Richard, Trump is not executing his former followers, but his treatment of them is nevertheless characteristic of authoritarianism, another hallmark of toxic leadership.[54]

LEARNING FROM SHAKESPEARE'S KINGS

These parallels are important to recognize because if we keep following the script of *Richard III*, things get worse before they get better. Although Trump has not murdered American citizens, the actions of Immigration and Customs Enforcement have resulted in the deaths of dozens of asylum seekers in detention centers, and the promised repeal of the Affordable Care Act would have caused the deaths of a not insignificant number of disabled Americans. The denial and subsequent mishandling of the COVID-19 global pandemic by the administration that shut down the American Pandemic Response Team undoubtedly contributed to much higher rates of infection and mortality in the United States (and possibly around the globe) than a prepared and responsive government would have. The Biden administration's rapid dispersal of vaccines and booster shots, for instance, demonstrated responsiveness to the situation rather than denial of political and social realities. Richard's refusal to read the proverbial writing on the wall—not unlike Trump's inability to see beyond the range of his followers' enthusiasm—is similarly short-sighted. Shakespeare's *Richard III* was meant as a cautionary tale disguised as propaganda; while it celebrated the rise of Henry VII and his triumph over Richard, it also called attention to the fact that the factionalism being perpetuated by the Elizabethan government (Catholic versus Protestant) was setting the country up for potential violence and civil war when Elizabeth died.

Richard's refusal to recognize his defeat on the eve of battle—despite the flight of his followers and the nightly visitation of ghosts cursing him to "despair and die" (*R3* 5.3.163)—also provides us with a precursor to the Trump faction's denial of the 2020 election results and subsequent refusal to withdraw from campaigning in early 2024, despite ongoing trials for defamation, obstruction of an election, mishandling documents, and fraud.[55] Shakespeare's Richard, who persists in attempting to defeat Henry Tudor, Earl of Richmond, in battle as his followers deserted him (or had been killed by him), presents us with the model of an authoritarian leader unable to accept the loss of power—an image echoed by Trump's insistence that the 2020 election results were the consequence of fraud, theft, and lies. Although at the time of writing, the outcome of the investigation into the January 6, 2021, insurrection has not been entirely resolved, we can compare Trump's speech given on that day to the circumstances of the Battle of Bosworth Field in *Richard III*, in which both Richard and Richmond (Henry Tudor) urge their followers to battle. Trump spoke as follows:

All of us here today do not want to see our election victory stolen by emboldened radical-left Democrats, which is what they're doing. And stolen by the fake news media. That's what they've done and what they're doing. We will never give up, we will never concede. It doesn't happen. You don't concede when there's theft involved. . . .

You will have an illegitimate president. That's what you'll have. And we can't let that happen. . . .

If we allow this group of people to illegally take over our country because it's illegal when the votes are illegal when the way they got there is illegal when the states that vote are given false and fraudulent information.

We are the greatest country on Earth and we are headed and were headed in the right direction.[56]

The speech, of course, is much longer, but at its core, it is fundamentally divisive. The essential rhetoric of this speech is us-versus-them, warns about the impending arrival of immigrants ("But now, the caravans, I think Biden's getting in, the caravans are forming again. They want to come in again and rip off our country. Can't let it happen"), and focuses specifically on stopping "them": Democrats, liberals, immigrants, and weak Republicans.[57] Trump emphasizes Biden's illegitimacy, talks about weakness, and repeats the word "illegal" with reference both to actions and people, using the rhetorical link to immigrants to otherize anyone who voted for Biden or supported the outcome of the 2020 election.

In his final speech of the play, Richard similarly seeks to otherize Richmond and his followers, using insults and alienating terms rather than attempting to bring unity to England:

RICHARD Remember whom you are to cope withal,
A sort of vagabonds, rascals and runaways,
A scum of Bretons and base lackey peasants,
Whom their o'ercloyed country vomits forth
To desperate adventures and assured destruction.
You sleeping safe, they bring you unrest;
You having lands and blessed with beauteous wives,
They would restrain the one, disdain the other.
And who doth lead them but a paltry fellow?
Long kept in Bretagne at our mother's cost,
A milksop, one that never in his life
Felt so much cold as over shoes in snow.
. . .
If we be conquered, let me conquer us,
And not these bastard Bretons, whom our fathers
Have in their own land beaten, bobbed and thumped,
And in record left them the heirs of shame. (R3 5.3.315–26, 332–35)

Richard's speech, although far different in tenor, makes several of the same rhetorical moves evident in Trump's speech from January 6. He otherizes the opposition, insulting them, calling them un-English (rather than un-American); he situates these Others as a threat to the safety, wealth, and masculinity of his followers; he insults the prowess of Richmond as "paltry" and calls him a "milksop," similar to Trump's repeated invocations of Biden's weakness and age; and he, also like Trump, invokes illegitimacy (albeit literal rather than political). Each line is meant to vilify the out-group rather than focus on unity and inclusivity.

But if Richard employs divisive tactics, then Richmond acts as his foil. Richmond's speech to *his* followers is one that explicitly promises peace and unity, the diametric opposite of Richard's:

RICHMOND God, and our good cause, fight upon our side.
The prayers of holy saints and wronged souls,
Like high-reared bulwarks, stand before our faces.
Richard except, those whom we fight against
Had rather have us win than him they follow.
. . .
But if I thrive, the gain of my attempt
The least of you shall share his part thereof. (*R3* 5.3.240–44,
    267–68)

While Richmond does insult Richard, calling him "A bloody tyrant and a homicide" (*R3* 5.3.246), his complaints about Richard have to do with his violence and (yes) illegitimacy of rule, since he stole the throne from his nephew (by killing said nephew). But Richmond does not explicitly insult Richard's person, despite Richard's physical infirmities, nor does he suggest that Richard's followers are inhuman—instead, he provides a point of unity between his own followers and Richard's, suggesting that *all* of them will be better off with Richmond's victory.

And when he does achieve that victory, he issues—like Henry V—a "pardon to the soldiers fled / That in submission will return to us" (*R3* 5.5.16–17), forgiving them for being loyal to their liege lords. The final speech of the sequence—the one alluded to at the conclusion of *Henry V* in the chorus's mention of the Wars of the Roses—brings together both sides, uniting them and establishing a new dynasty:

RICHMOND We will unite the white rose and the red.
Smile heaven upon this fair conjunction,
That long have frowned upon their enmity.
. . .
England hath long been made and scarred herself:
The brother blindly shed the brother's blood;
The father rashly slaughtered his own son;

The son, compelled, been butcher to the sire.
All this divided York and Lancaster,
Divided in their dire division.
O, now let Richmond and Elizabeth,
The true succeeders of each royal house,
By God's fair ordinance conjoin together;
And let their heirs, God, if Thy will be so,
Enrich the time to come with smooth-faced peace,
With smiling plenty and fair prosperous days. (*R3* 5.5.19–21,
    23–34)

The theme of unity—bringing together the two houses, ending the violence that has pitted England against itself—is central to the play's conclusion and to the summative intention of the whole two-tetralogy sequence. It is because of this that we can say that Shakespeare was ultimately optimistic, because although *Henry V* was written last and promised violence, we—and Shakespeare's audience—already knew that the eventual telos of the plays was the inauguration of the Tudor dynasty and the Elizabethan golden age. What ends the Wars of the Roses is the reunification of the houses of Lancaster (Henry) and York (Elizabeth) through the marriage, which could only take place because of the agreement of the elder Elizabeth, the queen. In short, Henry (another Henry) brings about reconciliation through unity and inclusivity rather than division and otherization.

In the twenty-first century, those who resisted Trump and what he has come to represent often occupy minority positions: women, people of color, Muslims, Jews, immigrants, LGBTQ folks, environmentalists, and socialists, among others. Even as hate crimes and acts of white supremacy are on the rise in the United States, state and local governments are increasingly held by a widely diverse and Democratic population. The US Congress, too, shows growing diversity along demographic lines: the 116th Congress included 56 Black members (up from 48 in 2016), 50 Hispanic (from 38), 20 Asian and Pacific Islander (from 14), and 4 indigenous persons (from 2).[58] The number of women also increased from 108 to 131 in the same period.[59] Across the United States, state and local elections saw similar demographic shifts as voters—like the citizens of *Richard III*—reacted against the Trump administration.

What these figures have in common is a refusal to accept fearmongering (accusations of witchcraft or instability; declarations of an emergency at the border), the desire to strengthen those who resist authoritarianism (supporting Richmond; supporting the American Civil Liberties Union and other pro-democratic organizations), seeking out "leaders who dis-illusion us" (Stanley and Richmond; the Green New Deal, which recognizes the imminent threat of climate change), and "rejecting the we/they dichotomy" by embracing a diversity of peoples and viewpoints (accepting Richmond's Burgundian allies and defectors from Richard; voting for people and policies that embrace diversity). These strategies—rejecting anxiety, shoring up democratic processes, selecting new leaders unafraid of "hard truths," embracing diversity—all appear in Lipman-Blumen's paradigm as viable strategies to reject toxic charisma and improve leadership within a stressed community.[60]

The United States no longer has a monarchy reliant on inheritance, so it does not face the same kinds of succession crises that England faced in Shakespeare's day. However, US elections are increasingly problematized by an antiquated system that does not reflect the popular vote and that, we have now learned, can be compromised by foreign countries with agendas of their own. We, too, face our own crises of succession, crises exacerbated—not solved—by the polarization of politics by extremists on both the left and right.

What all of this means for us, looking four hundred years back at a play written in a tumultuous time of international, religious, and social uncertainty, is that these patterns of history are a part and parcel of what it means to negotiate leadership and society. When he wrote a series of plays that summoned the ghosts of the Wars of the Roses, Shakespeare was reminding his audience that England had survived worse than the death of a powerful and beloved monarch—and that it would do so again. And he was right. Elizabeth's death in 1603 did not cause a civil war, and the accession of James VI and I was smooth—just as, ultimately, the transition of power from Trump to Biden was successful (even if a bit fraught).

The point made by Shakespeare in the 1590s, which is still germane more than four centuries later, is that a society which rests on the fundamental principle of participation—limited participatory monarchy for Shakespeare and inclusive democracy for us—is capable of surviving tyranny, demagoguery, and all manner of partisan shenanigans. While susceptibility to toxic charisma put Trump in office, as the days pass it becomes increasingly clear that people who are unwilling to tolerate his (in)actions are not only capable of but also willing to intercede, speak out, and clear the path for the next leader to take his place, a leader who will, hopefully, like Henry Tudor, Earl of Richmond, be a practical voice for moderation and unity . . . at least for a little while. But the nation—and the people at its heart—will be strong enough to survive the tides of history because they have weathered them before and can learn, if they pay attention, from the stories of the past.

NOTES

1. Kristin M. S. Bezio and George R. Goethals, "Introduction," *Leadership* 14, no. 5 (2018): 507.

2. George R. Goethals, "Donald Trump, Perceptions of Justice, and Populism," *Leadership* 14, no. 5 (2018): 513.

3. Goethals, "Donald Trump," 513.

4. For more on the electoral college, see Drew Desilver, "Why Electoral College Wins Are Bigger than Popular Vote Ones," *Pew Research Center*, December 20, 2016, https://www .pewresearch.org/fact-tank/2016/12/20/why-electoral-college-landslides-are-easier -to-win-than-popular-vote-ones/. For hypotheses on motivations, see Goethals, "Donald Trump"; as well as Brian F. Schaffner, Matthew MacWilliams, and Tatishe Nteta, "Understanding White Polarization in the 2016 Vote for President: The Sobering Role of Racism and Sexism," *Political Science Quarterly* 133, no. 1 (2018): 9–34.

5. Shakespeare plays somewhat fast and loose with the facts of history regarding Richard III. While Richard was, in all likelihood, hunched due to severe scoliosis (confirmed with the discovery of his skeletal remains in 2013), he was not likely as physically impaired as the character in the play, and several of the events depicted in Shakespeare's tetralogy—including the battlefield death of Prince Edward and the murder of Henry VI—could not have been committed by the historical Richard, despite being attributed to him in Shakespeare's dramatization.

6. E. M. W. Tillyard, *Shakespeare's History Plays* (New York: Macmillan, 1946).

7. See Kristin M. S. Bezio, *Staging Power in Tudor and Stuart English History Plays: History, Political Thought, and the Redefinition of Sovereignty* (Farnham: Ashgate, 2015), 6–9; Howard Nenner, *By Colour of Law: Legal Culture and Constitutional Politics in England, 1660–1689* (Chicago: University of Chicago Press, 1977); Robert Eccleshall, *Order and Reason in Politics: Theories of Absolute and Limited Monarchy in Early Modern England* (Oxford: Oxford University Press, 1978); J. P. Sommerville, *Royalists and Patriots: Politics and Ideology in England, 1603–1640*, 2nd ed. (London: Longman, 1999).

8. Michael Swanton, ed. and trans., *The Anglo-Saxon Chronicle* (New York: Routledge, 1998), 145.

9. For more on the historical development of limited participatory monarchy in England, see Bezio, *Staging Power*, 9–36.

10. Alan Gordon Smith, *William Cecil: The Power Behind Elizabeth*, (London: Paul, Trench, Trübner, 1934; Forest Grove, OR: University Press of the Pacific, 2004), 139.

11. David Bevington, *Tudor Drama and Politics: A Critical Approach to Topical Meaning* (Cambridge: Harvard University Press, 1968), 230–31.

12. William Shakespeare, *King Henry V*, ed. T. W. Craik, Arden Shakespeare, Third Series (London: Routledge, 1995).

13. Tillyard, *Shakespeare's History Plays*, 199.

14. Kristin M. S. Bezio, "Drama and Demigods: Kingship and Charisma in Shakespeare's England," *Religions* 4, no. 1 (January 22, 2013): 37, https://doi.org/10.3390/re14010030.

15. Criteria for charisma taken from Ronald Riggio, "Charisma," in *Encyclopedia of Leadership* (Thousand Oaks: Sage, 2004).

16. Jean Lipman-Blumen, *The Allure of Toxic Leaders: Why We Follow Destructive Bosses and Corrupt Politicians—and How We Can Survive Them* (Oxford: Oxford University Press, 2005), 11.

17. Lipman-Blumen, *The Allure of Toxic Leaders*, 35.

18. Lipman-Blumen, 19–20.

19. Lipman-Blumen, 29.

20. Lipman-Blumen, 51.

21. William Shakespeare, *King Henry VI, Part 3*, ed. John D. Cox and Eric Rasmussen, Arden Shakespeare, Third Series (London: Thomson Learning, 2001).

22. It is worth noting that Shakespeare was not the inventor of Richard's evil—Sir Thomas More had written a prose history of Richard III's life, and an anonymous play entitled *The True Tragedy of Richard III* produced by the Queen's Men circa 1588 focused on a similarly vile Richard.

23. Nina Taunton, *1590s Drama and Militarism: Portrayals of War in Marlowe, Chapman, and Shakespeare's "Henry V"* (Aldershot: Ashgate, 2001), 177; Sara Munson Deats, "Henry V at War: Christian King or Model Machiavel," in *War and Words: Horror and Heroism in the Literature of Warfare*, ed. Sara Munson Deats, Lagretta Tallent Lenker, and Merry G. Perry (Lanham: Lexington Books, 2004), 83–101; Malcolm Pittock, "The Problem of 'Henry V,'" *Neophilologus* 93 (2009): 188.

24. Bezio, "Drama and Demigods," 41.

25. William Shakespeare, *King Henry IV, Part 1*, ed. David Scott Kastan, Arden Shakespeare, Third Series (London: Thomson Learning, 2006).

26. Hamlet, the second most verbose, has 1,495 lines. Richard's lines are spread across three plays, with 24 in *Henry VI, Part 2* and 404 in *Henry VI, Part 3*, leaving 1,171 in *Richard III*.

27. And this concept would also have been reflected in the fact that it is a Henry (Henry Richmond, future Henry VII) who overthrows Richard, but also in the staging of the deposition scene of Richard II (in *Richard II*) by Henry Bolingbroke (Henry IV), in which Richard employs the bucket-and-well metaphor of down and up to describe his removal from the throne. It is also likely that Burbage would *also* have played Richard II, emphasizing to the audience the cyclical nature of power across multiple kings.

28. In engaging in *civil* war, Richard is arguably worse, in that he kills "enemies" who are also his subjects, where Henry is threatening the French, something Shakespeare's audience likely would have seen as far more acceptable.

29. Bert Alan Spector, "Carlyle, Freud, and the Great Man Theory More Fully Considered," *Leadership* 12, no. 2 (2016): 258.

30. Bezio, *Staging Power*, 89.

31. Lipman-Blumen, *The Allure of Toxic Leaders*, 130–31.

32. William Shakespeare, *King Richard III*, 3rd ed., ed. James R. Siemon, Arden Shakespeare, Third Series (London: Arden Shakespeare, 2009).

33. Don Gonyea and Domenico Montanaro, "Donald Trump's Been Saying the Same Thing for 30 Years," *NPR*, January 20, 2017, https://www.npr.org/2017/01/20/510680463/donald-trumps-been-saying-the-same-thing-for-30-years.

34. Kristin M. S. Bezio and George R. Goethals, "Introduction to *Leadership, Populism, and Resistance*," in *Leadership, Populism, and Resistance*, Jepson Studies in Leadership (Cheltenham, UK: Edward Elgar, 2020), 2.

35. Farid Hafez, "Shifting Borders: Islamophobia as Common Ground for Building Pan-European Right-Wing Unity," *Patterns of Prejudice* 48, no. 5 (December 2014): 480.

36. Lipman-Blumen, *The Allure of Toxic Leaders*, 40–41.

37. Michelle Ruiz, "Donald Trump Is Doing Yet Another Thing He Criticized Hillary Clinton Over," *Vogue*, February 3, 2017, https://www.vogue.com/article/donald-trump-hillary-clinton-five-attacks; Blythe Roberson, "Things Donald Trump Has Said About Hillary Clinton That Could Double as My Tinder Bio," *New Yorker*, July 5, 2016, http://www.newyorker.com/humor/daily-shouts/things-donald-trump-has-said-about-hillary-clinton-that-could-double-as-my-tinder-bio.

38. Lipman-Blumen, *The Allure of Toxic Leaders*, 244–45.

39. Peter Overby, "Trump's Efforts to 'Drain the Swamp' Lagging behind His Campaign Rhetoric," NPR, April 26, 2017, https://www.npr.org/2017/04/26/525551816/trumps-efforts-to-drain-the-swamp-lagging-behind-his-campaign-rhetoric.

40. Overby.

41. Overby.

42. Thomas Gallagher, "The Outsider on the Inside: Donald Trump's Twitter Activity and the Rhetoric of Separation from Washington Culture," *Atlantic Journal of Communication* 27, no. 3 (May 27, 2019): 185, 187.

43. Overby, "Trump's Efforts."

44. Mike Toole, "I Just Want a Candidate I Can Have a Beer With or One That Will Help Me Bury This Body," *Slackjaw* (blog), November 22, 2019, https://medium.com/slackjaw/i-just-want-a-candidate-i-can-have-a-beer-with-or-one-that-will-help-me-bury-this-body-5161a22a875b.

45. Center for Responsive Politics, "Top Contributors, Federal Election Data for Donald Trump, 2020 Cycle," OpenSecrets, accessed February 4, 2020, https://www.opensecrets.org/2020-presidential-race/contributors?id=N00023864; Pew Research Center, "An Examination of the 2016 Electorate, Based on Validated Voters," *Pew Research Center for the People and the Press* (blog), August 9, 2018, https://www.people-press.org/2018/08/09/an-examination-of-the-2016-electorate-based-on-validated-voters/.

46. Tim Wallace, Karen Yourish, and Troy Griggs, "Trump's Inauguration vs. Obama's: Comparing the Crowds," *New York Times*, January 20, 2017, https://www.nytimes.com/interactive/2017/01/20/us/politics/trump-inauguration-crowd.html.

47. Amy Wang, "'I Had to Be Real': #PlaidShirtGuy Removed from Trump Rally after Viral Facial Expressions," *Washington Post*, September 8, 2018, https://www.washingtonpost.com/politics/2018/09/08/i-had-be-real-plaidshirtguy-removed-trump-rally-after-viral-facial-expressions/.

48. Glenn Kessler, "Donald Trump's Revisionist History of Mocking a Disabled Reporter," *Washington Post*, August 2, 2016, https://www.washingtonpost.com/news/fact-checker/wp/2016/08/02/donald-trumps-revisionist-history-of-mocking-a-disabled-reporter/.

49. Schaffner, MacWilliams, and Nteta, "Understanding White Polarization."

50. Griffin Sims Edwards and Stephen Rushin, "The Effect of President Trump's Election on Hate Crimes" SSRN, January 14, 2018, 3, https://papers.ssrn.com/abstract=3102652.

51. Lipman-Blumen, *The Allure of Toxic Leaders*, 103, 52, 57.
52. Patricia Mazzei, "'It's Just Too Much': A Florida Town Grapples with a Shutdown after a Hurricane," *New York Times*, January 7, 2019, https://www.nytimes.com/2019/01/07/us/florida-government-shutdown-marianna.html.
53. Kathryn Dunn Tenpas, "Tracking Turnover in the Trump Administration," *Brookings* (blog), December 20, 2018, https://www.brookings.edu/research/tracking-turnover-in-the-trump-administration/.
54. Lipman-Blumen, *The Allure of Toxic Leaders*, 20.
55. Devlin Barrett, Perry Stein, and Josh Dawsey, "The Election Calendar's Set. Trump's Trial Timing? Deeply Unclear," *Washington Post*, January 15, 2024, https://www.washingtonpost.com/national-security/2024/01/12/trump-trial-schedule-when/.
56. Brian Naylor, "Read Trump's Jan. 6 Speech, a Key Part of Impeachment Trial," *NPR*, February 10, 2021, https://www.npr.org/2021/02/10/966396848/read-trumps-jan-6-speech-a-key-part-of-impeachment-trial.
57. Naylor, "Read Trump's Jan. 6 Speech."
58. Jennifer E. Manning, "Membership of the 116th Congress: A Profile," Congressional Research Service, January 14, 2020; Jennifer E. Manning, "Membership of the 114th Congress: A Profile," Congressional Research Service, December 5, 2016.
59. Manning, "Membership," 2020; Manning, "Membership," 2016.
60. Lipman-Blumen, *The Allure of Toxic Leaders*, 239–42.

PART IV

History

CHAPTER 9

Lincoln and Leadership in a Racist Democracy

Paul Escott

From scholars to schoolchildren, all agree that Abraham Lincoln was a great leader. At a critical time in the nation's history, he earned enormous credit for building a new political party, prodding the North to face the problem of slavery, issuing the Emancipation Proclamation, and directing a war that preserved the Union. Only George Washington and one or two other presidents rival Lincoln's stature, and he has become a cultural icon—a cherished national figure, a symbol of all that is good in American society.

The importance of Lincoln in our collective patriotic memories and myths complicates the task of historical analysis. One danger is the product of mythological distortions: seeing Lincoln as a symbol of the nation's mission and greatness can distort our view by abstracting him from the realities of his time and clothing him in the aspirations of our era. His role in addressing the nation's original sin of slavery and racism has encouraged exaggerations about his contributions to equality. Thus, one historian has explained Lincoln's racist statements or shortcomings by arguing that the man known as Honest Abe was "an artist in the Machiavellian uses of power" who supposedly used "some very crafty methods" to pursue equality and move "toward the goal of political equality for blacks."[1]

The obverse of that danger is the risk of being unfair to Lincoln. He was a man of the early and mid-nineteenth century, and to judge his actions simply by the morality and expectations of our time risks an unjust anachronism. Yet viewing Lincoln from the perspective of our time can help us see *his* time more clearly, even if the disjunctions between myth and fact are sometimes jarring and disturbing. Awareness of the racist realities of his time helps us to see the limits and inadequacies of democratic leadership in what was a nearly lily-white electorate. For racism was rampant in the North. It shaped the culture, it infected Lincoln's mentality and the vision of his Republican Party, and it buttressed nearly ubiquitous assumptions of white supremacy—a belief that the country was for white people. Racism constrained the majority-based politics that Lincoln practiced and demonstrated the need for a radicalism that was consistent with America's ideals.[2]

LINCOLN'S LEADERSHIP IN THE 1850S

The passage of the Kansas-Nebraska Act in 1854 began a new phase in Lincoln's life. Like many other Northerners, he was shocked when Congress approved Stephen Douglas's bill that opened to slavery a vast territory on the Great Plains. That land had been placed off-limits to slavery in 1820, and many land-hungry Northern farmers feared that the presence of slavery would destroy their opportunity to gain a better life west of the Mississippi River. Lincoln emerged from private life to speak out against slavery's growing influence over national policy.

Lincoln did more than criticize Douglas's legislation—he also made major contributions to the creation of a new political party, the Republican Party. That task required prying voters loose from existing loyalties to the Whigs or Democrats and welding them together behind new goals and leaders.[3] His challenge was to divide and then to unify. To achieve his goal, Lincoln used ideals and threats, inspiration and fear, and his tactics changed during the decade. Between 1854 and 1858 he shifted his emphasis from idealistic values to frightening threats.

In 1854 at Peoria, Lincoln eloquently invoked the ideals of the Declaration of Independence, insisting that the United States was a nation of liberty and freedom. Slavery, he declared, was a "monstrous injustice" at war with the nation's ideal of freedom. The zeal to spread slavery was something he "hate[d]" because the institution was wrong in itself and "because it deprives our republican example of its just influence in the world." Worse, "it forces so many really good men amongst ourselves into an open war with the very fundamental principles of civil liberty—criticizing the Declaration of Independence." Lincoln pointed out that the "moral principle" that underlay the outlawing of the international slave trade was indistinguishable from the 1820 ban on carrying slaves into Nebraska. Moreover, nothing was more important to "the WHOLE PEOPLE" than the preservation of "their own liberties." By focusing on liberty and freedom, Lincoln attached his cause to an enduring, central idea in American political culture: freedom. More than one hundred years later, Martin Luther King Jr. would voice faith that *his* cause would triumph "because the goal of America is freedom."[4]

At the same time Lincoln avoided a direct challenge to the racism that was nearly ubiquitous in society. Quoting from the Declaration of Independence, he read beyond the words that "all men are created equal" to emphasize instead that governments derive "THEIR JUST POWERS FROM THE CONSENT OF THE GOVERNED." Slavery in Nebraska would deny consent, for "if the negro *is* a man, is it not . . . a total destruction of self-government to say that he too shall not govern *himself?*" To make a slave of another man "is *more* than self-government—that is despotism." To avoid any suspicion that he was an abolitionist, Lincoln added, "Let it not be said that I am contending for the establishment of political and social equality between the whites and the blacks." His argument was against "the EXTENSION of a bad thing," and that became the consistent position of the prewar Republican Party.[5]

In addition to these appeals to American values of liberty and self-government, Lincoln reminded his listeners of their self-interest. "We want" the territories, he declared, "for the homes of free white people. This they cannot be, to any considerable extent, if slavery shall be planted within them," for "poor white people" flee from slavery and move to free states in order to "better their condition." Moreover, the slave South already enjoyed extra representation due to slavery—so much so that although Maine had more than twice the white population of South Carolina, the two states sent the same number of representatives to Congress.[6]

Lincoln did not attack or criticize Southerners in the Peoria speech, saying "they are just what we would be in their situation." Perhaps he hoped to preserve some bonds with Southern Whigs. But by 1858, in the wake of the *Dred Scott* decision, Lincoln put caution aside in favor of alarming his supporters and fomenting resentment of the Slave Power. Intensifying his rhetoric, he used threats and fear to mobilize voters. For in the House Divided speech and later, Lincoln charged that there was a conspiracy afoot to establish slavery even in the North.[7]

In the 1858 House Divided address, he made the exaggerated and incendiary claim that there was a conspiracy at the highest levels of government to fasten slavery on the entire nation. Describing four men who came from different places to build a house or a mill, he asked how it was possible that timbers brought separately by the four all fit together "exactly" and in proper "lengths and proportions." There must have been "preconcert . . . a common *plan.*" The four men in his story were Stephen, Franklin, Roger, and James, and his listeners immediately understood their last names to be Douglas, Pierce, Taney, and Buchanan—two presidents, a senator, and the chief justice of the Supreme Court. In case anyone missed the import of Lincoln's story, he listed a series of events that, he claimed, were preparing the way for a new Supreme Court decision that would make slavery "lawful in all the States. . . . We shall *lie down* pleasantly dreaming that the people of *Missouri* are on the verge of making their State *free,* and we shall *awake* to the *reality,* instead, that the *Supreme* Court has made *Illinois* a *slave* State."[8]

Lincoln continued to raise these fears during his debates with Stephen Douglas and deepened his emphasis on the "moral question about slavery." Douglas's view that "liberty and slavery are perfectly consistent" would erase any "barrier . . . against slavery being made lawful every where." Lincoln insisted that slavery was "a moral, a social and a political wrong." Restricting it territorially placed it "upon the original basis—the basis upon which our fathers placed it." The founders had understood that slavery needed to be "in the course of ultimate extinction." To distance himself from abolitionists, Lincoln told a questioner that he opposed "making voters or jurors of negroes, [or] qualifying them to hold office, [or] to intermarry with white people." The "physical difference" between the races prohibited "social and political equality," and therefore Lincoln, like "any other man," was "in favor of having the superior position assigned to the white race."[9]

Although the Illinois legislature reelected Douglas to the US Senate, Lincoln's growing popularity and his sense of the deepening national crisis fed his determination and his ambition. By 1860 he had jettisoned a moderate tone toward Southerners and positioned himself as a determined, insistent champion of Northern interests and of a nation that would be free of slavery at some indefinite, distant time in the future. In his speech at the Cooper Union in New York City, he dismissed Southerners as people who "will not" listen and who "speak of us Republicans . . . only to denounce us as reptiles, or, at the best, as no better than outlaws." In response, he urged Republicans to hold their ground, defy "Disunionists," and have faith "THAT RIGHT MAKES MIGHT." At length and with great care he set forth evidence that the Founding Fathers had intended to control and limit slavery in the territories.[10]

Elected president, Lincoln faced an unprecedented crisis: the secession of seven slaveholding states before he could even take office. Despite pressures from various groups to find a compromise and pacify the South,

Lincoln stood firm on the territorial issue. He instructed Republican leaders in Congress not to give way, and without a compromise on the territories, events moved inevitably toward conflict.

LINCOLN'S LEADERSHIP AS PRESIDENT

In the nation's highest office, Lincoln's strategy of leadership changed. No longer was he mobilizing a new party in an atmosphere of sectional conflict. Lincoln now saw himself as the elected leader of a larger entity with a constitutional duty to preserve the whole nation, including the South. Even after war came and four more Southern states seceded, he repeatedly offered conciliation to the rebellious Southern states. In wartime Northern politics, Lincoln never forgot that his Democratic opponents were a vigorous and very sizable minority. They frequently attacked the Republicans as radical abolitionists who planned to destroy slave property and make African Americans equal. President Lincoln tried to prove them wrong and maintain essential unity. Thus, his policies were more moderate, more centrist, than his divisive prewar rhetoric would have predicted, and he succeeded in aggregating and building support for emancipation as a necessary war measure.

In his inaugural address, Lincoln reminded Southerners that he had consistently pledged not to disturb slavery where it already existed. Going far beyond that, he gave his support to a constitutional amendment that Congress had already proposed—an amendment to prohibit Congress, permanently, from interfering with slavery in the states. In addition, Lincoln promised not to initiate a war, argued that a reasonable adjustment of fugitive slave laws should be possible, pledged not to force "obnoxious" appointees upon the South, and argued for the practical and transcendent value of Union. These steps did not appease the seceded states, but Northern Democrats remembered his words about not attacking slavery and would frequently remind the public of them.[11]

Once the war was under way, Lincoln worked to retain support in the Union's slaveholding border states and among Northern Democrats. Congress and much of the Northern public soon saw that slavery aided the rebel cause and must be attacked, but Lincoln moved more slowly. He repeatedly recommended gradual emancipation and colonization of freed Black people "in a climate congenial to them." He called only for financial aid to states that might voluntarily choose to emancipate. When two military commanders issued declarations of emancipation, in August 1861 and May 1862, Lincoln overruled them both. Though he was criticized for slowness and weak policies, Lincoln retained the support of many Democratic editors for more than a year.[12]

By the summer of 1862, however, a lack of military progress was causing great public dissatisfaction, and Lincoln decided that he had to change his policy or lose the game. On September 22, 1862, he issued the Preliminary Emancipation Proclamation, whose terms are little remembered by most citizens today. In fact, on the sesquicentennial of that proclamation, the Associated Press distributed an article incorrectly declaring that Lincoln required the South to give up slavery and return to the Union. In fact, he gave the rebellious states one hundred days to return to the Union and *keep* their slaves. The offer was real, for Lincoln dispatched envoys to urge rebels to accept his offer. Politically, this formula also allowed Republicans to put the blame for any emancipation on the rebels. In addition, Lincoln justified his action as a necessary war measure issued by the commander in chief, whose purpose remained the preservation of the Union, not the abolition of slavery. A racist backlash that Lincoln had feared did contribute to substantial Republican losses in the fall congressional elections. But with time more Northerners came to accept, as a necessary war measure, the final Emancipation Proclamation, issued on January 1, 1863.[13]

Within a week of that date, Gen. John McClernand reported that some prominent Southern slaveholders wanted to reenter the Union, if they could keep their slaves. Defending his declaration of emancipation, Lincoln replied that it would stand and that "broken eggs can not be mended." That colorful phrase is frequently mentioned in praise of Lincoln's antislavery firmness. Yet Lincoln was willing to extend his deadline, for at the end of his letter he wrote that McClernand's "friends" could "have peace upon the old terms" if they "should act at once . . . with entire safety, as far as I am concerned."[14]

Another important conciliatory step came only two and a half weeks after the Gettysburg Address. On December 8, 1863, Lincoln proposed a lenient "10 percent plan" of Reconstruction, whose terms showed that the "new birth of freedom" invoked at Gettysburg included little for African Americans beyond emancipation. This plan sacrificed the interests of freed people in order to appeal to Southern whites, whom he called a "deeply afflicted people." As long as returning rebels accepted emancipation and provided some form of education for Black people, Lincoln would allow them to establish "temporary arrangements" defining the status of the freed people. Candidly he explained to Congress that he "hoped that the already deeply afflicted people in the States may be somewhat more ready to give up the cause of their affliction," slavery, if "this vital matter be left to themselves." His "new birth of freedom" would fall far short of equal rights.[15]

The "slowness" or moderation in all these policies was criticized by some Republicans, but toward the end of the war and in later generations, it has won praise. In a sustained crisis, while presiding over a deeply divided and racist electorate, the president had been careful not to move too rapidly for Northern opinion. As the *North American Review* observed in January 1864, Lincoln had understood the politician's duty not "to anticipate public opinion" but to wait for the "maturing of popular conviction," which often was "slow." He wisely avoided "try[ing] to lead [the people] where they were averse to follow." The *Atlantic Monthly* agreed, saying, "Many of us thought that the President issued his Emancipation Proclamation at least a year too late; but we must now see that the time . . . was as skillfully chosen as its aim was laudable."[16]

Once the Emancipation Proclamation was issued, many elected Democrats and a large majority of Democratic newspapers savaged Lincoln for hypocrisy and racial radicalism. But a key segment of that party's leadership viewed themselves as War Democrats and gave considerable support to the administration. By 1864 Republicans, aspiring to as broad a base of support as possible and courting those War Democrats, renamed their party the Union Party. Eighty-three percent of the congressional contests in 1864 featured a Unionist—who was often a prowar Democrat—running against a Democrat irreconcilably opposed to Lincoln's policies. Lincoln's failure to embrace racial equality had paid dividends in his racist Northern society.[17]

NORTHERN RACISM AND WHITE
SUPREMACIST BELIEFS

Republican shortcomings become easier to understand when one looks seriously at the depth of racist, white supremacist attitudes in the North, especially in the Democratic Party. In the first place, for many Northerners slavery simply was not a problem. "The right to hold slaves," said one Democratic congressman, "is as clear and defined as the holding of any other species of property." Another admitted that "the free States dislike slavery . . . as they have the right to do." But "the slave States," he insisted, "have provided for and tolerate its existence, as they have an *equal* right to do." Democratic leaders believed that it was completely possible for the United States to be a nation half-slave and half-free. Even *Harper's Magazine*, which was one of the few major publications to denounce prejudice, accurately observed that "we of the North have never liked slavery. But the bulk of us have believed that it was not our business to interfere with it where it existed."[18]

Democrats and many others believed that the United States was a white man's country. Stephen Douglas, the most prominent Northern Democrat until his death in 1861, had declared, "This government was established on the white basis. It was made by the white men for the benefit of white men and their posterity forever, and never should be administered by any except white men." Democrats like Delaware's Senator Willard Saulsbury frequently repeated this formula in Congress on numerous occasions. To applause from the galleries Saulsbury thundered that "this country is the white man's country. . . . You cannot bring up the filthy negro to the elevation of the white man. . . . the white man shall govern." The danger posed by the Republican Party was that it would not protect "the social and political supremacy of the white race over the black." To Democrats, Republicans like Lincoln were trying to conceal radical, abolitionist goals that would overthrow the Constitution and break up the Union. Republicans supposedly aimed to subjugate whites and turn "loose 3,500,000 slaves . . . to devastate the country and prey upon its inhabitants."[19]

Democratic newspapers went far beyond these arguments to indulge in virulent, scurrilous invective against African Americans. The *New York Journal of Commerce* condemned Black people as "savages," and the *Cincinnati Daily Enquirer* called them "cousins" of gorillas and chimpanzees. Standard commentary by other papers agreed that Black people were a "distinct species of brutes," a "degraded and brutal" race, a barbarous people markedly inferior to whites. African Americans were "worthless," a "debased and irreclaimably barbarous" race, lazy, ignorant, and cowardly. Such vicious and hostile attitudes were general in Northern society, and to multiply examples, especially those that use even more vile language, would simply offend modern morality.[20] Even the *New York Times*, whose editor, Henry Raymond, became chair of the Republican National Committee in 1864, denied that Republicans "believe the negro race to be the equal of the white race." Only "a very small and insignificant portion" of the population favored equality, declared the *Times*, and "we do not advocate, because we do not believe in, negro equality."[21]

Upsetting the racial order was certain to bring catastrophe, argued Democrats. The "imbecile" Lincoln was "making a God of Sambo" and "inciting slaves to insurrection" through acts of "arson, rapine, and slaughter." His intention was to "flood the North" with free Blacks and "take the bread from the white man's mouth." "Swarms" of Black soldiers would come North, worried a Vermont newspaper. The Republicans wanted to send "Negro Paupers Northward" and then pass "laws to compel social equality and the association of the races." The "Negro Invasion," warned a Democratic newspaper in

Illinois, would deprive "white children of the necessaries of life" and begin "the Conflict of White Labor with Negroes." The massive "influx" that would Africanize the North meant poverty and suffering for white laboring men and their families.[22]

Democrats charged that the Emancipation Proclamation was "a gigantic usurpation," an act of "superlative wickedness" that would bring about "the destruction of the liberties of the people and the death of the Republic." Lincoln, they said, cared only about the Negro, and under his leadership, "The white race is to be burdened to the earth for the benefit of the black race."[23] Lincoln did not understand that "there is an utter repugnance on the part of the white race to any association on terms of equality with the negroes of the country."[24] "White people are forgotten," complained a Wisconsin critic. Lincoln's "unconstitutional crusade" would make "one half of the country a howling wilderness" and "elevate to the status of citizenship a worthless and improvident race."[25]

Before the end of the war, Democrats found ways to intensify their racist threats. The Emancipation Proclamation signaled that "in about a year [the Republicans] will cry, political equality for slaves—social, civil political equality" of the races. "Freeing a few millions of miserable negroes" meant ruin for the nation, said Democrats, and some charged that the North was already "Africanized" by a part-Negro president.[26] Black Union troops, according to the *New York World*, committed "all manner of atrocities" in North Carolina, and the *Chicago Times* charged that Black soldiers in Vicksburg "committed the greatest possible outrages" on white women.[27]

Worse, it was supposedly the purpose of the fanatical Republicans to promote race mixing, a sexual scenario that appalled most Northern whites. When Frederick Douglass spoke to the Ladies Loyal League of Chicago, the *Chicago Times* complained that "whites amalgamated lovingly" with Black people, and the ladies "crowded around the lecturer and communed with him very lovingly."[28] Such a disgusting display gave "strong confirmation to the advancing doctrine of miscegenation." "Miscegenation" was itself a new word, invented by two Democratic journalists to spread fear of racial mixture. These two men published a pamphlet entitled *Miscegenation: The Theory of the Blending of the Races, Applied to the American White Man and Negro,* which praised interracial sex as "essential to American progress." Race mixing would make Americans "the finest race on earth." Disguising their purpose, these writers succeeded in obtaining endorsements of their ideas from several incautious abolitionists. Then Democratic newspapers and Congressman Samuel Sullivan Cox denounced these "abominations" and charged that "progressive intermingling" was supposedly "the Republican solution."[29]

Cox's speech on the floor of the House "got enormous attention from the press." An Indiana editor, for example, asserted that miscegenation "is the platform the abolition party is destined ere long to occupy." The national Democratic Party distributed reprints of the pamphlet as Campaign Document no. 11 under the title "Miscegenation Indorsed by the Republican Party." Other campaign documents featured drawings of Black men with huge lips kissing white women. Soon, Democrats warned, "Our legislators will be of the thick-lipped and wooley-headed fraternity" and "the white laboring man" would be reduced "to the despised and degraded condition of the black man."[30]

This kind of vile propaganda was not the only sign that racism was a potent force in the period of emancipation. Urban race riots across the North gave further proof of white supremacist attitudes, especially from the summer of 1862 through the summer of 1863. Newspapers warned that Ohio was "to be Africanized" and reported that more than forty thousand citizens had signed a petition to keep African Americans out of the state. In Cincinnati a mob stripped Black men naked and in seven days of "riot, terror, and vandalism" attacked Black homes, property, and churches. Only a few days later "a fearful riot" broke out in Toledo, with "the loss of one or two lives" and "several wounded."[31]

By 1863 labor competition turned to conflict in Calumet, Indiana; Columbus, Ohio; and Belleville, Illinois. "Failed labor strikes in Boston, Brooklyn, Albany, Cleveland, and Chicago were all blamed on black competition. White strikers in Buffalo killed several blacks and injured many others," and longshoremen along New York's East River "set out upon a Negro hunt." A frightening riot in Detroit in March 1863 was based on rumors that a Black man raped a white girl or ran an "amalgamation den." Newspapers elsewhere commented that the affair proved the "radical hostility of the white race of the North" toward "all political schemes that would elevate the negro to political equality with the white man." Federal troops fought Black people in Harrisburg, Pennsylvania, just a few weeks before the infamous New York City race riot. Estimates of the number of killed in New York were at least 105, and a committee of merchants declared that "atrocities" committed on the body of one man were "so indecent, they are unfit for publication." The *New York Tribune* called the draft "merely the occasion of the outbreak; absolute disloyalty and hatred to the negro were the moving cause." Modern scholarship has agreed that an antidraft riot quickly turned into an effort "to erase the post-emancipation presence of the Black community."[32]

REPUBLICAN STRATEGIES, LINCOLN'S COMPASSION, AND THE NEED FOR RADICALISM

Given these realities, Lincoln and most Republicans shrank from endorsing equality and the principle that "all men are created equal." The Emancipation Proclamation had made them vulnerable to the charge that they were going to overturn racial mores and destroy white supremacy. In response they insisted that emancipation was solely a necessary war measure, and in addition they developed another important strategy. Republicans argued that, whatever the future of the former slaves, either they would stay in the South, or at some time and in some way they would leave the nation. In no case would they move into the North to challenge its customs and practices. Although some progress had occurred in Northern racial attitudes, especially among some soldiers who had fought beside Black regiments, the vast majority of whites vigorously opposed equality. Society's racism infected the Republican Party and its leadership, and few today appreciate how much the party of emancipation conformed to racist social norms.

Except for a minority of abolitionists in their ranks, wartime Republicans believed that African Americans were entitled to freedom and some rights, but not to social or political equality. These attitudes were patent in Lincoln's Cabinet. Secretary of the Navy Gideon Welles "would not enslave the negro" but opposed enfranchisement and did not "want him at my table, nor do I care to have him in the jury-box, or in the legislative hall, or on the bench." Edward Bates, Lincoln's attorney general, issued a pathbreaking legal opinion that Black people were citizens. Still, he believed that "voting and holding office" were a "privilege . . . not essential to citizenship, no more so in case of a negro than in the case of a white woman or child." Bates viewed Republican radicals like Charles Sumner with hostility and hoped Lincoln would always be a barrier against their "reckless, revolutionary spirit." The *New York Times* represented most Republicans' views when it wrote that Black people were not equal but were entitled to life, liberty, and the pursuit of happiness. To the *Times*, African Americans were "the most ignorant and degraded race of beings to be found in any civilized country." If they should vote, then "there is no good reason why the franchise should be withheld from children and idiots—to say nothing of women."[33]

To blunt the Democrats' warnings of racial change, Republicans separated emancipation from equality. Freed people did not gain equal rights, and the end of slavery in the South would not disturb Northern racial arrangements. Republicans declared that freed people would not come to "the cold North" but would remain in the South or move farther southward out of the country. Thus, emancipation, according to the Republican argument, would not affect race relations at home.[34]

For example, Pennsylvania's Representative William Kelley contradicted Democratic warnings of an invasion of freed people into the North. Instead, Black people would drift southward, since "nature has given [them] the monopoly of the wealth" of "the tropical and malarious regions of Central America" and "will bless the world by making [themselves] the master of it." James Patterson of New Hampshire similarly argued that the "African . . . gravitates to the tropics as naturally and as certainly as the winged people of the air migrate at the approach of winter." The *New York Times* agreed that "emancipation would not only keep the enfranchised slaves at the South, but would also draw thither the free negroes of the Northern States." The *New York Tribune*'s editor, Horace Greeley, echoed the popular view that "the natural drift of the blacks is toward the tropics" and predicted that freed people in the upper South would move toward the Gulf states.[35]

Despite such theories of a drift to the topics, colonization continued to be discussed throughout the war. Most Northern newspapers and magazines decided such schemes were impractical or undesirable (since Black labor would be needed in the postwar South), but the idea did not disappear. In 1864 Kansas's Senator James Lane proposed "to set apart a portion of the State of Texas for the use of persons of African descent" since the "people of the North and Northwest" had a "repugnance to legal amalgamation with the African." Montgomery Blair, Lincoln's postmaster general, praised separation as "the highest wisdom" and an "instinct of self preservation." His brother Frank, an important congressman and general, repeatedly promoted colonization in Central America as a way to extend national influence and rid the United States of "a class of men . . . worse than useless to us." Wisconsin's Senator James Doolittle, convinced that Black people and white people "cannot live in the same Government," made detailed statistical arguments to prove that removal was possible. Thus, New York Democrat Horatio Seymour had a point when he said, "The South holds that the African is fit to live here as a slave" but "our republican government denies that he is fit to live here at all."[36]

Lincoln himself dispatched close to four hundred willing Black people to an island off Haiti in 1863. This experiment proved to be a costly failure, as some of his advisers had warned, and he had to bring back the survivors a year later. Still, the president reacted with interest during 1864 to overtures from various European nations that sought labor for their possessions in the

Caribbean.[37] As victory approached, however, Lincoln's concern for African Americans grew.

In the last months of his life, he developed a constructive moral vision that finally placed him ahead of public opinion. Fervently hoping to leave war's killing and destruction behind, an idealistic Lincoln called for "malice toward none" and charity and compassion for all. In this changed, forgiving spirit, he reached out to Blacks and Southern whites. First, he successfully urged the lame-duck Congress to approve the Thirteenth Amendment. Then, a few days before his death, he declared a personal preference that some Black men would be allowed to vote—the "very intelligent" and US Army veterans. Yet in that same speech he argued that defeated Southern whites should be allowed to vote on ratification of the amendment. Convincing a sufficient number of seceded states to accept emancipation would be problematic, but Lincoln wanted the rebels' cooperation to be voluntary. He was hoping for a reunion with reconciliation and racial progress, if not yet equal rights for all.

Thus, during the war neither Lincoln nor his party embraced political or social equality for Black Americans. They maintained a racist distance from the ideals of the Declaration of Independence. Although Charles Sumner and a few others advocated for Black rights, most Republicans did not agree and probably felt they had no choice as politicians in a society where racism was nearly ubiquitous. For those reasons, progress toward American ideals depended on radicals whom many deplored or despised.

Abolitionists outside government championed that unpopular cause, but Black leaders and enslaved people surpassed many of their white allies. Even William Lloyd Garrison argued that emancipation "would draw [the Black] race ... to the South," rather than demanding equal rights in the North.[38] Southern enslaved people influenced policy from the first days of the war, as thousands poured into Union lines and demonstrated their usefulness to the cause. Northern Black leaders such as Frederick Douglass immediately argued that the war was "a war for and against slavery." Only by "LET[TING] THE OPPRESSED GO FREE" could the Union find "DELIVERANCE AND SAFETY!" The "inexorable logic of events," he declared, would force the government to emancipate. Only four months into the war, when the Lincoln administration was returning runaway slaves to their owners, James McCune Smith lectured the white abolitionist Gerrit Smith that "the only salvation of this nation is Immediate Emancipation." Black leaders demanded that African Americans be allowed to serve in the army, for as Douglass put it, "Once let the black man get upon his person" the nation's uniform, "there is no power on earth which can deny that he has earned the right to citizenship in the United States."[39]

Military service and citizenship, these men asserted, entitled African Americans to equal rights. "Our fathers have fought for this country, and helped to free it from the British yoke," declared J. W. C. Pennington. "We are now fighting to help to free it from the combined conspiracy of Jeff. Davis and Co.; we are doing so with the distinct understanding, that WE ARE TO HAVE ALL OUR RIGHTS AS MEN AND AS CITIZENS, and that there are to be no side issues, no RESERVATIONS, either political, civil, or religious." A convention of Blacks in Kansas told whites that "to deprive any portion of the native population of this country of so essential a right as that of suffrage, is to do violence to the genius of American Institutions, and is a departure from the aims of the illustrious founders of the Republic." Black leaders would "hear nothing of degradation or of ignorance of the black man" as an excuse to deny him the ballot. "If he knows an honest man from a thief," said Frederick Douglass, "he knows more than some of our white voters." Any qualifications or tests for voting must be applied equally to all.[40]

Black newspapers pointed out the importance of economic opportunity for the freed people even before 1861 had come to an end. "What course can be clearer," asked the *Anglo-African*, "what course more politic . . . what course so just, so humane . . . as that the government should immediately bestow [confiscated] lands upon these freed men who know best how to cultivate them . . . lands which they have bought and paid for by their sweat and blood?" Boston's John Rock agreed and challenged all "talk about compensating masters. Compensate them for what? . . . It is the slave who ought to be compensated." Rock told a white audience that "if you do your duty, posterity will give you the honor of being the first nation that dared to deal justly by the oppressed."[41]

Black leaders from Louisiana told Northerners after the capture of New Orleans that "the character of the whole people must be changed. As slavery is abolished, with it must vanish every vestige of oppression. The right to vote must be secured; the doors of our public schools must be opened, that our children, side by side, may study from the same books, and . . . learn the great truth that God 'created of one blood all the nations of men.'" Northern leaders did not go so far. Fully aware of the depth of Northern racism, Frederick Douglass invoked a formula common to many Black spokesmen. "What we want is perfect civil, religious and political equality," said Douglass. Social equality "is something that will settle and regulate itself." "All we ask is equal opportunities and equal rights," said John Rock. The ballot and equal rights were essential; purely social discrimination could be allowed to disappear in future years as the stigma of slavery faded.[42]

Rejecting all talk of colonization, a huge majority of the North's Black leaders demanded their rights as American citizens. When Lincoln promoted colonization to Black leaders from Washington, DC, Douglass excoriated the president's "pride of race and blood, his contempt for negroes and his canting hypocrisy." Lincoln's words "furnish[ed] a weapon to all the ignorant and base." "We were born here," declared Robert Purvis, "and here we choose to remain. . . . Don't advise me to leave, and don't add insult to injury by telling me it's for my own good. . . . Sir, this is our country as much as it is yours, and we will not leave it." John Rock agreed and eloquently defined the task ahead: "This being our country, we have made up our mind to remain in it, and to try to make it worth living in." African Americans would focus on "working our way up in this country, and in civilizing the whites." Almost alone, these Black men grasped the full meaning of the ideals of the Declaration of Independence.[43]

Heeding their leaders' advice, Northern Blacks in many cities and towns pressed for equal treatment. In California in 1863 they won a repeal of laws banning Black testimony against whites, and in Illinois they successfully pressured the legislature to repeal its discriminatory Black Laws in early 1865. Lawsuits or protests against discrimination in public transport succeeded in Chicago, New York, Cincinnati, and Boston. In 1864 the Kansas legislature passed a bill "making local school boards responsible for the support and supervision of public schools for blacks." Such gains were partial and localized but important; they also presaged future organizational efforts by African Americans seeking justice.[44]

The progress of the war years often filled Black leaders with joy and hope, but they learned in the summer of 1864 that their gains remained insecure in a white democracy. Amid burgeoning war-weariness in the North, Lincoln met calls for peace negotiations by declaring that he would entertain any proposition that embraced peace, reunion, "and the abandonment of slavery." Immediately there were angry protests against making "the abandonment of slavery" a condition for peace. Democrats charged that Lincoln's "negro mania" would prolong the war and cost the lives of "tens of thousands" of whites. With his reelection in danger, Lincoln and his allies devised a slippery argument—he had *not* ruled out considering something "*else* or *less*," and therefore emancipation was not a "'sine qua non'" for reunion.[45]

Black leaders, meeting in convention in Syracuse, New York, were dismayed and angered. It was "very evident," they protested, "that the

Republican party . . . is not prepared to make the abolition of slavery, in all the Rebel states," a requirement for reunion. Fearing that the administration might be willing to make peace not only "with the Rebels, but . . . with slavery also," the convention condemned Republicans' "contempt for the character and rights of the colored race" that these events revealed.[46]

What we know about subsequent history confirms the fears of Black leaders. White supremacy, the idea that "this is a white man's country," did not end with emancipation or the Civil War's important steps toward equality. The virulent racist rhetoric of the period constituted a virtual tsunami in public discourse. For many, prejudice may have become more normal and acceptable due to the enormous volume of racist warnings, threats, and denunciations. In some respects, these pernicious ideas may have taken deeper root, even as war was pruning their branches. For all it accomplished, the Civil War did not realize completely the ideas of the Declaration of Independence. It achieved, at best, only a partial repudiation of the idea of "a white man's country."

The history of the next 154 years has shown that the passions and interests served by racism remain a central challenge for the United States. At a time when racism and white supremacy continue to infect American democracy, the Black leaders and abolitionists who courageously pressed for racial equality, pushing beyond Lincoln and other political leaders of the time, offer important examples for contemporary leaders seeking to challenge racism, expand representation, and secure liberty and justice for all.

NOTES

1. Richard Striner, *Father Abraham: Lincoln's Relentless Struggle to End Slavery* (New York: Oxford University Press, 2006), 2, 219.
2. It is important to remember that Lincoln aspired to gain majorities from a nearly lily-white electorate. White people comprised 99 percent of the population of the free states and 96.5 percent of the loyal states (including Missouri, Kentucky, Delaware, and Maryland). For these statistics, see Gary W. Gallagher, *The Union War* (Cambridge: Harvard University Press, 2011), 4.
3. Many who joined the new Republican Party were Whigs, like Lincoln, but antislavery Democrats (like the Blairs) also helped to form the new organization. This fact created an additional dimension of challenge for Lincoln in holding his coalition together during the crisis of the Civil War.
4. Abraham Lincoln, "Peoria Speech, October 16, 1854," available online at https://www.nps.gov/liho/learn/historyculture/peoriaspeech.htm; Martin Luther King Jr., "Letter from Birmingham Jail," https://www.africa.upenn.edu/Articles_Gen/Letter_Birmingham.html. The quotation appears near the end of King's letter.
5. Lincoln, "Peoria Speech."

6. Lincoln.

7. Lincoln; William W. Freehling, in *Becoming Lincoln* (Charlottesville: University of Virginia Press, 2018), 48, 100, 172, 147, argues that earlier personal and political setbacks taught Lincoln the benefits of moderation and of not outrunning public opinion. Perhaps Lincoln also agreed with a writer today who has observed that "Humans find it easier to bond over fear than hope" (Gideon Rose, "The Fourth Founding: The United States and the Liberal Order," *Foreign Affairs* 98, no. 1 [January/February 2019], 14).

8. William E. Gienapp, ed., *This Fiery Trial: The Speeches and Writings of Abraham Lincoln* (New York: Oxford University Press, 2002), 43–51.

9. These quotations from the Lincoln-Douglas debates may be found in Gienapp, *This Fiery Trial*, 54, 58, 56, 60.

10. Gienapp, 71, 80, 81, and the extensive first half of the speech, which may be found in *Abraham Lincoln: Selected Writings* (New York: Barnes & Noble, 2013), 579–86.

11. For the text of Lincoln's first Inaugural Address, see Gienapp, *This Fiery Trial*, 88–97. Many Democratic newspapers prominently displayed Lincoln's pre-emancipation pledges in order to discredit him.

12. See Paul D. Escott, *"What Shall We Do with the Negro?": Lincoln, White Racism, and Civil War America* (Charlottesville: University of Virginia Press, 2009), 34; Gienapp, *This Fiery Trial*, 118–20, 108–11, 122–24; and Lincoln's annual address to Congress in 1861, available online at https://www.presidency.ucsb.edu/documents/first-annual-message-9.

13. The text of the Preliminary Emancipation Proclamation may be found online at the National Archives and Records Administration, https://www.archives.gov/exhibits/american_originals_iv/sections/transcript_preliminary_emancipation.html. The text of the final Emancipation Proclamation may be found at the National Archives' "Milestone Documents" page, https://www.ourdocuments.gov/doc.php. Lincoln's efforts to encourage southern whites to take advantage of his preliminary proclamation are described in William W. Freehling, *The South vs. the South: How Anti-Confederate Southerners Shaped the Course of the Civil War* (New York: Oxford University Press, 2001), 111.

14. The letter to McClernand, dated January 8, 1863, may be found in Gienapp, *This Fiery Trial*, 153–54.

15. See Gienapp, 183–84 for the Gettysburg Address and 185–92 for his 10 percent plan of Reconstruction, with the accompanying message to Congress.

16. *North American Review*, January 1864, 249–50, 254–55, and January 1865, 14–15, 18, 19; *Atlantic Monthly*, November 1864, 639–40.

17. Jack Furniss, "States of the Union: The Rise and Fall of the Political Center in the Civil War North" (PhD diss., University of Virginia, 2018), 14–17. Furniss cites the important work of Michel Holt on the 1864 congressional races.

18. Representative John Law of Indiana, speaking on May 26, 1862, 37th Cong., 2nd sess., *Appendix to the Congressional Globe*, 271; Representative W. P. Noble of Ohio, speaking on June 6, 1862, 37th Cong., 2nd sess., *Appendix to the Congressional Globe*, 293; *Harper's Magazine*, May 4, 1861, 274. In May 1862 fifteen Democrats in Congress published an address that affirmed "the absolute compatibility of a union of the States 'part slave and part free'" ("Adress of Democratic Members of Congress to the Democracy of the United States," 1864, https://babel.hathitrust.org/cgi/pt?id=loc.ark:/13960/t2v40tv6h).

19. Douglas made this statement in his fourth debate with Lincoln in 1858; *Congressional Globe*, 37th Cong., 2nd sess., April 3, 1862, May 2, 1862, 1526, 1923; *Cadiz Democratic Sentinel*, June 4, 1862, 2, July 2, 1862; *Joliet (Illinois) Signal*, October 28, 1862, 2.

20. *New York Journal of Commerce*, August 23, 1861; *Cincinnati Daily Enquirer*, April 6, 1862, 1; *Dollar Weekly*, quoting the Lafayette, Iowa, *Democratic Herald*, January 8, 1863, 2; *Cincinnati Daily Enquirer*, December 12, 1962, 2; Indianapolis *Daily State Sentinel*, May 22, 1862, 2; *Congressional Globe*, 37th Cong., 2nd sess., March 12, 1862, 1180; *Chicago Times*, quoted in the Savannah, Georgia, *Daily News*, January 15, 1863. For more details and extensive evidence, see Paul D. Escott, *"The Worst Passions of Human Nature": White Supremacy in the Civil War North* (Charlottesville: University of Virginia Press, 2020).

21. *New York Times*, March 29, 1863.

22. Vermont *Watchman and State Sentinel*, February 6, 1863, 1; *Cincinnati Enquirer*, January 27, 1862, 2, January 3, 1863; *Hartford Times*, quoted in the *New Haven Daily Palladium*, October 29, 1862; Woodstock, Vermont, *Spirit of the Age*, October 15, 1862, 2; *Jasper (Indiana) Weekly Courier*, June 11, 1862, 1, and January 17, 1863, 1; *Cadiz Democratic Sentinel*, November 12, 1862, 1; *Joliet Signal*, October 7, 1862, 1; *Cincinnati Daily Enquirer*, October 14, 1862, 2; *Plymouth (Indiana) Weekly Democrat*, July 31, 1862, 2.

23. Resolution of the Illinois Legislature on the Emancipation Proclamation, January 7, 1863, http://plaza.ufl.edu/edale/Resolution%20of%20the%20Illinois%20Legislature%20 in%20Opposition%20to%20the%20Emancipation%20Proclamation.htm; Resolutions of the New Jersey Legislature, March 18, 1863, in *Documents of American History*, 7th ed., ed. Henry Steele Commager (New York: Appleton-Century-Crofts, 1963), 427–28; Congressman Richardson, speaking on December 8, 1862, 37th Cong., 3rd sess., *Appendix to the Congressional Globe*, 39; *Ebensburg Democrat and Sentinel*, January 7, 1863, 2.

24. Congressman Jas. S. Rollins, speaking on February 2, 1863, 37th Cong., 3rd sess., *Appendix to the Congressional Globe*, 45–46, 86, 104.

25. *La Crosse Weekly Democrat*, January 6, 1863, 2; *Chicago Times*, quoted in the *Indianapolis Daily State Sentinel*, January 6, 1863, 2; *Jasper (Indiana) Weekly Courier*, January 10, 1863, 2.

26. *New York World*, February 12, 1864, February 22, 1864; *Cincinnati Daily Enquirer*, April 21, 1984, April 25, 1864, 2, April 28, 1864.

27. *New York World*, March 5, 1864; *Chicago Times*, quoted in the Columbia *Daily South Carolinian*, May 6, 1864.

28. *Chicago Times*, quoted in the *Daily Richmond Examiner*, April 5, 1864.

29. See Escott, *"What Shall We Do with the Negro?,"* 126–28; Congressman Samuel Sullivan Cox, speaking on February 17, 1864, 38th Cong., 1st sess., *Congressional Globe*, 708–13; *New York World*, March 17, 1864.

30. Leonard Richards, *Who Freed the Slaves? The Fight over the Thirteenth Amendment* (Chicago: University of Chicago Press, 2015), 172; *Jasper Weekly Courier*, April 16, 1864, 1; *Miscegenation Indorsed by the Republican Party*, see especially quotations from pages 1, 5, 6, 7, 8, 2; *What Miscegenation Is!*, Samuel May Anti-Slavery Collection, Division of Rare and Manuscripts Collection, Cornell University.

31. *Daily Ohio Statesman*, May 24, 1862, 2; *Cincinnati Enquirer*, July 16, 1862, 2, and May 1, 1862, 2; Nikki M. Taylor, *Frontiers of Freedom: Cincinnati's Black Community, 1802–1868* (Athens: Ohio University Press, 2005), 197–98; *Cadiz Democratic Sentinel*, July 23, 2, June 18, 1862, 1.

32. Ottawa, Illinois, *Free Trader*, March 14, 1863, 2; David Williams, *I Freed Myself: African American Self-Emancipation in the Civil War Era* (New York: Cambridge University Press, 2014), 121–22; *Detroit Free Press*, March 13, 1863; *Anti-Negro Riots in the North, 1863* (New York: Arno Press, 1969), iv, 19, 10, 3; Barnet Schecter, *The Devil's Own Work: The Civil War Draft Riots and the Fight to Reconstruct America* (New York: Walker, 2005), 106. According to the Ashtabula, Ohio, *Weekly Telegraph* (March 14, 1863, 2), thirty-two homes of African Americans were destroyed, and eight hundred people in all were affected. *The Alleghanian*, June 4, 1863, 2. For studies of the New York City draft riots, see Iver Bernstein, *The New York City Draft Riots: Their Significance for American Society and Politics in the Age of the Civil War* (New York: Oxford University Press, 1990); James McCague, *The Second Rebellion: The Story of the New York City Draft Riots of 1863* (New York: Dial Press, 1968); Schecter, *The Devil's Own Work*; and Joel Tyler Headley, *The Great Riots of New York, 1712–1873* (Indianapolis: Bobbs Merrill, 1970). This brief account is based on the above as quoted and cited in Paul D. Escott, *Lincoln's Dilemma: Blair, Sumner, and the Republican Struggle over Racism and Equality in the Civil War Era* (Charlottesville: University of Virginia Press, 2014), 167–68. The quotation from the *New York Tribune* was from July 14, 1863, 1.

33. Gideon Welles, *Diary of Gideon Welles, Secretary of the Navy under Lincoln and Johnson*, vol. 2 (Boston: Houghton Mifflin, 1911), 373–74, 234, 237; *Jeffersonian Democrat*, January 9, 1863, 2 (quoting Attorney General Bates's views); *New York Times*, April 3, 1864, 4, June 8, 1864, 4.

34. *Goodhue (Minnesota) Volunteer*, October 22, 1862, 1.

35. Representative William Kelley of Pennsylvania, speaking on January 16, 1865, and James Patterson of New Hampshire, speaking on January 28, 1865, 38th Cong., 2nd sess., *Congressional Globe*, 282–82, 484; *New York Times*, December 5, 1861, 4, October 1, 1862, 4, October 7, 1862, 4; *Ashtabula Weekly Telegraph*, August 30, 1862, 1, *Cincinnati Daily Gazette*, September 23, 1862, 2.

36. *Congressional Globe*, 38th Cong., 1st sess., February 16, 1864, 673, April 25, 1864, 1844–1845; for the views of the Blairs see Escott, *Lincoln's Dilemma*, 34, 118, 112, 119; Senator James Rood Doolittle, speaking on March 19, 1862, and April 11, 1862, 37th Cong., 1st sess., *Appendix to the Congressional Globe*, 83–86 and 97–98; Horatio Seymour, Address at the Democratic State Convention at Albany, September 10, 1862, on receiving the nomination for Governor, in *Public Record: The Speeches, Messages, Proclamations, Official Correspondence, and Other Public Utterances of Horatio Seymour, from the Campaign of 1856 to the Present Time*, ed. Thomas M. Cook and Thomas W. Knox (New York: I. W. England, 1868), at https://books.google.com/books/about/Public_Record.html?id=7SpcAAAAcAAJ, 55.

37. See Phillip W. Magness and Sebastian N. Page, *Colonization after Emancipation: Lincoln and the Movement for Black Resettlement* (Columbia: University of Missouri Press, 2011); and Escott, *"What Shall We Do with the Negro?,"* 109.

38. *The Liberator*, February 14, 1862.

39. James M. McPherson, *The Negro's Civil War: How American Blacks Felt and Acted during the War for the Union* (New York: Ballantine, 1965, 1982, 1991), 16–17, 163; C. Peter Ripley, ed., *The Black Abolitionist Papers*, vol. 5, *The United States, 1859–1865* (Chapel Hill: University of North Carolina Press, 1992), 114.

40. McPherson, *The Negro's Civil War*, 76, 278, 275.

41. McPherson, 297–98.

42. McPherson, 284, 289; Ripley, *Black Abolitionist Papers*, 305.

43. McPherson, *The Negro's Civil War*, 94, 97–98, 83.

44. Hugh Davis, *"We Will Be Satisfied with Nothing Less": The African American Struggle for Equal Rights in the North during Reconstruction* (Ithaca: Cornell University Press, 2011), 15; Ripley, *Black Abolitionist Papers*, 287.

45. Gienapp, *This Fiery Trial*, 200; *New York Herald*, July 27, 1864; James M. McPherson, *Battle Cry of Freedom: The Civil War Era* (New York: Oxford University Press, 1988), 768–69.

46. *Proceedings of the National Convention of Colored Men Held in the City of Syracuse, NY, October 4, 5, 6, and 7, 1864; with the Bill of Wrongs and Rights and the Address to the American People* (Boston, MA: J. S. Rock and Geo. L. Ruffin), 50–52.

CHAPTER 10

Leadership from the Ground

Enslaved People and the Civil War

Thavolia Glymph

The question of leadership has been central to my scholarship in ways direct and indirect. I work in a field—nineteenth-century US history with a focus on slavery, the Civil War, and Reconstruction—where it is impossible to escape. It is a field that has long been defined and understood by its attention to leaders and leadership—presidential, military, and political. It has celebrated, venerated, and memorialized leading men like Abraham Lincoln, Ulysses S. Grant, William Tecumseh Sherman, Charles Sumner, Jefferson Davis, Robert E. Lee, Joseph E. Johnston, and Howell Cobb. Men have historically crowded the pages of history books and our historical memory. Many fewer women and non-white men find even occasional mention.

This essay argues for a consideration of less well-known men and women who held no formal political or military office as leaders in the story of Civil War leadership, and of the battlefields on which they fought as sites of the exercise of leadership. It offers a reconsideration of Civil War leadership to include enslaved people. Social history has encouraged us to look more closely at the actions and politics of ordinary people including the enslaved. Yet, with few exceptions, Black people do not typically come to mind when historians think about leadership in the Civil War. Harriet Tubman, the Black person most frequently cited in this category, is an exception to the rule. Even when enslaved people have been seen as bearers of military knowledge or as people who understood military tactics, that knowledge in not seen as applicable or germane to the study of leadership in Civil War classes at universities, military schools like West Point, or the US Army War College, the senior educational institution of the US Army. Nor, apparently, is it considered a legitimate topic of study in programs on Civil War leadership tailored to broader audiences interested in learning how military knowledge can be applied to other aspects of life such as staff rides offered by the US Army War College, the National Park Service, Gettysburg National Military Park, and private companies.

Ordinary people without political position or military rank, of course, do not typically lead men or women into battle. But sometimes they do, and sometimes the initiative they take can have a tremendous impact on the decisions of men who hold formal leadership positions. The Civil War provided many such instances. During the war, enslaved people drew on the knowledge of having lived in a state of war—the war zone that was slavery— and experienced the use of military-like tactics of punishment and control on plantations and beyond the plantation in the form of slave patrols. They drew on their knowledge of the political and geographical terrain of the South to map out strategies of resistance that included wartime flight. How then should we classify and understand the battlefield lines they, untrained cartographers, drew or the military knowledge upon which they called? How did Confederate and US military leaders understand and respond to enslaved people's conception of the battlefield?

In March 1863 Confederate Brig. Gen. William S. Walker, commander of the Third and Fourth Subdistricts of South Carolina, warned "all planters and owners of negroes in [his] military district to remove their negroes as far as practicable into the interior of the State, as otherwise they are liable to be lost at any moment."[1] The removal Walker called for recognized the agency of enslaved people moving under their own leadership and ideas about the battlefield and the meaning of the war. It revealed Walker's worries about a people who had decided to forge their own paths and follow their own leaders. But by rendering enslaved people in the passive voice as "negroes . . . liable to be lost," he removed any hint of their agency or leadership.[2] The language erased the antebellum slaves' war which had spread to the Civil War.

In early June 1862 Alexander, Robert, Samuel Quamer, Tony Duhar, Monday, and Thomas Hamilton took their freedom, or in the language of slaveholders, became "lost." The men fled slavery "in a rickety canoe," making it safely to a Union gunboat docked at Dewees Inlet, eleven miles north of Charleston.[3] Like other enslaved people who joined the wartime slaves' war, their flight forced US and Confederate political and military leaders to take account of them and of their battlefield plans. It forced a consideration of them in formally recognized political and military councils and the war plans of the two opposing governments. Union political and military leaders were forced to revise plans and policies to accommodate Black people. The United States eventually embraced the slaves' war against the Confederacy. The Confederacy would acknowledge that the slaves' war had spread to the battlefields of the Civil War, those mapped by white people as well as those mapped by the enslaved. The battlefield plans of Confederate leaders came to include formal acknowledgment of enslaved people as enemies and the adoption of military plans that targeted them as such as they made their way to freedom, gathered and settled in refugee camps, and were found on the battlefield enlisted as soldiers, nurses, cooks, and waged laborers.[4]

June of 1862 also saw a raid by Confederate forces on a refugee camp on Hutchinson's Island off Saint Helena Sound, South Carolina. Arriving on the scene, Union Flag Officer S. F. Du Pont reported that Black people had been "murdered in cold blood" by Confederate forces.[5] He and his men res-cued seventy survivors and carried them away from the island. Among them was a "man literally riddled with balls and buckshot (since dead); another shot through the lungs and struck over the forehead with a clubbed musket, leaving the bone perfectly bare; one woman shot in the leg, shoulder, and thigh; one far gone in pregnancy, with dislocation of the hip joint and injury to the womb, caused by leaping from a second-story window, and another with displacement of the cap of the knee and injury to the leg from the same cause."[6] The Confederate forces who attacked the refugee camp at Hutchin-son's Island no doubt saw the people there no less as enemies of the Confed-erate state than Black soldiers, and the site as a battlefield.

Largely deserted today, Hutchinson's Island is mainly salt marsh and bears no hint of the battle-scarred site it was in 1862.[7] But what if we viewed this place and others like it, similar to the way we view Gettysburg or Corinth, as battlefield sites where questions of war and leadership can be explored? What if corporations sent company officers to places like Hutchin-son's Island to learn leadership skills? What if the US Army War College con-ducted a Strategic Leader Staff Ride, one of college's most popular Strategic Leadership Experience programs, at such a site or on the grounds of what was once a refugee camp?

Army staff rides began over a hundred years ago as exercises in leadership training and command decision-making. Staff rides at Civil War battlefields like Antietam and Gettysburg are promoted to corporations as leadership development opportunities. Studying military command structures and decisions made on the battlefield, corporate leaders believe, provides unique opportunities to gain insight into decision-making, collaboration, and risk-taking. At Gettysburg National Military Park, Pickett's Charge, Little Round Top, the Wheatfield, Devil's Den, Culp's Hill, and Cemetery Ridge provide classic field sites, as does Gen. Horatio Gates's victory over the British at Saratoga.[8] One corporate executive puts it this way:

> American Revolution and Civil War battlefields contain crucial insights for the 21st century executives wrestling over issues of global decision-making, supply chain management, resource deployment, management changes, or efficient communications. Historic grounds, like Saratoga . . . or Antietam . . . are the ultimate classrooms for teaching leadership, decision-making, collaboration and risk-taking under extreme pressure. . . . Imagine walking behind Antietam Creek and standing where General McClellan watched as his Corps commanders battered Lee's army and discussing the trade-offs between the advantage of surprise vs. disruption in the marketplace. Or, standing next to the redoubt defense system at Saratoga and reflecting on the relevant role of technology/engineering and innovation in one's own corporation.[9]

It is unsurprising that staff rides and other leadership programs focus on military commanders, battles, battlefield plans, and matters of state, spaces in which men historically dominate. Yet in the case of the Civil War—and indeed in all wars—ordinary people, un-uniformed, also took up arms and the mantle of leadership and helped carry the nation through four years of war. They held no elective or appointed office. They included more well-known leaders like Harriet Tubman, Frederick Douglass, Susie King Taylor, and Robert Smalls and the less well-known like Samuel Quamer, Tony Duhar, Thomas Hamilton, Spotswood Rice, Ann Bradford Stokes, and Rose, an enslaved woman branded an outlaw by slaveholders and tracked down and killed by Confederate militia near the end of the war for her role in a wartime slave rebellion.[10]

During the Civil War, women served as laundresses, cooks, nurses, missionaries, teachers, leaders of aid societies, and manufacturers of war matériel (food and clothing for soldiers) on both sides of the conflict. Their service led to important changes in the perception of women in American society and unprecedented engagement by men with them as citizens, partisans, and leaders. When maintaining supply lines in the guerrilla-torn borderlands of Missouri and Kansas, for example, as LeeAnn Whites writes, Confederate women played a "systemic role" in the fight to establish a proslavery nation. Whites reminds us that these were not "women down on their knees begging for mercy from the Union military."[11] Whites's work helps to banish a long-standing picture of Southern Confederate women as mere passive recipients of war's brutalities. The women chronicled in her work do not fit that stereotype. Rather, they play a critical part on the Confederate front, including as leaders in their own way.

On the other side, enslaved people formed a critical part of the Union front, their leadership helping, as W. E. B. Du Bois argued, to shape the outcome of the war. In recent decades, scholars have sharpened Du Bois's argument, demonstrating the many ways Black people fought and died for the Union and freedom. Drawing on their knowledge of the South and organizational skills forged in prewar resistance to slavery, they provided leadership as they carried the slaves' war to the Civil War as soldiers and soldiers' wives, male and female military laborers, laborers on abandoned plantations managed or leased by the US government, and on the home/war front from where they continued the slaves' war.

Enslaved people helped make plantations, towns, cities, factories, and mapped military lines contested spaces. Rose's war, the slave insurgency in Pineville, South Carolina, for example, was ultimately part of the larger Union war that destroyed slavery and preserved the United States. We can find Black political and military leadership in these contests if we look. The idea of Black women combatants and Unionists did not cross the minds of most white Northerners, nor did it become a part of the everyday vocabulary about Civil War leadership. Yet when enslaved women like Rose waged war on the Confederate state or led an exodus from a plantation, we ought to pay attention to the skills honed in slavery this required.[12] President Lincoln was among those who began to pay attention.

Abraham Lincoln is one of the most studied presidents in American history and one of the most celebrated leaders. His leadership of the nation and its armies was vital to the Union victory and the destruction of slavery. But as crucial as Lincoln's talents as commander in chief and politician and the acumen of the generals under his command were to Union victory, victory was also the product of leadership and armies from below. Evidence that Lincoln increasingly recognized Black people's leadership capacity, or "the art of leading," is found in speeches and proclamations like the Preliminary Emancipation Proclamation of September 22, 1862, and the 1863 Emancipation Proclamation. Both presidential decrees acknowledged the leadership enslaved people provided to help secure their own liberation and Union victory. The Preliminary Emancipation Proclamation set a deadline of January 1, 1863, for the Confederacy to surrender or else face slave emancipation. It declared enslaved people in areas still in rebellion as of January 1, 1863, "thenceforward, and forever free," committed the federal government to use all of its powers, including its military, to "recognize and maintain" their freedom, and forbade agents of the federal government from doing anything "to repress" any efforts they made to secure "their actual freedom."[13] Lincoln thus placed a good deal of the work of making and giving meaning to "actual freedom" on the enslaved, marking his recognition of the important role enslaved people played in the work of abolition.

Prior to issuing the Preliminary Emancipation Proclamation, Lincoln urged border state slaveholders to adopt a plan of gradual compensated emancipation. Otherwise, he told them, they would witness slavery wither away "by mere friction and abrasion—by the mere incidents of the war." Appealing to their financial interests, he emphasized that gradual compensated emancipation would not only shorten the war but ensure that border state slaveholders received "substantial compensation for that which is sure to be wholly lost in any other event." "How much better for you," the president stated, "as seller, and the nation as buyer, to sell out, and buy out, that without which the war could never have been, than to sink both the thing to be sold, and the price of it, in cutting one another's throats."[14] The path Lincoln offered would have made the federal government a direct participant in the slave market as a buyer of human beings. It was not the president's best leadership moment, and he would later drop the idea.

On the question of emancipation, Lincoln faced a divided cabinet. Secretary of State William Seward, the cabinet member closest to Lincoln, advised the president to postpone any action on emancipation at least until the Union armies achieved a major victory. Otherwise, the policy might be seen as a sign of weakness, "the last measure of an exhausted government, a cry for help; the government stretching forth its hands to Ethiopia, instead of Ethiopia stretching forth her hands to the government."[15] Seward well knew, however, that "Ethiopia" had already stretched forth her hands. The evidence was in the hundreds of thousands of enslaved people who had reached out by fleeing slavery, depriving the Confederacy of valuable labor and redirecting their labor to the support of the Union. They had already done what Secretary Seward said he wanted to see. The federal government had insisted that they were extraneous to the fight. They had proven that they were in fact vital to it.

Though widely criticized for not offering freedom to all enslaved people, the Emancipation Proclamation did provide an officially sanctioned path to fight for "actual freedom" and for the enlistment of Black men as soldiers in the US Army. In these ways, it sanctioned the leadership enslaved people had already taken to make themselves free and partisans in the US Civil War.[16] Under the laws of the Confederacy, this made them outlaws subject to age-old customs of outlawry—which empowered anyone "to persecute or kill" an outlaw. Confederate proclamations of outlawry did not exempt Black women. To the scouts who executed Rose and the slaveholders who applauded the military action, Rose was an outlaw.

Despite assurances made in the president's proclamations and congressional measures, the federal government offered little protest when Confederate forces aimed their fire at enslaved women who took the path of war to make their actual freedom. Article 148 of General Orders No. 100 of April 1863 ("Instructions for the Government of Armies of the United States in the Field"), also known as the Lieber Code, denounced Confederate proclamations of outlawry as "relapses into barbarism" that would be met with "sternest retaliation."[17] It proved to be of little help to women and children refugees caught unprotected in refugee camps or on abandoned plantations.[18] Yet, Black women refugees and those who took up arms against the Confederacy on the home front, who led themselves in battle, have not found a place in scholarship on leadership, popular images of leadership, or how we imagine leadership looks. They simply do not fit.

Black people struck blows for freedom on their own accord. Their ability to score victories undoubtedly relied heavily on the presence and victories of US Army and Navy forces and on individual soldiers and sailors who practiced abolition on the ground. But they also took leadership in the work of opening a second front in the war against the Confederacy that helped to turn even terrain untouched by the opposing armies of the United States and the Confederacy into battlegrounds. These battlegrounds are largely invisible today, literally and figuratively. They do not appear on Civil War battlefield maps nor, for the most part, in Civil War history books.[19] The places where Black people fought and died and led movements against the Confederacy are not the subjects of staff rides. Yet they are as mappable as Gettysburg or Antietam. Over three days from July 1 to 3, 1863, Robert E. Lee's Army of Northern Virginia and George Meade's Army of the Potomac engaged in the largest and most deadly battle of the Civil War.[20] Today, soldiers and their officers, children on school trips, corporate leaders, families on vacation, and tourists from around the world travel by the thousands to Gettysburg National Military Park. They take staff rides and walk Devil's Den and Little Round Top and across the field to the site where the fatal Confederate assault known as Picket's Charge took place on the afternoon of July 3, 1863.

Staff rides and battlefield tours have much to teach us about the nation's history and the idea of a "new birth of freedom" immortalized in Lincoln's speech at Gettysburg. I want to suggest that we need more walking and riding of battlefields, just neglected ones, and that consecrated battlefields include the places and spaces on the home front and the battlefield where enslaved people fought and died. In walking and riding the Gettysburg battlefield and visiting other Civil War battlefields myself, I have wondered why there are no battlefield tours of the sites where refugee camps stood. One can take a tour of a former plantation and even get married on one, but there are no *plantation battlefield tours*.

While visiting a plantation on the Ashley River in South Carolina, I imagined a staff ride at the site. From the Great Cypress Swamp, the Ashley River winds through the South Carolina low country joining the Cooper River to form the Charleston Harbor before emptying into the Atlantic Ocean. More than two dozen large plantations were built here along the Ashley River Area built between 1670 and 1861 in what now comprises the Ashley River Historic District listed on the National Register of Historic Places in 1994.[21] The Magnolia Plantation is one of them. Facing financial ruin after the Civil War, Reverend John Grimké Drayton, owner of Magnolia Plantation, opened the plantation gardens—said to be the oldest public garden in the United States—in the 1870s.[22] European editions of the famous Baedeker tourist guides listed Magnolia Gardens alongside Niagara Falls and the Grand Canyon as the three "foremost attractions in America."[23]

Magnolia Plantation remains a source of revenue today and continues to be billed and seen as a site of pleasure and beauty for many. Like other plantation sites in the Ashley River Historic District, it offers up its gardens and the plantation house, the remnants of the infrastructure of rice fields—canals, trunks and dikes, rice mills—and cabins that housed enslaved people to tourists. Today, plantation tour guides are more likely to offer more historically accurate insight into the lives of the enslaved than in the past while continuing to remain problematic.

Visitors to Magnolia Plantation and its website are invited to celebrate a story of slave loyalty to the plantation South through the life of Sara Bennett Smith (1922–2019). Smith was the granddaughter of Adam Bennett, an enslaved man who tended the gardens during and after slavery and who, it is said, walked 244 miles from Magnolia to Flat Rock, North Carolina, during the Civil War to carry news to slaveholder John Grimké Drayton, who like many of his low-country neighbors had taken refuge in the mountain retreat. It is also said that Union soldiers strung him up to a tree at Magnolia and beat him during their occupation of the plantation.[24] The Magnolia Plantation website praises the Bennett family's long association with the plantation. It says nothing about slave resistance at Magnolia before and during the Civil War. It is silent on the roads enslaved men built before the war that became highways to freedom during the war and on the men and women who walked out of slavery on those roads. It is silent on the acquisition of knowledge that made it possible for Adam Bennett to travel 244 miles from the low country of South Carolina to the mountains of North Carolina and how such knowledge fueled leadership opportunities among the enslaved.

How might a staff ride over the battlefield of Magnolia Plantation help us to better understand this place as more than a site of loss for the slaveholder or an "embodiment of southern charm" and open up room for different questions about Civil War leadership? Did a leader emerge from among the six enslaved men who fled slavery "in a rickety canoe" and made it safely to a Union gunboat docked at Dewees Inlet near Charleston in 1862? Was there among them a Robert Smalls, an enslaved man who led a group of seventeen enslaved people, including his wife and two children, to Union lines aboard the Confederate steamer, the CSS *Planter*, a month later in the spring of 1862?[25] Or a Harriet Tubman who helped lead a raid that rescued over seven hundred enslaved people from several plantations in Colleton and Berkeley counties along the Combahee River the following year in an expedition known as the Combahee River Raid?

On the night of June 1, 1863, three Union gunboats moved out from Hilton Head, their destination twenty-five miles up the Combahee River from Saint Helena Sound. In his report to Secretary of War Edwin M. Stanton, Gen. David Hunter, commanding the Department of the South, called the expedition "but the initial experiment of a system of incursions which will penetrate up all the inlets, creeks, and rivers of this department. . . . injuring the enemy . . . and carrying away their slaves." It accomplished both goals, destroying rice, cotton mills, and plantation homes and carried some 725 enslaved people to freedom.[26] This is a well-known story in part because of the participation of Tubman, who had famously fled slavery in Maryland and returned several times to rescue others, and became known as General Tubman, the only woman to play an acknowledged military leadership role in the Union Army.

The site of the Combahee Ferry Raid is a potentially rich for a study of different kinds of leadership, but the battles that took place there are much less well known. We have not talked about the site of the raid as a battlefield. What was it like? What was the nature of Confederate opposition? What was the casualty rate? Did leaders emerge from among the local enslaved population? What happened when the tide turned against Union forces? These questions have generally not been incorporated into the story of the Combahee Raid.

Even the part that has been told is not considered material for exploring questions of leadership. Despite Harriet Tubman's role in the raid, military officers and business leaders do not look to her leadership to inspire soldiers or employees, or to the Black soldiers on whose intelligence she relied. There are no staff rides along the Combahee River. But what if we imagined such a program there? But what if we mapped the geography of this battlefield as we do others using contemporary sources for information on the commanders on each side, the location of the skirmishes, the casualty rate, the territory gained and lost, the property destroyed? What if, understanding that the Union expedition that moved up the Combahee River on June 2, 1863, supported an exodus of enslaved people that did not begin with it, we looked for clues of exceptional leadership and bravery beyond Tubman?

It was 4:00 A.M. on the morning of June 2 when Lt. William E. Hewitt, commander of the Fourth South Carolina Cavalry Guard, reported the presence of Union gunboats anchored off Field's Point, a small peninsula on a bend of the Combahee River, that had arrived around midnight on June 1. By 6:00 A.M. slaveholders and overseers in the area knew that Union boats were coming up the river, and a Confederate force of state troops and Combahee Rangers had assembled at William Middleton's plantation opposite the river from the Heyward plantation. Led by Col. James Montgomery and Harriet Tubman, Union forces attacked at Field's Point, dislodging a small Confederate picket protecting small earthworks built to block access to the river by Union gunboats. Leaving behind a small force to hold the site, the Union expedition continued up the river to Combahee Ferry Landing, the site of plantations belonging to Charles Lowndes and William C. Heyward.[27]

In the aftermath of the raid, some Confederate officers charged that the Confederate response to the Union incursion had been cowardly from the moment that the twenty-man Confederate guard moved on the morning of June 2 from Green Pond to Fields's Point. The reports of Confederate subordinate commanders in the aftermath of the raid spoke repeatedly of a lack of coordination, complete lack of knowledge of the local geography, and other lapses in command. "If it had not been for our ignorance of the country and of the position of the enemy at Fields' Point," one Confederate commander wrote, "we might have succeeded in capturing the greater portion of the enemy." Another admitted that "they knew nothing of the country or course of the river." The commander of the advance guard from Green Pond, unable to overcome Union forces at the Middleton mill house, quickly skedaddled back to Green Pond. Accusations abounded of Confederate soldiers delaying movement, taking up posts "very slowly," of pickets asleep at the ferry, and of general disarray.[28] A Confederate officer with 247 men, surveying the situation from Green Pond on the afternoon of June 2, delayed an attack and sent part of his command in a different direction in response to reports of fires before taking shelter from the rain. Gen. W. S. Walker ordered three companies and a cavalry unit to proceed by train to Green Pond and telegraphed Charleston requesting additional field rifles and infantry support. In the meantime, he went to Green Pond to wait for reinforcements. By that point Union forces had burned four plantations (those of William C. Heyward, William Kirkland, Joshua Nichols, and William Middleton), six mills, and removed more than seven hundred enslaved people. In the wake of the disaster for the Confederacy, Walker again called attention to the circular of March 27, 1863, that had called on slaveholders to remove enslaved people "as far as practicable into the interior of the State, as otherwise they are liable to be lost at any moment." He noted that the circular had been posted at local railroad stations and copies had been sent to two of the slaveholders who lost property in the raid.[29]

In general, one Confederate officer concluded, "there seems to have been confusion of counsel, indecision, and great tardiness of movement, an entire want of active and vigorous enterprise, without which, while they followed after the movements of the enemy, they neither opposed nor disturbed them in their work of wicked destruction." From among the many causes of the disarray, the assistant adjutant general singled out the command of Maj. W. P. Emanuel, Fourth South Carolina Cavalry, as not having "been properly drilled, disciplined, or taught by him." Emanuel's "system of outposts," he wrote, "is loose and men and officers badly instructed," and his "pickets were neither watchful nor brave," allowing "the enemy to come up to them unawares, and then retreated without offering resistance or firing a gun, allowing a parcel of negro wretches, calling themselves soldiers, with a few degraded whites, to march unmolested, with the incendiary torch, to rob, destroy, and burn a large section of the country." The result was a failure to take "intelligent and bold activity," which proved "mortifying and humiliating to our arms," he concluded, noting that steps were underway to "bring to trial the pickets at the several points named."[30]

The success of the Union expedition up the Combahee River was due, Confederate commanders concluded, not only to the incompetence of their own men. They credited the competence of the enemy "guided by persons thoroughly acquainted with the river and the country" and "the character and capacity" of Confederate forces, the enslaved.[31] "Several intelligent negroes had recently escaped to the enemy, among them a pilot reported to be thoroughly familiar with the river," Walker wrote. He believed this accounted "for the boldness and celerity of the enemy's movements." Moreover, he conceded, the enslaved "are believed to have gone with great alacrity and to some extent with preconcerted arrangements."[32]

Word of the role enslaved people on the Combahee plantations played in guiding Federal forces to and through the region quickly circulated among slaveholders, even those distant from the scene. Three days after the raid, Mary Lamont Clinch wrote from Wateree, South Carolina, about one hundred miles north of Field's Point, that "it is believed that it was all planned, for five of Mr. W. C. Heyward's negroes, went down, 5 or 6 days ago, and told them, that a good many soldiers had been removed, and brought them up to their master's place." On the Blake plantation, she added, "as soon as Mr. Blake's people heard *that they had come*, they left their work in gangs, and fled to them, evidently expecting them."[33] Confederate officers and civilians all pointed to the central role enslaved people in the region played in the success of the Union expedition. In assessing their failures in response to the Union incursion along the Combahee River, Confederate commanders, more so than Union commanders, documented the leadership of Black people that helped to turn the tide for Union military victory.

The battle at the Combahee River ferry crossing is one of many sites that could serve as a case study of Civil War military and political leadership from the perspective of the Confederacy, the Union, and the enslaved—from the failure of Confederate forces to Union military victory aided by the leadership of Black people. The latter included river boat pilots Solomon Gregory, Mott Blake, Peter Burns, Gabriel Cahern, George Chisholm, Isaac Hayward, Walter Plowden, Charles Simmons, and Sandy Suffum, who mapped out river channels and helped plot the way for Union gunboats, informed Union commanders where Confederate torpedoes had been planted, and alerted enslaved people in the region of the planned raid.[34]

William Kirkland lost the vast majority of the people he enslaved at Rosehill Plantation. According to the 1860 census, they numbered 96: 82 fled on the Union gunboats. At least half were women, girls, and infants. Kirkland valued this loss at $64,000 and reported sustaining additional losses of $27,000 in rice, damage to his home and furniture, and the loss of a threshing mill, stable and carriage house, mule stable, fodder and winnowing house, and "one servt house." Slaveholder Joshua Nichols lost nearly all of the men and women he enslaved. He reported seventy-four enslaved people on his Combahee plantation in 1860 and, following the raid, that seventy-three left with Federal forces.[35]

The site might also be remembered as a site of a strategic loss on the Union side. Despite the strategic mistakes made by the Confederate commands, hundreds of enslaved people did not make it to freedom. Union forces had more success on some plantations than others. At Nichols Landing, Confederate cavalry used "negro dogs" to prevent Black people from escaping, including a "negro girl" who made it within ninety yards of a Union boat. A Confederate officer reported that "he ordered the Negro girl to stop; she refusing, he shot her down; she got up and ran to where the others were; they all stopped; he ran up to them and brought them back." Despite the bungled Confederate response, the Union expedition left the vast majority of Black people on the Combahee River plantations enslaved. It is not clear how many of the 370 people enslaved by Charles Lowndes on his Oakland plantation made it to the Union gunboats, but a company of Confederate soldiers captured at least thirty people as they tried to make their escape. At Field's Point, Confederate commander Maj. W. P. Emanuel "discovered a good many negroes standing in the edge of the swamp, commanded by one white man" and "ordered the artillery to fire into them," which it did "several times." Confederate forces arrived at the Heyward plantation as it was going up in flames. A cavalry commander wrote that they fired on the "stolen negroes" fleeing to the Union gunboat. It is also unclear how many of the 491 people enslaved by Charles Heyward in 1860 made it to the Union gunboats, nor how many of the more than five hundred people enslaved by Daniel Blake.[36] In the aftermath of the raid, Confederate pickets in the area were reinforced. Slaveholder Mary Elliott praised the move. "I am very glad to hear of the new picket arrangement for guarding the negroes and trust it may arrest desertion on their part—it would be ruinous to have more of such raids as the [Combahee]," she wrote.[37]

I imagine a staff ride along the Combahee, where rice fields made profitable by the labor of enslaved people once stood. I think about how this field of battle, now reclaimed by marshes, might help tourists, elementary students, and even corporate executives think in new ways about "the art of leading," about victory and loss, how studying strategic decisions made here, limbs and lives lost, might contribute to a better understanding of war and history.

On the banks of the Combahee River in Beaufort County in a cemetery in the woods, lie the graves of Union soldiers Wally Garrett and James Sheppard, identified as belonging to Company G, Thirty-Fourth US Colored Infantry.[38] A team of historians and archaeologists have been working to have the site of the raid listed as the Combahee Ferry Historic District in the National Register of Historic Places. This could be an important step in the effort both to understand the site and the role that ordinary people played as leaders and followers in the Civil War, to expand the definition of what constitutes a Civil War battlefield and a leader. The Confederate earthworks that were erected here have eroded into the Combahee River. Colleton County owns the boat landing at Field's Point, and part of the surrounding land, the

Cheeha Combahee Plantation, is the site of an annual plantation tour by the Colleton County Historical and Preservation Society.[39] None of this makes the site less valuable for consideration for a staff ride or walking as a battle-field. Rather, it argues for change.

Some years ago, I was on a panel honoring the work of Civil War histo-rian James McPherson, where I raised many of the questions that inform this essay and others.[40] I asked, for example, what a battlefield tour of a planta-tion or the site of a refugee camp might look like. I said that I could imagine McPherson leading a staff ride at a plantation on the Ashley River. At the beginning of his career, McPherson wrote a great deal about abolitionists and African Americans in the Civil War. They were the subjects of his first two books, *The Struggle for Equality: Abolitionists and the Negro in the Civil War and Reconstruction* (1964) and *The Negro's Civil War: How American Negroes Felt and Acted during the War for the Union* (1965). It had been some three decades since the publication of W. E. B. Du Bois's *Black Reconstruc-tion* (1935) and Herbert Aptheker's *The Negro in the Civil War* (1938) and a little more than a decade since Benjamin Quarles's *The Negro in the Civil War* (1953) had appeared. In a review in the *Journal of American History*, H. L. Swint hailed McPherson's interventions as "important and timely." In the *American Historical Review*, Don E. Fehrenbacher deemed *The Negro's Civil War* a "moving and instructive" documentary history that made "plainly vis-ible" the "beginnings of a revolution that is still in progress."[41]

McPherson's work also drew the kinds of visceral reactions in major historical journals that had greeted the earlier work of Du Bois, Aptheker, and Quarles. A reviewer of Aptheker's work in the *Georgia Historical Quar-terly*, for example, called it "an absurd bit of propaganda based on a perver-sion of historical facts" whose "purpose is to show the Negroes today that they were not in slavery a meek servile people" and ridiculed the notion that Black people had played any part in the defeat of slavery or the Con-federacy.[42] More than three decades later, a review of *The Negro's Civil War* in the *Georgia Historical Quarterly* lambasted McPherson for making "the extreme statement that 'perhaps' the war could not have been won without the help of the Negroes" and thus taking "a leaf out of Aptheker's book." The unnamed reviewer wrote that the idea that Black people had contrib-uted to the defeat of the South was "the most amazing discovery the author makes" and questioned the existence of any supporting evidence. He found fairly incredulous the suggestion that "Negro slaves were restless during the Civil War and whenever they got a chance to run away, they did so, and joined the labor force of the Federal armies."[43] Such views no longer hold a respectable place in the profession, but they played no small part in sealing off considerations of Black people as leaders in the Civil War, leaving a legacy that remains potent.

In terms of the size of the armies, the strategic significance of the battles or military stakes involved, the war in low country South Carolina was not comparable to Gettysburg, Vicksburg, or Antietam. It was nonetheless a significant site of war where Black people's leadership is visible. Indeed, there were many such sites and many leaders, men like the elderly Rufus Campbell, a Methodist minister from Illinois and agent of the US Christian Commission. Hundreds of miles from home, in a Memphis hospital for Black refugees, Campbell stated that, while he had been too old to enlist, he "did so for example sake" as he wished "to do all he could for the government and the colored people."[44]

We are reminded that people at the time spoke of "an army of slaves and fugitives, pushing its way irresistibly toward an army of fighting men."[45] This "army" of men, women, and children together with those who remained behind to fight on the home front, the front slaveholders went to war to protect, grew rapidly after Lincoln issued the Emancipation Proclamation. Steven Hahn has asked why historians "have been so reluctant to entertain seriously the idea that the Civil War may have witnessed a massive rebellion of southern slaves." The answer, he writes, "has less to do with the plausibility of such an interpretation than with the politics of history writing and memory making and with the challenges of imagining slaves as political actors," despite the fact that slaveholders themselves spoke of "disturbances," "contagions," "mutinies," "strikes," and "states of insurrection."[46]

I still imagine that there will come a time when the battlegrounds on which Black people fought that have been overlooked and ignored will be seen as hallowed ground not for magnolia and mint julep fantasies but for understanding the leadership of Black people in the making of a new birth of freedom. Leadership from the ground mattered.

NOTES

1. By order of Brig. Gen. W. S. Walker (commander, Third Military District), Charleston, SC, March 23, 1863, *The War of the Rebellion: A Compilation of the Official Records of the Union and Confederate Armies* (Washington: Government Printing Office, 1885; hereafter cited as *OR*), ser. 1, vol. 14, 292–93.

2. Even though Confederate leaders and citizens understood that enslaved people were leaving on their own accord, designating those who warred against slavery as "lost to the enemy," not only removed their agency but permitted slaveholders to seek compensation from the state and take cover in proslavery ideology which insisted that enslaved people were content and would never leave on their own accord.

3. Report of Commander J. B. Marchand, US Navy, Off Charleston, June 5, 1862, *Official Records of the Union and Confederate Navies in the War of the Rebellion*, 27 vols. (Washington, DC: Government Printing Office, 1894–1922; hereafter cited as *ORN*), ser. 1, vol. 13, 77.

4. See Thavolia Glymph, *The Women's Fight: The Civil War's Battles for Home, Freedom and Nation* (Chapel Hill: University of North Carolina Press, 2020).

5. Report of Flag-Officer Du Pont, US Navy, Flagship Wabash, Port Royal Harbor, SC, June 16, 1862, 95, Encloses Report of Lt. W. T. Truxtun, US Dale, St. Helena Sound, SC, June 13, *ORN*, ser. 1, vol. 13, 95.

6. Report of Flag-Officer Du Pont, 97; Capt. John S. Bishop, *A Concise History of the War Designed to Accompany Perrine's New War Map of the Southern States* (Indianapolis: Charles O. Perrine, 1864), 60.

7. Located on the intercoastal waterway, the few homes on the island today are used mainly for hunters. There is no power on the island, and it is accessible only by boat.

8. Fact Sheet 1, Strategic Leadership Experience, US Army War College https://www.csl .army.mil/img/SLEPImages/1_SLEP_Fact_Sheet_Jan_2015.pdf; "Army War College Uses Battlefield Staff Ride to Carry Lessons in Leadership," US Army War College Archives, Carlisle, Pennsylvania, September 26, 2017, https://www.armywarcollege .edu/News/archives/13364.pdf; "Conduct of the Staff Ride Developed by Tactics Division," Amphibious Warfare School Quantico, VA, https://www.nps.gov /ande/planyourvisit/upload/Conductofthestaffride.pdf. The army's first staff ride is said to have taken place in 1906 when Major Eben Swift took twelve officer students from Fort Leavenworth's General Service and Staff School to the Chickamauga Battlefield on a staff ride.

9. Steven L. Ossad, "Washington and Lincoln's Battlefield Lessons for CEOs," CNBC Online, February 18, 2023, https://www.cnbc.com/id/100450192. See also Steven L. Ossad, "Why the Boardroom Needs to Visit the Battlefield: Using the Lessons of Historic Battlefields to teach 21st Century Leadership," *Training* Magazine, July 3, 2013. Ossad is a military historian and founder of Applied Battlefield Concepts LLC.

10. Thavolia Glymph, "Rose's War and the Gendered Politics of a Slave Insurgency in the Civil War," *Journal of the Civil War Era* 3, no. 4 (December 2013): 501–32.

11. LeeAnn Whites, "Forty Shirts and a Wagonload of Wheat: Women, the Domestic Supply Line, and the Civil War on the Western Border," *Journal of the Civil War Era* 1, no. 1 (March 2011): 64, 73.

12. Report Encloses copy of Col. R. D. Massey, Colonel, 100th USCT, Commissioner, Organization Colored Troops, Letter to Hood and Bostwick, Nashville, Tennessee, August 14, 1864, Headquarters Commissioner Organization US Colored Troops. See also Elizabeth Russell, *Indiana and Ohio Narratives*, supp. Ser. 1, vol. 5, 180; *OR*, ser. 1, vol. 51, pt. 1, supp., 991–92; On Black women Unionists, see also Thavolia Glymph, "'I'm a Radical Black Girl': Black Women Unionists and the Politics of Civil War History," in *Unequal Sisters: A Revolutionary Reader in US Women's History*, 5th ed, ed. Stephanie Narrow, Kim Cary Warren, and Judy Tzu-Chun Wu with Vicki L. Ruiz (New York: Routledge, 2023); Thavolia Glymph, "'She Wears the Flag of Our Country': Women, Nation, and War," *Journal of the Civil War Era* 12, no. 3 (September 2022): 305–20; and Glymph, *The Women's Fight*.

13. The limitations were immediately clear. Some commanders in the field continued to issue orders denying fugitive slaves access to Union camps and for their removal beyond

the guard lines. See, for example, Brig. Gen. J. T. Boyle, General Orders No. 2, Head-Quarters District of Western Kentucky, November 27, 1862, in *Freedom: A Documentary History of Emancipation, 1861–1867*, ser. 1, vol. 1, *The Destruction of Slavery*, ed. Ira Berlin, Barbara J. Fields, Thavolia Glymph, Joseph P. Reidy, and Leslie S. Rowland (Cambridge: Cambridge University Press, 1985), 549.

14. Abraham Lincoln, *The Collected Works of Abraham Lincoln*, 9 vols., ed. Roy P. Basler et al. (New Brunswick, NJ: Rutgers University Press, 1953–55), 5:317–19.

15. Francis S. Browne, The *Every-Day Life of Abraham Lincoln* (New York: N. D. Thompson, 1886), 545–46.

16. For an extended discussion of this point, see Thavolia Glymph, "Du Bois's 'Black Reconstruction' and Slave Women's War for Freedom," *South Atlantic Quarterly* 112, no. 3 (Summer 2013): 489–505.

17. "Instructions for the Government of Armies of the United States in the Field," prepared by Francis Lieber, Originally Issued as General Orders No. 100, Adjutant General's Office, 1863, *OR*, 162–63.

18. On the Lieber Code, see John Fabian Witt, *Lincoln's Code: The Laws of War in American History* (New York: Free Press, 2012), 242–44. Witt notes that Lieber was primarily interested outlawry proclamations against Union officers of Black soldiers.

19. See Thavolia Glymph, "Refugee Camp at Helena, Arkansas, 1863," in *The Lens of War: Historians Reflect on their Favorite Civil War Photographs*, ed. J. Matthew Gallman and Gary W. Gallagher (Athens: University of Georgia Press, 2015), 133–40.

20. The losses at Gettysburg included 10,000 killed or mortally wounded, nearly 30,000 wounded, and almost 10,000 captured or missing.

21. National Register of Historic Places Registration Form, Ashley River Historic District, National Park Service, US Department of the Interior, http://www.nationalregister.sc.gov/dorchester/S10817718009/S10817710158BI.pdf.

22. Magnolia Gardens, "History," https://www.magnoliaplantation.com/history; Mark Blitz, "The Southern Romance of the Nation's Oldest Public Garden," American South: A Smithsonian Magazine Special Report, *Smithsonian Magazine*, September 30, 2015 (updated February 10, 2017).

23. National Register of Historic Places, Ashley River Historic District, 69, http://www.nationalregister.sc.gov/dorchester/S10817718009/S10817710158BI.pdf. The garden's renown also earned it a mention in *Lolita* (Vladimir Nabokov, *Lolita* [1955; New York: Vintage, 1997], 154). See also its mention in Karl Baedeker, *The United States with an Excursion into Mexico*, 3rd rev. ed. (New York: Charles Scribner's Sons, 1904), 438.

24. See Bill Grimke-Drayton, "The Bennett Family, June 13, 2011, https://grimke.wordpress.com/2011/06/13/the-bennett-family/; see also Magnolia Gardens, "History"; and Mary Pinckney Battle, "Confronting Slavery in Historic Charleston Changing Tourism Narratives in the Twenty-First Century" (PhD diss., Emory University, 2013), 60–61, 68–69.

25. Report of Commander J. B. Marchand, US Navy, Off Charleston, June 5, 1862, *ORN*, ser. 1, vol. 13, 77. On November 7, 1861, a US expeditionary force captured Port Royal Sound, South Carolina. Slaveholders in the region fled, leaving some ten thousand enslaved people behind. The Union would hold the area, which became a beacon for enslaved people from the mainland and throughout the low country of South Carolina, Georgia, and Florida, for the duration of the war. The Combahee River Raid was launched from this base.

26. *OR*, ser. 1, vol. 14, 463.

27. *OR*, ser, 1, vol. 14, 301, 302, 305.

28. *OR*, scr, 1, vol. 14, 294–96, 298, 301, 303, quotes at 294, 301, 302.

29. *OR*, ser, 1, vol. 14, 297–98, 290–93, 296, 295, quotes at 291, 293.

30. *OR*, ser. 1, vol. 14, 304–6.

31. *OR*, ser. 1, vol. 14, 306.

32. *OR*, ser, 1, vol. 14, 291.

33. Margaret Belser Hollis and Allen Stokes, eds., *Twilight on the South Carolina Rice Fields: Letters of the Heyward Family* (Columbia: University of South Carolina Press, 2010), 30.

34. Catherine Clinton, *Harriet Tubman: The Road to Freedom* (New York: Little, Brown, 2004); Catherine Clinton, "'General Tubman': Female Abolitionist Was Also a Secret Military Weapon," *Military Times*, February 7, 2018; Beverly Lowry, *Harriet Tubman: Imagining a Life* (New York: Anchor Books, 2008), 317.

35. US Census, 1860 Slave Schedules; Colleton District Property Losses of Record, https://sciway3.net/clark/civilwar/ColletonDistLosses.html.

36. *OR*, ser. 1, vol. 14, 293–94, 300–303, quotes at 294, 303; Glymph, *The Women's Fight*; US Census, 1860 Slave Schedules.

37. Mary [Elliott] to Emmie [Emily Elliott], Beaumont 28th June [1863], Elliott and Gonzales Family Papers, 1701–1898, Southern Historical Collection, University of North Carolina.

38. Wayne Washington, "Work Uncovers Site Where Raid Freed 700 Slaves," *The State*, October 16, 2005, updated May 26, 2007; Eric C. Poplin, Gordon Watts, Edward Salo, Kristrina A. Shuler, Dave Baluha, Emily Jateff, Nicole Isenbarger, and Charles F. Philips, "Crossing the Combahee: Mitigation of the Combahee Ferry Historic District," Digital Archaeological Record, 2017, https://core.tdar.org/document/439872/crossing-the-combahee-mitigation-of-the-combahee-ferry-historic-district. The Thirty-Fourth US Colored Infantry was organized in February 1864. It is, therefore, unclear whether these Black soldiers took part in the Combahee River Expedition. But as the Thirty-Fourth US Colored Infantry was organized from the Second South Carolina Colored Infantry, it is possible that they were present at Combahee as soldiers of the Second. This seems likely given that the service records of the Thirty-Fourth do not indicate any expeditions along the Combahee. See "Search for Battle Units," National Park Service, https://www.nps.gov/civilwar/search-battle-units.htm#sort=Title+asc&q=34th+regiment,+United+States+Colored+Infantry&fq%5B%5D=Side%3A%22Union%22&fq%5B%5D=State%3A%22United+States+Colored+Troops%22.

39. "Two Historic Events at Fields Point," *The Colletonian*, http://thecolletonian.com/two-historic-events-at-fields-point/. The Cheeha Combahee Plantation sold for $8 million in 2016.

40. "Walking Battlefields: African Americans in the Civil War and Freedom and the Legacy of James M. McPherson" and "James M. McPherson: A Life in American History Panel," American Historical Association Annual Meeting, January 8, 2012, Chicago.

41. H. L. Swint, Review of *The Struggle for Equality: Abolitionists and the Negro in the Civil War and Reconstruction* by James M. McPherson and *The Negro's Civil War: How American Negroes Felt and Acted during the War for the Union* by James M. McPherson, *Journal of American History* 52, no. 3 (December 1965): 627–29, quote at 627; Don E. Fehrenbacher, Review of *The Negro's Civil War: How American Negroes Felt and Acted during*

the War for the Union by James M. McPherson, *American Historical Review* 71, no. 1 (October 1965): 315.

42. Review of *The Negro in the Civil War* by Hebert Aptheker (1938), *Georgia Historical Quarterly* 23, no. 4 (December 1939): 401–2.

43. Review of *The Negro's Civil War: How American Negroes Felt and Acted during the War for the Union* by James M. McPherson, *Georgia Historical Quarterly* 50, No. 1 (March 1966): 127. The unidentified author wrote that "the method used is to quote from Negro sources. . . . Those who do the speaking are free Northern Negroes, for, of course, the slaves were in no position to write down what they thought, even by those who could write" (127).

44. Edward Wasmuth Diary, 1865 (Southern Historical Collection, University of North Carolina), 21.

45. John Eaton, *Grant, Lincoln, and the Freedmen: Reminiscences of the Civil War* (1907; New York: Negro Universities Press, 1969), 2.

46. Steven Hahn, *The Political Worlds of Slavery and Freedom* (Cambridge, MA: Harvard University Press, 2009), 57–58.

PART V

Visual Arts

CHAPTER 11

Leadership in Bronze

Boston's Shaw Memorial and the Battle over Civil War Memory

David M. Lubin

While for decades Civil War monuments attracted little notice, today the situation has changed. Street protests mounted for or against their demolition in Southern cities such as Charlottesville, Richmond, Chapel Hill, Durham, and New Orleans have brought them back into public awareness, probably for the first time since they were installed in the late nineteenth and early twentieth centuries.[1]

The protests are based, of course, on ideological rather than aesthetic grounds. If the latter criterion were in force, they would have been removed long ago. As pieces of sculpture, they are formulaic in their manner of representation. Lacking artistic innovation, they simply are not capable of expressing complex ideas about the war over slavery and the persistent moral questions that that war continues to raise.

The Robert Gould Shaw Memorial, designed by the Gilded Age sculptor Augustus Saint-Gaudens and installed on the Boston Common in May 1897, is a notable exception to the conventional aesthetics and simplistic ideology of most public sculptures erected in the aftermath of the Civil War. Because of its remarkable artistry and moral complexity, the Shaw Memorial had something new and timely to say to Americans at the height of Jim Crow racism. The Supreme Court's notorious *Plessy v. Ferguson* ruling had been handed down only a year earlier. The domestic terror group known as the Ku Klux Klan was on the rise in the South. Northerners increasingly came

197

Figure 11.1 Augustus Saint-Gaudens, the Robert Gould Shaw Memorial, 1897, Boston. Bronze sculpture on stone base. Photograph no. 090156 (c. 1906), Detroit Publishing Co. Courtesy of Library of Congress, Prints and Photographs Division.

to accept revisionist claims that the war had been fought over states' rights, not slavery.[2] The Shaw Memorial resisted these reactionary developments. It insisted on the centrality of racial dignity and cross-racial solidarity to a humane vision of the republic.

The memorial also put forward a new vision of leadership. The traditional way of honoring a military leader was to aggrandize him as the man on a horse. The Shaw Memorial departed from this tradition by calling attention to the African American foot soldiers who surge forward in step with their mounted leader. Instead of representing the troops as a generalized, undifferentiated mass that exhibits no agency of its own, the relief encourages the viewer to regard the soldiers as sentient, self-directed, and unified individuals who themselves, collectively, embody moral leadership.

With its centralized military rider on a horse, the Shaw Memorial draws from but also departs from antique traditions. In ancient Greece, the consummate achievement of a sculptor was to represent warriors mounted on horseback, as in the Parthenon friezes of the fifth century BCE. These were relief statues, carved in marble, depicting unnamed riders. In imperial Rome half a millennium later, equestrian statuary was taken much further. Sculptors working in bronze created the first fully three-dimensional and life-size (or larger), pedestal-based equestrian monuments. The calm and intellectual demeanors of the seated leaders contrasted with the brute force of their mounts. The juxtaposition between man and beast conjured the dominion of man, not only over nature, but also over his own animal instincts. By extension, these equestrian monuments symbolized the leader's authority over the troops he commanded and the populations he ruled.

Most Roman equestrian bronzes perished during the Christian era. Viewed as remnants of paganism, they were melted down for their precious metals. The only large equestrian bronze to survive immolation is the great statue of Marcus Aurelius (c. 175 CE), which escaped destruction because it was misidentified as a statue of Constantine, the first Christian emperor. In the early sixteenth century, Michelangelo had the Aurelian statue moved from its original location in the Roman Forum to be the centerpiece of his architectural design of the Piazza del Campidoglio on Rome's Capitoline Hill. By then, Italian Renaissance sculptors had reinvented techniques to produce monumental equestrian bronzes. The first and greatest of these was Donatello's 1453 statue in Padua of a mercenary general known as Gattamelata ("Honeyed Cat").

The first equestrian statue in the United States was that of King George III, erected in New York in 1770. An angry mob tore it down on July 9, 1776, days after independence was declared. It took three-quarters of a century before Americans had the know-how and wherewithal to return to equestrian statuary. They did so in the decade preceding the Civil War with memorial statues to Andrew Jackson in 1852, George Washington in 1856, and Washington again in 1858. As sectional tensions boiled, Americans must have taken solace in the ancient theme of good governance by a stoical leader in command of his horse as well as his emotions.

After the death of Robert E. Lee in 1870, Virginians lobbied for a monument in Richmond to memorialize the unrivaled hero of the Lost Cause. The Lost Cause was a term that Southerners used to justify their failed secession from the Union. By means of the chivalric term, with its undertones of romantic quest against formidable odds, they insisted that the war had been fought over states' rights rather than slavery and thus was morally justified. A French Beaux-Arts sculptor named Antonin Mercié was selected to design the monument. The resulting statue of Lee on horseback, rising sixty feet over an imposing stone base, was installed in 1890 on what came to be known as Monument Avenue, as similarly colossal statues of other Confederate leaders were subsequently added.

The sculpture historians Kirk Savage and Maurie D. McInnis have each noted that the statue served not only to apotheosize General Lee and elevate him to equal footing with the other most venerated Virginian, General Washington. It also proclaimed to Black Virginians, in the age of the Ku Klux Klan, race lynching, and Jim Crow legislation, that white men remained firmly in the saddle.[3]

"The meaning of resurgent Confederate symbolism was not lost on local African Americans," writes McInnis, pointing out that equestrian statues such as Richmond's Lee monument were "a symbol of white supremacy and of the power and violence encoded in the system of racial slavery." She speculates that freed Black viewers of the Lee statue in 1890 would have been reminded of the not-so-distant days when white overseers on horseback supervised enslaved labor in the cotton fields.[4]

Some commentators have seen the Shaw Memorial as a paternalistic, Northern version of this Southern trope: the white overseer on horseback once again riding above "his" Black men—in this case, soldiers rather than slaves. "The noble, erect bearing of Shaw and his look of determination are contrasted with the listless and rumpled-looking troops," writes the art historian Albert Boime. "The horse's head—rearing, majestic—complements the regal bearing of Shaw's torso, while the body screens out a large number of soldiers, who are recognizable only by their boots." Boime concludes: "The net result of this motif is to visually promote the identification of troops and animal, who move in obedience to Shaw's command, further reinforced by his diagonally thrusting riding cropper."[5]

Boime's interpretation of the bronze relief as yet another instance of white privilege and embedded racism is compelling but not entirely credible. As a work of art, the piece is more complex, less programmatic, and certainly less heavy-handed than that. Boime supports his claims about the inherent racism of the Shaw Memorial's design by citing the bigoted views (typical of the time and place) of the individual who sculpted it. He does not, however, chart Saint-Gaudens's growth as an *artist* and the significance this had on his ability to transcend paternalistic racism in his making of the monument.

Born of a Franco-Irish family that emigrated to New York in his youth, Saint-Gaudens (1848–1907) was acclaimed in his day for his visually compelling three-dimensional depictions of Civil War leaders from the North, including Adm. David Farragut, Gen. William T. Sherman, and, above all, President Abraham Lincoln. He was also celebrated for his sensitive portrayals of artists such as the sickly, bedridden author Robert Louis Stevenson, whom he charmingly depicted writing in bed, and his haunting sculptural memorials for private citizens, most famously the shrouded, gender-ambiguous figure of death that keeps watch over the Washington, DC, gravesite of the historian Henry Adams and his wife, Marian.[6]

Since antiquity, the medium of sculpture has been an ideal mode for memorializing the dead, because the substances involved are relatively stable and permanent, intended to withstand the diminishments of time. In this regard, Saint-Gaudens was the nineteenth-century United States' greatest sculptor of memory. He molded and shaped the past for Americans in ways that may or may not have been entirely accurate but which were always visually compelling and emotionally resonant.

His *Standing Lincoln*, unveiled in Chicago in 1887, astonished viewers. With this monument, Saint-Gaudens provided his contemporaries with a remarkable image in the round by which to remember—or, if you will, misremember—their recent past. Along with Daniel Chester French's much later rendition for the *Lincoln Memorial* in the nation's capital (1927) and Matthew Brady's earlier photographic portraits of the Illinois congressman who became president, *Standing Lincoln* is responsible for creating the iconic image of Lincoln that we have today, as rendered in film, fiction, and the five-dollar bill. Saint-Gaudens brought to life for his contemporaries the tall and lanky, craggy-faced orator who shambles forward to speak, his brow ponderous with thought, and his clothes wrinkled as if not only from normal wear but also from the weight of responsibility bearing down on his shoulders.[7]

Until Saint-Gaudens entered the field, Lincoln monuments typically showed him as the Great Emancipator, with freed Black people groveling at his feet. They served up a Lincoln that, to modern eyes, seems outlandishly faux and sentimental, embodying an implicit, if not explicit, white supremacist paternalism. With their declamatory gestures and pious expressions, they lack the gravitas and leonine presence of Saint-Gaudens's later rendering of the assassinated president.

Saint-Gaudens exploits an array of small external details and gestures to convey the rich inner presence of the man. The wrinkling of his vest echoes the wrinkling of his brow. His head is down-turned, as if in thought. The watch chain dangling across Lincoln's torso serves as a memento mori, an iconographic reminder of the chains of time and hence the premature mortality that tragically awaited the president from the moment he took his first step forward into the office that would eventually consume his life.

His left hand clutches his lapel—a gesture, Saint-Gaudens learned, that was common for Lincoln when making speeches. The right hand, balled

Figure 11.2 "Augustus Saint-Gaudens beside the completed 'Standing Lincoln,'" 1887. Courtesy of US Department of the Interior, National Park Service, Saint-Gaudens National Historical Park, Cornish, New Hampshire.

in a fist, disappears behind his back. In more typical sculptural depictions of leaders, an arm extends outward, toward viewers, or upward, toward the heavens. The ancient prototypes for the arm-extended leader were the Etruscan statue known as *L'Arringatore* (*The Orator*), sculpted between 110 and 90 BCE, the imperial Roman *Augustus of Prima Porta* (first century CE), and the equestrian *Marcus Aurelius*. Retraction of the leader's hand behind his back was unheard of in public sculpture. Its unusual, if not unique, appearance in *Standing Lincoln* gives the piece a startling air of mystery, tension, and withheld power.

Perhaps the most extraordinary element was the vacant seat behind the orator. This was a novel idea for public sculpture, a standing figure beside an empty seat. It bespeaks absence: someone *was* sitting there and is doing so no longer; he has passed to a different realm. In essence, Saint-Gaudens translates into sculptural form the famous remark of one of the president's closest allies at his deathbed, "Now he belongs to the ages."[8]

Standing Lincoln managed to appear real and authentic while at the same time transcendent, an embodiment of moral, even spiritual, strength. What was lost, however, in this new, naturalistic view of Lincoln—Lincoln the man rather than the saint—was his role as emancipator. Those earlier, highly sentimental sculptural groups of Lincoln and freed people were racially condescending. Each implicitly celebrated white superiority. Nonetheless, they asserted that the war had first and foremost been waged to end chattel slavery—a truth systematically supplanted in the North as well as the South by the more flattering (to white adherents) mythology of the Lost Cause.[9]

The federal policy of Reconstruction collapsed in 1877. Jim Crow racism increased in violence and scope. Most white Americans, as noted, wanted to minimize the importance of slavery as the cause of the war, preferring instead to see the upheaval as an honorable and heroic clash of political philosophies, which Lincoln gave his life to resolve. By forsaking his predecessors' insistence on showing Lincoln as the Great Emancipator, Saint-Gaudens in 1887 may inadvertently have helped shift the public's memory of the president to that of the Great Unifier instead and, in doing so, contributed to the disappearance of racial justice from the national agenda.

Completed ten years later, in 1897, the Shaw Memorial can be regarded as an attempt to counter public amnesia. It was dedicated to Col. Robert Gould Shaw and the Fifty-Fourth Massachusetts Volunteer Infantry, the first regiment of Black soldiers organized in the North during the Civil War. Shaw died in 1863 along with nearly half his regiment during a futile charge against a Confederate stronghold know as Battery Wagner, which was strategically situated on a small island outside Charleston, South Carolina.[10]

Set within a columned granite and marble frame, Saint-Gaudens's bronze relief occupies a terrace at the edge of Beacon Street, directly across from the State House and above Boston Common. Bearing laurel and poppy, symbols of victory and death, an angel soars like a ponderous cloud over the heads of the men, whom Saint-Gaudens depicts solemnly marching off to war. The angel presses close to the soldiers, as if she were an abiding thought

Figure 11.3 Augustus Saint-Gaudens, the Robert Gould Shaw Memorial. Photograph no. 090157 (c. 1900–1905), Detroit Publishing Co. Courtesy of Library of Congress, Prints and Photographs Division.

emanating from their heads. A Latin phrase appearing beneath her extended arm says in eulogy, "He left everything behind to save the Republic."[11]

Unlike the *Standing Lincoln*, this is a bas-relief rather than a free-standing statue. As such, its mood is reticent. Young Colonel Shaw seems almost to resist the viewer's attention. He's "lean as a compass-needle," to borrow Robert Lowell's arresting phrase, which refers not only to Shaw's physical but also his moral bearing. Lowell's well-known poem from 1960 "For the Union Dead" describes the rider on the frieze as having "an angry wrenlike vigilance, a greyhound's gentle tautness; he seems to wince at pleasure and suffocate for privacy."[12] Even though the Shaw Memorial is a major monument in the heart of a busy city, it is intimate and discreet, more along the lines of Saint-Gaudens's other masterpiece, the private and secluded Adams Memorial.

The idea for the Shaw Memorial was conceived in 1865 by an African American businessman in Boston, Joshua B. Smith, who had previously been employed in the Shaw household. Smith's idea was taken up by a group of prominent Bostonians and former abolitionists.[13] They wished to commemorate a great military leader: great not in the sense that he had commanded a successful assault, for his mission had been a distinct failure, but rather in the sense that he had sacrificed his life on behalf of a tremendous cause. These civic leaders were disheartened by the recent demise of Reconstruction and the resultant amnesia that was causing Americans to misremember the war as a glorious contest between chivalrous heroes rather than the awful but necessary cataclysm over slavery that it truly was.

The commissioners sought a memorial that downplayed military valor and paid tribute instead to the principle for which the young colonel and his "colored troops," as they called them, had rendered their lives—hence the sorrowful rather than celebratory nature of this monument. In the ongoing battle of symbols and ideas as to how the war would be remembered, it insisted—especially with the angel of death hovering overhead—that failure, tragedy, and loss are inalienable aspects of any victory, and that true leadership is about advancing, rather than impeding, human progress.

A related explanation as to why this monument looks so different from the others—so much more personal—is that the family of the individual being honored was actively engaged in the creative process. Robert Gould Shaw was a twenty-six-year-old, Harvard-educated Boston Brahmin raised by a family long committed to the belief that slavery was wrong and should be abolished at any cost. With the blessing of his parents and their associate Frederick Douglass, and perhaps an idealistic sense of noblesse oblige as well, young Shaw requested leadership of a regiment that no other white officer was willing to assume (and which racial politics of the time dictated could not be commanded by a Black officer, regardless of his rank or qualifications). When the war ended and proud New Englanders called for the colonel's martyred body to be disinterred from its mass grave and reburied with honors in his ancestral city of Boston, his parents refused, explaining that their son would have preferred to remain with his men, even in death.[14]

Later, when Saint-Gaudens received the commission for the memorial and planned to make a heroic equestrian statue of it, Shaw's parents again intervened. They objected that their son was not an important military commander, and a statue portraying him as a hero on a horse would be inappropriate. Once more, they insisted that he would have wished to remain with his men. Saint-Gaudens dropped the idea of a free-standing equestrian statue and began designing a multifigure monument instead. This necessitated a frieze because, under the financially restricted terms of the commission, it would have been impossible to sculpt a whole ensemble of secondary statues in the round.

Figure 11.4 Augustus Saint-Gaudens, the Robert Gould Shaw Memorial, 1901, Washington, DC. Gilded plaster cast on long-term loan to the National Gallery of Art from the US Department of the Interior, National Park Service, Saint-Gaudens National Historic Site, Cornish, New Hampshire.

In the design that resulted (fig. 11.4), the foot soldiers bunch up behind the mounted colonel, like a steel spring compressed in space, ready to uncoil. A sharp, angular linearity defines the scene, but these hard angles are relieved at intervals by the circular bedrolls, canteens, and drum, as well as the curving flanks of the horse and his involuted tail. Other softening elements are the angel's mantle, which undulates in a breezy swoop, and the elongated arch that encloses the frieze. Shaw's charger seems more emotional than the stoic colonel or his equally stoic men. The scene is fraught, but all the human agents within it exhibit self-control equivalent to that of the rider over his mount.

Indeed, one of the most innovative aspects of the Shaw Memorial was its dignified individualizing of the Black troops. Saint-Gaudens has given each of the sixteen or so fully or partially visible faces distinct characteristics, offering the viewer a range of race-appropriate, but also age-appropriate, facial structures and types. Thus, for example, he suggests that while some of the older soldiers haven't touched a razor in years, some of the younger have yet to use one. The reason it took Saint-Gaudens thirteen years to fulfill the commission—by far his longest period of completion—is that he sculpted some forty portrait studies of African American men before arriving at the much smaller cadre of faces he incorporated into the final version.[15]

Sad to say, Saint-Gaudens entertained some of the typically racist attitudes of his time and place. He patronized his Black models, regarding them as children in adult bodies; he called them "darkies." And yet, as art historian Kirk Savage has persuasively argued, the internal logic of the piece compelled the sculptor to transcend his own limited and bigoted beliefs, for how could he render tribute to Colonel Shaw without granting the officer's men an equivalent seriousness and respect? "As an artist," notes Savage, "Saint-Gaudens was not content with simply multiplying a generic Black soldier in order to create an undifferentiated mass of troops. Everything in his artistic makeup pushed him against the sort of repetition found in conventional war memorials." Rather than treat Blackness as a blanket trait, the sculptor found it, in Savage's words, "a field in which to create a rich interplay of internal differences."[16]

Whatever Saint-Gaudens's intentions may have been, the work that resulted is unique in nineteenth-century American art for the dignity and depth of humanity it accords people of African descent. In this the artist was going very much against the tide of racial representation in the late nineteenth-century United States, where Black soldiers were typically depicted as lazy, overgrown children incapable of standing on their own two feet. Simply by depicting African Americans on their feet instead of their backs, bellies, or knees, he afforded them an unusually high degree of respect. Contrasting the benighted racial views expressed by Saint-Gaudens in his memoirs with the racially progressive attitude exhibited by the memorial, Savage writes, "In the text [Saint-Gaudens] creates caricatures; in the relief he gives them room to live as individuals."[17]

With its multiple rows of military figures lined up four abreast, each row dissolving from high to low relief into the bronze background, the Shaw Memorial provides a plethora of individual faces gathered across the narrowly raking three-dimensional sculptural space. Their separate bodies and faces form a united front wedged between an adverse past and a benign future. The advancing foot soldiers, this is to say, are themselves leaders. They lead their people out of bondage and, from a wider perspective, lead the nation out of its vestigial barbarism.

The monument was unveiled on Memorial Day 1897, exactly thirty-four years after the event it commemorates, which is not the attack on the

Figure 11.5 Detail of marching men from the gilded plaster cast at the National Gallery of Art.

Confederate stronghold but rather the regiment's departure from Boston six weeks earlier. The sculptor chose, that is, to emphasize a moment of hope and promise rather than defeat. Nonetheless, sadness pervades the work. All who attended the unveiling would have known that this march to war resulted in the death of the hero and the decimation of the regiment.

Their regiment long disbanded, the veterans of the Fifty-Fourth reconvened for the unveiling. These were the survivors of the bloody assault that claimed their comrades and their commander and of the hardships of being poor and Black in the post-Reconstruction United States. They were survivors, too, of old age. The memorial depicts them as mostly young, marching south with their leader on Beacon Street, away from the Massachusetts State House, as they had done on a bright May morning in 1863. On this misty gray morning in May a third of a century later, none of them young anymore, the veterans paraded uphill along the same street.

Saint-Gaudens was moved by their presence at the ceremony. Years later he recalled watching them confront the monument: "The impression of those old soldiers, passing the very spot where they left for the war so many years before, thrills me even as I write these words. They seemed as if returning from the war, the troops of bronze marching in the opposite direction, the direction in which they had left for the front, and the young men there represented now showing these veterans the vigor and hope of youth."[18]

Over the years, the Shaw Memorial elicited forceful responses from artists and intellectuals who were captivated by its power. The speakers at the dedication ceremony were two famed leaders, Booker T. Washington, the most honored spokesperson for Black America, and the Harvard psychologist and philosopher William James. James vehemently opposed the jingoism and saber-rattling that would soon lead the nation into war with Spain for colonial possessions. He took the occasion of the dedication ceremony to remind his audience that Colonel Shaw and his men had fought and died for a great principle, the abolishment of slavery, and not for personal gain or glory or nationalist pride.[19]

In the years to come, the Shaw Memorial served as a muse to a range of American artists and writers. Charles Ives set it to music in 1911 as "The 'Saint-Gaudens' in Boston Common," which he later included in his *Three Places in New England*. Ralph Ellison was guided by it as an artistic model when he began writing his novel about racial injustice, *Invisible Man*, which was published in 1952 ("it was ... to remind me that war could, with art, be transformed into something deeper and more meaningful than its surface violence"). In 1960 Robert Lowell wrote "For the Union Dead," the poem quoted earlier, which contrasts the moral urgency of Colonel Shaw

Figure 11.6 Veterans of the Massachusetts Fifty-Fourth Regiment, May 31, 1897. Commonwealth of Massachusetts, Massachusetts Art Commission.

as depicted on the monument ("an angry wrenlike vigilance, a greyhound's gentle tautness") with the modern age of moral laxness and materialistic consumption. Other major poets who wrote about it include Paul Laurence Dunbar ("Robert Gould Shaw," 1900) and John Berryman ("Boston Common: A Meditation upon the Hero," 1942). In a personal appreciation delivered at the centennial celebration of the monument in 1997, Gen. Colin Powell, then chairman of the Joint Chiefs of Staff, recounted that the memorial inspired him, as a young Black man, to dedicate his life to service in the US military.[20]

In a sense, then, the memorial itself played a leadership role. It was inspiring, perhaps even racially transformative. But it did not cleanse Shaw's hometown of Boston of its persistent racial injustice. In the 1970s, the city became the national center of resistance to compulsory student busing initiated by court order to comply with school desegregation. A shocking, Pulitzer Prize–winning news photograph shows a young, white anti-busing protestor in Boston's City Hall Plaza thrusting the pole of an American flag at an African American attorney whose arms appear to be pinned behind his back by another protestor, though it was later determined that the young man who appears to be pinning back the arms of the assaulted man was actually trying to help him to his feet after he had been knocked down. The Shaw Memorial was just around the corner from where this shameful incident occurred, impotent to prevent it.[21]

Indeed, by the early 1970s, the memorial had fallen into a sad state of disrepair. The critic Lincoln Kirstein wrote eloquently of the ongoing relevance of the monument in the post–civil rights era, and the photography of his collaborator, Richard Benson, turned its stained and streaked surfaces into hauntingly beautiful images of decay.[22] After the busing crisis ended and Bostonians were rightfully ashamed of their city's national disgrace, there were calls to restore the monument to pristine condition. And in response to the installation of Washington's Vietnam Veterans Memorial in 1982, with its inclusive wall of names, the previously absent names of the fallen foot soldiers of the Massachusetts Fifty-Fourth Regiment were inscribed on the Shaw Memorial's limestone base. The memorial attracted newfound attention.

In the mid-1980s, Hollywood film producer Freddie Fields, crossing the Common after a business meeting, noticed the monument. He sensed that the events it memorialized would make a stirring subject for a movie. Four years later, in 1989, the Civil War drama *Glory* reached the screen. Directed by Edward Zwick and written by Kevin Jarre, the movie stars Matthew Broderick as young Colonel Shaw. Morgan Freeman and Denzel Washington, playing fictionalized composite characters, brought to life two of the unnamed soldiers in the relief.[23]

Unlike the Lincoln as Emancipator monuments and their latter-day incarnation as civil rights–era message films such as *To Kill a Mockingbird* (1962), Zwick's movie was not simply another white-liberal fantasy of a Caucasian hero coming to the defense of poor helpless African Americans, though it has widely, and I think wrongly, been criticized as such. As *Glory* makes abundantly clear, Shaw is the titular leader of the regiment, but the real leaders are the volunteers themselves, who educate him over the course

Figure 11.7 Richard Benson, *The Robert Gould Shaw Memorial* (detail), 1973. Inkjet print. Gift of Peter and Susan MacGill in honor of Anne Wilkes Tucker. Museum of Fine Arts, Houston.

of the narrative and stiffen his resolve. The film ends with him sharing their mass grave at the foot of Battery Wagner. He is now literally one with his troops, differences in skin color irrelevant, his lifeless body equal to theirs, neither better nor worse. The ending takes a parting shot at white privilege rather than memorializing it.

Saint-Gaudens memorably portrayed rich and famous citizens of the Gilded Age but also, as with the ancillary figures of the Shaw Memorial, individuals who lacked privilege, money, or fame. Through the nuance and stylistic versatility of his sculptural oeuvre over a series of decades, he shaped the way that generations of Americans and visitors to the United States encountered its history. He pictured the nation in ways we still wrestle with today.

We can argue about the ultimate meaning of the Shaw Memorial in terms of its racial politics. Is it a work of paternalistic liberalism, in which a white man rides literally above, and figuratively on, the shoulders and backs of

African Americans? Or, to the contrary, does it constitute for today's viewer an eloquent and powerful call for racial dignity and respect at a moment in US history when Jim Crow racism, characterized by systemic violence toward African Americans, seems once again on the rise?

Regardless of how we might answer these vexed questions, we cannot deny that the Shaw Memorial is unusual, if not unique, as a Civil War monument because it asks citizens, regardless of their color, to take the cause of racial justice seriously. It advances, too, an expanded view of leadership. More than celebrating a single leader, as most Civil War monuments do, this memorial provides a model for good leadership, viewing it as a collective enterprise and an ongoing, reciprocal relationship. Recall the meaning of the Latin phrase inscribed on the frieze: "He left everything behind to save the Republic." More accurately, and in the spirit of the sculpture itself, it might have said, "*They* left everything behind to save the Republic."

NOTES

1. A former mayor of New Orleans, Mitch Landrieu, explains his controversial decision to remove the city's Civil War monuments in Landrieu, *In the Shadow of Statues: A White Southerner Confronts History* (New York: Viking, 2018), 161–200.

2. David W. Blight, *Race and Reunion: The Civil War in American Memory* (Cambridge, MA: Belknap Press of Harvard University Press, 2001).

3. See Kirk Savage, *Standing Soldiers, Kneeling Slaves: Race, War, and Monument in Nineteenth-Century America* (Princeton: Princeton University Press, 1997), 129–61; and Maurie D. McInnis, "'To Strike Terror': Equestrian Monuments and Southern Power," in *The Civil War in Art and Memory*, ed. Kirk Savage (Washington, DC: National Gallery of Art, in conjunction with Yale University Press, 2016), 125–46.

4. McInnis, "'To Strike Terror,'" 139, 134–35.

5. See Albert Boime, *The Art of Exclusion: Representing Blacks in the Nineteenth Century* (Washington, DC: Smithsonian Institution Press, 1990), 199–219, quote 209. Boime conscientiously reproduces praise of the Shaw Memorial ("sublime in its expressiveness and mighty in its moving power") from the early twentieth-century African American art writer Freeman Henry Murray, whose father was a survivor of the attack on Fort Wagner; see Boime, *Art of Exclusion*, 204, for the quotation above; and Freeman H. M. Murray, *Emancipation and the Freed in American Sculpture: A Study in Interpretation* (Washington, DC: published by the author, 1916), 164–74, esp. 164, 168, and 173–74. See also Michael Hatt, "Sculpting and Lynching: The Making and Unmaking of the Black Citizen in Late Nineteenth-Century America," *Oxford Art Journal* 24, no. 1 (2001): 1–22, and Charles H. Karelis, "The Problem of Racial Hierarchy in the Shaw Memorial," in Savage, *Civil War in Art and Memory*, 203–12.

6. For biographical details about Saint-Gaudens and his career as a sculptor, see Burke Wilkinson, *Uncommon Clay: The Life and Work of Augustus Saint-Gaudens* (San Diego: Harcourt, Brace Jovanovich, 1985). See also Augustus Saint-Gaudens, *Reminiscences*, 2 vols. (New York: Century, 1913).

7. On the visual iconography of Abraham Lincoln, see Harold Holzer, Gabor S. Boritt, and Mark E. Neely Jr., *The Lincoln Image: Abraham Lincoln and the Popular Print* (Urbana: University of Illinois Press, 2005); and Frederick Hill Meserve, *The Photographs of Abraham Lincoln* (1944; repr., Gottingen: Steidl, 2015); see also Cara A. Finnegan, *Making Photography Matter: A Viewer's History from the Civil War to the Great Depression* (Urbana: University of Illinois Press, 2015), 51–80.

8. On the lore surrounding War Secretary Edward Stanton's remark, which has been called the most famous epitaph in American history, see Adam Gopnik, "Angels and Ages: Lincoln's Language and Its Legacy," *New Yorker*, May 21, 2007, 30–37.

9. This topic is most notably examined in Blight, *Race and Reunion*. See also David W. Blight, "The Shaw Memorial in the Landscape of Civil War Memory," in his *Beyond the Battlefield: Race, Memory, and the American Civil War* (Amherst and Boston: University of Massachusetts Press, 2002), 153–69.

10. For a rich compendium of literature on the Shaw Memorial, see Martin H. Blatt, Thomas J. Brown, and Donald Yacovone, eds., *Hope and Glory: Essays on the Legacy of the Fifty-Fourth Massachusetts Regiment* (Amherst: University of Massachusetts Press, in association with Massachusetts Historical Society, 2001). For a detailed study of the regiment that Shaw commanded, see George H. Junne, *A History of the Fifty-Fourth Regiment of Massachusetts Volunteer Colored Infantry in the Civil War: The Real Story behind the Movie "Glory"* (Lewiston, NY: Edwin Mellen, 2012); and for a regimental history by a former captain in the regiment, see Luis F. Emilio, *A Brave Black Regiment: History of the Fifty-Fourth Regiment of the Massachusetts Volunteer Infantry* (1887; repr., New York: Arno Press, 1968). The most recent and extensive account of the monument's history is Kathryn Grover, *To Heal a Wounded Nation's Life: African Americans and the Robert Gould Shaw/54th Regiment Memorial* (Cornish, NH: Saint-Gaudens National Historical Park, National Park Service, 2021).

11. *Omnia relinqvit servare rempvblicam*, the motto of the Order of Cincinnatus, literally translates as "He forsook all to preserve the public weal." After the memorial was dedicated, its Latin grammar was found technically incorrect, but Saint-Gaudens elected not to change it. See Gregory C. Schwarz, "The Shaw Memorial: A History of the Monument," in Gregory C. Schwarz, Ludwig Lauerhass, and Brigid Sullivan, *The Shaw Memorial: A Celebration of an American Masterpiece* (Cornish, NH: Saint-Gaudens National Historic Site, 1997), 21–22. For an excellent overview of the Shaw Memorial, its patrons, and its evolving reception, see Katie Mullis Kresser, "Power and Glory: Brahmin Identity and the *Shaw Memorial*," *American Art* 20, no. 3 (2006): 32–57.

12. Robert Lowell, "For the Union Dead (*Relinquunt Omnia Servare Rem Publicam*)" (1960), in *For the Union Dead* (New York: Farrar, Straus and Giroux, 1966), 70–72. See Ludwig Lauerhass, "A Commemoration: The Shaw Memorial in American Culture," in Schwarz et al., *The Shaw Memorial*, 60–61; and Steven Axelrod, "Colonel Shaw in American Poetry: For the Union Dead and Its Precursors," *American Quarterly* 24, no. 4 (October 1972): 523–37.

13. On Joshua B. Smith, the African American businessman, abolitionist, and philanthropist who first proposed the idea for the Shaw Memorial, and his fellow commissioners of the monument, see Kresser, "Power and Glory," 41–42.

14. On Shaw's life and military career, see Peter Burchard, *One Gallant Rush: Robert Gould Shaw and His Brave Black Regiment* (New York: St. Martin's, 1965); Russell Duncan, ed., *Blue-Eyed Child of Fortune: The Civil War Letters of Colonel Robert Gould Shaw*, (Athens:

University of Georgia Press, 1992); and Russell Duncan, *Where Death and Glory Meet: Robert Gould Shaw and the 54th Massachusetts Infantry* (Athens: University of George Press, 1999). The family letters indicate that young Shaw was initially reluctant to accept the commission, but his mother's urgent desire for him to do so eventually prevailed.

15. Saint-Gaudens, *Reminiscences*, 1: 333–35. See also Henry J. Duffy, "Consecration and Monument: Robert Gould Shaw, the 54th Massachusetts Regiment, and the Shaw Memorial," in Savage, *Civil War in Art and Memory*, 195–98 and 201–2n17.

16. Savage, *Standing Soldiers*, 201.

17. Savage, 201. Copious examples of vicious caricatures of Black Americans are found in Guy C. McElroy, *Facing History: The Black Image in American Art 1710–1940*, exhib. cat. (Washington, DC: Corcoran Gallery of Art, 1990), especially McElroy, "Introduction: Race and Representation," xi–xxvii; and Henry Louis Gates Jr., "The Face and Voice of Blackness," xxviii–xlvi.

18. Saint-Gaudens, *Reminiscences* 2: 83.

19. On William James's participation in the dedication ceremony, see Robert H. Bell, "William James, the Memory of Glory, and the Work of Mourning," in Savage, *Civil War in Art and Memory*, 227–43.

20. On Ives, see Denise Von Glahn, "The Musical Moment of Charles Ives," in Blatt et al., *Hope and Glory*, 191–201; and, on Lowell and Berryman in the same volume, see Helen Vendler, "Art, Heroism, and Poetry: The Shaw Memorial, Lowell's 'For the Union Dead,' and Berryman's 'Boston Common: A Meditation upon the Hero," 202–14. For Powell's tribute to the memorial in the same volume, see "Hope and Glory: The Monument to Colonel Robert Gould Shaw and the Fifty-Fourth Massachusetts Regiment," xiv–xx. Ralph Ellison's reminiscence is in his preface to the special thirtieth-anniversary edition of *Invisible Man* (New York: Random House, 1982), xvi–xvii, quotation on xvii.

21. The 1976 photograph by Stanley Forman, *The Soiling of Old Glory*, won a Pulitzer Prize in 1977. See Louis P. Masur, *The Soiling of Old Glory: The Story of a Photograph That Shocked a Nation* (New York: Bloomsbury, 2008), 87–90.

22. Richard Benson (photography) and Lincoln Kirstein (essay), *Lay This Laurel: An Album on the Saint-Gaudens Memorial on Boston Common Honoring Black and White Men Together Who Served the Union Cause with Robert Gould Shaw and Died with Him July 18, 1863* (New York: Eakins Press, 1973), 87–90.

23. On *Glory* and its relationship to the Shaw Memorial, see Martin H. Blatt, "'Glory': Hollywood History, Popular Culture, and the Fifty-fourth Massachusetts Regiment," and Thomas Cripps, "'Glory' as a Meditation on the Saint-Gaudens Monument," in Blatt et al., *Hope and Glory*, 215–35 and 236–52. These essays air important criticisms of the film for being too "white" in its orientation. Conversely, the historian Robert J. Cook asserts, "Although *Glory* was only a modest success at the box office, its stirring account of a black Union regiment garnered significant attention from African Americans, many of whom knew nothing of blacks fighting for the United States in the Civil War. In November 1998, a poll carried out by the glossy magazine *Ebony* rated it fifteenth in a list of 'the top black films of all time.'" See Robert J. Cook, *Civil War Memories: Contesting the Past in the United States since 1865* (Baltimore: Johns Hopkins University Press, 2017), 188.

CHAPTER 12

Visual Leadership

The Power of Art in the
Obama Presidency

Gwendolyn DuBois Shaw

> In the making of our presidents, the political gathering begins the
> operation, and the picture gallery ends it.
> —Frederick Douglass, "Lecture on Pictures," December 3, 1861

> That is the story of this country . . . the story of generations of
> people who felt the lash of bondage, the shame of servitude, the
> sting of segregation, but who kept on striving and hoping and doing
> what needed to be done so that today I wake up every morning in a
> house that was built by slaves.
> —Michelle Obama, July 25, 2016

Portraiture has long played an important role in the social and cultural construction of national leaders in the United States of America. From the first
administration of George Washington in the late eighteenth century to that
of Barack Obama in the twenty-first, individual portraits and artistic representations of national symbols in the official spaces of the nation have helped
to shape our conception of political gravitas and an individual's ability to lead
effectively.

The images of American leaders that circulate in visual culture and hang
in the Smithsonian Institution's National Portrait Gallery in Washington,
DC, do much to affect our impression of their power and humanity. Art
installed in the White House functions as a visual tool to communicate the

current president's leadership style, cultural vision, and political agenda. As such, these images and objects can help us understand some of the ways in which such choices—made by or with the ultimate approval of the First Family—impact the polity and shape the vision of the larger American self. This chapter focuses on the role that racial difference has played, and continues to play, in the formation of ideals of national citizenship, self-worth, and belonging. It begins with a historical consideration of the use of photographic portraiture by activist Frederick Douglass in the nineteenth century before moving to a contemporary discussion of art in the making of the Obama presidency and its role in the formation of its legacy. In this way, it will examine the larger cultural role of art in the construction of historical and contemporary American identity.

By the time he ran as the vice presidential candidate on the National Equal Rights Party ticket in 1872, Frederick Douglass, the self-freed son of his mother's enslaver, understood the ability of portraiture to create visions of power in the public sphere and the political arena. After his first autobiography was published in 1845, Douglass's persuasive arguments for the humanity of the enslaved people whose status he had once shared vaulted him into the national ranks of serious activists fighting against slavery, racism, and social inequality. In surviving images, exemplified by a daguerreotype of around 1850 in the collection of the Smithsonian's National Portrait Gallery, Douglass's incisive gaze cuts as deeply as the fiery rhetoric he deployed in his public lectures. Through these fiercely self-possessed exchanges with the camera lens, Douglass sought to end debate about the fact of Black humanity and what qualities constituted a man. As historian John Stauffer explains, "the look of the public persona was crucial to him because he wanted to enter into the public sphere with an equal voice with an equal image and have the same rights as any other citizen."[1]

In addition to his impressive rhetorical skills on paper and on stage, Douglass used the photographic image as a political tool. Compared to a well-painted portrait, early daguerreotypes and paper photographs were inexpensive and quick to make, and as technology progressed over the course of the nineteenth century, they could be reproduced cheaply and infinitely. Douglass used photography to distribute his own image widely over the fifty-four years between the taking of his first daguerreotype in 1841 and the printing of his last authorized cabinet card in 1895.[2] He had scores of photographs taken of himself. With 160 distinct surviving portraits, it has been argued that he was the most photographed American of the nineteenth century.[3] By comparison, there are 130 photographs of his contemporary President Abraham Lincoln.

Figure 12.1 Frederick Douglass (1818–1895), c. 1850, after c. 1847 original. Sixth-plate daguerreotype. National Portrait Gallery, Smithsonian Institution.

During the summer of 1863, at the height of the Civil War, Douglass visited the White House. As he sat in the waiting room, he reflected on those around him. "They were white; and as I was the only dark spot among them, I expected to have to wait at least half a day."[4] There were, of course, other African American bodies in the White House that day, including Mary Todd Lincoln's seamstress Elizabeth Keckley and President Lincoln's personal messenger William Slade, but Black guests during the 1860s were limited to Douglass and fellow abolitionist Sojourner Truth, who met with Lincoln in 1864.[5]

The dilemma of how to enter and inhabit the space of the White House as a Black body, a space that was built by both free and enslaved Black laborers, was important to Barack Obama when he assumed the presidency in January 2009. His resolution to this question may be seen in the photographs of the president taken by Pete Souza, who was given exclusive access within the White House, and the art that was installed in the executive mansion during his two terms in office. Art within the Oval Office, the architectural space most closely associated with the executive branch of government in the United States, was very thoughtfully installed during the Obama presidency. A photograph from 2009 of President Obama and Secretary of State Hillary Clinton, for example, shows Norman Rockwell's 1946 painting of the *Statue of Liberty*, her outstretched arm holding a torch being cleaned and maintained by a diverse group of American men including an African American figure at right, and Childe Hassam's World War I–era painting of American flags, *The Avenue in the Rain* (1917), flanking the *Resolute* desk (see fig. 12.2). While both paintings deploy signs of nationalist fervor and patriotic signification, they also point to a high level of aesthetic and cultural appreciation for American art.

Further, the president's appreciation of the art hung on the walls of his workspace is emphasized in other pictures taken by Souza that show Obama contemplating or otherwise engaging with the art in his main workspace. In these images, Souza makes the visual proposal that the paintings were not in the executive mansion solely for decorative purposes; rather, they had been chosen for the personal delectation of the president, as though President Obama turned to artistic depictions of our nation in search of philosophical or aesthetic guidance. These photographs create a visual argument for what might be read as the president's highly developed aesthetic sensibility, an educated appreciation of American art, or a natural inclination toward "the finer things." By demonstrating that the United States' first Black president possessed a specific type of cultural currency, Souza and Obama collaborated in the deployment of an image of belonging within a space that had never had a similar-looking occupant.

In addition to the strategic placement of paintings in the space of the Oval Office and in photographs of the president, the Obamas oversaw the installation and constant rotation of numerous important works of art by established icons of both American fine and popular art, like Hassam and Rockwell, throughout the public and private space of the White House. In 2009 White House curator William Allman described the Obamas'

Figure 12.2 President Barack Obama meets with Secretary of State Hillary Clinton, January 21, 2009. Photo by Pete Souza. Official White House Photo.

borrowings as expressing a very strong "interest in truly modern art."[6] They clearly took great care in selecting the location and then spending personal time considering and appreciating the works themselves.

More than any other recent First Family, the Obamas used the White House as a public and private space to display a whole range of modern and contemporary art that presented an expanded and more inclusive vision of American culture, history, and experience. Their intervention is important given the historical placement of art in the public and private spaces of the White House. For example, let us consider two official photographs of the Old Dining Room made a year apart during the second administration of President Theodore Roosevelt. On the left (fig. 12.3) we see a large empty space that is framed by two candelabra sconces and anchored by the mute presence of Black member of the service staff, eyes cast downward as though he was just another piece of furniture. The white space of the wall beside him creates a kind of visual white noise drowning out and subsuming the possibility of Black voice or vision. He serves as a kind of staffage for this domestic interior—present for size and scale, but also to connote the purpose of the space and the social rank of its intended inhabitants. In the other photograph (fig. 12.4), the Black figure had been replaced by the installation of a rather large portrait of President John Tyler over the sideboard, a bold

PRIVATE DINING-ROOM

Figure 12.3 Private [Family] Dining Room at the White House. Printed in Esther Single-ton, *Story of the White House* (New York: The McClure, 1907), vol. 2, 259.

Figure 12.4 Family Dining Room under Roosevelt renovation, 1902. White House Collection, White House Historical Association.

antidote to the silent blackness and glaring blankness that had been there before.

Once on the wall, the portrait of President Tyler became a familiar fixture in the room, as integral a part of its milieu as the candelabra sconces and architectural millwork. Subsequent presidents and their families continually reinstalled the painting in the space after various renovations over the century, up through the administration of President Lyndon Johnson. It was not until the 1990s that the artistic program in this room and the other spaces in the mansion began to change. During the Clinton administration, First Lady Hillary Rodham Clinton had the White House purchase its first work of art by a woman, *Mountain at Bear Lake—Taos* (1930), a landscape painting by Irish American artist Georgia O'Keeffe, which was installed in the formal living room. Several years later, First Lady Laura Bush doubled down by borrowing O'Keeffe's 1932 painting *Jimson Weed* from the O'Keeffe Museum in New Mexico and having it installed in the Family Dining Room.[7]

First Lady Michelle Obama expanded this interest in showcasing art by women at the White House, marking another first in 2015 when she had the White House purchase and install an abstract painting by the African American woman artist Alma Woodsey Thomas in the Old Dining Room above an area rug designed by Jewish American designer Anni Albers. While Thomas's work was the first by a Black woman artist to enter the collection or to be hung on the walls, it was not the first piece by an African American to be installed in the White House. In 2009, a few years before, the Obamas had borrowed an oil stick text piece by Glenn Ligon, *Black Like Me #2*, from the Smithsonian's Hirshhorn Museum. Here, Ligon has stenciled across the surface of the canvas a quote from the 1961 book *Black Like Me*, a memoir by white journalist John Howard Griffin, who transformed himself into a Black man so that he could write about his experiences and help support the cause of African American civil rights in the era leading up to the Voting Rights Act of 1965. "All traces of the Griffin I had been were wiped from existence," "All traces of the Griffin I had been were wiped from existence," "All traces of the Griffin I had been were wiped from existence." Stenciled over and over again until the once clear message has itself slipped away into a sticky smudge of black illegibility covering over again the meaning within itself into the obscure. By working with the kind of repetition found in the early twentieth-century poetry and prose of Gertrude Stein (a rose is a rose is a rose is a rose), Ligon reemploys an enduring modernist mode to destabilize a present sense of selfhood and social knowledge.

In 2011, when more of Ligon's work came to the Corcoran Gallery of Art in Washington, DC, as a part of the traveling exhibition *30 Americans*,

Figure 12.5 Library room, ground floor of the White House, after its refurbishment during the administration of President George W. Bush, 2007. White House Historical Association.

Figure 12.6 President's Dining Room during George W. Bush administration. Photo by Peter Vitale, 2007. White House Historical Association.

Figure 12.7 The Old Family Dining Room of the White House, February 9, 2015. Photo by Amanda Lucidon. Official White House Photo.

Michelle Obama took her daughters to see the show. In addition to works by Ligon, *30 Americans*, drawn exclusively from the Miami-based collection of Don and Mera Rubell, includes works by Jean-Michel Basquiat, Robert Colescott, Kara Walker, Mickalene Thomas, and twenty-seven other African American artists. The challenge of avant-garde contemporary art was clearly something that all members of this particular First Family were prepared to embrace.

"It's in the private quarters of the White House," Ligon told *The Guardian* newspaper in 2013 when he was asked about the placement of *Black Like Me #2*,

> So I can't see it. But I met Obama once, backstage at the Apollo in Harlem. I was with my friend and a woman said, "I wonder if you have a moment to meet the president?" And, you know, we had dinner reservations—but OK. So we go downstairs and there's Obama with the chief of staff, who says, "Mr President, this is Glenn Ligon. Black Like Me No 2 is in your personal quarters." And Obama looks at me and goes, "Oh, yeah, we have a set of prints too! But they had to move them out, because of the light. I really miss them." . . . I thought, "Oh wait, this is real! They live with art, they take their children to look at

art, they're not scared of artists. This is not some bullshit. This is not on his talking points." I was super impressed.[8]

The way that the Obamas welcomed dynamic and challenging art into their daily lives during their eight years in the White House surpassed that of previous First Families, including John and Jacqueline Kennedy, who were strongly committed supporters of contemporary American artists such as color field painters Morris Louis and Elaine de Kooning, who painted the portrait of President Kennedy that now hangs in the National Portrait Gallery.[9] For example, the White House borrowed *The Problem We All Live With*, Norman Rockwell's 1963 painting of school desegregation in New Orleans, in preparation for a visit by the painting's subject, Ruby Bridges, in 2011 (fig. 12.8). Here, Rockwell skillfully sites meaningful leadership in the body of a small girl walking purposefully forward into a future of opportunities despite the insults being hurled at her body and the bodies of all others that her color and form signify.

In the winter of 2016–17, as he prepared to leave office, President Obama began consulting with the staff of the Smithsonian's National Portrait Gallery regarding the commissioning of the official presidential portrait and portrait of the First Lady destined to be installed in the ongoing *America's Presidents* and *First Ladies* exhibitions. A year later, on February 13, 2018, when the portraits of the by-then-former president and his wife, by Kehinde Wiley and Amy Sherald, respectively, were revealed, they created a national sensation. These distinctive portraits quickly became the most viewed images in the history of the National Portrait Gallery, logging over 2.3 million visitors in their first year.

Kehinde Wiley's portrait of Obama shows him sitting on an ornate chair surrounded by lush foliage and white jasmine flowers native to his birthplace in Hawaii and to Indonesia, where he spent his childhood; the African lily, representing his Kenyan heritage; the multicolored chrysanthemum, symbolizing his life in Chicago; and the rosebud for love and courage.[10] In person, the portrait has an almost mesmerizing effect on viewers. Some have detected hidden meanings or seen coded script embedded in the green leaves that curl about Obama's body as he perches on his modest throne, leaning in toward the picture plane and almost into the space of the viewer. Secret language or no, there is nothing else even remotely like it in the *America's Presidents* exhibition. While most of the presidential portraits assert the power embodied in their subject through the direct and penetrating gaze of the subject, none of them seems to go as fiercely deep as that of Wiley's Obama. Perhaps this is because Wiley's composition channels a spectral

Figure 12.8 President Barack Obama, Ruby Bridges, and representatives of the Norman Rockwell Museum view Rockwell's *The Problem We All Live With,* hanging in a West Wing hallway near the Oval Office, July 15, 2011. Photo by Pete Souza. Official White House Photo.

return of the barely visible and historically silenced Black bodies, including Elizabeth Keckley, William Slade, and the unnamed footman who served in the Roosevelt household in 1908, that have always been in the White House yet rarely seen, heard, or acknowledged in any formal way. And perhaps it is because the portrait also strongly echoes the penetrating gaze of Frederick Douglass. The presence of an unbending Black gaze within the National Portrait Gallery's *America's Presidents* exhibition, the field of portraiture in which the visual legacies of the face of American power are perennially at stake, is a very threatening prospect for those who hold a white supremacist vision of the United States.[11]

Proof of these specular anxieties appeared in spring 2019 among the creatives working for the visual propaganda machine of Obama's successor, Donald J. Trump. A parody T-shirt appropriating Wiley's painting was offered for sale on the Trump 2020 Campaign website.[12] Here, the sensation that the viewer has of being captured within Obama's penetrating gaze in Wiley's portrait is doubled by the addition of a pair of binoculars held up to the face of the former president. Signs of sight and sites of a powerful gaze, these binoculars are used to "spy" on one of the least difficult figures to miss: President Donald Trump.

I close this consideration of the visionary power of photographic portraits and paintings in the creation of presidential vision and leadership in the contemporary United States by considering the impact of Amy Sherald's portrait of Michelle Obama on one very specific and often overlooked group of American viewers: African American and other girls of color. In Sherald's composition, the First Lady sits on a low platform facing the viewer, wearing an evening gown from Milly, designed by Michelle Smith. "It has an abstract pattern that reminded me of the Dutch artist Piet Mondrian's geometric paintings," Sherald explained in her comments at the portrait's unveiling. "But Milly's design also resembles the inspired quilt masterpieces made by the women of Gee's Bend, a small remote black community in Alabama, where they compose quilts in geometries that transform clothes and fabric remnants into masterpieces."[13] A painterly statement about sartorial history and women's arts, the patterns of quilts made by women ancestors are spread out below Michelle Obama's bare and legendarily well-toned arms.

The profound and very particular importance of Amy Sherald's portrait was witnessed just two weeks after its unveiling when Jessica Curry took her two-year-old daughter, Parker, to see the painting. Parker was stunned by the image of a beautiful Black woman, whom she described to her mother as a "queen." A photograph of that moment taken by another museum visitor quickly went viral. "This is what America is all about," retweeted an Atlanta man. "This young girl can now dream about being someone like Michelle Obama."[14] When Sherald posted the image to her Instagram account, she wrote:

When I look at this picture I think back to my first field trip in elementary school to a museum. I had only seen paintings in encyclopedias up to that point in my life. . . . There was a painting of a black man standing in front of a house. I don't remember a lot about my childhood, but I do have a few emotional memories etched into my mind forever and seeing that painting of a man that looked like he could be my father stopped me dead in my tracks. This was my first time seeing real paintings that weren't in a book and also weren't painted in another century. I didn't realize that none of them had me in them until I saw that painting. . . . I knew I wanted to be an artist already, but seeing that painting made me realize that I could. What dreams may come? #representationmatters[15]

A week later, Michelle Obama posted some photos and a video of her and Parker dancing in the family room of the Kalorama mansion that the

Obamas moved to in January 2017. She wrote: "Parker, I'm so glad I had the chance to meet you today (and for the dance party!) Keep on dreaming big for yourself and maybe one day I'll proudly look up at a portrait of you." More than 1.5 million people liked this image, but only a few noticed that in the background of photos from that day we can see a print by Kerry James Marshall and a firehose piece by Theaster Gates. They are evidence of the continuous commitment that the Obamas have made to contemporary art and to Black Chicago artists. The following Halloween, now three-year-old Parker Curry chose to go as Sherald's vision of Michelle Obama. So too did an untold number of other young girls of color choose to envision themselves as the former First Lady in her designer dress, elegantly posed for her official parting portrait.

Sherald's painting has become a unique image that represents not just the culmination of Michelle Obama's process of "becoming," as she titled her best-selling memoir, but also a key icon leading the positive identity formation of young girls of color, giving them a way to visualize the possibility of themselves as beautiful, powerful women with leadership potential. And while the photos of girls dressed and posed as Sherald's painting are tremendously moving, another little girl's Halloween costume choice to go as "Amy Sherald, American artist" is equally inspiring. For this shows us that both art and the ability to create art can have the power to lead and inspire us in many ways, not just to propel us to occupy a seat of power, but also to envision ourselves as the creators of culture. This picture of a little Black girl who does not want to be a queen or the accomplished wife of a former president but a famous woman artist fills one with hope for the future—a future in which the people who pursue the roles of political and cultural leadership in the United States will be as rich and diverse as the country itself.

NOTES

1. John Stauffer, interview by Michel Martin, "Picture This: Frederick Douglass Was the Most Photographed Man of His Time," *All Things Considered*, December 13, 2015, accessed January 20, 2019, https://www.npr.org/2015/12/13/459593474/picture-this -frederick-douglass-was-the-most-photographed-man-of-his-time. See John Stauffer, Zoe Trodd, and Celeste-Marie Bernier, *Picturing Frederick Douglass: An Illustrated Biography of the Nineteenth Century's Most Photographed American*, 1st ed. (New York: Liveright, 2015).

2. David W. Blight, *Frederick Douglass: Prophet of Freedom* (New York: Simon & Schuster, 2018).

3. Stauffer et al., *Picturing Frederick Douglass.*

4. Frederick Douglass, *Proceedings of the American Anti-Slavery Society at its third decade, held in the city of Philadelphia, Dec. 3rd and 4th, 1863, with an appendix and a catalogue*

of Anti-Slavery publications in America from 1750 to 1863 (New York: American Anti-Slavery Society, 1864), 116.

5. "African Americans in the Lincoln White House," White House Historical Association, accessed May 31, 2019, https://www.whitehousehistory.org/african-americans-in-the-lincoln-white-house. For more on African Americans in the Lincoln White House, see William Seale, *The President's House* (Washington, DC: White House Historical Association, 1986); William Seale, "Upstairs and Downstairs: The 19th-Century White House," *American Visions*, February–March 1995, 16–20; Adele Logan Alexander, "White House Confidante of Mrs. Lincoln," *American Visions*, February–March 1995, 18; and Elizabeth Keckley, *Behind the Scenes: Or, Thirty Years a Slave, and Four Years in the White House* (1868; repr., Oxford: Oxford University Press, 1988).

6. Blake Gopnik, "On Loan to the White House: Art to Ponder," *Washington Post*, October 7, 2009, accessed April 20, 2019, http://www.washingtonpost.com/wp-dyn/content/article/2009/10/06/AR2009100601824.html.

7. In 2014, when the O'Keeffe Museum chose to sell *Jimson Weed* to raise much-needed funds, the painting fetched $44.5 million at auction, setting a record price not just for the artist herself but also for any work of art by a woman. It is now in the collection of the Tate Modern in London. Here, the visionary leadership of these two First Ladies to spotlight the work of a particular American artist, by linking it to the spaces of the presidency (and vice versa), yielded tremendous results for the promotion and validation of American women's creativity on an international scale.

8. Jason Farago, "He's Barack Obama's Favourite Artist. But Is Britain Ready for Glenn Ligon?," *Guardian*, April 2, 2015, accessed April 20, 2019.

9. For more on the Kennedy's interest in contemporary art, see Alexander Nemerov, "Morris Louis Court Painter of the Kennedy Era," in *Morris Louis Now: An American Master Revisited*, ed. Kelly Morris and Lori Cavagnaro, 1st ed. (Atlanta: High Museum of Art, 2006), 21–38.

10. Kim Sajet, "In Obama's Official Portrait the Flowers Are Cultivated from the Past," February 20, 2018, accessed April 19, 2019, https://www.smithsonianmag.com/smithsonian-institution/obamas-official-portrait-flowers-cultivated-from-past-180968200/.

11. Mieke Bal and Norman Bryson, "Semiotics and Art History," *Art Bulletin* 73, no. 2 (June 1991): 207.

12. Zachary Small, "Trump Satirizes Kehinde Wiley's Obama Portrait to Fundraise 2020 Reelection Bid," accessed April 19, 2019, https://hyperallergic.com/495444/trump-satirizes-kehinde-wileys-obama-portrait-to-fundraise-2020-reelection-bid/.

13. Ellen C. Caldwell, "What Amy Sherald Tells Us with Michelle Obama's Dress," JSTOR Daily, February 13, 2018, accessed July 26, 2020, https://daily.jstor.org/what-amy-sherald-tells-us-with-michelle-obamas-dress/.

14. Michael S. Rosenwald, "'A Moment of Awe': Photo of Little Girl Captivated by Michelle Obama Portrait Goes Viral," *Washington Post*, March 4, 2018, accessed January 20, 2019, https://www.washingtonpost.com/local/a-moment-of-awe-photo-of-little-girl-staring-at-michelle-obama-portrait-goes-viral/2018/03/04/4e5a4548-1ff2-11e8-94da-ebf9d112159c_story.html.

15. Amy Sherald (@asherald), "Feeling all the feels," Instagram, March 2, 2018, https://www.instagram.com/p/Bf06igcHKwr/.

PART VI

Performing Arts

CHAPTER 13

"O Clap Your Hands!"

Leadership Lessons from the
Experience of Music

Pegram Harrison

Orlando Gibbons was, by any estimation, a leading musician. Born in Oxford in 1583, he established himself in London as a prominent keyboard player, becoming a member of the Jacobean Chapel Royal at the early age of nineteen; his contemporaries described him as "the best finger of the age" and "the best hand in England."[1] At the height of his career he returned to Oxford to supplicate for his doctoral degree. The procedure involved composing an impressive piece, in this case an anthem for eight-part choir with words from Psalm 47, "O Clap Your Hands." If the choice of text was intended to elicit approving applause, it worked: Gibbons was granted his doctorate, and his anthem was first formally performed at his own degree ceremony in 1622. The piece demonstrates superb compositional skill. It also provides an excellent teaching device for exploring leadership: the story of its origins, the way it is composed, and the process of performing it, both in the past and in the present, all provide vivid and memorable insights into aspects of leadership that resonate far more powerfully than much other pedagogic material. Moreover, because the University of Oxford is home to such cultural artifacts and their history, it is well positioned to draw on the arts and humanities in teaching leadership. Gibbons's anthem is but one example informing an MBA class at Oxford's Saïd Business School called Leadership Perspectives from the Humanities that makes extensive use of the opportunities Oxford provides.[2] Gibbons proved himself worthy of an Oxford degree by the exercise of his skill and virtuosity; current-day Oxford MBA students are challenged to engage with the same art forms and creative expressions as they shape themselves into leaders for our time.

THE STATE OF THE ART

Many MBA students and professional managers have experienced workshops involving music to develop leadership skills, drawing on similar inspirations and working in similar ways. In the main, these workshops assume that musical ensembles provide examples of highly expert, high-performance, dynamic human systems akin to professional teams in business, and that the leadership skills necessary to assemble, motivate, and coordinate them are transferable. This process is neither mechanistic nor straightforward, though. Leadership is assumed to be something that—like creativity—can be learned if not taught, fostered if not commanded, so the format of these experiential workshops aims for a learning experience that is more emotive than cognitive. And though there is not much rigorous evidence about their effectiveness, there is research on the practice of arts-based leadership learning, as well as on the mechanics of leadership in orchestras.[3] Outside the formal academy, anecdotal impressions about the effectiveness of such interventions are plentiful. In the United States, for example, Boston-based conductor Benjamin Zander has run successful workshops with business leaders and managers for many years.[4] In Europe, Danish conductor Peter Hanke has developed superb activities with small groups of executives, delving into many aspects of leadership and innovation, "transforming knowledge and experience from the performing arts into core leadership principles that can be understood and used across any industry."[5] These instances use mainly classical music; others use the improvisatory nature of jazz, the rhythmic drive of drums, the physical immediacy of dance, and so forth.[6] All add nuance to the general idea that performance—in artistic as well as professional contexts—has some relationship to leadership, and that leadership effectiveness can be enhanced by involvement with musical performance, just as musical performance can be enhanced by leadership.

However, what these approaches do not do, really, is inquire into the contributions that the discipline of *music itself* can make to understanding leadership. If music does anything more than merely supplying an entrancing metaphor about teamwork and coordination, what else might that be? And how might it happen? Essential elements of leadership do align with elements of music—empathy, listening, operating both cognitively and emotionally—and there is some research on leadership in practice based on observation of sensemaking and emotion in musical organizations.[7] Such work pushes well beyond the metaphor of the leader/conductor. But still, it concerns musical performance mainly and does not extensively explore how music itself—as composition, sound, social phenomenon, et cetera—might contribute to and enhance an understanding of leadership.

What other alignments between music and leadership might be valuable to explore? For example, music and leadership alike can be functional or inspiring, can imitate or innovate, can perpetuate or challenge institutional structures and expectations. Both motivate, both set goals and facilitate their achievement, both generate values to be shared and promoted. There is also something similar about their operational mechanisms for achieving outputs though synchronicity, entrainment, and rhythm. Composition techniques such as counterpoint work by giving the listener something to follow, to be involved in, and to share in achieving. How can making connections such as these improve our understanding of both music and leadership?

I grapple with these questions all the time, and I have no answers. Nonetheless, it is important to acknowledge the challenge. That, after all, is something art does: instead of offering answers, it poses questions and provides the conditions for consideration and reflection and contemplation and whatever else might enable one to deal with not knowing the answers. Leadership does the same: it enables progress toward something without controlling every aspect of it. Grappling to bring leadership and music together is itself instructive.

The great American lyric soprano Joyce DiDonato took up this challenge in an article offering "Lessons for the Economy from the Stage."[8] Why can't the world mimic the opera stage? she asks. In opera many things that seem undervalued or valueless in the real world are placed center-stage: capable leaders who project authority with beauty and finesse more than force, artistic accomplishment, equal pay for women, and so on. Her message is personal and universal: "I'm not arguing with reality. . . . I just call on us all to think and act with more operatic audacity." DiDonato's own career, as well as her article, demonstrate that opera offers more than mere lessons for the economy: it offers insights into how leadership as understood and practiced in an artistic profession can provide a model for leadership more generally— precisely because it is so rooted in a holistically humane, and not a merely economic, understanding. "There is so much that the operatic world gets right about humanity," DiDonato concludes, citing especially how empathy with its characters is achieved through singing. With such empathy, "we might dare to be a bit more vocal, a bit more loud, a bit more audacious—dare I say, operatic—in how we speak up for those who are not 'allowed' to carry power in our current society."[9] In short, *experiencing* opera can be a leadership lesson as potent as any other, and even more so.

However, it is hard to harness opera for the classroom. Recordings and videos are simply too mechanical; bringing real performers into a class is logistically complicated; and opera singers lose potency without all the additional accoutrements of orchestra and stage and sets and costumes and appropriate acoustics. And again, DiDonato's message—her medium—is mainly about performance. Insights from the music itself remain hard to grasp.

Even for musical professionals, for whom the value of music often derives from its ability to articulate the ineffable, it can be difficult to explain in words what happens in music. Musicians who, like DiDonato, are also good explainers—Leonard Bernstein, Aaron Copland—emphasize the vital importance of *not* explaining away the mystery.[10] Instead, like all great musicians, they strive always to keep music innately musical, not merely a metaphor for something else. For these reasons, in thinking about leadership through the experience of music, it is important not to delve too deeply into the mechanics of either phenomenon and instead to dwell a while in the mystery—a realm somewhat abstract, and more revealing because of that.

So from now on I want to use a more personal voice to explore ideas about leadership and music that prioritize personal experience as the most valuable pedagogic element in music-based leadership development, and to demonstrate how and why that is so.

EXPERIENCING THE MUSIC

An audience assembles, lights dim, the hall falls utterly silent as the conductor raises her arms. Following her gestures, the hugely complex machinery of an orchestra fuses art and science and humanity with miraculous coordination. Together, the performers and audience create a shared experience of head, heart, and hand that is at once exhilarating and mystifying. Such a musical experience, presided over by a conductor, is one of the most emblematic and yet also intriguing metaphors for leadership. How does it happen? Can others harness that same power in different contexts? How does it feel to lead like an orchestral conductor? And how can one learn to do so?

As with opera, it is hard to bring an orchestra into the classroom, so my classes on leadership use choral music and singers to ask these questions. Pieces such as Orlando Gibbons's anthem, supported by carefully designed activities for engaging students, can provide accessible leadership lessons. I have the great good fortune of being able to do this in a place with a strong appetite for experiential learning, a ready supply of highly accomplished singers, and ancient traditions of composition and performance, as well as inspiring architectural and acoustic spaces. Drawing on these resources and working with like-minded colleagues have enabled me to develop the learning experience described here.

Class begins normally. I stand in front of the students, explain who I am, and introduce the singers who are joining me for the session. So much, so normal, so comfortable. But soon, I begin to do unexpected things: I ask students to stand, and wave their hands about, and feel their arms moving. The goal is to get out of the head and into the body, to change students' usual perspective and point of view from rational to physical. I want them to become excited, even uncomfortable—no longer sitting, no longer sure what is going on, no longer "in control" of their relationship to each other and to me. At base, I want to start detaching the notion of leadership from the notion of control.

As in some pieces of music, this opening phase of the class works like an anacrusis: an unstressed beat before the first bar line of a piece, an upbeat that helps to define where the repeating stress of the line will occur. "Happy Birthday" starts with an anacrusis:

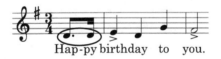

Hap-py birthday   to   you.

Similarly, in ancient Greek drama, anacrusis (ἀνάκρουσις) can take the form of a loud chaotic noise before a play starts, to clear out demons and distractions, to focus attention, and to enable the suspension of disbelief. Much later, in eighteenth-century Europe, symphonies often began with a slow, quiet, and unsettled introduction to attract the attention of the audience before beginning the real material of the piece. Jazz musicians will be familiar with the similarly intended instruction to "vamp till ready." In this spirit, I use incidental activities to distract, displace, and discomfort students, before beginning in earnest with a more readily responsive audience. Even the vignette of the orchestra at the start of this section is such an incidental activity. All are examples of a pedagogic tactic, an anacrusis, that is innately and intentionally musical.

Keeping the focus on hands and gestures, I then ask students to imitate my own gestures. While this might look like a means of further focusing attention on a leader standing in front of a group of followers, it is actually intended to problematize that image. "Imitate me" is leadership in only the most superficial way: "do what I do" presumes I know what to do and how to do it. Yes, there is a time and a place for such a directive leadership style—for example, an urgent moment of crisis—but it is not always the most appropriate model of leadership.[11] Control is necessary for getting out of a burning building perhaps ("Follow me! Now!"), but not for many other functions. Likewise, the command-and-control implications of a leader as a focal point can be set up so as to be torn down. The image of a drill sergeant, or of a prison guard at the center of a Panopticon—or indeed, to those who have not thought about it much, of a conductor standing before an orchestra—represents a thin understanding of leadership, easily debunked. Put simply, "Do what I say" does not result in art or innovation; drilling might build skill or maintain discipline, but it more often undermines creativity than enhances it.

In more detail, asking people to imitate my gestures but then making those gestures too complex to copy shows that someone who cannot enable followers is no leader. Similarly, asking students to imitate a pattern of clapping—simple at first but then too fast or random to follow—demonstrates that imitation is fundamentally at odds with innovation, and that command and control is only the most basic form of leadership. I ask students to think about all this in a musical context: if all the players had to do was obey instructions, they wouldn't be making music, and a robot could replace them. Instead, when their leader enables them to exercise their skill together, then they make music. I ask the students to consider for themselves what this might mean in a managerial context.

Clapping is a useful pedagogic tool for more lessons than this. Students can quickly learn to synchronize their clapping to a simple pattern, after which it is possible to push them further by setting up a new, more complex pattern—but this only works if I ask them to take ownership of it. The rhythmic motif of Beethoven's Fifth Symphony is useful for this:

Everyone knows it; it is apparently the most familiar musical motif in the world,[12] and it is persistently easy to hear and, therefore, also easy to work with. First, the whole class learns to clap the pattern; then half the group does the first part, and the other half follows with the second. But this is not as straightforward as it sounds: it is messy at first, until some student eventually points out that the silent upbeat is relevant. The rest after the first statement of the pattern provides the springboard for the next, like an anacrusis, without which the second group cannot coordinate its entry:

This exercise challenges students to listen to the pattern, to the silence, to the other group, and to each other; it creates ensemble and cohesion. Without this challenge—far more subtle than being told what to do—the activity is impossible. With it, however, there is far less need for a focal leader to give the cues and bring people in at the right time and so forth. If everyone is listening and coordinating properly, the teacher can step back after starting the process and simply let it run. It takes a few iterations, but once the groups realize what is expected—not by the teacher but *by the music*—they begin to feel empowered and motivated to perfect this more complex activity. Now they are no longer imitating nor following orders; they are working together, with each other and with Beethoven and, least importantly, with the individual who respects their skill enough to let them proceed without further intervention. In Beethoven's symphony, the initial four-note motif pervades the rest of the piece, from very beginning to very end. So, too, does the leadership lesson of this exercise about team ensemble: the leader's role is most often not to control but to enable.

Another exercise involving clapping can be very powerful. American composer Steve Reich's 1972 piece "Clapping Music" consists of a single rhythmic motif that performers vary:

Two performers start the sequence together (at number 1 below); after several iterations, one performer starts at a different time, as in a round (2); and then continues to shift the pattern (3):

clap 1
clap 2

The stresses of the pattern come at different times for each performer, as do the rests. The challenge for the performers is both sticking to their own specific roles and listening carefully to the others; the challenge for listeners is hearing the whole effect and becoming aware of the slow-changing precession of stresses and silences that gives the piece dynamism and interest beyond its basic motif. The overall leadership lesson—building on the earlier ones about imitation, coordination, listening, and releasing control—is that with enabling (not controlling) leadership, quite complex shared endeavors can achieve much that would be impossible otherwise.

The class has come far already, in about thirty minutes, and only with clapping. At this point, I introduce more sophisticated music, as well as the local Oxford context—and maintain the clapping theme. The next piece is the one cited earlier, Orlando Gibbons's eight-part anthem for double choir, "O Clap Your Hands." The piece provides excellent teaching opportunities for exploring imitation and innovation, leadership and followership, power and empowerment, speaking and listening, independence and coordination, coordination and ensemble, and much else. Because Gibbons divides the eight-part choir into two halves of four, which entails a high level of professional expertise to coordinate, students can recall earlier lessons about coordination and empowerment from the clapping exercises with Beethoven's Fifth and Reich's "Clapping Music."

The complexity of "O Clap Your Hands" invites attentive listening and watching. I ask the students why the choir seems to have split into two groups of four: the answer is that the music suggests it, even requires it. This answer comes easily to those who can hear the way the music works antiphonally at times—the two halves in dialogue with each other (for example, singing the phrase "O sing praises" back and forth to each other)—and at other times in full ensemble, when all voices converge on particularly appropriate moments of text (such as the word "together"). Some students hear this easily; some need to see the physical movements of the choir (two groups forming, mouths opening and closing); still others need to have all of this pointed out to them. Instead of doing that myself, I ask questions and stand back as the students first discuss with each other and then eventually start to ask the singers for information and advice. The singers are, after all, the ones who know best. In time, with enhanced understanding of how the music works and why certain performance decisions are taken, the students listen as the singers sing the whole piece, and everyone's overall engagement with the music is significantly heightened. When the singers begin to sing the piece, this florid, elaborate, and emphatically impressive music amply demonstrates their skill and grants them professional credibility. They achieve a high level of performance merely by being enabled in the exercise of their expertise—which is itself a leadership lesson. Again, as the notional "leader" of the class, I have done almost nothing to achieve this deeper engagement other than to set up the scenario and to invite people to think about it. The leadership lessons expand with the experience of the music: leadership is a distributed activity, it is very much about trusting in others' expertise as well as accessing it to enhance one's own contribution, and it is legitimated and enhanced through the direct appreciation of others' perspectives. The music demonstrates this, not the conductor.

At this point, I often ask if someone in the class would like to volunteer to help me, a device learned from my colleague Peter Hanke and his workshops with Exart Performances.[13] Without explaining what the volunteer will be asked to do, I put some pressure on the class to ensure that a self-confident and extroverted person, almost invariably a young man, will step forth in front of his peers, to take a risk or be the center of attention, or both. Imagine this young man: he is often North American, he is tall and sturdy and popular, and so forth; he is conventional leadership material. And he is happy to stand up in front of the class, with all eyes focused on him. Then I reveal what he has volunteered for: I ask him to conduct the choir. "How hard can it be? You've seen this before, on TV or in real life. Just wave your arms." Confidently, he jumps right in. And predictably, everything falls apart fast. He raises his arms, and nothing happens; or he waves them around meaninglessly or confusingly; or he gets things started and then cannot stop them; or because his gestures are peculiar, the singers interpret them differently and get out of sync; or they look stressed, sound bad, and get worse. The others start to laugh at their classmate, whose confidence drains away rapidly. It is a harsh and obvious lesson: being in a position of responsibility is no guarantee of leadership effectiveness. Like the vain Malvolio in Shakespeare's *Twelfth Night*, who is set up to fail in a similar way (in Act II, scene 5), those who have greatness "thrust upon 'em" face an especially hard task. In some ways, people who seem to be natural leaders—those who conform to conventional ideas of what leadership means, how it works, and who can do it best—are less often called upon to reflect on the hollowness of such assumptions and have less opportunity to learn leadership properly. This lesson seems particularly appropriate for an elite student, such as anyone in an MBA program or a position of social, professional, and financial security—and for that reason, it is even more important to emphasize.

In any case, it is fun for everyone (except perhaps the brave and foolish volunteer) to see the mighty stumble; this is important, too, insofar as it renders the lessons more resonant and personal. Leadership is not abstract but physical, vulnerable, and changeable, like any human being. The situation of the singers also comes to the fore: they are disabled, not enabled, by inept or inappropriate intervention in their activity—by micromanagement. Still, they do need something from the person in front, and figuring out what this is can be harder than identifying what it is not. The volunteer might realize he does not know what he is doing, but he is rarely quick to identify why this is a problem or how to fix it. In brief, he continues to think about himself instead of others and fails at first to seek the assistance of those who can best support him, who in turn need his support. He might realize that he should turn to the singers for feedback, but rather than ask "what am I doing wrong?" he will benefit most from asking "what do you need from me?" Instead of assuming he knows already what they need, he should find a way to direct attention where it needs to be—to the expertise in the room. It is not about him; instead, his role as a leader is to *enable* the others' expertise, not to be "in control." And until he realizes that, the music will sound terrible. This leadership lesson is often obvious to the classmates observing, and only eventually dawns on the poor guy in the spotlight: ask for help, and you will become a more effective leader; by not doing so, you will lose trust and power.

Gibbons's piece provides many more leadership lessons; one could craft a whole class around it. Gibbons lived and wrote at a time—the early Jacobean Era—when ideas of authority were being interrogated by many artists, including his older contemporary Shakespeare. Choral music was a means of projecting power, not merely by sumptuary means but as a statement of faith, of loyalty, of conformity, of privilege, of patronage.[14] And the role of Oxford as an incubator of leaders—the ecclesiastical and secular clerisy that ran the institutions of early modern England[15]—is exemplified in this complex piece, in its artistic demands, in its performance history, in its reception then and now. But there is other music, and other lessons to explore, and to these the class now turns.

LISTENING FOR LEADERSHIP LESSONS

Listening is such a crucial leadership skill, and such an important lesson, that it is worth exploring from more angles. Almost any contrapuntal piece would serve to demonstrate how important listening is to any act of understanding. I use several pieces written in Oxford by an Oxford composer, John Sheppard (1515–1585), who wrote for the chapel of Magdalen College, where he led the choir on and off between 1541 and 1548, tumultuous years spanning the end of Henry VIII's reign and the aggressively Protestant period of his son Edward VI. Though much of Sheppard's music was composed after his Oxford years for the Roman Catholic liturgy, during Queen Mary's attempts to roll back the Reformation, his earlier Oxford compositions reflect a pragmatism in conforming to institutional power.[16] These facts provide an opportunity to make interesting and rich historical points about how music and artistic expression were used like advertising or branding are today. Such points are easier to make in situ, where students can walk into Magdalen College and its chapel, hear its choir, and reflect on what has changed and what has not in the last five hundred years.

Sheppard's pieces also provide an opportunity to demonstrate how contrapuntal music invites close listening, as exemplified by any piece with the same phrase repeated between voices at different times, a recurring motif that holds listeners' attention. To emphasize this, I ask the singers to perform sitting down, except when they are singing the repeating motif itself, at which times they stand temporarily. In this way, students can both hear and see the motif, observing how it moves around and how it is shared. Then, the singers stay seated and sing again, while I ask the students to raise a hand when they can hear the motif (without also seeing it). It is remarkable how much more easily people can detect the motif once they know what to listen for. The discipline of knowing what to listen for, and when, and how—and how to screen out distractions—is a useful skill for leaders.

The sitting posture of the singers is key to another exercise—also developed by Peter Hanke—that emphasizes how both the students' and singers' experience of the music is intimately connected, like the conjoined roles of leader and follower. With a new volunteer conductor, I make sure he or she knows the basics of what is needed: providing a steady beat, not distracting the singers, asking them for help or advice even if only to establish trust and acknowledge an interdependent relationship. After establishing all that through a few trial runs of one piece, the volunteer will attempt to conduct a new piece. The singers stay seated until each one starts to feel connected to and engaged by the conductor; they show this by standing or, if the connection is lost, by sitting down again. The conductor's task is to get and keep every singer standing. It is remarkably difficult. Often the conductor gets a few people standing by paying them very close attention, but then they sit down when that attention turns elsewhere; or some singers might never stand because they do not feel motivated or do not trust the conductor, who becomes increasingly frustrated by this real-time feedback about his ineffective leadership, often losing more of the singers as a result. The ensuing panic is obvious, and the vicious feedback loop provides a stark lesson: a leader must find ways to motivate when direct connection is impossible, and to motivate a whole team, not just some part of it. As people rise through organizational hierarchies and have increasingly broad and varied responsibilities, with less direct contact and more delegated authority, an ability to communicate deeply and widely through an organization is crucial to leadership effectiveness. And importantly, though many leadership lessons here derive from experiencing performance, they also come from other aspects of the music itself: its workings, its history, its influence.

Sheppard's music is austere. A later Oxford composer, Thomas Weelkes (1576–1623), wrote pieces that are more accessible. Some of his madrigals published in 1600 provide examples of music leading the listener's ear. For example, "As Vesta Was from Latmos Hill Descending" has many instances of "word-painting" in which the music illustrates the meaning of the words—two singers sing the phrase "two-by-two" while only one sings "all alone"; the word "long" lasts a long time; and so forth. Such tricks were popular and common in Elizabethan madrigals, like the elaborate wordplay in poetry and prose of the same period. More deeply, this music is an expression of another aspect of the era: economic exploration. English ships of this time were beginning to explore global trading opportunities and this music is a direct expression of that. The words of one madrigal even manage to equate the personal experience of being in love with international business!

> The Andalusian merchant, that returns
> Laden with cochineal and China dishes,
> Reports in Spain how strangely Fogo burns,
> Amidst an ocean full of flying fishes!
> These things seem wond'rous, yet more wond'rous I,
> Whose heart with fear doth freeze, with love doth fry.[17]

This vivid language is set to music that is harmonically and contrapuntally adventurous to suit the adventurous words. More usefully for students of business, the rhetoric of trade is equated with emotion through the marriage of words and music. There is an entrepreneurial creativity in the composition, in which the merchant demonstrates his passion and his trade through motivic exchanges: a musical phrase is loaned from one voice to another, elaborated, and then returned to its source—as it were, with interest. Though the performance is clearly a corporate activity requiring skill and coordination, it is also an act of musical exploration and innovation at once geographic, economic, and personal. Understanding the music in these ways enables insights into business and leadership as activities that are as innately human as music.

Other leadership lessons can be explored through other music. Often, ideas occur in the moment: the singers provide enormously valuable comments in each class, and students themselves often suggest unexpected insights as they reflect on what they are being asked to hear and watch and do. Oxford's musical and social history provide rich resources to draw on in expanding the teaching material. Sometimes we teach in a chapel of architectural significance; sometimes we use compositions by contemporary composers to demonstrate other aspects of listening, enabling, humility, power, responsibility, engagement, even joy. The class evolves, yet its lessons remain copious, immediate, and (literally) resonant. Deliberately, I offer no list of "Leadership Lessons from Conducting Choirs" or suchlike. Instead, I let the sound hang in the air. I ask students to remember how they felt, how beautifully the singers sang, how unlike most other learning experiences this has been. And I ask them to consider that leadership is most powerful when it is somewhat mysterious—like music.

CODA

There is a delicate and remarkable moment in Gibbons's anthem, which I hadn't noticed until a very attentive MBA student brought it to my attention. After the words of the psalm firmly assert the idea of divine leadership—"For God is the King of all the earth"—Gibbons adds a subtle flourish. The choir, having split into two clearly distinct halves to toss the words "Sing praises!" back and forth like a ball, now begins smoothly to fuse back together into one whole on words about clarity: "Sing praises *with the understanding.*" At this point, and rather unusually for music of this period, Gibbons begins modulating the key, lifting the tonality slightly higher and leading the listener's attention to words about power: "God reigneth.... God is highly exalted." The modulations do make one sit up and listen. At a time when composers were refining how to do this, the gesture demonstrates Gibbons's skill and learnedness. But mainly, it is joyful. The effect is to lead listeners to a new awareness, a new "understanding," and a new appreciation of the artist who has so skillfully and humanely enabled this perception. I wish that all leadership lessons were so beautiful.

NOTES

1. Peter Le Huray, "Gibbons, Orlando," in *Grove Dictionary of Music*, ed. John Harper (Oxford: Oxford University Press, 2001); Paul Vining, "Orlando Gibbons: The Portraits," *Music & Letters* 58, no. 4 (October 1977): 415–29.
2. "What Businesses Can Learn from the Arts: The Merits of Firms and MBA Programmes That Think Creatively," *The Economist*, December 12, 2019, https://www.economist.com/business/2019/12/12/what-businesses-can-learn-from-the-arts.
3. AACORN, JISCMail Email discussion lists for the UK Education and Research communities, 2023, https://www.jiscmail.ac.uk/cgi-bin/webadmin?A0=AACORN; "Artistic Interventions in Organizations, 2008–2017," WZB, https://www.wzb.eu/en/research/digitalization-and-societal-transformation/science-policy/projects/artistic-interventions-in-organizations; Ulla Johansson Sköldberg, Jill Woodilla, and Ariane Berthoin Antal, eds., *Artistic Interventions in Organizations: Research, Theory and Practice* (London: Routledge, 2015); Cayenna Ponchione-Bailey and Eric Clarke, "Technologies for Investigating Large Ensemble Performance," in *Together in Music: Coordination, Expression, Participation*, ed. Renee Timmers, Freya Bailes, and Helena Daffern (Oxford: Oxford University Press, 2022), 119–28.
4. Benjamin Zander and Rosamund Zander, *The Art of Possibility* (Cambridge, MA: Harvard Business Review Press, 2000).
5. Peter Hanke, *Performance & Lederskab: Passionen som drivkraft* (Børsens Forlag, 2008), extracts in English, *Performance and Leadership*, https://www.peterhanke.com/.
6. Dominic Alldis, https://www.dominicalldis.com, 2023; Sewabeats, https://sewabeatsusa.com, 2023; Robert Denhardt and Janet Denhardt, eds., *The Dance of Leadership: The Art of Leading in Business, Government, and Society* (London: Routledge, 2006).
7. Jutta Allmendinger and J. Richard Hackman, "Organizations in Changing Environments: The Case of East German Symphony Orchestras," *Administrative Science Quarterly* 41 (1996): 337–69; Sally Maitlis and Thomas Lawrence, "Orchestral Manoeuvres in the Dark: Understanding Failure in Organizational Strategizing," *Journal of Management Studies* 40, no. 1 (2003): 109–39; Sally Maitlis and Thomas Lawrence, "Triggers and Enablers of Sensegiving in Organizations" *Academy of Management Journal* 50, no. 1 (2007): 57–84.
8. Joyce DiDonato, "Lessons for the Economy from the Stage," *Capitalism & Society* 14, no. 1 (2019): 3–6, https://ssrn.com/abstract=3497785.
9. DiDonato, 5.
10. Leonard Bernstein, *The Unanswered Question: Six Talks at Harvard* (Cambridge, MA: Harvard University Press, 1976); Aaron Copland, *Music and Imagination* (Cambridge, MA: Harvard University Press, 1952).
11. Daniel Goleman, "Leadership That Gets Results," *Harvard Business Review* 78, no. 2 (2000): 4–17.
12. Matthew Guerrieri, *The First Four Notes* (New York: Random House, 2012).
13. Exart, http://www.exart.org, 2023.
14. Andrew Gant, *O Sing unto the Lord: A History of English Church Music* (London: Profile, 2015); Nicholas Temperley, *The Music of the English Parish Church* (Cambridge: Cambridge University Press, 1983).
15. Stefan Collini, *Absent Minds: Intellectuals in Britain* (Oxford: Oxford University Press, 2006).

16. Hugh Benham, *Latin Church Music in England, c. 1460–1575* (London: Barrie & Jenkins, 1977); Geoffrey Elton, *Reform and Reformation: England, 1509–1558* (London: Edward Arnold, 1977); John Sheppard, various compositions, in *John Sheppard: Hymns, Psalms, Antiphons and other Latin Polyphony*, ed. Magnus Williamson, Early English Church Music vol. 54 (London: Stainer & Bell, 2012).

17. Thomas Weelkes, "The Andalusian Merchant," in *Madrigals to 5 and 6 Parts* (London, 1600).

CHAPTER 14

Acting to Uncover

Theater and Inclusive Leadership

Melissa Jones Briggs

Acting is doing. The sum total of the actions, what you do from
moment to moment, reveals your character. Your selection and
execution will also be the determining factor of the degree of your
artistry.

—Uta Hagen, *Respect for Acting*

We must use the relative freedom of adulthood to integrate the
many selves we hold. This includes uncovering the selves we buried
long ago because they were inconvenient, impractical or even hated.
—Kenji Yoshino, *Covering: The Hidden Assault on Our Human Rights*

Leaders navigate complex power dynamics every day. The current global
leadership crisis extends beyond the world stage, revealing oppressive and
exclusionary patterns in our organizations, communities, and homes. The
argument of this chapter is that theater can provide powerful tools for people
seeking to advance inclusive leadership practices. The aesthetic and creative
rigor of the modern acting craft, however, is often misunderstood by non-
actors, and the field of applied theater is expansive. Introducing key acting
mindsets and methods of revealing the self through the roles we play, a form
of "uncovering," can embolden leaders to embrace the artistry both inherent
to and necessary in their leadership roles.

We know both from ancient dramatic texts—from Sophocles to
Shakespeare—and from current social science research that power

transforms individual psychology.[1] Powerful people think and act in ways that lead to the acquisition and retention of power, whether they are aware of it or not.[2] Leaders who are committed to advancing inclusive processes and organizations can act with the power they hold to mitigate its negative effects in undermining relationships and reducing inhibitions.[3] They can do this by honing their awareness and performance—as the actor does—and thereby calibrating their performance effectively and authentically. This performance of their leadership role, in service of the group, may mean summoning the humility to stay in, or emerge from, a philosophical cave.[4] It may also require the courageous and adept revelation of self to set the stage for the inclusive expression of other, diverse voices—in other words: acting.

In what follows, I examine the current direction of diversity and inclusion practice and the role of leaders in expanding the range of expected behaviors. Then I discuss the related concepts of covering and uncovering. Finally, I explore performance insights on uncovering from the theater and how techniques of performative repression and oppression in current leadership styles may be reclaimed and leveraged for good.[5] The Acting with Power course I co-teach at Stanford University will provide a case study. As a teaching artist, my career is dedicated to theater as a tool for social change. I am interested in how access to the arts can unlock creativity, confidence, and compassion in everyday relationships. Though my role on campus at Stanford is academic, this chapter is somewhat personal, drawing from my experience as an actor and acting teacher. I hope to share some personal insights from the classroom at the intersection of theater and leadership studies through the lens of inclusion. While the case described here is from an MBA classroom, my perspective is also informed by my work coaching executives in leading organizations around the world and from my work as a theater artist teaching youth, both privileged and underserved, including those with profound functional needs, to express their voices and achieve their goals.

INCLUSION

Theater has revealed truths about social systems for millennia. In ancient Greece, where roots of Western theater took hold around 400 BCE, theater was the primary mode of civic engagement and gathered people by the thousands. The tradition was developing in the East around the same time; in the second century BCE, Sanskrit plays were staged all over India.[6] Shakespeare's work reached masses during a tumultuous period of history. His work contained coded social comment calibrated to engage his audience but avoid punishment for heresy or treason from the crown.[7] Theater can reinforce oppressive systems of violence, as Thingspiel, the propaganda theater of Nazi Germany, did in the 1930s. Or it can give voice to marginalized people, ideas, and ways of being, as Augusto Boal's important social-justice-focused Forum Theater did in Brazil in the 1960s.

As an embodied art form, theater has the power to reflect the ways individuals and societies themselves perform and to engage, enlist, and transform audiences. This action may be embedded in applied theater work, or it may use the platform of the work to engage audiences directly. Lin-Manuel Miranda's revolutionary rap musical, *Hamilton*, has done both. At one performance in 2016, the actor Brandon Victor Dixon addressed Vice President Mike Pence, who was in the audience: "We, sir—we—are the diverse America who are alarmed and anxious that your new administration will not protect us, our planet, our children, our parents, or defend us and uphold our inalienable rights. We truly hope that this show has inspired you to uphold our American values and to work on behalf of all of us."[8] The riveted audience stood and cheered. This is one example of inclusive leadership in action.

Yet despite such examples of inclusive leadership, divisive and violent rhetoric is on the rise, both on the world stage and in our everyday communities.[9] At the same time, quality communication across difference is plummeting as people retreat to the safety of their identity groups.[10] Ironically, this phenomenon coincides with an increased awareness in organizational literature of the positive effects of diversity. Linked to increased revenue, innovation, and team performance, diversity in organizations is good for people and good for business.[11] If a leader cares about outcomes and the performance and engagement of their people, they should care about inclusion. Inclusion is the practice of involvement, respect, and connection. This richness of ideas, backgrounds, identities, and perspectives can be harnessed to create value of all kinds.

Research on the mechanisms of inclusion that most effectively unlock the benefits of diversity are evolving rapidly, but it can feel like high drama for the individuals and leaders implementing them. Individuals often struggle to evolve, and many of these struggles involve tensions between role expectations, interpersonal or group dynamics, and effective communication. Expression, not repression, of our unique selves is an important aspect of inclusion practice. Those unique selves, of course, do not act or exist in a vacuum. Inclusion is active; it is a social interaction, a *practice*. Social scientists know that behavior (B) is a function of the environment or social situation (E) and the person (P). This foundational theory is known in the field of social psychology as Lewin's equation, $B = f(P,E)$.[12] In the performing arts, behavior in the specific context of given circumstances (environmental, social, personal) is known as the craft of acting.

Leadership is a role. Inclusion, on an interpersonal level, requires expanding the mold of expected behaviors in leadership roles to accommodate the growing diversity of leadership teams. Straight white men are still being hired in most leadership roles, but that is changing, as is ensemble composition throughout organizations. When there is a misalignment of our expected social role behaviors (e.g., what it means to be a "good" woman) and expected leadership role behaviors (e.g., what it means to be a "good" leader), there can be backlash effects, with social and economic reprisals for those that transgress expected behaviors.[13] Fear of these consequences lead people to downplay aspects of their identity that may not align with role expectations or the group majority. This everyday performance technique is called "covering."[14] A leader of character seeking to advance equity in their organization or community faces the task of overcoming cultural dynamics of entrenched systemic oppression and exclusion in an increasingly complex climate. It feels like an overwhelmingly tall order. But change is happening, on the personal and organizational level.

Renowned sociologist Shelley Correll devised what she and her team at the Women's Leadership Innovation Lab at Stanford call a "small wins" approach.[15] They synthesized decades of research on concrete, small, implementable actions that are producing visible results. An example of a small win might be increasing equity in performance review feedback.[16] The five-step model involves educating people in the organization, diagnosing bias, developing tools, intervening by rolling out new tools in groups, and, finally, evaluating progress. It is a change model that shifts the focus away from changing individuals toward organizational systems and processes while simultaneously empowering organizational actors to perform as change agents at all levels of the corporate hierarchy. Small, data-driven actions have a big impact. This approach allows small organizational changes—for example, gendered feedback—to become the building blocks to larger organizational transformation. The intervention stage of this model interests me most in the ways that social, cultural, and organizational norms are reshaped on a day-to-day, individual level. Everyday social interactions are critical to the process of creating a more equitable world. The processes of inclusion are performative and personal.

COVERING

Introduced by the sociologist Erving Goffman in 1963, the term "covering" is defined as the downplaying of stigmatized identities.[17] The identity may be apparent, but the individual downplays various aspects of it to assimilate in a majority group. For example, they might alter their hair, clothes, or accent, or distance themselves from causes, events, or people. In *Covering: The Hidden Assault on Our Human Rights*, Kenji Yoshino, a professor of law at New York University, describes how everyone covers in some way, which enables all people to find common cause with the issue.[18] Men and women, for example, may cover within an organization that has a strong "masculinity contest culture" by bragging about long work hours or strategically distancing themselves from caregiving identities.[19] One report spearheaded by Christie Smith on covering in the corporate setting found that 61 percent of people reported covering in the previous year.[20]

Covering is a performance. It is a dynamic act of emotional intelligence. Many people cover in ways that they may or may not even be aware of, and outsider groups particularly face pressure to cover.[21] Yoshino proposes a framework that invites us to reflect on what he identifies as the "axes" of four A's: *appearance*, ways people alter their self-presentation; *affiliation*, ways people avoid behaviors affiliated with their identity; *advocacy*, ways people stick up for their group; and *association*, ways people manage contact with other group members.[22] Within these axes, people may downplay aspects of their race, gender, sexual orientation, military status, disability, age, citizenship, political alignment, socioeconomic status, or other characteristics for particular purposes in different contexts. For example, consider a leader who is a woman and a mother in a competitive, male-dominated workplace. She may seek to hide a pregnancy (appearance), avoid mentioning her children or the needs related to them (affiliation), not speak up when after-work team drinks are proposed (advocacy), or avoid women-focused events (association). She represses her motherhood identity to assimilate with the male majority because she may face disadvantages in terms of daily job experience and pay, among others.[23] (She may or may not also know that even if the male majority are parents, fathers are often rewarded, not penalized, for their parental status.)[24]

As this example demonstrates, the problem with covering is that it undermines our fundamental human desire for authenticity and perpetuates cultures of assimilation. If we have diversity at the table but we are all covering to assimilate or pressuring others to cover, inclusion is not possible. Covering is detrimental to our sense of self.

Pressures to cover also limit our opportunities and our commitment. Yoshino describes the act of covering as a hidden assault on our civil rights. While civil rights laws protect immutable and innate traits, such as skin color or gender, they cannot reach many of the behavioral aspects of personhood. In a leadership culture of covering, the pressures to assimilate even further hide the roots of repression, including white supremacy, patriarchy, and homophobia, to name a few. This pressure to assimilate is the covering's hidden assault.

"Uncovering," according to Yoshino, serves a person's fundamental desire for authenticity, "our common human wish to express ourselves without being impeded by demands for conformity."[25] Of course, there are benefits and costs to both covering and uncovering, and skepticism about uncovering is well placed. There are very real risks, not least of which include psychological safety and survival in some extreme cases.[26] Moreover, there are many good reasons people need to cover group identities and needs, for example, to avoid discrimination or violence. But there are also both personal and organizational costs to covering that range from detriment to sense of self and decreased opportunities to a decreased commitment to the group.[27] These costs echo the research on the costs of code-switching and other forced assimilation performances. Leaders who hold some form of power already may see great benefits in seeking and revealing previously covered selves. And in doing so, leaders may create cultures where communication across difference can more effectively thrive.

How might leaders who are committed to furthering inclusion effectively engage the pressure to cover that confronts minority groups? Since we all experience the covering demand, as Yoshino and Smith argue, we can all relate to and invest in this new civil rights paradigm based on our desire for authenticity.[28] As one high-level executive at a large multinational retail corporation, a woman of color, asked at the end of one of my recent lectures on gender and power: "I have been acting to assimilate for so long, and it's gotten me really far. Now I finally have the power to show more of myself and my range, but how do I do it? Won't everyone now think this is the act?" The internal and external pressure to cover is evident in this questioning, and she is not alone. These questions arise all the time.

The short answer to the second question is "no." If a leader's behavior is aligned with the objectives of her group, team, or organization and her own espoused values, they will likely believe her, if they even notice. (In fact, there is even some data that show norm-breaking behavior can increase power affordance.)[29]

The answer to the first question is more complex. The very performance strategy of covering can be deployed in its inverse to uncover buried selves and invite others to uncover as well. Covering and uncovering are both cali-brated performances. In accord with gender scholar Joan Williams's import-ant insights on the art of gender judo, leaders can leverage their covering strength in surprising ways.[30] Techniques from the theater can help us navi-gate the dynamics in which we seek to uncover and avoid backlash while we do it. Acting teaches us to uncover, and it sets the stage to allows others to uncover as well.

ACTING TO UNCOVER

Most people think the craft of "acting" is about faking it. Pretending. But the-ater professionals know the craft of acting is about revealing. As the Nobel Prize–winning dramatist Bernard Shaw observed about actors, "Far from being a mere mask with no individuality . . . individuality is concentrated, fixed, gripped, in the emotionally gifted man . . . who is preeminently him-self."[31] This concept of the "emotionally gifted" actor aligns with psychol-ogy's understanding of emotional intelligence, whereby "verbal and non-verbal appraisal and expression of emotion," along with the calibration of emotion in the self and others, evokes emotional content that can be uti-lized in problem solving.[32] Acting is the practice of self-awareness and self-expression through role.

Acting to uncover may reveal someone's physical manifestation of iden-tity, disclose their cultural identifications, display their political persuasion, or divulge one's chosen community. Theater director and theorist Jerzy Gro-towski articulates the actor's craft of unmasking and its power to influence others to do the same: "casting off his everyday mask [an actor] makes it pos-sible for the spectator to undertake a similar process of self-penetration."[33] But uncovering and authentic leadership in general need not be about extreme candor or baring one's soul. The actor's way—knowledge of that soul, analysis of one's objective, assessment of the given circumstances, and exploration in role—can facilitate authentic performance safely.

In lectures when I tell students or executives that they are acting every day, full auditoriums ripple with discomfort. Most people think of acting as a form of cynical manipulation in service of self-interest—pulling one over on us, making us believe they are someone that they are not to advance their own agenda. We are all uncomfortable with a perceived lack of authenticity, whether it is our own or someone else's. We bristle under the pressure to be something we are not, and we dislike fake people and bad actors. And rightly so—trust is important. Trust, emerging from behavioral integrity, is the perceived alignment of words and deeds.[34] Signaled through physical and vocal behaviors, it is something one "does," like the communication of status.[35] Within minutes of getting these very same audiences up on their feet doing something—breaking the lecture hall or virtual classroom norm, using their bodies and voices, engaging with each other—laughter, acknowledgment, and even a sense of relief follows. Uta Hagen says "acting is doing," and as educators know, doing is learning.

Deep learning requires trust, especially between leaders and teams, teachers and students. And trust is active. For leaders developing in their roles, they may be forgiven for occasional competence lapses, but the data show perceived cold behavior may be enough to change trust forever. This is scary news for the new parent focused on racing off to daycare pickup while coworkers head leisurely to the bar. Amy Cuddy, Peter Glick, and Anna Beninger suggest that leaders can manage the impressions they make along these dimensions of competence and warmth—the linchpins of trustworthiness—by honing their nonverbal behaviors.[36]

I know about having to build trust quickly. I teach acting to non-actors, often in non-theatrical settings. Whether in a three-hour- or a three-month-long class, the objective is often the same: grow performance range by experiencing more ways to bring more of yourself to more of your roles. Students report that relationships improve, tensions both internal and organizational disappear, and they feel empowered to be fuller versions of themselves. I have come to view this work—acting with non-actors—as a process of safe, calibrated, and courageous uncovering.

A CASE STUDY: ACTING WITH POWER

Educators, corporate learning and development professionals, and not-for-profit leaders and activists are all looking more and more to the embodied arts like theater to engage people and uplift diverse voices. The course Acting with Power is a good case study of one such application of the arts. It is also a good pedagogical example of acting to uncover. I was a founding member of the teaching team for this course when experimental social psychologist Deborah Gruenfeld introduced a pilot version of the class to the Stanford Graduate School of Business curriculum with Kay Kostopoulos from the Department of Theater and Performance Studies. The course has grown into an extremely popular quarter-long, second-year MBA offering that is almost always oversubscribed. The teaching team has expanded and currently includes Benoît Monin, a social psychologist who has published widely on social perception, self-presentation, and self-image, and Dan Klein, an award-winning theater department lecturer. A deep and talented bench of professional theater artist coaches used to support student rehearsals and exercises as well, but with curriculum innovations over time, we developed a robust peer-coaching methodology that empowers student feedback. Our purpose, as detailed in the syllabus, acknowledges that "the ability to function within a social hierarchy—that is, to accept without cynicism and move gracefully among different ranks—is critical for professional and personal success." We give students the experience, the knowledge, and ultimately the courage to act outside of their comfort zones so they can perform all kinds of roles with agility and impact.

Lectures and discussions focus on power as a force for good. Power and status dynamics are brought to life through acting training and scene work. Application exercises drive home the importance of role-taking in social and organizational life. Through this work students uncover unfamiliar sides of themselves. With direction and coaching, students are pushed to challenge ideas about themselves, identities they lead with or hide, and beliefs about who they can and cannot be on all kinds of stages. All of this work is in service of discovering where the truth is in a scene and where the truth about oneself intersects with the truth about one's character or role.

Gruenfeld's decades of research on power and the effects of power acquisition underpin the course's purpose and philosophy.[37] Other supporting research from the global field of social psychology ranges from recent data on power and power preferences and dimensions of social perception to leading work on personality and emotional expression.[38] But in large part it began as an acting class. Kostopoulos's own decades of teaching acting to non-majors undergird the performance material. The techniques we teach are drawn from the theater. In an earlier version of the class, students even rehearsed and performed scenes from the canon of (mostly English language) dramatic literature. We adapted the curriculum to teach virtually during the COVID-19 pandemic. These adaptations inspired continued valuable course innovations back in person on campus.

On day one in the first intensive session of the course, we explore students' individual comfort zone of power and performance. Within moments of sitting down, we launch them onto their feet, disassemble the room, and push the limits of even the physical boundaries of the classroom walls. Through Boal-inspired, highly interactive activities that explore archetypal roles, our non-actor students begin their acting training. Like a conservatory, our strict attendance and participation policy requires students' full immersion, and given the nature of the experiential work and partnership responsibilities, tardiness is verboten. Physical and emotional safety is paramount. We ensure everyone feels safe and responsible for each other's well-being, while stretching outside of their comfort zone and revealing unfamiliar behaviors in unfamiliar roles. Students' eyes are wide, and their breath is short for much of the time.

In following sessions, we explore how and why we "do" power through performance exercises inspired by improvisational experts such as Keith Johnstone. As the course progresses, we deepen the performance training to explore power, status, and authority in dynamic exercises (e.g., raising, lowering, and exchanging status with others). And we introduce an introductory analytical acting tool to decode and communicate given circumstances (e.g., context details of character, relationship, location, objective). A more robust actor's inventory tool is used in theater classes to study character, and these personal inventories surface many of Yoshino's four A's (appearance, affiliation, advocacy, and association). In developing authentic leaders who embody inclusive virtues in their leadership roles, this acting foundation can be used to create character—in both senses of the word.

We also study the psychology of power, helping students to reflect on their own relationship to power, train in beginning acting craft, and ultimately grow their performance range in scene work. In a previous version of the course, which included a series of Acting Intensive sessions with Kostopoulos, students examined concepts like objective (e.g., what you want), obstacle (e.g., what is in your way), and action (e.g., what you do to get what you want). In neutral scenes (contextless, alternating lines of text), students practice using these concepts and are given circumstances to grow their range. They are coached by professionals, and they coach each other too.

In an earlier version of the course, using scenes from great plays, students rehearsed vocal technique, cold reading (speaking unfamiliar text in front of an audience), blocking (movement and use of furniture), and secondary activity (use of props, handheld items). Students commonly played roles profoundly outside their comfort zone. A confident second-year MBA man may explore the limits of his range playing down his power as Victor in *Four Dogs and a Bone* by John Patrick Shanley or play up his power as Roma in David Mamet's *Glengarry Glen Ross*. Alternatively, a naturally deferent, soft-spoken student might explore playing her power up to fiercely protect her daughter as Joyce in Caryl Churchill's *Top Girls* or excoriate their brother as Lee or Austin in *True West* by Sam Shepard. When using scenes, we would sometimes cross-gender cast since it is impossible to decouple gender and power in this classroom, and this proved an enlightening tool. We grappled with questions of identity and authenticity through role. We selected scenes that have dramatic exchanges of status, in which students experience sending and receiving a wide range of possible dominance and deference signals within minutes. Plays we might pull scenes from included Joanna Murray-Smith's *Honour*, Lanford Wilson's *Burn This*, Theresa Rebeck's *Seminar*, David Rabe's *Hurlyburly*, David Mamet's *Glengarry Glen Ross*, and Lynn Nottage's *Intimate Apparel*, among many others. We often vetted scenes first in Kay Kostopoulos's popular Acting for Non-Majors class at Stanford's Department of Theater and Performance Studies.

The artistic training is not rigorous by conservatory standards, but it is experiential, disciplined, and immersive. Curriculum innovations, like incorporating more student-devised scenes, have heightened this classroom experience. As a teaching team, we introduce non-actors to an accessible version of acting training techniques. Such training takes many forms, but in a very simplified view, there are two dominant modern schools, often referred to by the shorthand terms "inside-out" and "outside-in."[39] These phrases refer to the actor's process of crafting their performance, sometimes described as psychological and the sociological modes.[40] In the inside-out process, actors rely on their internal emotional life to determine the actions of their character. In the outside-in process, they rely on external actions to motivate internal responses. But rarely do actors use just one method to craft a role—rather, they use a combination of techniques unique to their training, experience, and the demands of the role. In Acting with Power, we give students a peek at a few different methods.

Most non-actors are familiar with the term "method acting," which refers to the largely psychological, or inside-out, style of acting. Developed under Konstantin Stanislavski at the Moscow Art Theater at the beginning of the twentieth century with a focus on realism and naturalism, this method is still popular today, having been honed in New York's midcentury theater community by the famous teachers Lee Strasberg, Stella Adler, and Sanford Meisner. We teach Meisner's concept of the "reality of doing" through exercises that reveal techniques for moving off oneself and focusing on one's scene partners.[41]

The other form, outside-in, refers to a form initiated by Vsevolod Meyerhold, a former Moscow Art Theater actor who evolved the sociological and biomechanical mode famous for its more demonstrative style.[42] In this training mode, actors focus on learning gestures and movements as a way of expressing emotion physically. These styles of training were born in Russia but developed throughout the twentieth century in the United States. Because a primary instrument of communication is the body, we spend a lot of time in class warming up and training physical awareness and agility.

Kostopoulos sums up the importance of this work neatly: "when our physical cues are misaligned with our verbal cues, we always believe the body." In class we explore student's default physical reactions to interpersonal and environmental dynamics more than we explore their psychological or even emotional reactions.

Most training programs today integrate these two styles of training, along with other international training methods, such as Augusto Boal's political-educational work originating in Brazil, the French movement school of Jacques Lecoq, Tadashi Suzuki's psychophysical technique from Japan, and the work of Tasmanian posture pedagogue Frederick Matthias Alexander, along with countless others. The field of study and breadth of techniques are vast. Regardless of our depth of knowledge about acting methodology, we might answer yes to this question from Konstantin Stanislavski: "Haven't you noticed, whether in real life or on stage, during mutual communication, sensations of strong-willed currents emanating from you, streaming through your eyes, through your fingertips, through the pores of your body?"[43] Those strong-willed currents are our natural impulses and responses. The job of the actor is to channel them, in role, to influence an audience.

We also lead real-world application exercises in which the students craft everyday scenarios that matter to them to rehearse. In fact, almost all of the scene work from plays is now replaced with exercises that include student-sourced and student-written high-stakes interactions. Overseen by faculty, students calibrate physical, vocal, and mindset strategies from the lessons in these scenes. The social science research on power from the lessons provide both the foundation and backdrop for this work. We teach and deploy non-evaluative observations and link behaviors to the motivations of the character in role. Criticism is discouraged. Rather, we mine student reactions to others' performances for what they surface about their own unique experience with the work and their feelings about power and identity. Peer-coaching is scaffolded throughout the acting training, rehearsal, and application exercises. Coaching techniques are rigorously modeled and enforced since giving effective feedback is an important learning outcome. The related learning objective, harnessing the unique expertise in the room, is inherent in artistic ensemble work and echoed in Pegram Harrison's "ask the expert" approach.[44]

As in most arts education outside the conservatory setting, the focus is on process, not product. However, students may be expected in any class to perform or rehearse in front of the whole group. Pedagogically, we seek to mirror the pressure and stakes familiar in leadership. Leaders face many of the same day-to-day challenges actors face—challenges of physical and vocal technique, mindset, and identity in role. In an early version of the course, final scene performances took place on the very stage on campus where world leaders and titans of global industry may have spoken to students the evening before. We do not evaluate students based on talent or the artistic value of their performances. Rather, we ask: Did they experiment? Did they courageously try something new? Did they commit to doing it even if it felt inauthentic or unfamiliar? Did they expand their authentic range? As we see it, rehearsals and performances create space to grow as students uncover aspects of themselves to these roles that they often have previously hidden. We teach students how to act on their knowledge, not just think, talk, or write about it. By the end of this course, students know good performances demand complex awareness, deeper intimacy, and greater presence. They are practiced at revealing other versions of themselves to use their power more responsibly and inhabit their roles more effectively.

CONCLUSION

Inauthentic performances, in life and on stage, are empty, and the performers are often driven by trying to affect how other people see and experience them. Counterintuitively, acting training teaches students to release control of how others view them in a way that is not typical in other professional realms. Authenticity demands committed expression of ourselves in alignment with the needs of others and the situation. Acting training helps people identify, reveal, and use underdeveloped parts of themselves. This calibrated uncovering enables them to serve the role and the material and own the truth of the situation and the truths of the other people involved.

Leaders seeking to deepen trust to amplify diverse voices can harness these techniques too. Ethical leadership, on a personal level, involves the cultivation and embodiment of virtues that serve the common good of an organization or community.[45] To be effective, however, these virtues must also be embedded in the larger culture and systems in ways that are impactful and measurable. The master acting teacher Uta Hagen illustrates how actors bring themselves to the character, as in the role or part played on stage: "The sum total of the actions, what we do from moment to moment, reveals our character. Our selection and execution will also be the determining factor of the degree of their artistry."[46] This also applies to people offstage, and to the other definition of character, as in the mental and moral qualities distinctive to an individual.[47] Hagen also demonstrates here the performer's act of revelation. Performance, yes, but calibrated to uncover.

Establishing and maintaining trust is critical for personal and professional success. Wake Forest University Professor Patrick Sweeney articulates three C's of trust—competence, caring, and character—in his pioneering field research while on active duty in the military.[48] Competence is easy enough to show (if you have it, of course), but character and caring are much more difficult to demonstrate. It is important to note that caring, according to Sweeney, is about a commitment to doing the right thing for the group. This critical element is well known to any trained ensemble of actors. Actors work constantly in service of the group. On- or offstage, when an audience or collaborator senses an actor is not aligned with the needs of their team or production, trust suffers. The retail sector executive cares about her work and colleagues; their trust matters. The stakes are high, but she is well equipped to uncover. Beginning with an actor's inventory, through the lens of Yoshino's four A's, serves leaders like her.

People in power are responsible for expanding the mold of expected behaviors in leadership roles. They are also responsible for creating space and implementing systems to amplify a variety of voices. It requires adept integration of our many selves because of the complex power dynamics at play. Covering is a form of performance agility that we are likely already doing, to varying degrees. It might involve aspects of our gender, race, sexual orientation, political affiliation, military status, citizenship, or socioeconomic status. Inclusive leadership roles require trust and collaboration across all areas of intersectional difference. Engaging the perspective of the theater artist is relevant to growing agility in this area since actors are trained revealers of self. The insights and practices of this rigorous creative discipline can help leaders deepen their understanding of themselves and calibrate the execution of their roles with authenticity.

If you are reading this book, you are a power holder. You act in ways that may assert or undermine, cover or uncover, your power and the power of others, all the time. You are always acting.[49] You are sending crucial physical and vocal cues that affect the way others perceive you and the way you perceive yourself. At the beginning of her lectures on voice, Kostopoulos suggests that "if you care passionately about what you are saying, but you are using a limited vocal range, you are denying yourself the right to speak." The same is true for leadership performance. If you care passionately about your role but are showing up with a limited range or sharing a limited self, you are denying yourself and others your full leadership potential.

Regardless of your level in an organizational or social hierarchy, you can serve the group or organization by allowing a wide range of previously covered selves to have voice and presence in your leadership. The practice of this art will expand the mold of expected behaviors for emerging leaders and advance cultures of inclusion. Major systemic change is made up of many minor acts in which mindsets and behaviors evolve and concrete steps are implemented, evaluated, adapted, and scaled. Dramatic little structural changes and small performance wins can reveal big leadership strengths. We can broaden our awareness of covering by observing in the way that the trained actor observes, and we can uncover the selves we hold and reveal by growing our own performance range and inviting the unique humanity of other actors to our daily stages. Like leadership, inclusivity requires artistry.

It is your right and responsibility to harness your power, as effectively and authentically as possible, to achieve organizational objectives. It is your right, and responsibility, to inhabit and embody your everyday roles with maximum agility. To make relationships work better. To bridge gaps in communities. To expand the mold of expected behaviors of people in leadership. According to Herminia Ibarra, "we only increase our self knowledge in the process of making changes. We try something new and observe the results. . . . We act like a leader and then think like a leader."[50] This is why leaders must act.

NOTES

1. See Hall, "Tragedies of Leadership," ch. 2; Miles, "Shakespeare, His Books, and Leadership," ch. 7; and Bezio, "Crooked Politics," ch. 8 herein.
2. Joe C. Magee and Adam D. Galinsky, "Social Hierarchy: The Self-Reinforcing Nature of Power and Status," *Academy of Management Annals* 2, no. 1 (2008): 351–98.
3. Ena M. Inesi, Deborah H. Gruenfeld, and Adam D. Galinsky, "How Power Corrupts Relationships: Cynical Attributions for Others' Generous Acts," *Journal of Experimental Social Psychology* 48, no. 4 (2012): 795–803; Cameron Anderson and Jennifer L. Berdahl, "The Experience of Power: Examining the Effects of Power on Approach and Inhibition Tendencies," *Journal of Personality and Social Psychology*, 83, no. 6 (2002): 1362–77.
4. See Lopez, "Leadership Lessons from Plato's *Republic*," ch. 3 herein.
5. While the professional field of theater has its own diversity problem, with most jobs skewing white and male, according to a recent study by Actors' Equity Association, the inclusion landscape in the American theater is improving in terms of race and gender. In most industries however, the opposite is true, and diversity has stalled in both the United States and UK.
6. John Russell Brown, ed., *The Oxford Illustrated History of Theatre*, vol. 1 (Oxford: Oxford University Press, 2001), 15.
7. On Shakespeare's relevance for leadership, see, e.g., Miles, "Shakespeare, His Books, and Leadership," ch. 7; and Bezio, "Crooked Politics," ch. 8 herein.
8. Christopher Mele and Patrick Healy, "'Hamilton' Had Some Unscripted Lines for Pence. Trump Wasn't Happy," *New York Times*, November 19, 2016.

9. Amnesty International, "Amnesty International Report 2017/18: The State of the World's Human Rights," February 22, 2018; Joseph Zompetti, *Divisive Discourse: The Extreme Rhetoric of Contemporary American Politics* (San Diego: Cognella Academic, 2019).

10. Most people have densely interconnected confidants similar to them. Miller McPherson, Lynn Smith-Lovin, Matthew E. Brashears, "Social Isolation in America: Changes in Core Discussion Networks over Two Decades," *American Sociological Review* 71, no. 3 (2006): 353–75.

11. Cedric Herring, "Does Diversity Pay? Race, Gender, and the Business Case for Diversity," *American Sociological Review* 74, no. 2 (2009): 208–24; Christian R. Østergaard, Bram Timmermans, and Kari Kristinsson, "Does a Different View Create Something New? The Effect of Employee Diversity on Innovation," *Research Policy* 40, no. 3 (2011): 500–509; Katherine W. Phillips, Katie A. Liljenquist, and Margaret A. Neale, "Is the Pain Worth the Gain? The Advantages and Liabilities of Agreeing with Socially Distinct Newcomers," *Personality and Social Psychology Bulletin* 35, no. 3 (2009): 336–50.

12. Kurt Lewin, *Principles of Topological Psychology* (New York: McGraw Hill, 1936), 4–7.

13. Laurie A. Rudman and Julie E. Phaelan, "Backlash Effects for Disconfirming Gender Stereotypes in Organizations," *Research in Organizational Behavior* 28 (2008): 61–79.

14. Erving Goffman, *Stigma: Notes on the Management of Spoiled Identity* (New York: Simon and Schuster, 2009), 103.

15. Shelley J. Correll, "SWS 2016 Feminist Lecture: Reducing Gender Biases in Modern Workplaces: A Small Wins Approach to Organizational Change," *Gender and Society* 31, no. 6 (2017): 725–50.

16. Shelley J. Correll and Caroline Simard, "Vague Feedback Is Holding Women Back," *Harvard Business Review*, April 29, 2016.

17. Goffman, *Stigma*, 102.

18. Kenji Yoshino, *Covering: The Hidden Assault on Our Civil Rights* (New York: Random House, 2007).

19. Jennifer L. Berdahl, Marianne Cooper, Peter Glick, Robert W. Livingston, and Joan C. Williams, "Work as a Masculinity Contest," *Journal of Social Issues* 74, no. 3 (2018): 422–48.

20. Christie Smith and Kenji Yoshino, "Uncovering Talent: A New Model of Inclusion," Deloitte University, The Leadership Center for Inclusion, 2013, 5.

21. Yoshino, *Covering*, 27: "In America today, all outsider groups are systematically asked to assimilate to mainstream norms in ways that burden our equality."

22. Yoshino, 79, 125.

23. Shelley J. Correll, Stephen Benard, and In Paik, "Getting a Job: Is There a Motherhood Penalty?" *American Journal of Sociology* 112, no. 5 (2007): 1297–1339; Deborah J. Anderson, Melissa Binder, and Kate Krause, "The Motherhood Wage Penalty Revisited: Experience, Heterogeneity, Work Effort, and Work-Schedule Flexibility," *Industrial and Labor Relations Review* 56, no. 2 (2003): 273–94.

24. Correll et al., "Getting a Job."

25. Yoshino, *Covering*, xii.

26. Anthony V. Alfieri, "(Un)Covering Identity in Civil Rights and Poverty Law," *Harvard Law Review* 121, no. 3 (2008): 805–44.

27. Smith and Yoshino, "Uncovering Talent," 11.

28. Smith and Yoshino.

29. Gerben A. van Kleef, Astrid C. Homan, Catrin Finkenauer, Nancy Blaker, and Marc W. Heerdink, "Prosocial Norm Violations Fuel Power Affordance," *Journal of Experimental Social Psychology* 48, no. 4 (2012): 937–42.

30. Joan C. Williams, "Women, Work, and the Art of Gender Judo," *Washington Post*, January 24, 2014.

31. G. B. Shaw, *The Drama Observed, Volume 1: 1880–1895*, ed. B. F. Dukore (Pennsylvania State University Press, 1993), 97.

32. Peter Salovey, Marc A. Brackett, and John D. Mayer, eds., *Emotional Intelligence: Key Readings on the Mayer and Salovey Model* (Port Chester, NY: Dude Publishing, 2004), 16.

33. Jerzy Grotowski, *Towards a Poor Theatre*, ed. Eugenio Barba (London: Methuen Drama, 1975), 34.

34. Tony Simons, "Behavioral Integrity: The Perceived Alignment between Managers' Words and Deeds as a Research Focus," *Organization Science* 13, no. 1 (2002): 13, 18–35.

35. Keith Johnstone, *Impro: Improvisation and the Theatre* (Routledge, 1987), 36.

36. Amy J. C. Cuddy, Peter Glick, and Anna Beninger, "The Dynamics of Warmth and Competence Judgments, and Their Outcomes in Organizations," *Research in Organizational Behavior* 31 (2011): 73–98.

37. Deborah H. Gruenfeld, *Acting with Power: Why We Are More Powerful than We Believe* (New York: Currency, 2020).

38. Adam D. Galinsky, Deborah H. Gruenfeld, and Joe C. Magee, "From Power to Action," *Journal of Personality and Social Psychology* 85, no. 3 (2003): 453; C. Anderson, Robb Willer, Gavin J. Kilduff, and Courtney E. Brown, "The Origins of Deference: When Do People Prefer Lower Status?," *Journal of Personality and Social Psychology* 102, no. 5 (2012): 1077–88; Amy J. C. Cuddy, Susan T. Fiske, and Peter Glick, "Warmth and Competence as Universal Dimensions of Social Perception: The Stereotype Content Model and the BIAS Map," *Advances in Experimental Social Psychology* 40 (2008): 61–149; Solomon E. Asch, "Forming Impressions of Personality," *Journal of Abnormal and Social Psychology* 41, no. 3 (1946): 258–90; Paul Ekman, Richard J. Davidson, and Wallace V. Friesen, "The Duchenne Smile: Emotional Expression and Brain Physiology II," *Journal of Personality and Social Psychology* 58, no. 2 (1990): 342–53.

39. Robert Gordon, *The Purpose of Playing: Modern Acting Theories in Perspective* (Ann Arbor: University of Michigan Press, 2006).

40. Bruce McConachie, Robin Nellhaus, Tamara Underiner, and Carol Fisher Sogenfrei, *Theatre Histories: An Introduction*, 3rd ed. (London: Routledge, 2016).

41. Vera Soloviova, Stella Adler, Sanford Meisner, and Paul Gray, "The Reality of Doing," *Tulane Drama Review* 9, no. 1 (1964): 155.

42. Alison Hodge, ed., *Twentieth Century Actor Training* (London: Psychology Press, 2000), 39.

43. Konstantin Stanislavski, *An Actor's Work on Himself, Part I*, ed. Oleg N. Efremov, *Collected Works in Nine Volumes*, vol. 2 (Moscow: Iskusstvo, 1989).

44. See Harrison, "'O Clap Your Hands,'" ch. 13 herein.

45. On "servant leadership," see, e.g., Robert K. Greenleaf, *Servant Leadership: A Journey into the Nature of Legitimate Power and Greatness* (Mahwah, NJ: Paulist Press, 2002); and Dirk van Dierendonck, "Servant Leadership: A Review and Synthesis," *Journal of Management* 37, no. 4 (2011): 1228–61.

46. Uta Hagen and Haskel Frankel, *Respect for Acting* (New York: Macmillan, 1973), 184–85.

47. *Oxford English Dictionary*, 3rd ed., s.v. "character," 2019.

48. Patrick J. Sweeney, *Trust: The Key to Combat Leadership*, in *Leadership Lessons from West Point*, ed. Doug Crandall (Hoboken, NJ: John Wiley & Sons, 2007), 252–77.

49. Erving Goffman, *Presentation of Self in Everyday Life* (New York: Doubleday, 1959), 12, 15.

50. Herminia Ibarra, *Act like a Leader, Think like a Leader* (New York: Perseus, 2015), 1–3.

Demos and Deep Democracy

Leadership, the Humanities,
and a New Human

Corey D. B. Walker

The designers and perpetrators of the Holocaust . . . were the heirs
of Kant and Goethe. . . . In most respects the Germans were the
best educated people on earth, their education did not serve as an
adequate barrier to barbarity. What was wrong with their education?
—Elie Wiesel

The study of leadership is experiencing a renaissance. Given the multiple crises facing the global community—environmental, political, and societal—it
is no wonder there is a keen interest in leadership and a veritable cottage industry of popular and academic studies of leadership. It is generally assumed that,
with proper leadership, we may not only address these issues in significant
and consequential ways but do so in a manner that will enhance human flourishing. To this end, there remains a need to furnish today's expanding interest
in the study of leadership with fresh sources and new perspectives that can aid
in cultivating the forms of leadership required to meet the challenges in this
pivotal moment in human history.

Edward Brooks and Michael Lamb's *The Arts of Leading: Perspectives
from the Humanities and the Liberal Arts* offers critical insights for the study
of leadership at this propitious time. Instead of beginning with the assumption of what constitutes proper leadership and then highlighting exemplars
of those assumptions, they begin with a more foundational question of how

266

to rethink leadership beyond a "science of leadership."[1] This question seeks not only to excavate new ground for thinking through the complexities of leadership—indeed, if not the very idea of leadership itself—but also to develop new methods for understanding how leadership is an ongoing conversation between people and society. Leadership has never been one thing. Nor is it confined to just those dominant personalities that occupy the center of traditional leadership models, methods, and principles. Leadership is best approached as a cluster of competing, contrasting, and complementary ideas and ideologies that are seemingly inexhaustible. It is this dynamism that captures our attention and offers us dramatic renditions of exemplary forms of human relationship and societal formation and reformation. It is this dynamic tension that led Brooks and Lamb to gather a broad and diverse group of thinkers to shift the terrain of traditional leadership studies from the social sciences and professions, particularly psychology and management, to the rich and variegated terrain of the humanities. By reterritorializing leadership in this manner, new opportunities are revealed for fundamentally rethinking the idea of leadership as well as revealing new resources for thinking through leadership in our moment.

Now, to be sure, it is not enough to just assert that the humanities offers new perspectives for reconceptualizing leadership. It must be clearly demonstrated. All too often, the quest for the new often leaves us looking askance and wondering if it is really new. This is where this volume breaks new ground: by maintaining acute attention on the openness that is *constitutive* of the humanities. The openness of the humanities is the distinctive character that unfolds, as Brooks and Lamb write in the introduction, "new ways of acting and knowing in the world, often in ways that challenge contemporary orthodoxies." Indeed, if the humanities are to contribute to this renaissance in the study of leadership, they must offer something beyond a nostalgia of an imagined culture that Matthew Arnold deemed "the best which has been thought and said in the world."[2] Instead, they must reveal how and in what ways a style and tradition of inquiry about the depth and complexity of what it means to be human may contribute to new elaborations of human being and belonging in a complex, challenging, and changing world. In other words, the humanities may be critically engaged as both reservoir and resource in an ongoing conversation between cultures, peoples, and traditions to yield fresh perspectives on leadership. In this regard, the signature strength of this collection is in modeling a style of inquiry that is shaped and reshaped by a fundamentally open question—how do we rethink leadership beyond a "science of leadership"?

The essays by Joy Connolly, Edith Hall, and Noah Lopez that open the collection reveal fresh ideas of leadership drawn from the deep wells of classics and philosophy. While these two intellectual formations are often taken to constitute a traditional and somewhat static notion of the humanities, each of these thinkers excavates novel insights. The "newness" of the ideas lies in opening the idea of the humanities in yielding critical insights for understanding the principles and practices of leadership. This is best exemplified in the statement by Noah Lopez in chapter 3: "Where leadership today seeks to transcend mere concern for efficiency and a bottom line, there is need for resources to imagine, create, and sustain richer conceptions of leadership—leadership that seeks to ignite and mobilize diverse minds, hearts, and bodies; leadership that holds ongoing learning and wisdom as relevant and desirable aims." Along with the other contributors, Lopez underscores the requisite idea for a distinctive humanistic contribution to the renaissance of leadership in our moment. Such a contribution is grounded in and retrieves the fundamentally open character of the humanities that reads and rereads the classics and philosophy, as well as other scholarly areas contributing to the humanities, as ongoing dialogues and open inquiries into the vibrant conversation that is human existence. What the humanities contributes to a critical understanding of leadership is not mere disciplinary expertise but rather a style of thinking and a mode of inquiry into those foundational ideas that shed new light and fresh perspectives on the triumphs and tragedies of the human experience. The newness of ideas that underscores the critical turn (or return) to the humanities lies in an attentive practice of human understanding and interpretation of tradition as not fixed and static but rather open and responsive to new times and new challenges.

If the humanities draw our attention to new ideas about leadership, then the humanities also encourage us to think anew about the institutions that cultivate the requisite disposition for renewed leadership. Our considered interest in the study of leadership occurs concomitantly with a decline in the authority and legitimacy of some of our most revered social and political institutions. Robert Putnam's *Bowling Alone* is a classic statement of the decline in late twentieth-century social life and served as a harbinger of the divides that would widen and grow more rigid in democratic societies across the globe.[3] Of course, the rise and decline of human institutions is not new in human history. Yet what is new and profound in our contemporary moment is the deep legitimation crisis—to borrow from Jürgen Habermas's classic text—of some of our most significant institutions in a moment of planetary precarity.[4] At a time when global solidarity is needed to confront the most significant challenges in human history—which constitute nothing less than the present and future prospects of humanity itself—leadership and traditional institutions for cultivating leadership are sources of some of the deepest antagonisms that militate against meeting the challenge of this moment. It is here where the contributors to this volume harness the power of the humanities to renew the possibilities of leadership.

The stories we tell about ourselves, our pasts, and our ultimate commitments hold out the distinct possibilities for renewing the ways in which we view our collective lives and how we may shape and renew our institutions. To be sure, religion, literature, and history lie at the root of some of our deepest antagonisms in the modern world. Yet they also point toward some rich possibilities for a renewal of leadership appropriate for our age, as the essays by Alan Mittleman, Tahera Qutbuddin, and Marla Frederick reveal. Through an open thinking of the humanities, the religions that form the Abrahamic tradition yield powerful insights about leadership that are not bound by an absolute theological vision open only to the requisite communities of believers. As scholars in social and political philosophy have drawn on the figure of Caliban in Shakespeare's *The Tempest* to yield new philosophical insights appropriate to contemporary configurations of power and politics, Kristin M. S. Bezio and John Miles invoke Shakespeare in similar ways to illuminate the practices of leadership.[5] In a similar vein, Paul Escott and Thavolia Glymph engage the complex and conflicted history of democracy in the United States to reveal new opportunities for rethinking leadership in the midst of a fraught and fractured polity. These two essays take the opportunity of pressing the humanities to critically engage American democracy and the forms of leadership that have developed in spite of the contradictions of the unique American experiment. If, as Thavolia Glymph presciently argues in chapter 10, the humanities and liberal arts enable a more expansive vision of leadership that elevates "ordinary people without political position or military rank," investigations into these democratic institutions and examples may shed new light on the institutional matrix that has shaped and formed a broad array of actors, stories, and traditions. The disclosure of the power of the humanities in these essays serves as a poignant reminder that the complex cultures and requisite practices of leadership are linked to a renewal of the very institutions that animate our deepest antagonisms and fuel our highest aspirations.

The focus on the humanities in the service of developing new formulations of leadership also empowers us to create new imaginaries for thinking about leadership in this moment of renaissance. The humanities are more than just a collection of areas of study and more than just a tradition waiting to be tapped and pressed into service when we seek to examine the multiple meanings of our humanity. The humanities generate new horizons for imagining ways of being human beyond the tyranny of tradition and the calculus of the present. The humanities raise new questions in examining the changing styles of representing our worlds, our ideals, and ourselves. It is quite appropriate for this collection to end then with a humanistic consideration of how the arts of the humanities reveal new vistas for thinking through fresh ideas of leadership. Portraiture and monuments provide appropriate points of entry for reconsidering how the changing cartography of American democracy opens up a new imaginary for an iconography of leadership. Equally important are the performative arts, which unfold the critical potential of embodied dimensions of representations of leadership. While the arts are being deployed to reinvigorate business and management, as Pegram Harrison discusses in chapter 13, the critical potential of the focus on music in particular lies in its ability to create a soundscape of possibility for novel conceptions of leadership. This soundscape opens up the imagination and reconfigures our disciplinary domains and institutional locations in considering new forms of leadership. The embodied element reminds us of the communal quality of leadership and the possibilities of inhabiting and moving through our world in new and dynamic ways. Form, gesture, and technique are imbued with new and resonant meaning in this context, which revises the horizons of possibility for leadership. In the unfolding of imagination, as Harrison highlights, leadership is like music: though ineffable, it is "innately human."

By leveraging a robust understanding of the humanities, *The Arts of Leading* advances a critical understanding of the possibilities in our contemporary leadership for our moment. This collection invites us to begin again the critical task of formulating fresh conceptions of leadership beyond mere convention and tradition. Yet a question remains; a specter haunts the very mobilization of the humanities in this task. While the humanities demonstrate new ideas and imaginaries that may cultivate new frameworks and practices of leadership, is this but a variation on the same theme? In other words, must we subject the humanities—and by extension the liberal arts—to a more rigorous and fundamental interrogation if we are to critically confront the key question that animates this enterprise? This collection opens up with a recognition of the need for broader representations of leadership and leaders. As Brooks and Lamb write in the introduction, "Because of various and often intersecting forms of discrimination, injustice, and exclusion, those who are often perceived to be 'leaders' in Western societies have historically tended to be wealthy, white, and male, representing only limited and sometimes distorted experiences of what it means to lead." Yet, as this collection demonstrates, it is more than just examining the *effects* of forms of social, political, and economic power and injustice that guides us to reconsider the humanities and leadership. It is the very constitution of the discourses of both the humanities and leadership that beckons us to take up this critical task in this moment of planetary crisis. It is here where I think these essays open up to even further and more critical considerations animating our inquiry into how to rethink leadership.

In their introduction to the collection, Brooks and Lamb reference the towering theorist and historian of religion Charles H. Long and his germinal essay, "The Humanities and 'Other' Humans." They aptly note that Long's essay presents a "critique of how the humanities have typically been practiced in the Western world and a call to expand the scope to other expressions of being human." Indeed, the essays in this collection, most notably those by Marla Frederick and Thavolia Glymph, have done just that in considering new formulations of the humanities in rethinking leadership.

Importantly, Long's critique is more expansive than inventorying the practices of the humanities in the West along with generating a more expansive scope of representations, ideas, and concepts of being human. Long's critique calls us to undertake a virtual inventory of the ideas, institutions, and imagination that have fueled and continue to fuel our understanding of the requisite sources, frames, and formulas that define the humanities. The task is nothing less than critique in the sense argued by Long, that is, "a critique from the point of view of a form of life."[6] The humanities—as the dominant and traditional intellectual expressions of the very idea and form of life of being human in the world—are the proper object of Long's critique. At this level of critique, mere expansion and extension without requisite attention to the very form of the humanities itself traps us in a prison house of *the* humanities. As such, rethinking leadership from the vantage point of an unreconstructed humanities becomes mere decoration of the same house. To echo Long, "The 'humanistic sentence' remains intact in the midst of the reforms; the structure still holds."[7] Thus, the function of critique involves taking into account the limits of the humanities while always already thinking the possibilities of the humanities and "other" humans.

It is only at the conclusion of our intellectual journey that the critical challenge represented by this collection is revealed as nothing less than a foundational and categorical rethinking of the humanities to confront the intensity of the arts of leading in our moment. And it is none other than Charles H. Long, by way of a footnote, who (un)consciously directs us to this critical confrontation:

> One of the crucial issues in the humanities today has to do with a definition of the meaning of totality in terms of human worlds. In the

first instance, how are we to define the human species? Are all human cultures, both past and present, to be included in the study of the humanities? Are all human situations part of the possible constituting data of the humanities? *In other words, the question is raised, given the actual or possible worlds we live in, is it adequate for the humanities to derive its fundamental orientation, meaning, and data from simply the Hebraic, Greek, Christian meanings of our culture?*[8]

If we are to reconstruct leadership beyond a paradigmatic science of leadership and its categorical dictates, then the humanities cannot operate within a logic of the same. This is the force of Long's imperative. It is a challenge not only to rethink the concept of leadership with the aid of the humanities but to reconceive leadership within the space of a reconstructed humanities. Thus, the issue is not one of merely returning to the humanities—its traditional sources, norms, and frameworks—but to rethink the fundamentals of the humanities in disclosing new regimes for thinking the forms of human life and human possibility. In the space of Long's open question, we are invited to undertake an excavation and inventory of the infinite possibilities of forms of human life and in so doing uncover fresh formulations of leadership. It is this spirit that haunts the critical intellectual task assembled in this text. Much like Jacques Derrida's *Specters of Marx: The State of the Debt, the Work of Mourning, and the New International*, it is not one of mere hauntings or a pervasive nostalgia but rather one of a deep responsibility and a fidelity to taking up the gift of responsibility to an/other way of life—"Someone, you or me, comes forward and says: *I would like to learn to live finally.*"[9] The quest to learn to live is intimately connected to our quest to rethink leadership, or to learn to lead, as instructed by the gift of the humanities. Yet this responsibility cannot be met with a humanities of the same that has led us to our current cul-de-sac of thought. Rather, it must be enacted by rethinking the humanities—its ideas, its institutions, and its imaginations. If this is taken as the task to which we have gestured throughout this text but have not formalized until we have completed but a phase of our journey, the task now confronts us fully and directly, as Long—who we recognized at the beginning but could not *read* until the end—invites us to continue our journey in a way that is a restatement not of how we are mobilizing a tradition of thinking of the humanities but rather how a *thinking* of the humanities uncovers new regimes of thinking about leadership beyond its present forms.

Edward Said reminds us that beginnings—beyond the mystical and the magical—afford new opportunities to think anew if and only if we critically rethink beginnings.[10] One of the world's truly great humanists, Said offers a provocation that creates an intensity of thought that can only be met by beginning again. Perhaps the end is the beginning, and in this context we are empowered to move beyond the calculus of the humanities caught within a tradition and temporality of *studia humanitatis*. In this respect, we can do no better than re/turn to the *demos* in cultivating new modes of thinking to leverage new conceptions of the humanities as revealed by the knowledges and practices of the *demos* across space and time. The re/turn to the *demos* is not a nostalgic move of returning to "the people" as already constituted, nor it is a recourse to a collective *mentalité* of the *demos*. Rather, it is an invitation to think with the languages and practices that fall outside of the frame of the humanities proper. In a moment of crisis and a critical rethinking of leadership, the *demos* not only holds out the promises of reinvigorating the very idea of the humanities along the lines suggested by Charles H. Long, but it also portends a new opportunity for a renewal of politics to realize new forms of life together. In this regard, Wendy Brown's important book *Undoing the Demos: Neoliberalism's Stealth Revolution* catalogs the myriad ways in which the *demos* has been undermined historically and in our contemporary moment, yielding to an elite politics that diminishes the chances of planetary human life itself.[11] In this regard, a provincial preoccupation with leadership—even a rethinking of leadership within the confines of the humanities—is not one that can meet the challenges of our contemporary moment. This is why *The Arts of Leading* is vitally important and why we must not rest at the closing of this book but must continue and deepen the conversation. The humanities beyond the rhetoric of a critical thinking in and through the humanities calls for a return to the *demos*—understood as the multiple and varied languages and practices of human life constituted by the people—as fundamentally reconstituting the idea, institution, and imagination of the humanities. The *demos* serves as the fountain of new ideas and practices of the humanities in all of their multiplicity, density, and diversity. In so doing, it transforms the humanities from a linear formation captured by the beginning of a traditional classical world to rhizomatic formation that erupts with new possibilities arising from a planetary humanity. The *demos* unleashes a theoretical freedom to rediscover a humanities without boundaries and a humanities open to the novelty of the multiple expressions of being human in the world. Such a freedom for the humanities creates the conditions of possibility for a creative dialogical formulation of the humanities with the *demos* that holds out the distinct possibility for elaborating new conceptions of human being and belonging in the world. In a world confronting the very real challenge of the future of organized human life and society, it seems that this form of humanities—a humanities for a new human—is the critical one that must be excavated to reveal new ideas of leadership.

Famed leader of the twentieth-century Black freedom movement in the United States Ella J. Baker elegantly stated, "I have always thought what is needed is the development of people who are interested not in being leaders as much as developing leadership among other people."[12] Baker overturns the relationship between leaders and people by redefining the very foundation of leadership. Instead of the exclusive preserve of a singular, exemplary individual, Baker democratizes leadership across the *demos*. In so doing, she reveals the multiple theories and models of leadership always already available when reterritorializing leadership from the provincial space to a planetary horizon. This move is underwritten by a conception of "other people" analogous to Long's "other humans"—that is, the variety and diversity of humans existing in the world. If we are to truly harness the humanities for leadership beyond the science of leadership, then, at a minimum, we must cultivate a humanities beyond the traditional grammar of the human. We must begin to critically comprehend the failure to attend to other humans and not merely restate the humanities with additives. The call is not for a re/turn to the humanities in a moment of crisis of humanistic thought and critique. Rather, it is a call to a renewed humanities that can aid our democratic aspirations, a humanities that can enliven our civic culture, and a humanities that can renew the liberal arts. Such a vision of the humanities holds out the distinct possibility of a new human that is not a repeat or reproduction of the old human of the old humanities.

In closing, I return to the epigraph by Elie Wiesel. Wiesel's statement is a poignant and singular warning of the horrors of tradition. The order of the humanities inaugurates and elaborates a classificatory schema that all too often limits conceptions of the human. Indeed, it may be argued that, through the logics of the human, we may find ourselves constituting a logic and practice that reinscribes us within the prison of thought and practice from which we seek escape. In this manner, we must ask ourselves, "What [is] wrong with [our] education?" In so doing, we may excavate other archives and come upon new resources in the ruins of civilization in founding an/other humanities of the *demos* that may renew and democratize our conceptions and visions of and for the arts of leading.

NOTES

1. Brooks and Lamb, "Introduction," herein.
2. Matthew Arnold, *Culture and Anarchy: An Essay in Political and Social Criticism* (London: Smith, Elder, 1869), viii.

3. Robert D. Putnam, *Bowling Alone: The Collapse and Revival of American Community* (New York: Touchstone, 2001).
4. Jürgen Habermas, *Legitimation Crisis* (Boston: Beacon Press, 1975). See also Judith Butler, *Precarious Life: The Powers of Mourning and Violence* (London: Verso, 2004); and Guy Standing, *The Precariat: The New Dangerous Class* (London: Bloomsbury, 2011).
5. See the classic text by Paget Henry, *Caliban's Reason: Introducing Afro-Caribbean Philosophy* (New York: Routledge, 2000) and subsequent work inspired by this text, including Jane Anna Gordon, *Creolizing Political Theory: Reading Rousseau through Fanon* (New York: Fordham University Press, 2014); and Neil Roberts, *Freedom as Marronage* (Chicago: University of Chicago Press, 2015).
6. Carolyn M. Jones and Julia M. Hardy, "From Colonialism to Community: Religion and Culture in Charles H. Long's Significations," *Callaloo* 35 (Spring 1988): 261.
7. Charles H. Long, "The Humanities and 'Other' Humans," in *Morphologies of Faith: Essays in Religion and Culture in Honor of Nathan A. Scott, Jr.*, ed. Mary Gerhardt and Anthony C. Yu (Atlanta: Scholars Press, 1990), 203–14, at 211.
8. Long, "The Humanities and 'Other' Humans," 204, emphasis added.
9. Jacques Derrida, *Specters of Marx: The State of Debt, the Work of Mourning, and the New International*, trans. Peggy Kamuf (New York: Routledge, 1994), xvi.
10. Edward Said, *Beginnings: Intention and Method* (New York: Columbia University Press, 1985).
11. Wendy Brown, *Undoing the Demos: Neoliberalism's Stealth Revolution* (New York: Zone, 2015).
12. Ella Baker, "Developing Community Leadership," in *Black Women in White America*, ed. Gerda Lerner (New York: Vintage, 1973), 345–52. See also Barbara Ransby, *Ella Baker and the Black Freedom Movement: A Radical Democratic Vision* (Chapel Hill: University of North Carolina Press, 2003).

CONTRIBUTORS

KRISTIN M. S. BEZIO is professor of leadership studies and associate dean for academic affairs at the Jepson School of Leadership Studies at the University of Richmond. Her research focuses on leadership in literature and film, leadership in performance, and cultural and political history in early modern England. She integrates the study of literature into the curriculum by teaching classes such as Leadership and the Humanities and Leadership on Stage and Screen. She is especially interested in how literature, drama, film, and video games have influenced society and approaches to leadership and followership. She is the author of *The Eye of the Crown: The Development and Evolution of the Elizabethan Secret Service* and *Staging Power in Tudor and Stuart English History Plays: History, Political Thought, and the Redefinition of Sovereignty*. In addition, she is coeditor of the *Interdisciplinary Journal of Leadership Studies*, as well as six edited volumes addressing questions of leadership, religion, drama, and play.

ELLEKE BOEHMER is professor of world literature in English and director of the Oxford Centre for Life-Writing at the University of Oxford. Previously, she served as director of the Oxford Research Centre in the Humanities, where she was principal investigator of an Andrew W. Mellon Foundation–funded project on "Humanities and Identities." A Rhodes Scholar from South Africa with a doctorate from the University of Oxford, she is a founding figure in the field of postcolonial studies and internationally known for her research in anglophone literatures of empire and anti-empire, which pays special attention to dynamics of leadership, identity, race, gender, and culture. A fellow of the English Academy, Royal Society of Literature, and Royal Historical Society, she is the author of *Postcolonial Poetics: Twenty-First-Century Critical Readings*; *Indian Arrivals, 1870–1915: Networks of British Empire*; *Nelson Mandela: A Very Short Introduction*; *Empire, the National, and the Postcolonial, 1890–1920: Resistance in Interaction*; *Stories of Women: Gender and Narrative in the Postcolonial Nation*; and *Colonial and Postcolonial Literature: Migrant Metaphors*. In addition to editing numerous volumes in postcolonial studies, she is the general editor of the Oxford Studies in Postcolonial Literatures series (Oxford University Press). She is also an acclaimed novelist and short story writer. Her fiction includes *To the Volcano, and Other Stories, The Shouting in the Dark, Sharmilla and Other Portraits, Nile Baby, Bloodlines, An Immaculate Figure,* and *Screens against the Sky*.

MELISSA JONES BRIGGS is a lecturer in organizational behavior at the Stanford University Graduate School of Business. She also serves as an associate fellow of the Oxford Character Project at the University of Oxford. An alumna of Wake Forest's Department of Theater and Dance, she trained as a theater artist in London and New York and now combines performance techniques with social science research to offer new approaches to leadership. Focusing on relationships between power, status, and authority, her courses and coaching equip leaders with the capacities and skills to negotiate diverse personal and professional roles. At Stanford, she co-teaches a popular class called Acting with Power, where students examine their relationship to power through in-class performances, social psychological research, and reflection exercises. Outside academia, she designs, directs, and deploys global leadership and inclusion programs for corporations, NGOs, and academic and federal institutions.

EDWARD BROOKS is executive director of the Oxford Character Project and director of the Programme for Global Leadership in the Department of Politics and International Relations at the University of Oxford. He is also cofounder of Oxford's SDG Impact Lab. His research lies at the intersection of virtue ethics, leadership, and character development, and he has a particular interest in the virtue of hope. He has led major research projects on character and global leadership and on character, culture, and leadership in UK business. His work on leadership has been featured in media outlets including *Brunswick Review, Executive Excellence, Financial Times,* and *New Scientist*. He was named by Thinkers50 on their radar list of emerging business influencers. He is coeditor of *Cultivating Virtue in the University* and *Literature and Character Education in Universities*. He holds a BA in modern history from Magdalen College, Oxford, and a DPhil in theology from Oriel College, Oxford.

JOY CONNOLLY is the president of the American Council of Learned Societies. Previously, she served as provost and interim president of the Graduate Center at the City University of New York, where she was also distinguished professor of classics. She has held faculty appointments at

New York University (where she served as dean for the humanities), Stanford University, and the University of Washington. She is the author of two books, *The State of Speech: Rhetoric and Political Thought in Ancient Rome* and *The Life of Roman Republicanism*, and more than seventy articles, reviews, and short essays. Her current book project maps out a new path for what we now call "classical studies." Deeply interested in contemporary art, she served as an interpreter/player for the artist Tino Sehgal and is at work on a translation of Vergil's pastoral poetry. She was elected a fellow of the American Academy of Arts and Sciences in 2021.

PAUL ESCOTT is the Reynolds Professor (Emeritus) of History at Wake Forest University. A specialist in the history of the American Civil War, he has published eleven books and edited eight volumes exploring the causes, effects, and aftermath of the Civil War, with a particular focus on leadership. His books include *After Secession: Jefferson Davis and the Failure of Confederate Nationalism, Military Necessity: Civil-Military Relations in the Confederacy, "What Shall We Do with the Negro?": Lincoln, White Racism, and Civil War America, Uncommonly Savage: Civil War and Remembrance in Spain and the United States, Many Excellent People: Power and Privilege in North Carolina, 1850–1900, Lincoln's Dilemma: Blair, Sumner, and the Republican Struggle over Racism and Equality in the Civil War Era, Rethinking the Civil War Era: Directions for Research, The Worst Passions of Human Nature: White Supremacy in the Civil War North*, and most recently, *Black Suffrage: Lincoln's Last Goal*. He also served for nine years as dean of the college at Wake Forest. He has received fellowships from the Whitney Young Jr. Foundation and the Rockefeller Foundation, and twice won an award for the best nonfiction book published by a resident of North Carolina.

MARLA FREDERICK is the dean of Harvard Divinity School. An authority on religion, race, and ethnography, she pursues research on the study of religion and media, religion and economics, and the sustainability of Black institutions in a "post-racial" world. She is the author of *Between Sundays: Black Women and Everyday Struggles of Faith* and *Colored Television: American Religion Gone Global* and coauthor of *Televised Redemption: Black Religious Media and Racial Empowerment*. In 2007 her coauthored book *Local Democracy under Siege: Activism, Public Interests, and Private Politics* won the Best Book Award for the Society for the Anthropology of North America. Previously, she was the Asa Griggs Candler Professor of Religion and Culture at Emory University and professor of African and African American studies and of the study of religion at Harvard University. She has served as the president of the Association of Black Anthropologists and president of the American Academy of Religion.

THAVOLIA GLYMPH is the Peabody Family Distinguished Professor of History and professor of law at Duke University and faculty research scholar for the Duke University Population Research Institute. A historian of the United States, her work focuses on the nineteenth-century US South. She is the author of *Out of the House of Bondage: The Transformation of the Plantation Household*, which won the 2009 Philip Taft Book Prize and was a finalist for the Frederick Douglass Prize, and *The Women's Fight: The Civil War's Battles for Home, Freedom, and Nation*, which won the Tom Watson Brown Book Award from the Society of Civil War Historians and the Watson-Brown Foundation; the Albert J. Beveridge Award and the Joan Kelly Memorial Prize from the American Historical Association; the Julia Cherry Spruill Prize from the Southern Association for Women Historians; the Civil War and Reconstruction Book Award, the Mary Nickliss Prize, and the Darlene Clark Hine Award from the Organization of American Historians; and the John Nau Book Prize awarded by the John L. Nau III Center for Civil War History; she was also a finalist for the 2021 Gilder Lehrman Lincoln Prize. Glymph is coeditor of two volumes of *Freedom: A Documentary History of Emancipation, 1861–1867*. She is an Organization of American Historians distinguished lecturer and an elected member of the Society of American Historians, American Antiquarian Society, and board of directors of the Gettysburg Foundation. She is past president of the Southern Historical Association, 2023–2024 Rogers Distinguished Fellow in Nineteenth-Century American History at the Huntington Library, San Marino, California, and president of the American Historical Association.

EDITH HALL is a professor of classics and ancient history at Durham University. Previously, she held posts at Cambridge, Oxford, and King's College London, among others. A leading international expert on the study of ethnicity, class, and gender in ancient sources, ancient theater, and the continuing influence of ancient Greek and Roman culture on modernity, she has published more than thirty books, including *Inventing the Barbarian, The Return of Ulysses, Greek Tragedy: Suffering under the Sun, Introducing the Ancient Greeks, Aristotle's Way: How Ancient Wisdom Can Change Your Life*, and, most recently, *Facing Down the Furies: Suicide, the Ancient Greeks, and Me*. She cofounded the Archive of Performances of Greek and Roman Drama at Oxford and is chair of the Gilbert Murray Trust. Her research has been funded by the Arts and Humanities Research Council, Leverhulme

Trust, British Academy, European Research Council, UK Research and Innovation, and Center for Hellenic Studies in Washington, and she has been awarded a Humboldt Research Prize, the Erasmus Prize Medal of the European Academy, and an honorary doctorate from the University of Athens. In 2022 she was elected a fellow of the British Academy. She appears regularly on BBC Radio and has acted as consultant to productions of ancient drama at the Royal Shakespeare Company, the National Theatre, and other professional companies.

PEGRAM HARRISON is a senior fellow in entrepreneurship at the Saïd Business School at the University of Oxford, where he teaches on the MBA program and is director of undergraduate studies in management. Previously, he taught entrepreneurship and strategy at the European Business School, London, and was director of the Emerging Leaders Programme at the London Business School. He also taught literature and history at New York University and Birkbeck College at the University of London. A humanities scholar by training, educated at Yale and Cambridge, he studies the role of the arts and humanities in business. He contributes to the Oxford Cultural Leaders program, a senior executive education program for arts and heritage professionals. Beyond Oxford, he works with various cultural institutions and policy bodies (the British Council, the Art Fund, the National Trust, the Arts Council, and others) on research projects and initiatives for enhancing cultural leadership capabilities.

MICHAEL LAMB is the F. M. Kirby Foundation Chair of Leadership and Character, executive director of the Program for Leadership and Character, and associate professor of interdisciplinary humanities at Wake Forest University. He is also an associate fellow of the Oxford Character Project, where he helped to develop the liberal arts–based leadership curricula for the Oxford Global Leadership Initiative. He also helped to integrate humanistic perspectives in the leadership programming of the Rhodes Trust, where he served as dean of leadership, service, and character development. He holds a PhD in politics from Princeton University, a BA in political science from Rhodes College, and a second BA in philosophy and theology from the University of Oxford, where he studied as a Rhodes Scholar. A principal investigator on several multimillion-dollar grants to educate leadership and character, his interdisciplinary teaching and research focus on leadership and character development and the role of virtues in public life. He is the author of *A Commonwealth of Hope: Augustine's Political Thought* and coeditor of *Everyday Ethics: Moral Theology and the Practices of Ordinary Life* and *Cultivating Virtue in the University*.

NOAH LOPEZ is currently an online learning facilitator at Harvard Business School. Previously, Lopez was assistant director of equity and inclusion and a Learning Lab fellow for ethics and critical engagement at Harvard's Derek Bok Center for Teaching and Learning. They have taught philosophy at Boston College and were a postdoctoral fellow at Harvard. Lopez earned a DPhil in philosophy at the University of Oxford on a Rhodes Scholarship, and their research has focused on ethics, justice, and the philosophy of love, particularly in the thought of Plato. In their current work, Lopez collaborates with students, faculty, staff, and administrators to support pedagogical effectiveness, especially in response to inequities in the classroom. Their approach to pedagogy is informed by years of competitive athletics and multimedia artistic practice as well as their study of ancient Greek philosophy as the pursuit of wisdom and a flourishing life.

DAVID M. LUBIN is the Charlotte C. Weber Professor of Art at Wake Forest University. He has published seven books on American art, film, and popular culture, including *Picturing a Nation: Art and Social Change in Nineteenth-Century America*, *Grand Illusions: American Art and the First World War*, and *Shooting Kennedy: JFK and the Culture of Images*, which won the Smithsonian Institution's Charles Eldredge Prize for distinguished scholarship in American art. His awards include a Guggenheim Fellowship and research residencies at Harvard, Stanford, and the National Gallery's Center for Advanced Study in the Visual Arts. In 2016–17, he served as the inaugural Terra Foundation Visiting Professor of American Art at the University of Oxford. He is currently writing a book on the making of the classic film *Sunset Boulevard*.

JOHN MILES is founder and chief executive officer at Inkpath, the skills and career development platform, and a former research associate at Wadham College at the University of Oxford. Before spinning Inkpath out of the University, he served as training officer for the University of Oxford's Humanities Division and the Oxford Research Centre in the Humanities, where he led the professional and personal development program for doctoral students and early career researchers across the humanities. Prior to this, he taught Shakespeare and Renaissance literature in the English Department at Royal Holloway, University of London, where he was a Caroline Spurgeon Research Fellow.

ALAN MITTLEMAN is the Aaron Rabinowitz and Simon H. Rifkind Emeritus Professor of Jewish Philosophy at the Jewish Theological Seminary. His teaching and research focus on the intersection between Jewish thought and

Western philosophy in ethics, political theory, and metaphysics. He is the author of eight books: *Between Kant and Kabbalah, The Politics of Torah, The Scepter Shall Not Depart from Judah, Hope in a Democratic Age, A Short History of Jewish Ethics, Human Nature and Jewish Thought, Does Judaism Condone Violence? Holiness and Ethics in the Jewish Tradition,* and *Absurdity and Meaning in Contemporary Philosophy and Jewish Thought.* He is editor of *Holiness in Jewish Thought* and coeditor of *Jewish Virtue Ethics.* He has received numerous awards and fellowships, including an Alexander von Humboldt Foundation Research Fellowship, a Harry Starr Fellowship in Modern Jewish History from Harvard University's Center for Jewish Studies, and a fellowship at the James Madison Program at Princeton University. He has been a visiting professor at the University of Cologne and Princeton University.

TAHERA QUTBUDDIN is the AlBabtain Laudian Professor of Arabic at the University of Oxford. Previously, she served as professor of Arabic literature and chair of Interdisciplinary Studies in the Humanities at the University of Chicago. Her scholarship focuses on intersections of the literary, the religious, and the political in classical Arabic poetry and prose. She is the author of *Al-Mu'ayyad al-Shīrāzī and Fatimid Daʿwa Poetry: A Case of Commitment in Classical Arabic Literature* and the editor and translator of two medieval ethical compilations: *A Treasury of Virtues: Sayings, Sermons, and Teachings of ʿAli* and *Light in the Heavens: Sayings of the Prophet Muhammad.* For her book entitled *Arabic Oration: Art and Function,* she was awarded fellowships by the Carnegie Corporation of New York and the American Council of Learned Societies and won the 2021 Shaykh Zayed Book Prize. Recently, she published an edition and translation of the preeminent tenth-century compilation of Ali's words entitled *Nahj al-Balaghah: The Wisdom and Eloquence of ʿAli.* She is now working on a book supported by the Guggenheim Foundation in which she draws primarily on Ali's orations to reconstruct his biography and thought.

GWENDOLYN DUBOIS SHAW is the Class of 1940 Bicentennial Term Associate Professor of the History of Art at the University of Pennsylvania. Previously, she served as senior historian and director of history, research, and scholarship at the National Portrait Gallery. An expert on African American art, she is the author of *The Art of Remembering: Essays on African American Art and History, First Ladies of the United States, Represent: 200 Years of African American Art in the Philadelphia Museum of Art, Portraits of a People: Picturing African Americans in the Nineteenth Century,* and *Seeing the Unspeakable: The Art of Kara Walker.* She is also a curator, and in the past decade, she has helped mount exhibitions at the Philadelphia Museum of Art, the Institute of Contemporary Art in Philadelphia, the Addison Gallery of American Art, the Arthur Ross Gallery at the University of Pennsylvania, and the University of Pennsylvania's Museum of Archaeology and Anthropology. She has also partnered with numerous institutions, including the Whitney Museum of American Art, the Metropolitan Museum of Art, the National Portrait Gallery, and the Museum of Fine Arts, Boston, to develop and implement numerous exhibitions, public programs, and scholarly events.

COREY D. B. WALKER is the dean of the Wake Forest University School of Divinity, Wake Forest Professor of the Humanities, and director of the Program in African American Studies at Wake Forest University. His research and teaching interests include African American philosophy, critical theory, ethics, leadership studies, and religion and public life. His publications include *A Noble Fight: African American Freemasonry and the Struggle for Democracy in America*, *Community Wealth Building and the Reconstruction of American Democracy: Can We Make American Democracy Work?* (coedited with Melody Barnes and Thad Williamson), *African Americans and Religious Freedom: New Perspectives for Congregations and Communities* (coedited with Sabrina E. Dent), and more than sixty articles, essays, book chapters, and reviews in a wide range of scholarly journals. He also codirected and coproduced the documentary film *Fifeville* with acclaimed artist and filmmaker Kevin Jerome Everson. A prominent academic leader, he previously served as vice president and dean of the Samuel DeWitt Proctor School of Theology at Virginia Union University, dean of the College of Arts and Sciences and John W. and Anna Hodgin Hanes Professor of the Humanities at Winston-Salem State University, chair of the Department of Africana Studies at Brown University, and director of the Center for the Study of Local Knowledge at the University of Virginia. He has held visiting faculty appointments at Friedrich Schiller Universität Jena, Union Presbyterian Seminary, and University of Richmond, where he taught in the humanities and leadership studies in the School of Arts and Sciences and in the Jepson School of Leadership Studies.

ACKNOWLEDGMENTS

A core insight of this volume is that good leaders do not act alone. They depend on the collaboration, support, and effort of many others to realize a shared vision and advance a common good. As editors, we are grateful to all those who have supported this collective effort. We owe special thanks to our generous and generative contributors, whose keen intellect, scholarly creativity, and deep commitment to the humanities and liberal arts have made this volume possible.

This volume originated as a conference on The Arts of Leading: Perspectives from the Humanities and Liberal Arts, cosponsored by the Oxford Character Project at the University of Oxford and the Program for Leadership and Character at Wake Forest University. We are grateful to Wake Forest University for hosting this interdisciplinary conference, to the talented university events team for helping us to organize it, and to more than forty Wake Forest departments, offices, programs, and schools that offered their support as cosponsors, including several who provided funding for the conference: the A. C. Reid Philosophy Fund, Department of Philosophy, Humanities Institute, Intercultural Center, Office of Alumni Engagement, Office of Diversity and Inclusion, Office of Global Affairs, Office of the Provost, School of Business, and Women's Center. We are also grateful to the foundations and donors who helped to fund the conference and support the research and work of the Oxford Character Project and Program for Leadership and Character over the last few years, including the F. M. Kirby Foundation, John Templeton Foundation, Kern Family Foundation, Laidlaw Foundation, Legatum Foundation, Lilly Endowment Inc., National Endowment for the Humanities, Oxford Pastorate, and Templeton World Charity Foundation. The ideas, views, and opinions expressed in this volume are those of the editors and contributors and do not necessarily represent the views of any of our colleagues, sponsors, or supporters.

A number of friends and colleagues provided valuable feedback on the design of the conference and the content of the volume. We are especially grateful to Jonathan Brant, Michele Gillespie, Nathan Hatch, Jack McNichol, Cameron Silverglate, and Kenneth Townsend. Three anonymous reviewers offered helpful feedback and encouragement, and Jocelyn Krauss and William Morgan provided careful research assistance. Fábio D'Almeida kindly assisted in sourcing figures and permissions for chapter 13.

Georgetown University Press has been a wonderful partner in stewarding this volume to publication. We are especially grateful to our editor, Al Bertrand, for believing in this book and to the Faculty Editorial Board for supporting it so enthusiastically. Elizabeth Sheridan shepherded the book through the production process, Billie Smith-Haffener provided excellent copyediting, and Francys Reed and Stephanie Rojas offered valuable assistance with marketing.

Finally, we want to thank all of our teachers, colleagues, and students over the years who have taught us the value of engaging the arts and humanities to deepen, unsettle, and expand our understanding of leadership. Their insight and example affirm the vital necessity of practicing the arts of leading.

INDEX

Pages in *italics* refer to figures